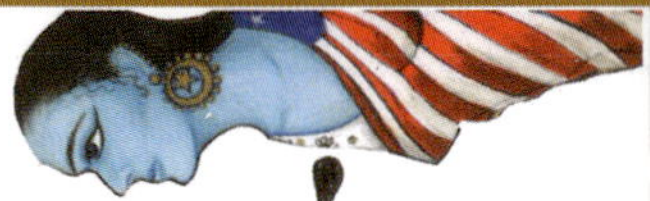

Jews have lived in Ernakulam for centuries... Some claim that the original synagogue was constructed in the early 13th century... The current building has elements from the early 18th & 19th century... members left for Israel... In 1975 a storm caused serious damage to the synagogue

...and the roof with its deep overhangs is an exposed wooden structure covered with traditional terracotta tiles...

1972 thieves broke into the building and stole some of its contents... 1972 the synagogue closed

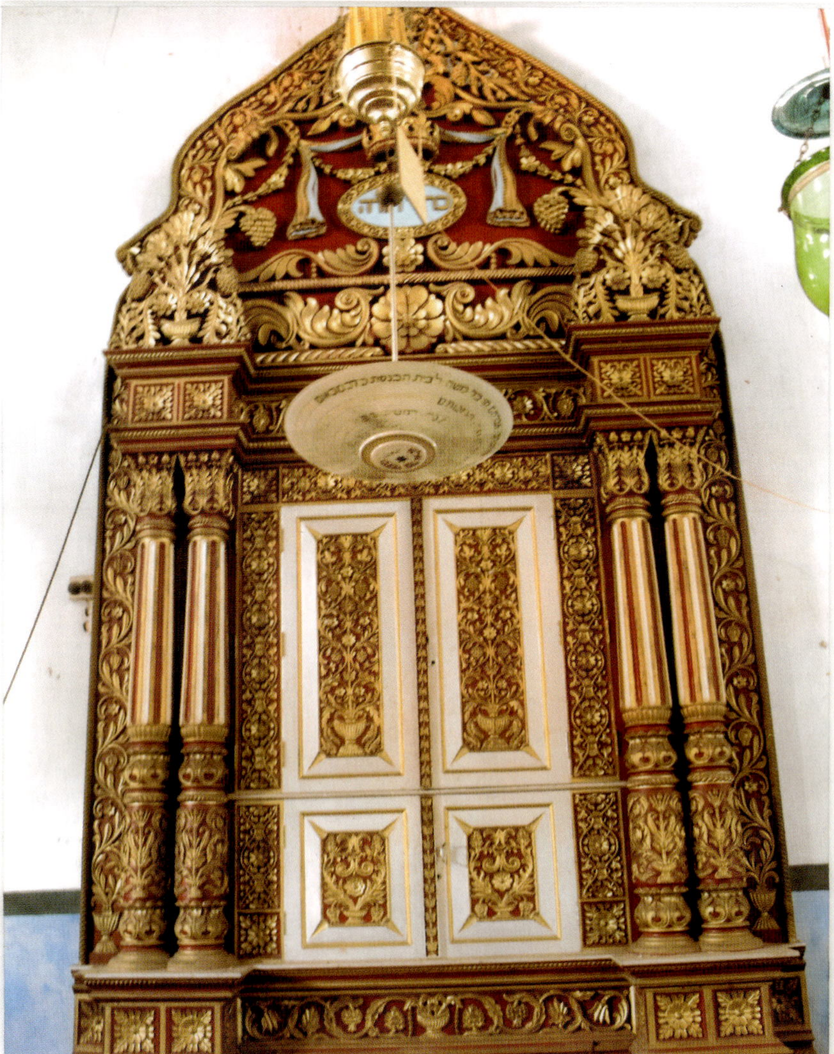

Siona in Cochin 2016

Growing Up Jewish in India

Synagogues, Customs, and Communities from the Bene Israel to the Art of Siona Benjamin

Editor
Ori Z. Soltes

NIYOGI BOOKS

This book was made possible by the generous support of
Indian Jewish Heritage Center

Published by
NIYOGI BOOKS
Block D, Building No. 77,
Okhla Industrial Area, Phase-I,
New Delhi-110 020, INDIA
Tel: 91-11-26816301, 26818960
Email: niyogibooks@gmail.com
Website: www.niyogibooksindia.com

Editor: K.E. Priyamvada
Design: Misha Oberoi

Cover image: Finding Home (*Fereshteh*) #77: Miriam,
Siona Benjamin, 2006, see p. 270.
Frontispiece: Kadavumbhagam-Ernakulam Synagogue *heikhal,*
Siona Benjamin, 2011

ISBN: 978-93-89136-81-4
Publication: 2021
Reprint: 2025

Printed at: Niyogi Offset Pvt. Ltd., New Delhi, India

Contents

Acknowledgments

There are three particular groups of individuals and organizations whom I would like to thank for making this volume possible. Each of the writers, it goes without saying—and yet it bears saying—has expended significant effort to provide what has emerged as a work that looks at India, and Jews in India, from a range of different angles—historical and cultural, art historical and ethnic-religious. I am thus grateful to Erica Lyons for framing our book so elegantly within the larger context of the Jewish presence in southern and eastern Asia. Jael Silliman, Barbara C. Johnson and Orna Eliyahu-Oron contributed impressive discussions of two of the three primary Indian Jewish communities—the Baghdadi and Cochini Jews—to complement my own essay on the Bene Israel. Each of these three discussions has managed to represent its subject from different perspectives, including history, culture and above all, synagogue architecture.

Both Siona Benjamin's eye-opening memoir and the following discussion of her art, toward which her essay organically leads, carry the overall narrative forward from past to present and future, while also returning it full circle to the observation in the Introduction regarding India's long history of diversity and hospitality—the experience of which provided a stepping off point for Benjamin's ongoing efforts to use her art as an instrument that can help to improve the world by broadly opening the minds of her visual audience.

Siona was also the key member of our two-person organizational team who pursued funds from the outside to help elevate the production possibilities of this volume, making it feasible for the publisher to spend more energy on the production itself. With this in mind, I wish also to thank a trio of organizations that have assisted this publication with generous subventions. I—we—offer heartfelt gratitude to the Bene Israel Heritage Museum & Genealogical Research Centre, in Mumbai, India; as well as to Marvin and Dan Tokayer and the Foundation for Remote Jewish Culture, in the United States. Both the Centre's president, Ralphy Jhirad, and the Tokayers, have long been supportive of Siona's artwork and also of my own writing, so that it proved a wonderful meeting between our worlds not only for Siona and me to share in a project that includes both of our respective areas of focus, but to re-encounter patrons whom both of us have reasons beyond this project to admire and appreciate.

Above all, I thank the Indian Jewish Heritage Center in Nevatim, Israel. In the midst of their own important cultural center project (briefly discussed in Chapter Six) they stepped forward to assure that our own project could proceed with as little fiscal pain as possible—and we look forward eagerly to the publication of this volume in a Hebrew translation that they will subsequently undertake.

I also wish to thank the staff of Niyogi Books for the attentive and sensitive job that they consistently accomplished at long distance. I am particularly grateful to Professor Nirmal Kanti Bhattacharjee and K.E. Priyamvada, who shepherded this project through the final stages of the process, bringing it to fruition as they brought their talents as editors and—in Nirmal's case, as a translator—to bear. We have never met, yet I feel as if both of them are colleagues and friends, a relationship that has evolved through myriad emails and their discussions.

The same is true of Siddhartha Banerjee. Indeed, Siddhartha's demise was a shock to everyone at Niyogi and to both Siona Benjamin and myself, who enjoyed such an extensive email correspondence with him during the initial stages of this project. It is with respect and affection that I would like to dedicate this book to Siddhartha Banerjee's memory.

ORI Z. SOLTES
Washington, D.C.

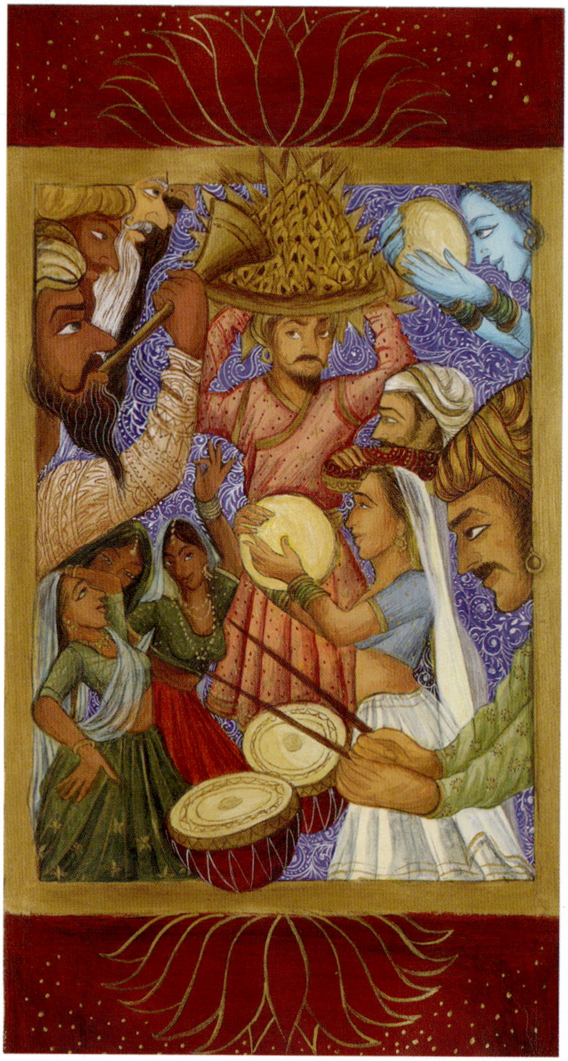

Detail from the *Megillat Esther* (Esther Scroll) by Siona Benjamin, 2007, depicting the Judaeans rejoicing after the defeat and destruction of Haman

Foreword

The three main Indian Jewish communities —the Bene Israel, Baghdadi and Cochini—are easily remembered as the 'BBC Jews of India'. These communities are unique in the manner in which they exhibit a most dynamic combination of the Jewish and Indian heritages. The Jewish communities in India have experienced Philo-Semitism rather than the Anti-Semitism that many Jewish communities across the Diaspora have faced; they are an important part of the mainstream Indian world, well-integrated within Indian society, yet retaining their distinctive Jewish traditions and culture.

Scholars from around the world have over the years researched these Indian Jewish communities. Fascinating narratives record diverse times of immigration into India during the past many centuries, as well as more recent emigration from India to Israel and Europe, to North America and Australia—creating an unusual diaspora within the Diaspora. Researchers have produced a growing library of books and

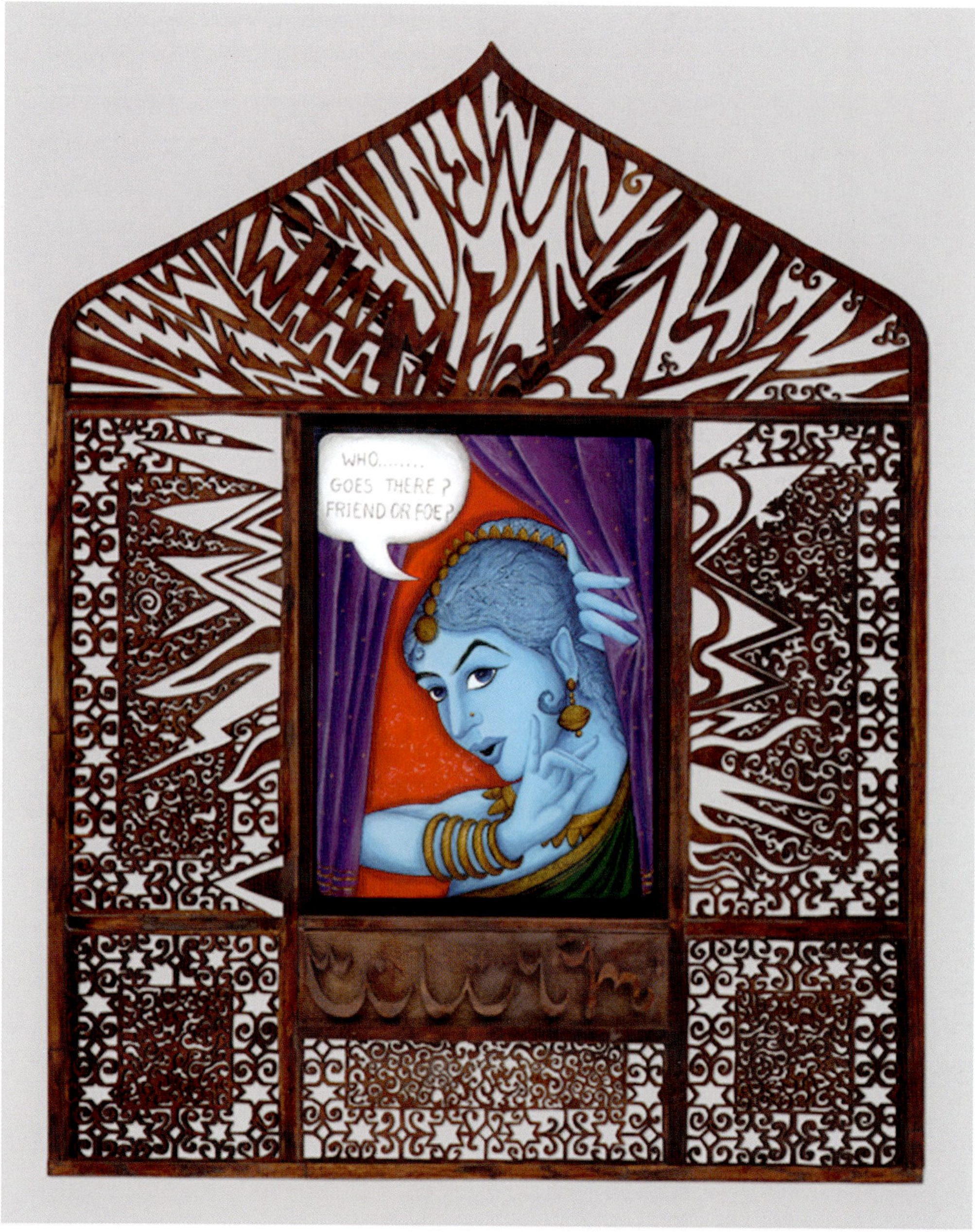

Finding Home (*Fereshteh*) #102: Lilith (with finely carved wooden frame), Siona Benjamin, 2009

articles—and yet a new book such as this one is most significant. It enables the reader to explore a range of newly uncovered information regarding the three well-known Jewish communities as well as learning about new and emerging groups eager to be a part of the Indian Jewish world. The narratives present the rich Indian Jewish heritage in its migrations within the Indian subcontinent, the development of its distinctive synagogues and customs, the emergence of new Indian Jewish communities, and its own dispersions in the past seven decades.

Two particularly important and interesting chapters are the personal account and the discussion of the work of the renowned artist, Siona Benjamin—a great source of Indian Jewish pride. Siona's discussion of growing up Jewish in India and becoming an artist is inspiring; the analysis of her work is enlightening and will introduce many readers for the first time to a singularly important part of the Indian Jewish heritage that extends a rich past into a powerful present and dynamic future.

I wish to congratulate the editor and writer, Ori Z. Soltes; the authors and scholars, Erica Lyons, Barbara C. Johnson, Orna Eliyahu-Oron, and Jael Silliman; the artist, Siona Benjamin; Niyogi Books—as well as those who directly and/or indirectly helped to make this publication possible.

I enthusiastically welcome the many readers who will find this volume so very useful in fulfilling their desire to learn more about the Indian Jewish communities in an illuminating and enriching manner.

RALPHY JHIRAD
Mumbai, India

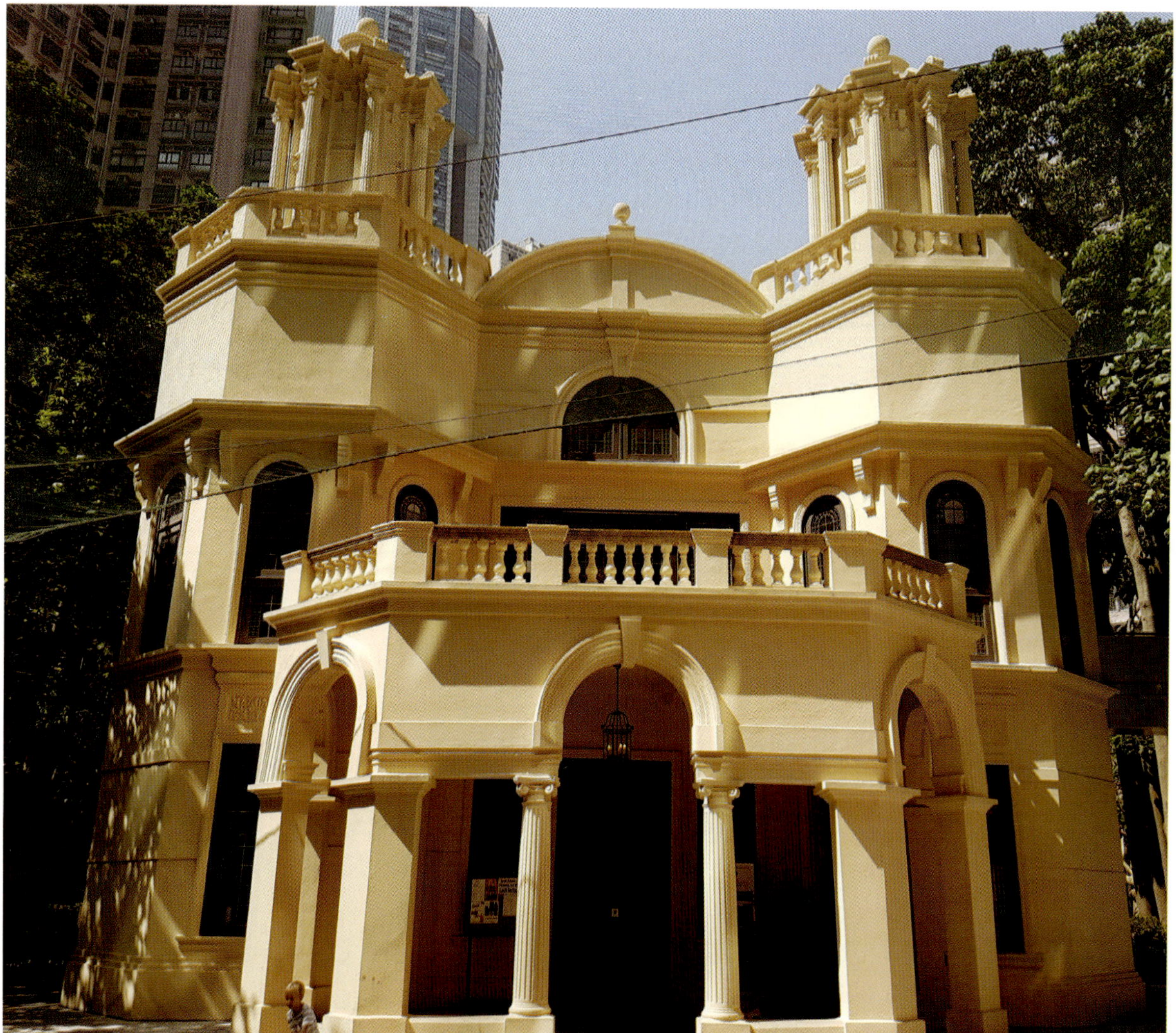

Fig. 8. Ohel Leah Synagogue, Hong Kong

PREFACE

Jewish Migrations to the Far East

Erica Lyons

The Jewish story is ultimately a story of migrations and resettlements, exiles, expulsions, and returns. These themes present themselves as early as Genesis, the first book of the Torah, with the expulsion of Adam and Eve (and Lilith) from the Garden of Eden. Following this, Abraham leaves Ur, and later Joseph and ultimately his entire family migrate to Egypt. The entire second book of the Torah is titled Exodus, the movement of the Israelites anticipating the migratory and resettlement patterns of the Jewish people throughout its long history.

Most scholars agree that despite these early Biblical period expulsions and dispersions, the Jewish identity as a Diaspora people begins just after the destruction of the Temple in Jerusalem by the Romans in 70 CE. With the destruction of the Temple—and even more emphatically after the Bar Kokhba revolt of 132–135 CE—many Jews left Judaea, with many ending up after generations in the four corners of the earth. It is following this mass expulsion that the Jewish people began to develop the complex institutions that had begun to take early shape well before the Temple fell—such as synagogues, rabbinic Judaism and the Talmud—to insure that the Jewish identity survived, even outside the Jewish homeland. This continued for the nearly two thousand years that followed with a continuous focus on the promise, in Isaiah 11:12 (among other places), that they would one day be ingathered from the four corners of the earth and returned home. Different places around the world certainly did not see an equal distribution of Jewish people. As such, it is the dominant regions, those that are demographically most significant, whose stories are, by and large, canonized in the West, thus shaping a significant part of our collective memory.

An article was recently published about a Japanese man who identifies as Haredi (ultra-Orthodox) and who has made his home in Israel. One United States-based Jewish reader asked, 'Is he real?' as if Jews actually hailing from among the four corners of the world, as foretold in Isaiah, are some sort of mythical creatures like unicorns.

The coming to America story is a Diaspora story that resonates with millions, particularly the countless stories of Jewish Eastern European immigrants. These have been recorded, memorialized in memoir, literature, and film, but it is by no means the Diaspora story. What of those stories in which Ellis Island doesn't take focus at all? The Jewish Diaspora narrative, while encompassing the story of the massive waves of Ashkenazi migration to the United States near the turn of the 20th century, must be expanded to include the smaller stories that take place in corners of the earth far from New York City's Lower East Side, in places that include China, Japan, Myanmar, Singapore, the Philippines, and—of course—India, too.

As to what drove Jews to the Far East, the answer is quite the same as the answer as to what drove Jews to any of the places in which they settled across the globe. For the most part, the waves of migration were powered by numerous forces that include economic opportunity, escape from persecution, expulsion and, undeniably, part luck. There were even those who were drawn to the Far East without any compelling force beyond their own quest for adventure. Irrespective of the forces that drove them, once settled, the Jews in the Far East operated as Jews do elsewhere in the Diaspora: they formed communities the basis of which began with the erection of communal structures and organizations, such as synagogues, cemeteries, and schools.

Perhaps, other than the Jews of India, there is no Far Eastern community better illustrative of the Diaspora story in all its intricacies than the story of the Jews in China and Hong Kong. The China story is inextricably linked with the story of the Jews in India at points in time, as well as that of other Diaspora communities in the Far East. Just as in India, Jewish history in China spans centuries and merges together Jews of diverse backgrounds with regard to observance level, geographic origin, economic circumstances, and political reality.

The earliest recorded Jewish settlement in China was that in Kaifeng-Fu. Their arrival in Kaifeng dates somewhere between the seventh and the ninth centuries during the Song dynasty. These Jews came as Silk Road traders and then were invited to settle. The community faced a number of challenges in the centuries to come including assimilation, economic depression, isolation from the main arteries of Jewish life, and a series of floods—through the rising of the Yellow River—and fires. The community established a synagogue and a cemetery, trained rabbis, and had a collection of holy scrolls (Fig. 1).

A massive flood in 1642 marked the beginning of the community's

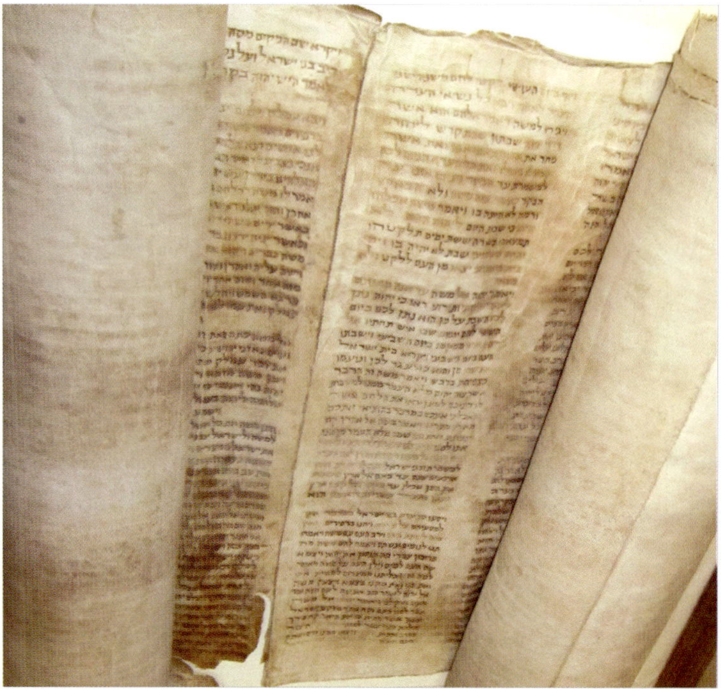

Fig. 1. Kaifeng Torah scroll

decline. Although they repaired the synagogue and scrolls, the community never returned to its former position and each natural and economic disaster that followed further contributed to its ultimate demise. A later flood-based destruction of the synagogue in the 1860s accelerated the disintegration of this community. Unlike India's Bene Israel community, who date their own arrival in the Far East much further back, the community of Kaifeng Jewry exists only in memory today (Fig. 2).

Another early wave of migration at the turn of the 20th century brought Jews to multiple cities in China, like Harbin, Tianjin, Hailar, and

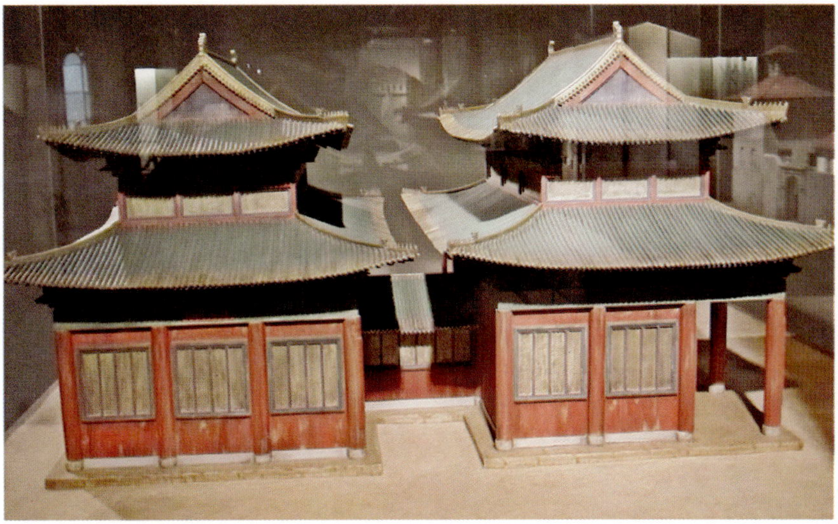

Fig. 2. Model of Kaifeng Synagogue

Hengdaohezi, places nearly forgotten in history books save for occasional footnotes. The main commonality that links these Jewish communities is the fact that they were all comprised of Russian Jews. Persecuted in Russia, they found economic opportunity in China and temporary relief from political upheaval. Another commonality is the demise of each of these communities dating to the mid-1940s. Harbin, with approximately 10,000 Jewish residents at its peak, and Tianjin, with approximately 5,000 Jewish residents at its peak, were the largest of these, boasting multiple communal Jewish organizations that included synagogues, Jewish publications, youth movements, Jewish schools, Jewish relief organizations to provide aid to the impoverished, cemeteries, and Zionist associations. In Harbin alone there were 20 Jewish newspapers and periodicals. Moreover, in addition to its synagogues and schools, Harbin had an established library, soup kitchen, home for the aged and

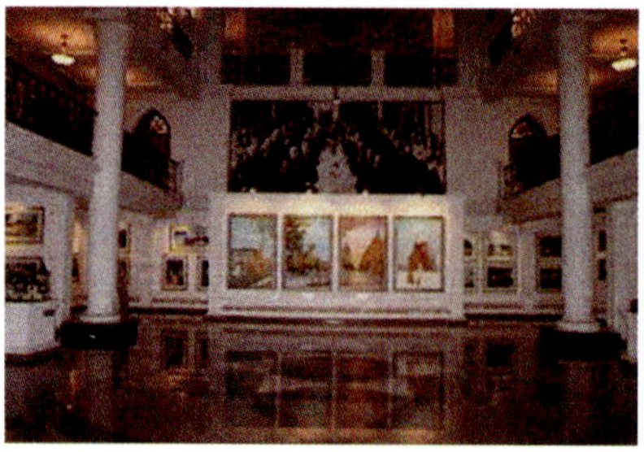

Fig. 3a. Harbin Synagogue interior, now a museum

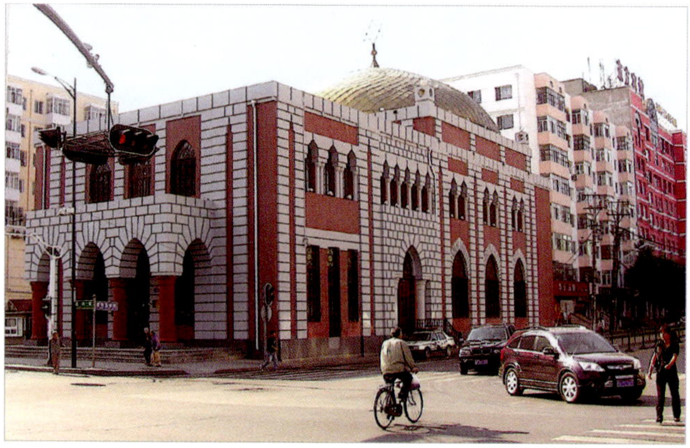

Fig. 3. New Synagogue, Harbin (built in 1918)

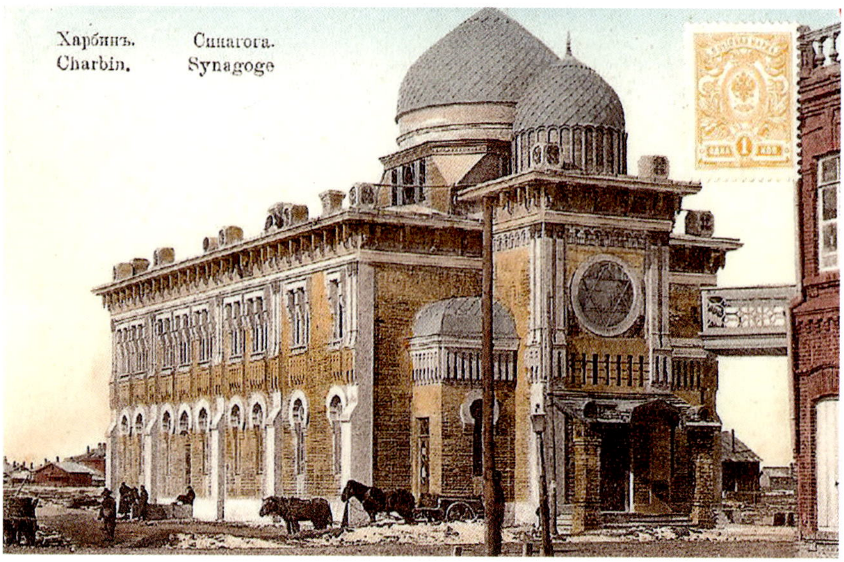

Fig. 4. Harbin Old Synagogue

Jewish hospital, covering every facet of Jewish life.

The synagogue and other communal structures in Tianjin, left empty once the community migrated from the city, were soon reduced to poverty. The synagogue building deteriorated and the cemetery, without caretakers and in the presence of great upheavals in China, has disappeared. Jewish Harbin, though the community never returned, has surprisingly become if not a hub of Jewish communal life, at least a hub of Jewish tourist activity and interest. The community's two main synagogues still stand and have both undergone major renovations. The so-called New Synagogue, built in 1918 and completed in 1921, houses a Jewish Museum that aims to preserve the history of the Jews of Harbin (Figs 3 and 3a). The Main Synagogue, also referred to as the Old Synagogue, built in 1909, became a hostel and housed a number of assorted businesses, once Jewish residents left the city. It underwent a massive renovation in 2014 when it was transformed from a home of bric-a-brac to an impressive modern concert hall (Fig. 4). The former Jewish Secondary School, located adjacent to the Old Synagogue, together with two other buildings form the Harbin Music Center.

Tumult in the 1940s overwhelmed these communities founded by the wave of immigration from Russia. Just as the Japanese occupation ended and they were beginning to attempt to understand the depths of utter destruction the Holocaust had brought upon Jewish life in Europe, the Chinese Communist Revolution overtook China. The subsequent exodus of Jews from China in this period, culminating in about 1949 and ending within just a few years, was, in part, a massive aliyah to Israel as these communities were unified by pre-State Zionist fervor. China, with the exception of Hong Kong, was nearly emptied of its Jewish residents. Following their immigration to Israel, many of the former Jewish residents of China remained connected by their ties to China. A housing project for new olim (immigrants to Israel) was even aptly named Shikun Shanghai. While some of these Jews did return home to what was by then the USSR, still others migrated to the United States, Australia, and anywhere they were able to make new lives for themselves. Thus began yet another chapter in the long story of great Jewish migrations.

While these smaller and perhaps less known Jewish migration stories in China partially illustrate the breadth of the Jewish Diaspora story, they are focused almost entirely on the migration of Jews from Eastern Europe, specifically Russia. Jewish Shanghai presents an altogether different and much broader view of Jewish Diaspora communities in the Far East. The Shanghai Jewish community dates its origins to the arrival of the Baghdadi Jews, migrating from India in order to expand their trading empires. The Baghdadi Jews, of course, didn't begin their Diaspora story in India but can trace their own family histories from Spain, from which they were expelled in 1492 in the context of the Spanish Inquisition, to Baghdad, where they prospered but then faced persecution, to India and then onwards throughout the Far East in search of business opportunities.

In Shanghai the Baghdadi Jews, arriving in the mid-1800s, achieved the pinnacle of success. In particular, families like the Sassoons, Kadoories, Ezras, and Hardoons were all visible figures in Shanghai society (Fig. 5). They established businesses and thrived, helping Shanghai to earn its name as the Paris of the East. The imprint the Baghdadi Jews had on Shanghai extended into Jewish communal life where institutions were quickly established to cater to the needs of the expanding community. The Sassoons, as they did elsewhere, maintained Jewish religious lives while enjoying their mercantile success as well as social status. They remained closely linked to India where many of their businesses were founded and they brought over other Baghdadi Jews and Indians to help further expand their interests.

In contemporary Shanghai, a visitor can catch a glimpse of Ohel Rachel Synagogue, built in 1917 by Jacob Sassoon as the successor to the Beth El Synagogue (Fig. 6). In 1952 when the community was forced to migrate from Shanghai following the Japanese occupation and on the eve of the Chinese Communist Revolution, the synagogue was seized by Chinese authorities and stripped. It has been in control of the Chinese government since. Also established by a prominent Baghdadi Jew to serve the community, Beth Aharon was built in 1927 by Silas Hardoon, replacing Shearith Israel Synagogue. Beth Aharon was later used by Jewish refugees who arrived in Shanghai's third wave of Jewish migration. It should be noted that the Shanghai community, while worthy of separate mention because of its unique role in history, certainly did not exist in isolation from the other Jewish communities in China. Numerous Jewish residents of Harbin made their way to Shanghai and settled there. The

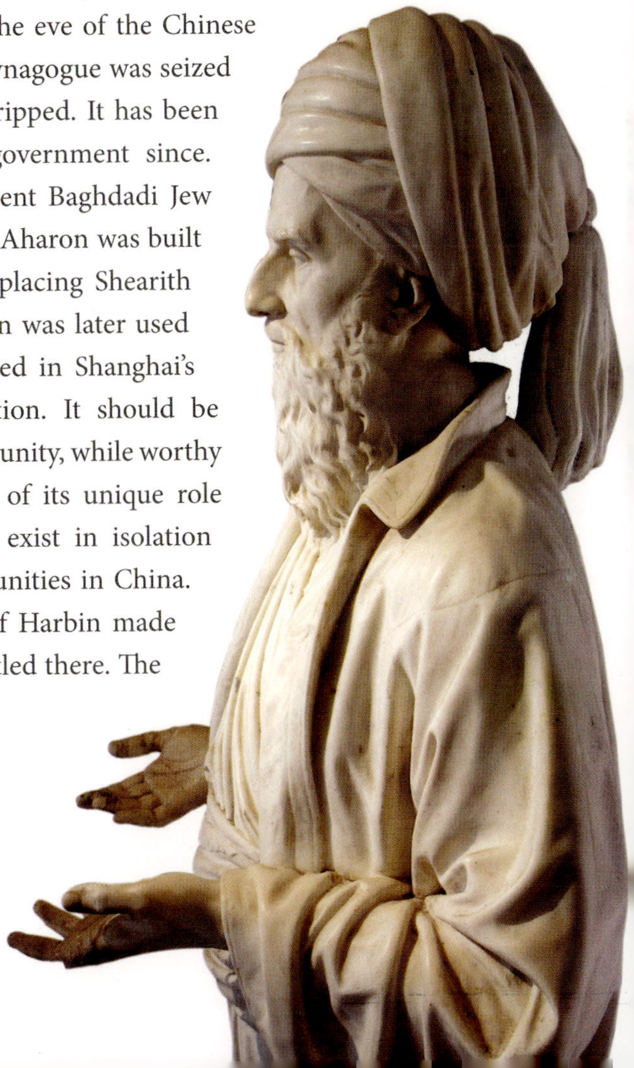

Fig. 5. Portrait statue of David Sassoon

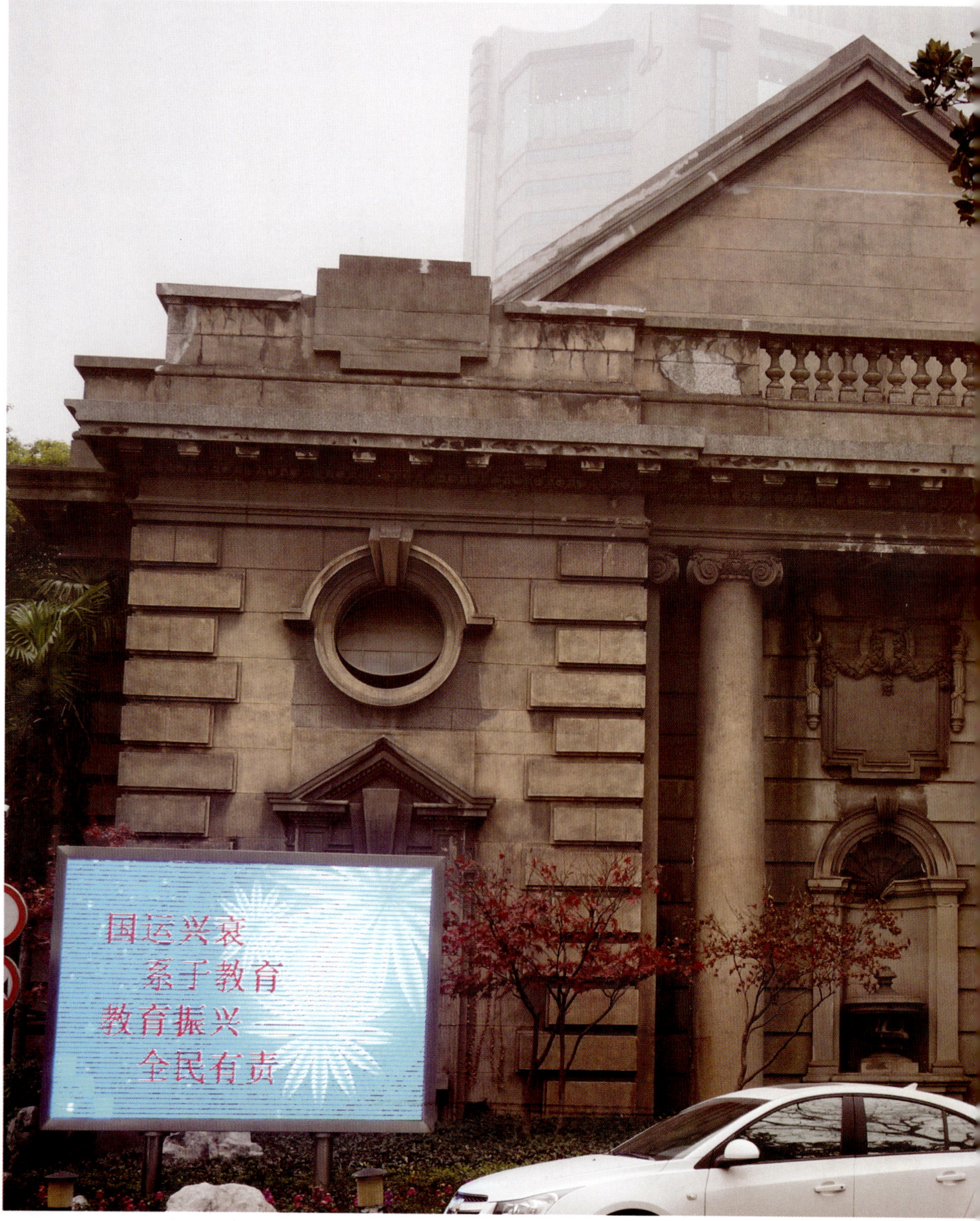
国运兴衰
系于教育
教育振兴
全民有责

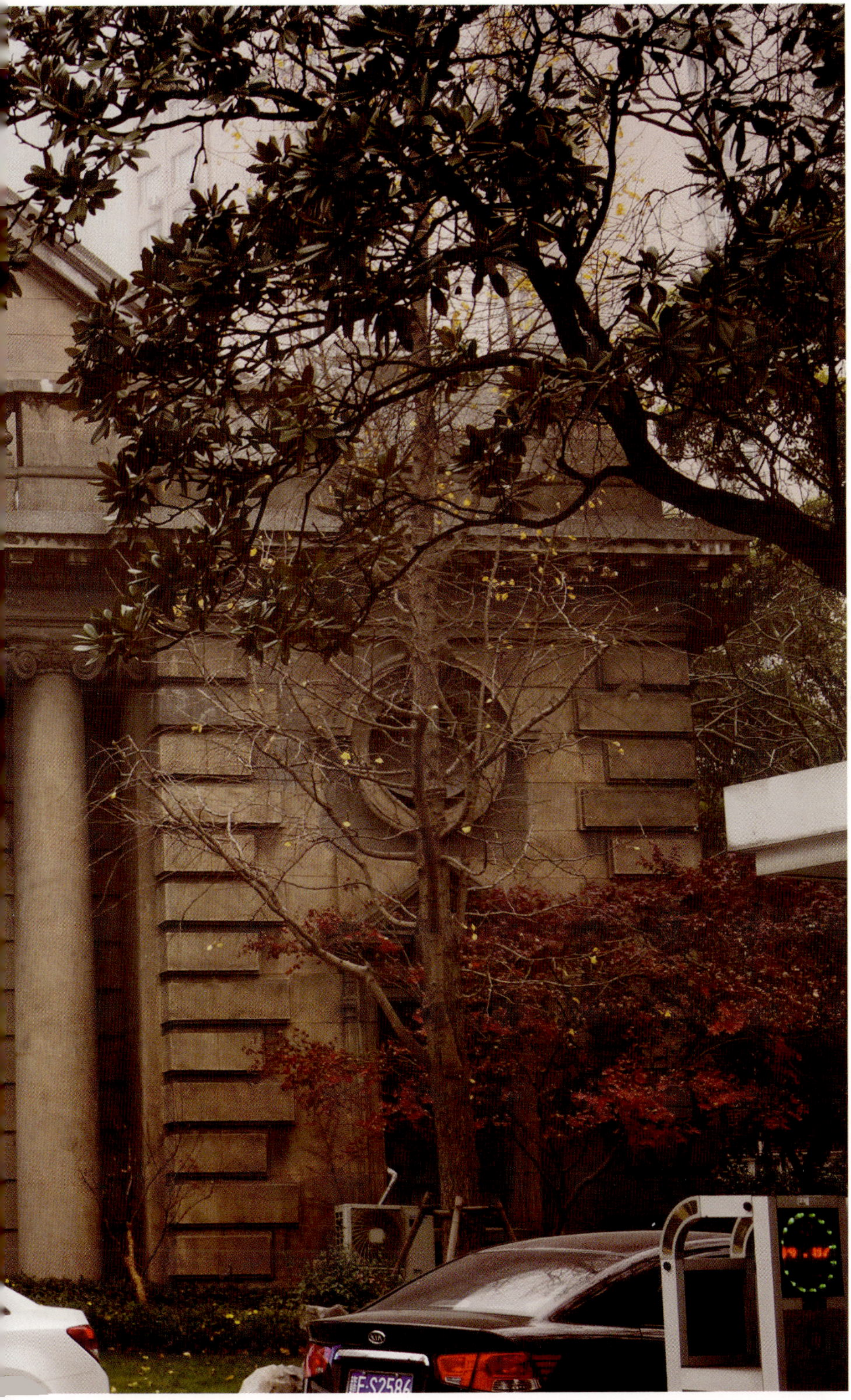

Fig. 6. Ohel Rachel Synagogue, Shanghai

Shanghai community was in contact with the then all-but-disappeared Jewish community of Kaifeng.

Additionally, many Jewish residents in Shanghai maintained significant contacts and business interests in Hong Kong. These are but a few of the community's relationships with other communities in China, which they developed in addition to maintaining their strong ties to India.

In contrast to well-off Jews with established roots in the Far East, in the early part of the 20th century, Shanghai saw an influx of Ashkenazi Jewish immigrants fleeing persecution and the Bolshevik Revolution. These made up the second wave of Jewish migration to Shanghai. This group of Eastern Europeans quickly overtook the Baghdadi Jews, population-wise, though the Baghdadis remained the dominant force in the city's economic and social landscapes.

While the Jewish population of Shanghai prior to World War II, numbering approximately 6,000 by the early part of the 1930s, was well integrated in the international community and played no small role in the development of the city, their Diaspora story is often overshadowed by the third and final wave of Jewish migration to the city. This is the arrival of Holocaust refugees in the late 1930s. Shanghai was one of the only remaining open ports left in the world to Jews fleeing Europe before and during World War II. Approximately 16,000 Jewish refugees settled in Shanghai for the duration of the war. The already-established Jewish residents, in particular the Kadoorie family, played key roles in aiding these refugees, along with the notable assistance received from the American Jewish Joint Distribution Committee.

Institutions created to serve Shanghai's pre-WWII residents adapted to include the new Jewish immigrants to the city. The Shanghai Jewish School grew exponentially with the admission of the Jewish refugees' children. Ohel Moshe Synagogue, built in 1927 for Russian Jewish immigrants, played a central role in the life of the Holocaust refugees and sat at the heart of what later became designated as the Shanghai Ghetto for Stateless Refugees. Likewise, the Beth Aharon Synagogue housed the Mir Yeshiva's 2,400 students and teachers who had fled Lithuania on an escape route that took them first to Japan. They ultimately found a safe haven in Shanghai, where they remained until they immigrated to pre-State Israel and the United States in 1945–1946. Additional institutions were established for the benefit of Jewish refugees, including the Shanghai Jewish Youth Association (S.J.Y.A) in 1937.

Most recently, a contemporary expatriate Jewish community began to establish itself in Shanghai toward the end of the 20th century. There are reminders of the history of the community that once boasted countless Jewish institutions. Given the fact that the city was virtually without Jewish residents from the 1940s on, however, in the aftermath of the Chinese Revolution, it isn't surprising that much was lost. Only two synagogues remain standing as Beth Aharon was entirely demolished after Jews had been forced to abandon the city. Ohel Rachel Synagogue, a shell of its former self, continues to be under the control of the Chinese government and therefore off limits to the Jewish community, with a few exceptions. Ohel Moshe, though no longer a house of worship, has been restored and converted into the Shanghai Jewish Refugees Museum (Fig. 7). The Museum offers a glimpse at the city's role as a safe-haven for Holocaust refugees. The community's cemetery, forcibly abandoned like Beth Aharon and the other Jewish institutions, was demolished by the government. An effort is underway to locate and restore Shanghai Jewish gravestones to rescue them from being entirely lost to history.

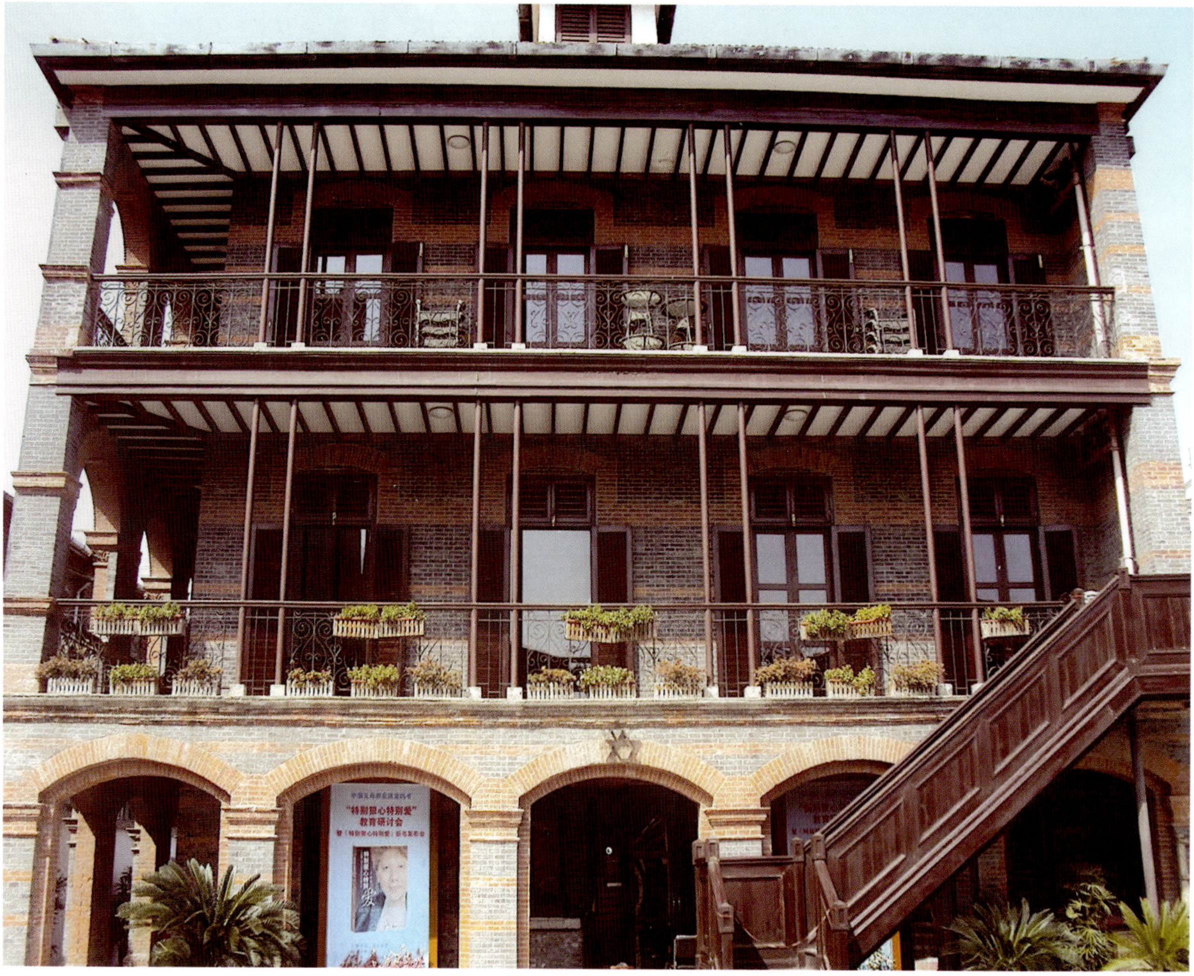

Fig. 7. Ohel Moshe Synagogue, Shanghai (1907), now Jewish Refugees Museum

The Jewish Hong Kong story stands in strong contrast to the Shanghai story. Though it is a quieter history, it is nonetheless extraordinary, having nothing to do with the fact that I have made it my home for nearly two decades. The founders of Hong Kong's Jewish community, like Shanghai's, were the Sassoons, Baghdadi Jews expanding their trading empire from India. They were soon followed by other Baghdadi families seeking and amassing fortunes and thus the Hong Kong Jewish community's origin story is virtually identical to that of early Shanghai.

As with Shanghai's first wave of Jewish immigration, it is impossible to tell the Hong Kong Jewish story without first referencing the history of the Baghdadi Jews in India. The Hong Kong community began to diversify with an influx of Eastern European Jews escaping pogroms toward the end of the 1800s and the early 1900s. Hong Kong's Ohel Leah Synagogue, funded by the Sassoons, was completed in 1902 (Fig. 8). It was actually the third and final synagogue built by the Sassoons in Hong Kong and was created as a replacement for an earlier synagogue, in order to meet the growing community's needs. Further, the Sassoons also established the Jewish cemetery in 1855. The Jewish Recreation Club was established in 1905 and expanded in 1909 by Sir Elly Kadoorie. What differentiates Hong Kong from other communities in Greater China, is that Hong Kong's Ohel Leah Synagogue is the only historical synagogue in Greater China that is still in use for its original intended purpose (Fig. 9). Likewise, the Hong Kong Jewish cemetery is the only Jewish cemetery in Greater China still in its original location and still in use today.

While this community's origins may have mirrored the origin story of other communities in many respects, history has been far kinder to Hong Kong's Jewish community whose Jews have thrived, and continue to

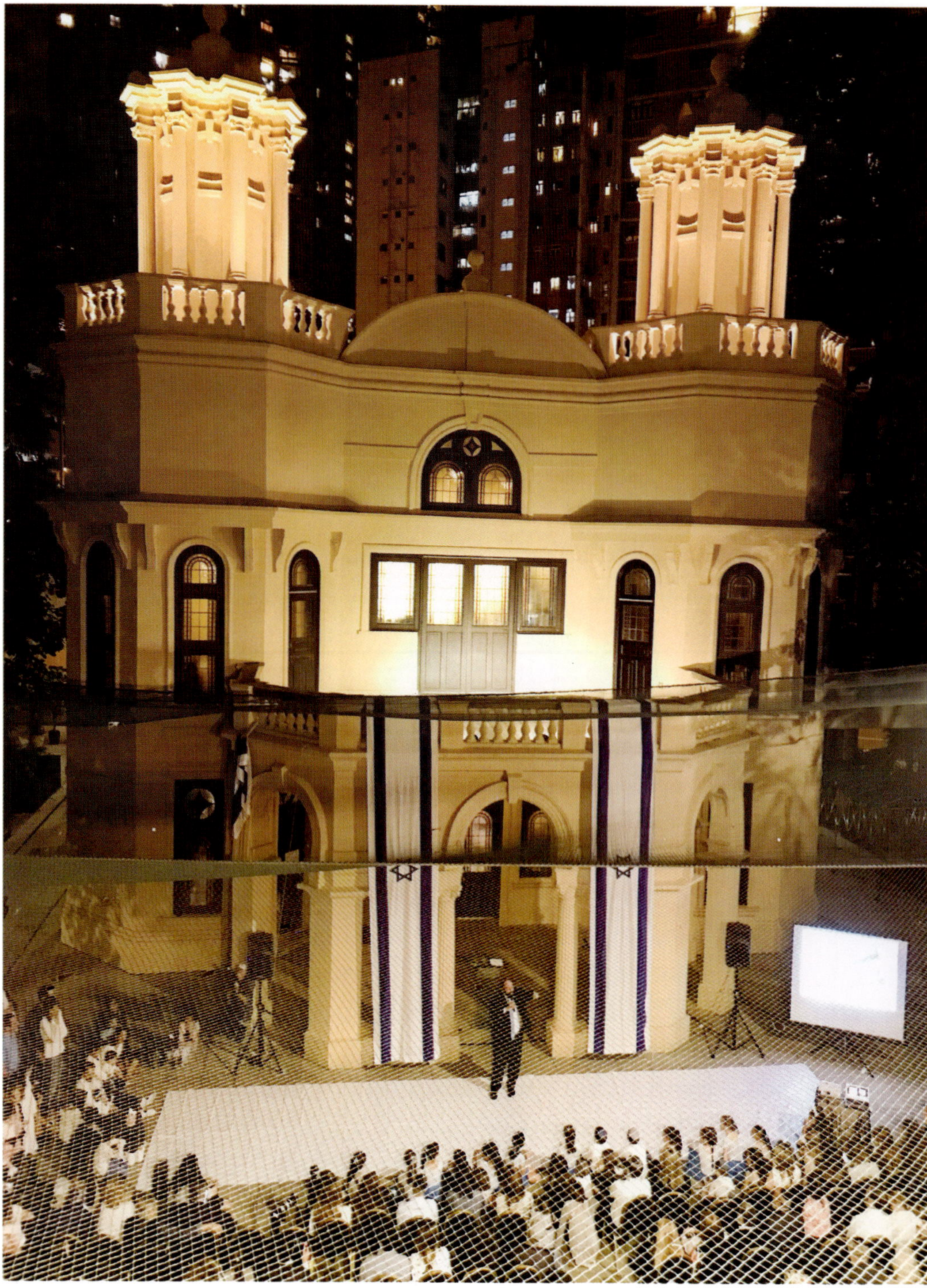

Fig. 9. Ohel Leah Synagogue on Israel's Independence Day

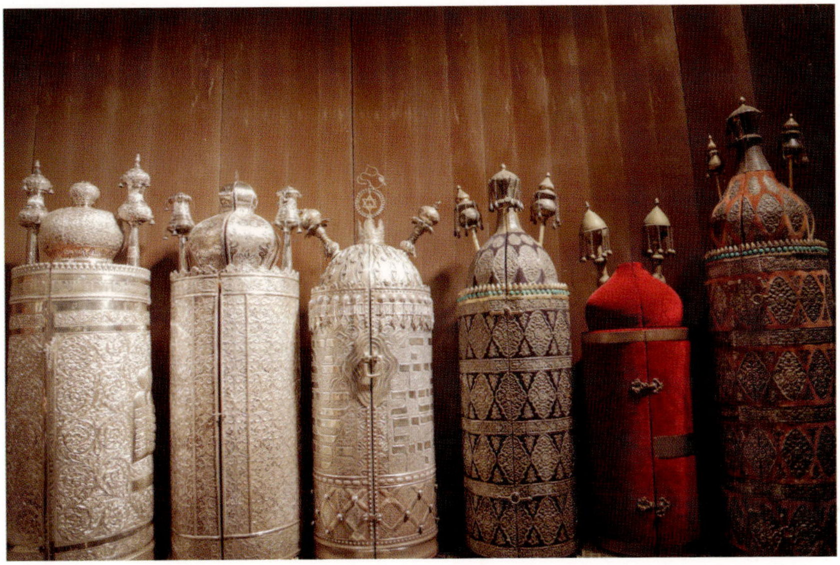

Fig. 10. Torah scrolls in Ohel Leah Synagogue, Hong Kong

do so, since the 1840s. Much of this has had to do with Hong Kong's own history, diverging from mainland China's, being under British rule during, for example, the turbulent years of the Cultural Revolution. Despite the relative longevity of the Hong Kong community in comparison to other modern communities in Greater China, the mere existence of this community, as is the case of Asian Jewry generally, continues to surprise people wholly unaware of the breadth of the Diaspora.

Jews are Indian and Chinese and Japanese just as they are Eastern European and Latin American. The Jewish story is broad and vast. It begins with a single narrative that branches out and reaches to the four corners of the globe. If this story of Jewish migration seems a bit all over the map, so to speak, then it has succeeded in its breadth and it has given at least a brief glimpse at the Jewish story in Asia and around the world (Fig. 10).

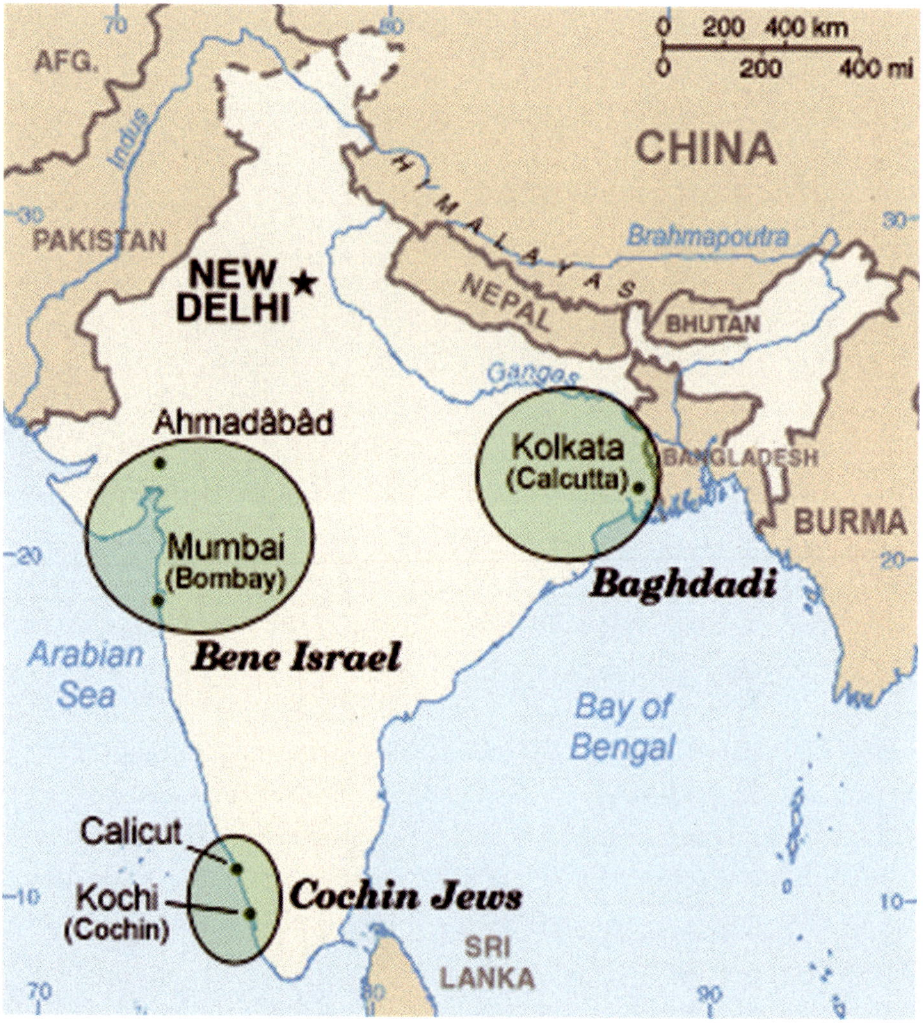

Map not to scale

Fig. 1. Map of India depicting the location of primary Jewish communities

Disclaimer: This map is for representation purposes only. The external boundaries of India depicted in the map are not an accurate depiction of the actual borders of the country.

INTRODUCTION

Indian Jews as a Diverse Diaspora

Ori Z. Soltes

This volume is intended to be a bit idiosyncratic. The library of books devoted to the Jews of India—or to this or that part of its overall community—has grown slowly but steadily over the years. There is also one recent and very important book that focuses on the Jews of India through the specific lens of the visual arts.[1]

Our intention is not to offer another study that mimics other extant works. It is to encompass, in part, a general history, but with a particular focus on the material culture of Indian Jews as Jews in the first place—with somewhat of an emphasis on synagogues and ceremonial objects—and to use the broadest of Jewish Indian contexts as a stepping off point for a narrowed focus on a singular contemporary Indian Jewish artist. Her experience might be viewed as somewhat paradigmatic of the Jewish Indian experience, and her art eventuates as a complex and unique instrument of synthesis.

---

[1] See Kenneth X. Robbins and Marvin Tokayer, eds., *Jews and the Indian National Art Project* (New Delhi: Niyogi Books, 2015).

Her work not only overtly acknowledges an intriguing array of cultural and religious influences, but is intended by the artist herself as an instrument of multi-cultural and transnational import. As such, she intends it to be a means for furthering a responsibility articulated in and out of the long history of art: to push viewers to recognize the ease with which diversity can find itself in universality.

So the arc of this book has a logic to it: Erica Lyon's preface introduces the reader to the concept of Jewish dispersion in both a broad historical sense and with a particular focus on East Asia—part of which connects directly to the diasporic phenomenon as it is associated with the diverse community of Indian Jews (in fact, part of one of the Indian Jewish communities—the so-called Baghdadi community—would continue its migration eastward and end up in Shanghai and Hong Kong, in China). What follows Lyon's preface is this broad introduction to the diverse history of Jews in a historically diverse India, which continues in the next several pages, followed in turn by three essays that focus on the three largest and historically most significant Jewish communities in India: the Baghdadi Jews, (written by Jael Silliman) the Bene Israel Jews,[2] (written by Ori Z. Soltes), and the Cochini Jews, (written by Orna Eliyahu-Oron and Barbara C. Johnson). These three, together with other, smaller groups, arrived from different places at different times to find a home in the vast Indian subcontinent. Each of these three articles follows a slightly different path with regard to concept and composition, reflecting the inclinations of the authors,

[2] Strictly speaking, the more accurate transliteration of the Hebrew word that yields 'Bene' in English should be 'Bnei' or 'Bnai', but it has long been a convention to transliterate it as 'Bene'—thus, Bene Israel, Bene Menashe, Bene Ephraim, and so on. We shall follow that convention throughout this volume.

but all of them offer strong degrees of emphasis on the synagogues and ceremonies of these communities.

The narrative then focuses on Siona Benjamin—a child of the Bene Israel world of Mumbai[3]—by way of her autobiographical essay 'Growing Up Jewish in India.' In her story the reader encounters both a very personal and not entirely atypical account that resonates with the diversity of the Jewish community in India, the large Indian community of which the Jews have long been part, and also the further diaspora of Indian Jews in the past 70 years or so—to England, the United States, Australia, and above all, Israel.

The chapter that follows is an examination by Ori Z. Soltes of Ms Benjamin's very interesting work as an artist, which reflects both the range of her personal experience growing up in India—and with that growing up, diverse cultural and religious inputs—and her subsequent experience as someone who has gradually become most comfortable as a trans-national and multi-cultural individual and artist. Her work carries from the illuminated manuscript tradition that associates her with specific elements of both Indian and Jewish art history—but in a uniquely different stylistic manner—to an ongoing series of small paintings that reflect on the culturally, socially, religiously, and politically dispersed world of which she—and we, the readers—are part. It extends to a series of works, the result of two Fulbright fellowships, which explore the intersection of the Indian Jewish community, as it remains situated within its home of so many generations' duration, together with that part of the community that has spread out in its own diaspora from

[3] Bombay began to be called Mumbai in 1995 as part of the program of disconnecting the city from its British colonial past.

within the Diaspora—which is in fact, a return to the point from which the original diaspora of Jews brought them to India, as to other places across the planet: Israel.

Indian Jews have historically lived across diverse parts of the Indian subcontinent over the centuries without experiencing the sort of anti-Semitism that has been so common in many other parts of the world—particularly Christian Europe, which exported its anti-Jewish sensibilities into the Muslim world eventually, particularly in the context of European colonialism and post-colonialism in the Middle East, culminating with World War I and its aftermath. Indeed, the most obvious exception to the rule of Jewish experience in India arrived with the control of Goa in the early 16th century by the Portuguese, who brought with them not only anti-Jewish feelings but the specifics associated with the development of the Spanish and Portuguese Inquisition that would affect New Christians suspected of secretly continuing to practice Judaism—and continue until the formal abolition of the Inquisition authority in 1812.

The general lack of hostility and persecution may be understood in part as a cultural phenomenon, but also as a function of the nature of Hinduism, by far the dominant religion across India, and its embrace of diverse perspectives regarding how, specifically, one might understand and address divinity. Within the singularity of Brahman—Being—what we term 'Hinduism' recognizes a nearly infinite possibility for divine manifestations: Brahma, Vishnu, Shiva, Devi, Krishna (and many other more minor figures) are both separate from each other and all understood to be part of each other and subsumed into a singularity that is Brahman.

Indian Jews are—obviously, by definition—both Indian and Jewish. As such, in the broadest of senses, they are part of two interwoven historical and geographical continua, each with its own unique features. India is not only a vast country with dynamic contrasts between its towering mountains and its coastal lowlands and all that lies between. It is historically complex in terms of ethnicity, religion, culture and language.

To begin with, its native Dravidian population was largely pushed to its southern climes with the arrival and expansion of the Indo-Europeans around 4,500 years ago. Among other things, this means not only that Indians fall into two very broadly different ethnic groups, but that, whereas the country is overrun by scores of different languages—23 'official' languages, today, just for starters—these languages also fall into at least two very different families or categories. Thus languages like Hindi, Bengali, and Marathi are ultimately related Indo-Aryan members of the greater Indo-European family, and are largely derived from Vedic and Sanskrit (earlier and somewhat later versions of a branch of the far-flung Indo-European language family that encompasses languages from extinct Tocharian in what is now China, eastward, to Portuguese, English, and Icelandic, at the western edges of the Eurasian continent).

Conversely, languages like Tamil, Kannada, and Malayalam with an ancestry in Tamil, are part of the more geographically concentrated family of Dravidian languages. This is apart from smaller groups of Afro-Asiatic and Sino-Tibetan languages—and some in the Himalayas that are still not classified. There are, overall, perhaps 415 different languages spoken in India.

India is as diverse religiously as it is linguistically. It is, as most people are aware, the country in which Hinduism was born—in fact the word 'Hindu' refers to the place, India, not to the form of faith. However, and more to the point, 'Hinduism' is also a misnomer in being used as if there is a monolithic form of faith that goes by that name, just as it is often misunderstood to be polytheistic: there are, after all, any number of gods and goddesses, it would seem, that occupy its pantheon. In truth, (to repeat), an Indian who is part of this spiritual tradition understands all of these 'gods' and 'goddesses' to be particularized manifestations of a single god of Being.

Thus 'Hinduism' may be understood by Westerners as a more complex version, in a sense, of Christianity in its understanding of God as triune, for instead of a threefold, Father/Son/Holy Spirit Godhead, 'Hinduism' offers a poly-une Brahman (Being) expressed as Brahma, Vishnu, Siva, Devi, and others. So one is typically a Saivite, say, or a Vaishnavite, believing that Siva or Vishnu represents the consummate expression of God, but embracing the legitimacy of other expressions, as well. Moreover, among the 10 avatars assumed by Vishnu over history, one of them is as a dark-skinned (blue or black) anthropomorph, Krishna, and over time, a growing community of Krishna's followers or Krishnaites views him as the consummate manifestation of God—not as an avatar of Vishnu: on the contrary, Vishnu is viewed as a manifestation of Krishna.

This idea is most straightforwardly and succinctly expressed in the 'Bhagavad Gita', an important part of the larger epic poem, the *Mahabharata*. In chapter nine of the 'Gita', Krishna himself explains to the warrior-prince, Arjuna, that

> Even those who are devotees of other gods,
> And worship them permeated with faith
> It is only Me, son of Kunti, that even they
> Worship, though not in the enjoined fashion.

And further, in chapter 10, Krishna continues:

> Of the Adityas I am Vishnu,
> Of light the radiant sun…
>
> Of Vedas I am the Sama Veda,
> Of gods I am Vasava (Indra)…
>
> Of Rudras I am Samkara (Shiva)…[4]

And so on. This religious complexity—a paradox, really—incidentally has a literary parallel of sorts. The 'Gita' is understood by Krishnaites to be a revealed text—'*sruti*' (literally, 'heard') is the Sanskrit term. It is embedded, however, in the *Mahabharata*, an enormous epic poem that is regarded as a '*smrti*' (literally 'remembered': humanly contrived rather than divinely revealed) text. Whereas for followers of Krishna the *Gita* is the virtual equivalent of the Bible for Jews and Christians, and the Qur'an for Muslims, for non-Krishnaites it is merely part of that extended *smrti* epic, without its own *sruti* identity.

If all of this is the tip of the iceberg of Hindu complexity, consider that one of the offspring of Hinduism is Buddhism, born in India—the original Buddha, Gautama Buddha, lived from ca 563 to ca 483 BCE. While much of what emerged and evolved as Buddhism migrated eastward to other parts of Asia, as well as diversifying in its details in accordance with various cultural and prior religious traditions, a small

[4] I am using the translation by Franklin Edgerton (Harper Torchbooks, 1944), out of convenience.

but critical mass of Buddhists remained in India, and monasteries and cave complexes, albeit mostly no longer active, with stunning wall paintings, may be found in some abundance in different parts of the country. So, too, another form of faith that shares many features in common with Buddhism, Jainism, presents a small but noteworthy presence in the country.

There is also, of course, a substantial Muslim community in India—by far the largest community after Hinduism. Most Indian Muslims are Sunnis and adhere to the Ahmadiyya order. Within the next generation it is projected that India will become the most populous Muslim country in the world, outdistancing Indonesia. It is symptomatic of India's enormous population that Muslims will still constitute less than 15% of the entire population—as compared with nearly 80% as adherents to Hinduism. Similarly, although Christians are a distant third group in size—about 2.3% of the population—this still amounts to nearly 25 million adherents. There are also important populations, still smaller in number, of Sikhs, Zoroastrians (in India, known as Parsis) and Baha'is—and again symptomatic of India's enormous demographic size, members of two of these groups are more numerous in India than anywhere else on the planet.[5]

Among the smallest religious groups in India is that of the Jews. This leads to the second half of the identity question for Indian Jews as Jews—and to the question: if participating in the Indian world clearly

[5] As of this writing, more than 20 million of the 23.5 million Sikh population worldwide resides in India. About 70,000 Parsis reside in India (they are called Parsis—'Persians'—by reference to their origin in Persia); about 1,400 reside in neighboring Pakistan. More than 2.5 million Baha'is dwell in India, out of a world-wide population of nearly 7.5 million. Iran offers the next largest population, numbering approximately 350,000.

means interacting with others of diverse faiths and diverse languages and of diverse ethnic and cultural backgrounds, what does it mean to be a Jew? The first part of the answer to that question carries well beyond India. If one considers definitional aspects of Judaism, one of the most prominent is that of having spent most of the last two millennia in varying states of dispersion—as noted by Erica Lyons in her preface to this volume. The Jewish Diaspora that began to take shape between the time of the destruction of the Temple in Jerusalem (70 CE) and the failed Bar Kokhba Revolt (132–135 CE) would over the centuries yield subsequently smaller expulsion-enforced diasporas from within the Diaspora—from the Rhineland in the 12th century, or from England in 1290, or from Spain in 1492, to name three prominent examples.

Jews are also typically referred to by different quasi-ethnic terms, depending upon what is regarded as their point of departure prior to dispersion. Thus Mizrahi Jews come from the Middle East—a subset of which, as Arab Jews, are properly referred to as Must'arabi Jews—and north Africa; Romaniot Jews trace themselves back through two millennia in Rome; Sephardic Jews associate themselves with Spain and Portugal, and Ashkenazi Jews are considered narrowly Rhineland Jews and more broadly Jews from the larger realm of northern and eastern Europe. India's Jewish community, as we shall subsequently note in more detail, is the consequence of several diasporic moments in Jewish history. It also consists of a range of different 'kinds' of Jews: mainly Mizrahis, Sephardis, and Ashkenazis.

Moreover, across most of history, 'Jewish' was a term used to refer primarily to adherence to a religion—with a common set of beliefs and accompanying prayers, ceremonies, and customs, within the synagogue and home as centering spaces of Jewish life, but with divergent details reflecting the nature of Judaism as a dispersed phenomenon—as a series of islands in vast seas of Christians, Muslims, Hindus and others. In the last two centuries or so, new terminology has come to reference new ways of thinking about Judaism as a religion: Reform, Orthodox, Conservative, and within the past century, Reconstructionist Judaism, as well.

Gradually, within that same time period, however, other ways of defining 'Judaism' have made their way into the thought and the vocabulary of Jews and those focused on Judaism. Thus it has been redefined as an ethnicity or a race (most straightforwardly by the German political and philosophical pamphleteer, William Marr, in 1879). In any number of countries, the idea that Jews are an ethnic group precluded accepting them as genuine citizens of and participants in that country. The definitional issue would become more complicated with the arrival of modern Jewish Nationalism—Zionism—onto the world stage by ca 1862, with the publication of Moses Hess' volume, *Rome and Jerusalem*; Jewish nationalist thinking reached full efflorescence by 1896, with the publication of Theodor Herzl's *The Jewish State*. By the late 1920s, the American Reconstructionist movement would carry the definition of Judaism as a culture to a further point, referring to it as a civilization. And by the 1960s there was a formally organized Secular Jewish Community that similarly sees itself as Jewish in historical, cultural, and possibly ethnic, but not religious terms.

The question of how to define Judaism leads, for this discussion, back to the subject of Indian Jews by raising the layered question: how and when did they arrive into India, from where and under what circumstances? And how do they define themselves exactly? The answer to the first question is that Jews arrived in the Indian subcontinent in several distinct waves at distinct if—in some cases—debated times, and from distinct and diverse places—a layered diaspora from within the Jewish Diaspora.

To this discussion must be added one further historical note that extends beyond India: the use of the terms 'Judaism', 'Jewish', and 'Jew' in thinking back conceptually through the past four millennia. Abraham, Isaac, Jacob and their spouses are referred to as 'Hebrews' in the Bible; Moses, Joshua, and the Kings Saul, David, and Solomon are all referred to as 'Israelites.' A millennium after the time of the united kingdom of Israel, when its descendants split into two groups—Jews and Christians—both laid claim to being the proper continuation of the Hebrew-Israelite tradition: the phrase that was used in the Latin-speaking Roman period, and for many centuries thereafter, in fact, was *verus Israel*—'true Israel'. Thus on the one hand, the word 'Jew' and its cognates are not found in the Torah (Five Books of Moses) or the prophetic books of the Hebrew Bible and on the other, what we think of as Judaism, with its fully canonized Bible, its emerging rabbinic tradition, its full complement of life-cycle and annual communal celebrations and commemorations, and above all, its existence as a far-flung diaspora, is not fully in place until well after the biblical period.

There is more complexity to this. Shortly after Solomon's death (ca 930 BCE), a civil war split the kingdom of Israel into two parts. Between the time of that break-up and the aftermath of the Crucifixion (ca 35 CE)—and the subsequent Destruction of the Second Temple (70 CE), and the push toward the Bar Kokhba Revolt (132–135 CE)—at least two crucial developments connected to this narrative took place. One, the northern 10 tribes of Israel—still called 'Israel'—ultimately disappeared from history in the aftermath of the Assyrian debacle of ca 722–721 BCE, while the southern two tribes, Judah and Benjamin—together referred to as 'Judah' since the split-up of the kingdom—continued, even surviving the debacle of the Babylonian destruction of Solomon's Temple (586 BCE) and the nearly half century of exile for many Judaeans that followed the destruction.

Two, in the slow aftermath of the return of some of the exiled Judaeans to Judah (in 538 BCE), and the rebuilding of the Temple, under Akhaemenid Medo-Persian patronage, the prophetic era came gradually to a close: with the final redaction of the Torah by Ezra the Scribe (444 BCE), mainstream Judaeans were led by a nomocracy centered on scribes and scholars who could read and interpret the word of God, not by a theocracy led by prophets and priests to whom God is understood to be speaking directly with some regularity.

It is the embrace or rejection of this nomocratic revolution that would yield the schism within the Judaean community half a millennium later that shaped Judaism and Christianity in spiritual (and, eventually, political) opposition to each other. And here is the linguistic complication: in the operative languages of that time and place—mainly Hebrew, Aramaic, Greek, and Latin (but others as well), one cannot make a distinction between 'Judaean' and 'Jewish'. Thus, in pure linguistic terms there would appear to be a straightforward continuum between these two terms and concepts, while both of them are distinguished from 'Christian'. However, historically speaking, this would be inaccurate: to repeat, what we identify as 'Judaism' is still in the process of taking shape in the century or more after the Crucifixion, and what is taking shape as Christianity perceives itself for at least several centuries after that moment to be the proper continuation of the Hebrew-Israelite-Judaean tradition beginning with Abraham. It will be some time until the smoke clears and we can clearly distinguish these two forms of faith from each other.

I have belabored the historical issue of the previous several paragraphs in order to add one further important element to the layered context of Indian Jewish history and culture. That history has several chronological beginning points and several points of geographic origin, since the Jewish community of India is a community of diverse communities (Fig. 1).

Thus the primary Jewish community in terms of size, the Bene Israel—at its height, around 1948, it numbered some 20,000 individuals—in and around Bombay, (specifically settling just to the south of the island city in the Konkan region of Maharashtra), is first mentioned in foreign documents in 1768, and these accounts assert that the Bene Israel ancestors had arrived originally 18 or 19 centuries earlier—and that by the time of the 18th-century references their understanding of Judaism had become minimal, reinforced only through their contacts with Cochini Jews. The Bene Israel community generally speaks Marathi and was traditionally divided into two lighter- and darker-skinned groups that typically did not intermarry.

The generally darker-complexioned part of the much smaller Jewish community of Cochin speaks Judeo-Malayalam (by which I mean Malayalam with a generous spicing of vocabulary and turns of phrase from Hebrew and Aramaic). Like the Bene Israel in traditional self-conception, they originate in the Middle East—the initial group of Cochini Jews carries a tradition of having arrived as traders to India during the time of King Solomon (which would mean that they were Israelites, not Jews when they first arrived), and/or that they arrived as traders to the port near Cochin within a generation of the destruction of Solomon's Temple in 586 BCE, with more arriving six centuries later, after the destruction of the Second Temple in 70 CE—but there is also a lighter-skinned community of Jews in Cochin, who arrived only in the 15th and 16th centuries, from Spain and Portugal. These Cochini Jews are also known as Paradesi Jews, and while they arrived speaking Judezmo (Judeo-Spanish/Portuguese; also known as Ladino), they also eventually acclimatized linguistically to Malayalam.

A third subset Cochini group apparently arrived in the 17th century from the Netherlands, and a fourth subset arrived in Cochin in the late 19th century—from Nagercoil, to which their Musta'arabi ancestors are alleged to have arrived in the first century from Syria, along with one of Jesus' disciples, St Thomas, who had travelled there to preach the word of Jesus. On the other hand, more Bene Israel Jews arrived from Pakistan after the partition of 1947, but others who arrived at that time from the Sindh, Punjab, and Pathan areas were not part of the Bene Israel community.

So, too, those Jews who settled in Goa, like the later additions to the community in Cochin, came from Portugal in the wake of the development of the Inquisition and Expulsion effected by the end of the 15th century and the Inquisition that continued in the several centuries that followed—which also means that their primary language was Judezmo. This last group was mostly comprised of Marranos—Jews who had been pressed to convert to Christianity but who secretly tried to live as hidden Jews; coming to India would have provided a respite and an opportunity to return to openly Jewish lives—and when the Portuguese Inquisition arrived in Goa, these Jews found themselves potentially subject to its dangerous depredations.

An altogether different group of Jews originated in Baghdad—and in other parts of the Middle East, such as Basra, Syria, Iran, Aden, and Afghanistan—arriving between the mid-18th and early 19th centuries. Referred to collectively as Baghdadi Jews, they arrived first in the city of Surat—the first Baghdadi immigrant mentioned by name was Joseph Semah, recorded as arriving in Surat in 1730—and then primarily settled in Bombay and Calcutta; some of them also settled in Pune. The Baghdadi Jews continued to speak mainly Arabic and in some cases Farsi, eventually acquiring English, rather than one of the Indic languages spoken by most other groups of Indian Jews.

There were still smaller settlements of Jews here and there across the subcontinent, as well: a further diaspora within this diaspora from among the broad Jewish diaspora. Thus a small number of Ladino-speaking Jews from Spain and Portugal, arrived by way of Britain, Holland, and Livorno, Italy, to Madras (now Chennai), soon after the city was founded in 1640. Most of these were coral merchants and became acculturated as Tamil-speakers.

There are two further, smaller groups that might also be mentioned in the interest of offering a fuller sense of the complexity of the Indian Jewish world. Thus, there is a group of roughly 9,000 individuals that refers to itself as the Bene Menashe—associating itself with one of the two sons of the patriarch, Joseph. Interestingly, this group is comprised of formerly animist Mizo and Kuki headhunting tribesmen in Manipur and Mizoram who converted to Christianity at the beginning of the 20th century and then began converting to Judaism in the 1970s. They assert, however, that they are actually returning to their original faith, having descended from one of the lost Ten tribes (that of Menashe) who disappeared from history after the (previously noted) Assyrian conquest of northern Israel in 722–721 BCE—which would make their ancestors Israelites, as opposed to Judaeans or Jews. In fact, the form of Judaism that they follow is more akin to biblical 'Israelitism' than to mainstream Judaism, in following the Bible with no regard for the rabbinic tradition that has evolved over the past two millennia.

The second such recent addition to the overall Indian Jewish community is a smaller group in Andhra Pradesh on the southeast coast, referred to as the 'Telugu Jews': they speak Telugu (one of the Dravidian languages in south India), and embraced Judaism in 1991. The 'Telugu Jews'—some of them came to follow an ultra-Orthodox life-style—refer to themselves as Bene Ephraim, tracing their ancestry in a manner analogous to the identity-sensibility of the Mizo and Kuki Bene Menashe, to the other son of Joseph—Ephraim—and to the lost Israelite tribe that is traditionally understood to have descended from him.

As India has emerged as part of the modern world since the country's inception in 1947, on the one hand, a majority of its diverse Jewish communities have emigrated, mainly going to Israel, which was born at virtually the same time. Conversely, Delhi, as the political capital of the country, with little Jewish history of its own, has not surprisingly acquired a small community made up largely of expatriates and diplomats (in particular from Israel) working in Delhi. Equally unsurprising is the fact that Chabad has established a synagogue and religious center in the Paharganj neighborhood in the central part of the city—an area frequented by young Israeli backpackers.

In the chapters that follow this brief introduction, a more detailed discussion of the Bene Israel, Cochini, and Baghdadi Jews will consider their respective origins and developments in more detail, as well as the current fate of each of them. We shall also observe that some of what defines each such community as unique will be the reflection of each in its synagogues and its ceremonial objects and customs.

The complexity of the Indian Jewish community is on the one hand an organic outcome of the complexities of India and of Jewish history and culture in general, and also reflects the broader dispersion of Jews throughout Asia. On the other hand, that organic complexity yields naturally to the sort of narrative articulated by Siona Benjamin's personal recollections and her family story—to say nothing of the creative outcome that becomes her transcultural visual art, with its diverse sources of inspiration and its rich colors and forms, which interweaves and transforms so many sources and influences in an unprecedented and exciting manner.

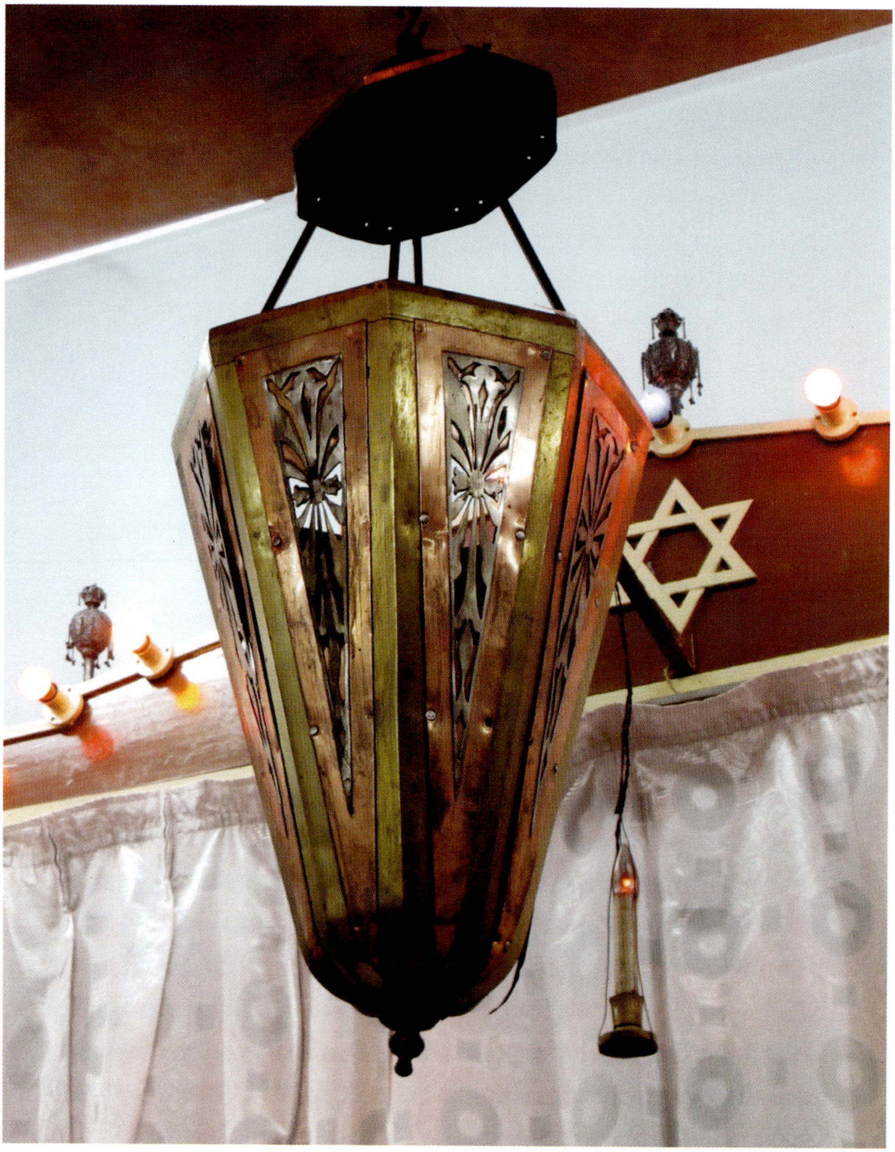

Fig. 5a. *Ner Tamid*, Magen Abraham Synagogue, Ahmedabad

CHAPTER ONE

The Bene Israel and their Customs and Structures

Ori Z. Soltes

The Intrigue of Origins

It is a truism across Jewish history and geography that it is always difficult to determine who was the first Jew to settle in almost whatever place to which a Jewish community has migrated, just as it is often difficult, if a community has all but disappeared, to assert definitively that the last Jew is gone: there always seems to have been somebody who was there before the standard narrative asserts a beginning, and someone still lingering after the narrative has pronounced the community completely vanished. Where Indian Jews are concerned this truism is even more emphatic, with its own particular chronological issues: which community really arrived first—and when, and from where? And where the largest of the Jewish Indian communities is concerned, the so-called Bene Israel, this sort of question is even more pronounced. For there are any number of theories regarding exactly when the first Bene Israel Jews arrived in India and from where they came.

Thus one tradition—one 'theory'—asserts that the Bene Israel originated as part of a trading group during the reign of King Solomon (r ca 965–930 BCE) which would place their arrival onto the west coast of the Indian subcontinent at nearly 3,000 years ago.[1] So, too, their origins would have been as Israelites, since the word 'Jews' and the mainstream Jewish tradition did not yet exist; in fact, neither the Torah nor the rest of the Hebrew Bible would have been redacted and canonized yet.[2] A variant of this idea is that they were part of the lost 10 tribes that disappeared from Northern Israel and from history in the context and aftermath of the conquest of the Israelite Kingdom by the Neo-Assyrian Empire, in 722–721 BCE. This would also, of course, make their ancestry Israelite, as opposed, strictly speaking, to 'Jewish'—and either of these theories might also account for the more Bible-based than rabbinic tradition-based sort of Judaism that they were practicing when 'rediscovered' in the modern era.

Nor are these the only theories of origin. A third proposal, adumbrated in the mid-19th century, is that they arrived around 175 BCE—this would be during the Hasmonean period, just prior to

---

[1] This theory was proposed by Shellim Samuel in his *Treatise on the Origin and Early History of the Bene Israel of Maharashtra State.*

[2] Regardless of whether or not one subscribes to the Documentary Hypothesis, as most academics and most non-academic Jews and Christians do—the simple form of which is that Ezra, in redacting (editing) the Torah into its final form, in 444 BCE, wove together four different authorial threads dating from between the time of David and the Babylonian exile—or as a traditionalist, (one who believes that the entirety of the text came through Moses at Sinai); the definitive written text is understood to have been prepared by Ezra. The remainder of the Hebrew Bible—the historical, prophetic, and literary books that constitute the 'Prophets' (Joshua, Judges, Samuel, Kings, Isaiah, Jeremiah, Ezekiel, and the 12 'minor' prophets) and the 'Sacred Writings' (Ruth, Job, Ecclesiastes, Psalms, Proverbs, Song of Songs, Ezra, Nehemiah, Esther, Daniel, Chronicles, et al.) were all included in the final canon around 140 CE.

the revolt against the Seleucids led by the so-called Maccabee brothers.[3] In fact this theory suggests that they were from the Galilee and fled the growing persecution being directed toward the Judaeans by Antiokhos IV, which itself led to the revolt of 168/7–165/4 BCE. This dating would therefore depict them as Judaeans—in possession of the fully redacted Torah, but not of a fully canonized Bible, and at most with the beginnings of an oral rabbinic interpretive tradition.[4]

A fourth tradition (and perhaps the most popular by now) is vaguely set in the first or second century CE, but with very specific circumstances of arrival. This tradition asserts that there was a group of Jewish trading vessels that were hit by a storm coming up through the Arabian Sea; the small flotilla was shipwrecked on its way to the port of Cheul, at the site of the dangerous outcroppings known as the Twin Rocks of Andheri-Underi. Most of the passengers and crew perished, but seven men and seven women managed to make it alive to shore along the Konkan coast, not too far south of Bombay, near Nowgaon—and the Bene Israel are the descendants of these 14 survivors.

Further details within this particular narrative offer the survivors, settling in among the locals and adopting Indian names similar to their biblically-based first names, but eventually becoming known by their '-kar' surnames, which references the particular village in which a given individual had settled. Thus, Nawgaonkar, for instance—and other names, like Penkar (from the village of Pen) eventuated into more than

[3] Haim Solomon Kehimkar, *History of the Bene Israel of India*, ed. Immanuel Olsvanger (Tel-Aviv: The Dayag Press, Ltd, and London: G. Salby, 1937). This also seems to be a hypothesis favored by many of the Bene Israel Jews themselves.

[4] For a slightly fuller discussion of the Israelite-Judaean-Jew/ish distinctions, see the Introduction, pp. 41–44.

a hundred such 'village' surnames among the Bene Israel. Meanwhile, all of the group's holy texts were lost in the shipwreck, so they eventually forgot all of the Hebrew prayers except 'Sh'ma Yisrael...' ('Hear O Israel...')

One of the obvious features of eyebrow-raising interest in this last origin story is its centering on the number 'seven' which has a long history and wide geography—in pagan antiquity; in Judaism, Christianity, and Islam; and in other cultural contexts in other parts of the world—of being understood as an important, sacred number. Among its many manifestations within the Jewish tradition alone is the commandment to keep the seventh day sacred and in the seven-branched Temple menorah—so it is, at the least, interesting and at most historically suspicious that this is the number of founding fathers and mothers that has been passed down in this subset account of origin.

Moreover, interestingly, the Chitpavan Brahmins from the same region have a nearly identical origin story: that they are the light-skinned descendants of a shipwreck; that the local (dark-skinned) inhabitants of that small strip of coast gathered the bodies of all those who had drowned and had been washed ashore and prepared a common funeral pyre; that as the pyre was about to be lit, a renowned sage, Parashurama—a figure referenced in a number of Hindu works, most importantly in the renowned Sanskrit epic, *Mahabharata*: the sixth avatar of Vishnu, who appears in this human form to quell the spread of evil on the earth—passed by. Parashurama saw in these fair-skinned bodies potential recruits for the Brahmin (priestly) caste in his campaign against the members of the Kshatriya (warrior) caste who had been abusing their power and thus sowing the seeds of evil—so he sprinkled some holy water on the bodies and recited some mantras and they sprang to life.

That group called itself the Chitpavan Brahmins. Their descendants, lighter-skinned Brahmins, do not intermarry with the darker-skinned Brahmins (Saraswat Brahmins) in the same region, keeping themselves somewhat apart from the other communities. They share many names in common, interestingly enough, with the Bene Israel—and the shipwreck origin story is apparently shared, as well.

Yet another—a fifth—suggestion is that the Bene Israel arrived in the fifth or sixth century CE, from either South Arabia or Persia. This would certainly present a classification of the Bene Israel as Jews, and Mizrahi Jews at that—and in the case of the South Arabian hypothesis, more specifically as Must'arabi Jews. If from Persia, this would either have occurred during the Sassanian era or toward the beginning of the Muslim era—the Muslim Arabs conquered Sassanian Persia in 643–647 CE; if from south Arabia, either from the last pagan or early Muslim era. The presumption in either of these two subset versions of this theory is that the Jewish community was under stress and therefore emigrated, ending up in India. Clearly that supposition would require a more precise dating proposal, since neither the Zoroastrian Sassanians nor the pagan Arabs are known to have persecuted the Jews, and the early Muslim Arabs both in the *hijaz* and in Persia were inconsistent, depending upon various circumstances, with regard to their relationship with the Jews. This does not mean that there could not have been a migration anyway, but not necessarily due to active persecutory pressures.

In any case, there is virtually no hard evidence to prove any of these theories; each of them is interesting in its own way, and offers intriguing possibilities as to its facticity. Regardless of when they arrived, the Bene Israel became isolated from the Jewish world at large and remained so for a good number of centuries. That may account for the limited but distinctive ways in which they celebrated their traditions—such as a strict, Torah-inspired observance of the Sabbath. In fact they came to be referred to locally as *Shaniwar Teli*—'Saturday Oil pressers'—a reference both to their keeping of that day as a day apart, in accordance with the Fourth of the Ten Commandments found in the Torah (Ex 20:9-11 and Deut 5:12-15) and also, presumably due to their primary profession.

Indeed, the origin hypothesis proposed in the 1830s by Haeem Samuel Kehimkar (that the first Bene Israel arrived around the time of the Maccabees) includes the notion that their primary and original profession as oil pressers reflects their descent from the tribe of Levi, since, he contends, that profession was reserved for those who served in the Temple—either the Levite tribe in general or perhaps only the higher priestly clan, a subset of the Levites, the *Kohanim*. A DNA study associated with Tudor Parfitt—an academic known for his work with out-of the-way remnants of ancient and isolated Jewish communities—asserts that the Bene Israel share a DNA link with a lineage going back to Moses and Aaron (from whose family the *Kohanim* derive). This, of course, does not clarify the question of when they arrived in India, and one might wonder, among other things, whether Kehimkar's claim is confuting the rabbinic tradition that has become a centerpiece of the Hanukah story—the miracle of the pure oil lasting eight days—with the idea that those associated with the Temple were uniquely pressers of oil, per se.

There are, to further complicate matters, two sub-communities that did not traditionally marry in the past: darker-skinned '*Kala*' and lighter-skinned '*Gora*' Bene Israel, which resonates with the 'shipwreck origin' story.[5] One further origin hypothesis, in fact, suggests that the latter group is derived from the aforementioned ship-wreck survivors, while the former, it is asserted, are descendants of concubinage of one or more of those seven males with local women.[6] Such a theory naturally introduces certain logistical complications: if the darker-skinned Bene Israel derive from local—presumably non-Jewish—females, then none of their descendants are halakhically Jewish. And at what time and under what specific circumstances did the two communities, one entirely and the other partially derived from the shipwreck survivors, who obviously interfaced, cease to interface? And do the two populations not have different percentages of DNA derived from the *kohanim*?

II. The Narrative of Rediscovery: An Old-New Community

Be these questions and issues as they may, beyond the origin theories are the slight variants on a rediscovery theory. One commonly held notion is that, at some uncertain point in history, an Indian Jew from Cochin named David Rahabi discovered the Bene Israel in their villages and recognized their vestigial Jewish customs.[7] Rahabi taught the

---

[5] Nathan Katz, *Who Are the Jews of India?* (Los Angeles: California University Press, 2000), 91ff.

[6] Ibid.

[7] Shalva Weil, 'Yom Kippur: the Festival of Closing the Doors,' in Hananya Goodman, ed. *Between Jerusalem & Benares: Comparative Studies in Judaism & Hinduism* (New York: State University of New York Press, 1994), pp. 85–100.

people about normative Judaism, allegedly re-introducing them to the festivals of Shavuot and Sukkot, among others. He trained some young men among them to be the religious leaders of the community.[8] Known as Kajis, these men held positions that became hereditary, assuming the roles of judges and adjudicators of disputes.[9]

What makes this rediscovery anecdote interesting is that one Bene Israel tradition places Rahabi's arrival around 1000 or 1400 (in and of itself offering a wide range of chronological possibility), however, outside historians more often conclude that he was not active until the 18th century. They suggest that the 'David Rahabi' of the Bene Israel folk tradition was actually a David Yehezkel (Ezekiel) Rahabi, (1694–1772), who resided in, and may have been a leader of, the Cochin Jewish community—the center, by then, of the relatively wealthy Malabar Jewish community along the southwest corner of the Indian peninsula—whereas others suggest that the reference is to David Baruch Rahabi, who arrived in Bombay from Cochin still later, in 1825.[10]

In any case, the earliest discussion of the Bene Israel to reach the outside world in the modern era is found in a letter written in 1768 by that first-noted David Yehezkel Rahabi to a Dutch trading partner, in which he comments on how the Bene Israel community is spread throughout the Maratha province, and that they recite the *sh'ma*, circumcise their sons on the eighth day after birth, do not eat shellfish,

---

[8] Shalva Weil, 'Religious Leadership vs. Secular Authority: the Case of the Bene Israel,' in *Eastern Anthropologist*, 49 (3–4), (1996): 301–316.

[9] Pushkar Sohoni and Kenneth X. Robbins, *Jewish Heritage of the Deccan: Mumbai, the Northern Konkan, Pune*. (Mumbai: Deccan Heritage Foundation; Jaico, 2017), pp. 16–17.

[10] Kehimkar, *The History of the Bene-Israel of India*, p. 66.

and rest on the Sabbath.[11] They are again referenced by Christian missionaries around 1813. These assert that, working among the Bene Israel, they are teaching them to read Hebrew and have also provided them with a Hebrew Bible in Marathi. It is interesting that, especially American Methodist and Scottish Presbyterian missionaries felt it essential to bring them up to a more complete condition of Jewishness, by way of Hebrew and Biblical instruction, before they could be brought into the fuller light of Christianity.

Anglican missionaries were more immediately and directly focused on the conversion process, but were frustrated by the fact that the Bene Israel 'closed their minds' when confronted with arguments demonstrating the divinity of Jesus.[12] It is of equal importance that however unaware the community had been of the centuries of mainstream Judaism, they clung fiercely to whatever limited knowledge they possessed. The attempt of outsiders to disconnect them from their Judaism by re-acquainting them with more of its biblical foundations,

[11] Consistent with the principle that when one believes one has located the first Jew in any given place, there turns out to have been one who arrived earlier, there may have been mention of the Bene Israel as early as 1732, when 'a Danish missionary, J.A. Sartorius, was told by "German and Indian [i.e. Cochin] Jews resident at Madras who gained their information from other Jews who came from Cochin" that there were people in Surat and Rajapore… "who do not call themselves Jews nor understand the name, but 'Bene Israel', children or descendants of Israel… What they know of religion is not yet ascertained except they make use of the word '*Shema*' as a formal of prayer or of doctrine."' This passage, from Benjamin J. Israel, 78, has embedded within it a passage from the article by Walter J. Fischel, 'David D'Beth Hillel: a hitherto unknown Jewish traveler to India in the nineteenth century,' in his volume, *Unknown Jews in Unknown Lands: the Travels of Rabbi David D'Beth Hillel, 1824-1832*. (New York, 1973).

[12] Interestingly, the turn of phrase was a quote from what one of the Bene Israel had said: 'When it came to the messiahship of Jesus, our Bene Israel just knew that the missionaries were wrong and simply closed their minds.' (See Shifra Strizower, *The Children of Israel; the Bene Israel of Bombay*, p. 41.)

rather than affirming for them the fallaciousness of rabbinic mainstream Judaism (as a misdirected form of post-biblical Judaism), provided them with a stronger intellectual and spiritual basis for resisting the conversionary efforts made toward them.

There were other interesting aspects of this part of the story. Britain only allowed missionaries into its Indian territories in 1813, after which both European and American Christian missions across India were centered in Bombay. The American Mission established a Hebrew school in 1827, at Alibag, in the Konkan, attended by some 30 Bene Israel children, 8 of them girls. By 1829 there were 130 Bene Israel children in schools run by the American Mission.[13] Most significantly for this narrative, John Wilson, a missionary from the Church of Scotland, arrived in that same year and worked in Bombay and the Kolaba district until his death in 1875. By 1836 there were more than 250 Bene Israel children in his schools—one third of them girls. It was Wilson who first suggested that the Bene Israel were a biblical 'remnant of Israel'; he wrote both *The Rudiments of Hebrew Grammar* in Marathi, in 1832, and the first serious account of Bene Israel customs, in 1838.

A still slightly different account that interweaves the role of Cochini Jews with that of English missionaries in the education and renewal of the Bene Israel is that a group of Cochini teachers came to Bombay in 1826, made aware of the community's existence through the larger publicity of it generated by Wilson and other missionaries. They lived among the Bene Israel community in Bombay and the Kolaba district in order to teach them about mainstream Jewish observance; and a second group of Cochini teachers arrived in 1833. This tradition

[13] Strizower, p. 40.

asserts that they spent weekdays teaching Hebrew reading and writing and Jewish religious ideas, and on Saturdays—Shabbat—they led the morning prayer service and then discussed Jewish rabbinic law (*halakhah*) and traditions in the afternoons.

So, aside from origin questions, even in this rather recent aspect of Bene Israel history there is disagreement as to etiology: was it the Christian missionaries or the Cochini Jews who first redirected the Bene Israel toward the mainstream—and/or to what extent was it simply a combination of both?

Regardless of who started the ball rolling—exactly when and by whom the Bene Israel were first 're-discovered' and/or regained contact with the larger Jewish world by the mid-18th century; and in spite of the apparent paucity of their knowledge of and isolated disconnection from the mainstream Jewish (i.e. rabbinic) world—the outcome of Wilson's efforts in particular opened up new possibilities for members of the Bene Israel community. Using his book as a starting point, and accepted into the college that he founded in 1857, a number of them became very proficient in Hebrew. Sometime thereafter, Bene Israel scholars published translations of classic Hebrew texts, prayer books, rabbinical commentaries, and even sermons available in textual form, into Marathi. They also studied English in Wilson's schools—thus exposing the community for the first time to the larger realm of Jewish spirituality and intellect as well as to the larger world of knowledge that was rapidly becoming available through English.

Yet their identity as a distinct community remained intact. They are a community not only identifiable by their customs but by their language, a dialect of Marathi—Judeo-Marathi—that is one of the more than 40 dialects of that language; clearly, regardless of when they arrived, they picked up the local language, although they embedded within it vocabulary and turns of phrase probably derived from Hebrew and/or Aramaic as well as words from Urdu that are themselves derived from Arabic and Persian.

Apparently, many of the terms used by them that refer to kinship relationships and to religion come from these diverse non-Marathi sources. Thus, for instance, *abba*, meaning father', is from Hebrew; *masjid* for 'synagogue', *namaz* for 'prayer', and *kabar* for 'grave', are all from Arabic. The plethora of such Arabic-based terminology underscores how close the Bene Israel community seems to have been with the Muslim community, as much as or more so than with the Hindu community. Interestingly, they may also have written Judeo-Marathi, as others did other dialects of Marathi, in the traditional *Modi* script, but eventually shifted—as Marathi in general did—to the use of *Devanagari* (the writing system used in Vedic and Sanskrit, and in the modern era used by Hindi and many other Sanskrit-based languages). The Bene Israel who served in the British army tended to speak Hindi, which was the Indian language in use by British troops—as well as picking up English.

One of the testaments to the power of the Bene Israel identity as Jewish throughout the centuries leading up to this 'rediscovery' period, is that the better part of a century of efforts to convert them to Christianity ultimately failed. Wilson himself, after 25 years of working among them noted, in 1854, that '...the labors of the Bombay Missions have not yet been blessed with the conversion of any of their number.'

III. The Reshaping of a Community in the Last Three Centuries

There is a handful of further chronological markers in the 18th and 19th centuries that bring the Bene Israel, if not into greater clarity regarding their origins, at least into greater clarity regarding how they have come to operate as Jews in the modern era—although, to repeat, for how long before this recent period it is impossible to say, with what is available in our current sources of information. By the early 18th century they were mostly concentrated in a small area just south of Bombay. Some were already probably migrating, however, across Dharamtar Bay from the Konkan area into the area of Bombay proper, gradually, after 1688, which is the year in which the Bombay islands were handed over by the Portuguese to the British as part of the dowry of Catherine De Braganza in marriage to Charles II. While the British East India Company held the island of Bombay proper, the area to the south was ruled partially by the hereditary Maratha Admirals known as the Angrias and the Maratha feudatory chieftain, the Pant Sachiv of Bhor, as well as partially by the Muslim Nawab of Janjira.

It is commonly asserted that the pioneers, strictly speaking, within the process of the Bene Israel arrival specifically into Bombay, were members of the Divekar family, moving there (given the family name, we might assume that they originated in the village of Dive) in 1746, where the British guaranteed their religious freedom. Some achieved employment in the East India Company; Samuel Ezekiel Divekar (born in Cochin in 1730) promoted to the rank of Native Commandant, established the first synagogue in Bombay in 1796—a year after escaping from the prison of Tipu Sultan, where he had been a captive during the

Second Mysore War, and a year before he died.[14] By then a significant-sized community had evolved.

The Bene Israel had previously served in the army and navy of the Marathas—and possibly, but not certainly, also under the Nawab of Janjira. Apparently, as the British began to develop an army by mid-century, to defend Bombay against these native forces, substantial numbers of Bene Israel enlisted in turn and served in that armed force, using the 'caste' name, 'Israel', and thereby beginning to reside in Bombay proper. Substantial Bene Israel service in the Bombay (British) military continued until toward the middle of the 19th century—certainly not the most familiar kind of role for Jews in other parts of the world.[15] Eventually as the Bene Israel gradually were engaged less frequently in the military, they transitioned to diverse areas of public service: education, medicine, accounting, as well as working as contractors and skilled carpenters. The knowledge of English that had become rather widespread among them through the missionary schools, to which they eagerly flocked, offered an obvious advantage.

[14] Divekar had been the native commandant of the Sixth Battalion of Britain's East India Company's army, and serving under General Matthews in the War, was among a handful of Bene Israel Jews taken prisoner by Tipu Sultan. They were to be executed, but upon learning that they were Bene Israel, the Sultan's mother begged for their lives, since she was familiar with 'Beni Israel' from the Qur'an—so they were placed in prison instead. Divekar swore to himself that if he were released, he would devote his life to reviving Jewish life among the Bene Israel in Bombay. When he escaped, he made the center of that effort the building of the synagogue. He died in Cochin; he had gone there to acquire some Torah scrolls for the new synagogue.

[15] Among the few exceptions to this in Europe—somewhat ironically, given subsequent history—was the demographically significant presence of Jews in the Hapsburg, Austro-Hungarian army, from 1783 through World War I; and somewhat less numerically significant, in the Prussian army between the mid-19th century and World War I. Part of what made Alfred Dreyfus such a viable target in Catholic France for the trumped-up charges of treason against him in the 1890s was that, as a Jewish Captain in the French army, he stood out as a rarity.

Nonetheless, a small number continued as soldiers under the British, often of high rank, and distinguished themselves in various wars and campaigns, such as the Anglo-Maratha Wars, the Mysore Wars, the Sind war, the Punjab wars, the Persian Campaign, the Afghan Wars, the Burma Wars, the Abyssinian Wars, as well as in World War I. It may be of particular interest, given subsequent history, that there is a record of a Bene Israel medical officer who served among Allenby's troops when they marched into Jerusalem in 1917 as part of Britain's Palestine Campaign against the Ottoman Turks.

Interestingly, part of the reason that many Bene Israel rose to prominence under British colonial rule was that they were perceived as racially different from the 'natives' against whom the English maintained their ongoing prejudices. There is, again, an irony to this: as Jews were gradually being treated more as a non-European ethno-racial group in Western Europe and on that basis, new forms and justifications for non-religion-based marginalization were often operative, on the other side of the world from England itself, and from Prussia and France in particular, they were re-visioned as, essentially, 'European'.[16]

As a consequence of this view, they were typically able to find higher, better-paying positions in the British army than were their non-

[16] I am thinking specifically of the discussion of Jews as a non-European, Asian race, which view emerged particularly in the works of the Prussians, Adolph Stoecker (1878) and Wilhelm Marr (1879) and the Frenchman, Edouard Drumont (1886), who sought to relegate German and French Jews, respectively, to the cultural and political sidelines by labeling them as inherently foreign—specifically, in Marr's case, by referring to them as 'Semites'. The same prejudices against non-Europeans that accompanied the development of anthropology—and with it the fabrication of theories of 'race'—in the Europe of the late 18th and 19th centuries, and which helped justify the expansion of colonialism, the enslavement of Africans, and the oppression and economic rape of Asia; and which helped reshape medieval religious anti-Jewishness into modern anti-Semitism, yielded a positive treatment of Jews by the colonial British in India.

Jewish—Hindu and Muslim—neighbors. Some of them remained tied to the British army when it governed Aden as a protectorate, moving to the Gulf with their entire families. Interestingly—and again this offers both irony and a reminder of the complexity of the Jewish community in India overall (and of human nature)—the newly anglicized Baghdadi Jews, absorbing the prejudices of their patrons, looked down upon the Bene Israel in the mid-19th century, because they regarded them as 'Indian' and therefore inferior—and in fact questioned the authenticity of their Judaism. It was in reaction to this attitude that the Bene Israel historian, Haeem Samuel Kehimkar (referenced above, p. 56 and fnn 10, 17) wrote vigorously regarding the Jewishness of his community in the later part of the century. To push its Jewish legitimacy, he emphasized its non-Indian origins, promoting the idea that there are two Bene Israel communities—one, 'white' (*gora*) that derived purely from outside India; and the other 'black' (*kala*), derived from the union of 'white' 'foreign' males with indigenous Indian females.[17]

As the 19th century pushed forward, various Bene Israel families moved away from the Bombay area and settled in Pune, Ahmedabad, Karachi, Delhi, and other Indian cities (as well as beyond—for example, in Karachi, which would eventually be located within Pakistan). Two job-related features of the community—both pertaining to its relative prominence within the British colonial infrastructure—contributed to its dispersal across the Indian subcontinent. On the one hand, civil service positions were available in many different locations. So, too, were positions in the government police services, the army, navy, merchant marine, and by the 20th century, the air corps. All of these vocations typically required temporary or, more often, permanent relocation far

[17] See Kehimkar, *The History of the Bene-Israel of India.*

from the main Bene Israel population centers. So the Bene Israel became increasingly diasporic, both within and beyond India.

For those stationed in remote places, the connection to their Judaism was maintained though life cycle and family rites of passage, including whatever Jewish customs they practiced at home and also including their adherence to the Jewish calendar. For major life cycle events or holidays, they would usually travel to Bombay, to the villages from which they had come to wherever they now resided, or to the nearest available Jewish congregation, in order to celebrate.

In the course of the rediscovery of the Bene Israel by the outside world, and their turn toward a more traditional Judaism than had apparently been their practice down through the centuries, they absorbed into their customs—perhaps instructed by Rahabi—not only major festivals like Shavuot and Sukkot, but several fasts. Thus, for instance, they came to observe a version of the fast of the ninth day of the (Hebrew) month of Av, commemorating the destruction of both the first and the second Temples in Jerusalem, known to the Bene Israel as *Bridacha Roza*: 'Lentil Fast'; and the *Sabbi Roza* (Fast of the fourth month) that takes place on the 17th day of the month of Tammuz, commemorating the first break in the walls in the Roman siege of Jerusalem; and most interestingly, the fast of Ramzan—clearly related to the Muslim fast of Ramadan—which is held throughout the month of Elul, leading up to the New Year and Day of Atonement festivals on the first and 10th days of Tishri.[18]

---

[18] The *Bridacha* Fast has a particular and unique connotation: Bene Israel tradition maintains that, 'when our ancestors were washed ashore in the Konkan, the first food they found growing close by that could be eaten was' a kind of bittersweet lentil bean—its Indian Jewish name is '*vhal*'. They thought of the prayer '*Ha M'haieh*' (Hebrew: 'He who brings back to life'), so they came to associate that moment with both God and these specific beans as the 'food that gave us life'—and the fast is also in commemoration of those who did not survive that shipwreck.

Even as late as the mid-19th century, at least some groups of Bene Israel had their own ways of celebrating some of the major Jewish holidays—and we possess no clear evidence, of course, to indicate how far back such observances may extend in time, or how they may have changed as the community resumed contact with the outer Jewish and general world in the 18th and 19th centuries. One particularly fascinating example is the Day of Atonement (Yom Kippur), which was known as *darfalnicha san*, meaning 'the holiday of door-closing'. A Jewish visitor to India in August, 1860, Jacob Saphir, noted in his memoir, *Eben Sappir*, that, on the day in question, the Bene Israel sat in their homes with the doors locked, until the end of the fast day. Saphir conjectured that, since the last service on Yom Kippur is called *ne'ilah* (locking)—or more fully, *ne'ilat she'arim* ('locking of the gates', referring to the gates of heaven and analogous to the notion that the book of life for the year to come is sealed at the end of that last day of the ten Days of Awe), they had interpreted this to mean that they should spend the entire day behind locked doors.[19]

This may not have been the custom of all the Bene Israel: certainly by 1860 there were at least two significant synagogues in Bombay alone, in which one might imagine many members of the community spent the Day of Atonement in prayer. Could it be that Saphir's experience was of members of the community who were located away from synagogues? And if he was there in August, he cannot have witnessed the celebration of Yom Kippur at that time, which would come somewhat later, in the early autumn. Could he have witnessed this custom on Tisha b'Av, which could have taken place in early August? Or did he arrive in India in August, but remain through, say, the end of the High Holidays? In any

[19] Jacob Sapphir, *Eben Sappir*, Vol I, pp. 33–5.

case, this practice was one of any number of customs apparently unique to at least part of the Bene Israel community.

There are, indeed, any number of practices accompanying not only holidays but life-cycle events that are associated specifically with the Bene Israel. One of these is their unique *malida* ceremony, which accompanies virtually every rite of passage and important occasion, and which combines a series of prayers—in particular blessings and prayers directed toward the prophet Elijah, and the chanting of the *Eliyahu HaNavi* (Elijah the Prophet) song that in the Ashkenazi and Sephardi worlds is only part of the Passover Seder and sometimes the Havdalah ceremony (marking the end of Shabbat)—together with the passing around of sweet foods (*malida*) to those present at the ceremony. The foods symbolize the offerings brought to the Temple in Jerusalem in antiquity—and also, piled high on the platter, the *malida* connotes Mount Sinai, from which Moses brought down the Torah (Fig. 1).[20]

---

[20] The allusion to Sinai is intended, in part, to connote the passage of the Israelites from Egypt to the Promised Land, in which journey Mount Sinai was so essential, which offers an analogue to the wandering Bene Israel who eventually arrived (at least the 14 who survived the shipwreck) to the coast of India. This additionally underscores the idea within the Bene Israel world of the past 70 years that they have two homelands: India is the motherland and Israel is the fatherland. The classic contents of the *malida* platter are *poha* (flattened rice), sugar, five (sometimes seven) kinds of dried fruits, as well as raisins and almonds, and shredded coconut—often garnished with flower petals. Tradition asserts that, when in the 16th century much of the Bene Israel community was living in Alibag, and would participate with their Hindu and Muslim neighbors in each other's celebrations, the Bene Israel lacked a specific dessert-like food to contribute to the feasts, and traders within the community came up with this combination of edibles derived in part from their travels. The *malida* dish came to have a specific association with Elijah, in part because of the tradition that asserts that the rock from which he ascended to heaven in that fiery chariot was in Alibag (and still bears the marks of the chariot wheels). There are also distinctly prescribed holidays (and the sabbath, as well), when the *malida* dish and ceremony do not play a role.

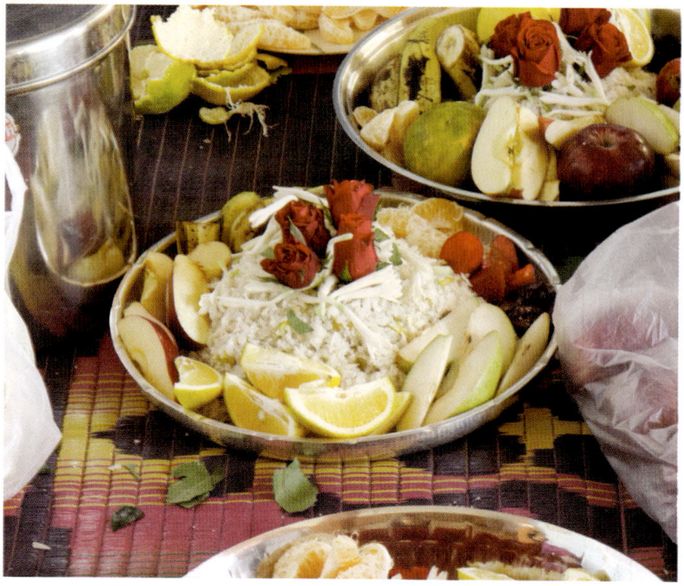

Fig. 1. *Malida* platter

Elijah is a uniquely ubiquitous figure within Bene Israel ritual. There is, in fact, a tradition asserting that it was Elijah who revived the original 14 Bene Israel who survived the shipwreck at Navagaon. As a consequence of this the community celebrates a unique annual *Eliyahu Hahhaniccha Urus*—'Anniversary of Elijah the Prophet', on the 15th day of Shvat (around mid-February)—the time when elsewhere in the Jewish world, the first fruits of the early spring are celebrated in commemoration of the first fruit offerings brought to the Temple in antiquity.

In the *malida* that accompanies the mehndi ceremony that precedes a wedding—when the bride's hands and feet are decorated with henna—fruit from the plate is wrapped in the upper edge of the

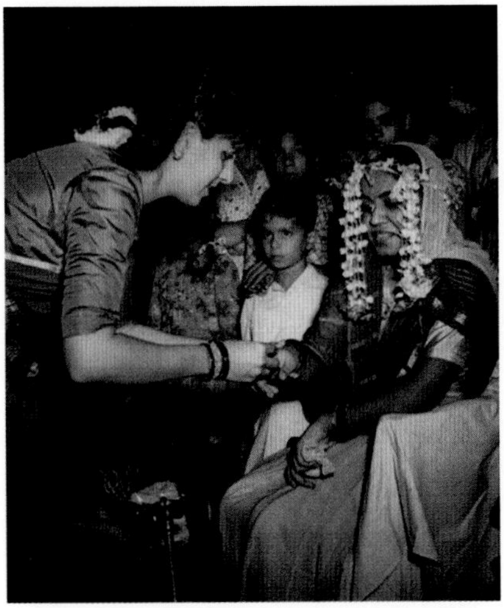

Fig. 2. Mehndi ceremony—Sophie Benjamin applies henna to the bride, her sister-in-law, Diana

bride's sari, placed near her belly, to assure her fertility (Fig. 2). So too, a Bene Israel wedding includes the singing by the groom of a unique 'groom song', as he awaits on the synagogue *teva/bimah* (pulpit) for the bride, dressed in a white sari, to come up to meet him there. The Bene Israel also place great emphasis on the baby-naming ceremony for a girl, called a *barsa*, which, typically on the 12th day after birth, offers an equivalent to the circumcision of baby boys that is non-existent in most of the Jewish world.[21]

It might be further noted—turning briefly back to the issue of professional achievement—that in the early part of the 20th century, as the film industry was establishing itself in India, a number of Bene Israel became very prominent in that field of enterprise, as well. Males sometimes became well-known as producers, directors, and actors. Thus, for instance, Ezra Mir (known in the industry as Edwin Myers; 1903–1993) became the first head of India's Films Division, and Solomon Moses was head of the Bombay Film Lab Pvt Ltd from the 1940s to the

[21] Only in recent years have some Jewish communities, particularly in the United States, added a baby-naming kind of ceremony for girls, called a *Brit Bat* ('Covenant of a Daughter') ceremony.

early 1990s. Hannoch Isaac Satamkar was a film actor and assistant director to Mehhoob Khan, a director of Hindi-language films.

It is estimated that there were about 6,000 Bene Israel in the 1830s, 10,000 at the turn of the 20th century, and in 1948—their peak in India—they numbered 20,000.[22] When at that time the establishment of the state of Israel coincided approximately with the post-colonial partition into a new India and two Pakistans, many Bene Israel (and other Jews) immigrated to Israel. Already at that time, the newly shaped Israeli chief rabbinate was presuming to define who could be considered a Jew (and therefore entitled to automatic Israeli citizenship according to the Law of Return) and questioned whether—or more truly, rejected the idea that—the Bene Israel were actually Jews. Gradually that attitude faded, dissipating by the mid-1960s, perhaps in part due to an increasing number of marriages between members of the community and other Israeli Jews.

In fact, in 1961, the Chief Rabbi Nissim convened a special meeting of the Supreme Rabbinical Council comprised of 10 rabbis who were acknowledged scholars of *halakhah* (rabbinic law)—in order to offer a final determination regarding the status of the Bene Israel as Jews. They posed the question of proof of their Jewishness, given the centuries of isolation, of whether they intermarried with non-Jews and if so, they asked who would have performed the conversions of non-Jewish spouses; similarly, might they have conducted marriages considered incestuous by rabbinic law; whether they conducted divorce proceedings according to rabbinic law (with a *get*) and followed the rabbinic custom

[22] Shalva Weil, 'The Bene Israel of India,' in the catalogue of The Museum of the Jewish People at Beit Hatfutsot, 1996.

of *halitsah* with respect to a widow and her living brother-in-law. To answer these questions, four of the rabbis were tasked with meeting with representatives of the Bene Israel in order to obtain information about their history and customs.[23] The outcome was that the 10-rabbi Council unanimously declared the Bene Israel an integral part of the Jewish people—thus, incidentally, reversing the ruling of the Baghdadi rabbis a century earlier, who were said not to have possessed sufficient information for their own ruling at that time![24] Nobody doubts the Jewish 'legitimacy' of Bene Israel Jews today.[25] Typically referred simply to as *Hodu'im* (Indians) in Israel,[26] Bene Israel Jews have risen to many positions of prominence there.[27]

IV. The Shaping and Reshaping of Bene Israel Synagogues

In India overall, in the gradual aftermath of the substantial migration to Israel, perhaps about 4,500 Jews remain, most of them Bene Israel, but as that community has shrunk, even if not as dramatically as the Cochini (ca 50) and Baghdadi (ca 250) communities have, many of the old synagogues—perhaps 34 of them overall, dating from the 16th

23 Dayan Dr Pinchas Toledano, *The Bene Israel of India*, pp. 42–5.

24 Ibid.

25 Joseph Hodes, *From India to Israel: Identity, Immigration, and the Struggle for Religious Equality* (Montreal: McGill-Queen's Press, 2014), pp. 98ff and p. 108.

26 Nathan Katz, *Who Are the Jews of India?*, pp. 91ff.

27 Shalva Weil. 'Religious Leadership vs. Secular Authority: the Case of the Bene Israel,' in *Eastern Anthropologist*, 49 (3–4) (1996): 301–316.

through 20th centuries, and in varied states of demise—have fallen into disuse.[28] The history of these structures is relatively brief, compared to the variously claimed history of the Jewish communities themselves. Indeed, what physical evidence we possess for specifically Bene Israel structures stretches back no more than a few centuries at most. But the brevity of time frame is compensated for by the range and substance of structures. As the Bene Israel spread delicate community tendrils away from Bombay and into other cities and towns, in the 19th century, prayer services were initially held in the homes of community members, but in time a substantial synagogue or—where there were still too few Jewish residents—an attractive prayer-hall would be erected. Synagogues became important centers of religious, social, and communal life. They often functioned without an ordained rabbi, served instead by a *hazan* (cantor)—most often a Cochini, Baghdadi, or Yemenite Jew who also served as *shohet* (kosher slaughterer), *mohel* (ritual circumciser), and *sopher* (scribe).

There are seven Bene Israel synagogues in Mumbai (and two more in Mumbai that are Baghdadi). Eleven other Bene Israel structures are located down the Konkan coastal region, beginning about 30 miles south of Mumbai and then extending for about 50 miles. There is another in Pune, just east of Mumbai and another in Ahmedabad, in Gujarat, as well as a more recent one, not surprisingly, in India's capital city, New Delhi. One might keep in mind that, as in so many other ways

[28] Cochini synagogues from the 12th through 14th centuries no longer exist; we do possess the foundation stone with its Hebrew inscription, however, from the 1344 Kochangandi Synagogue. It is now located within the Paradesi Synagogue. The oldest still-standing synagogue is also Cochini, and dates from 1568—it is located on land donated at that time to the community by the maharaja, adjoining his palace grounds, in fact. See Chapter Two, p. 126.

India's complexity would be reflected in the diversity of sacred sites that would have potentially influenced the architecture of synagogues (some of which are literally next to other houses of worship)—from Hindu, Buddhist, Jain, and Sikh gurudwaras to Christian churches and Muslim mosques, as well as Parsi agiaries, Buddhist rock-cut-and-painted cave monastic complexes, stupas, and pagodas. So there are diverse potential sources of stylistic inspiration, both indigenous and, during the periods when these synagogues were being built, colonial European. In several cases, moreover, very recent renovations have eradicated whatever distinctive details had originally been part of the various edifice exteriors.

It was, as far as our physical evidence indicates, during the era of religious revival and reconnection to the larger Jewish world that the first Bene Israel synagogue, Sha'ar HaRahamim, (Gate of Mercy), was built, in 1796 in Bombay/Mumbai—by Samuel Ezekiel Divekar—although it was completely rebuilt in 1860 (and renovated in 2009). This structure has the distinction of being one of the few synagogue buildings (Bene Israel or otherwise) that offers decorative elements that are indigenous: specifically, its exterior roof balustrade is composed of perforated, geometric-and-stylized-floral design 'screens'—*jali*—and surmounted by crenellations inspired by Mughal *kanjura* (Fig. 3).

It is also broadly consistent with a synagogue architectural tradition that began in antiquity, was borrowed into Christian ecclesiastical architecture, and returned to synagogue architecture across the world from the 18th century forward: specifically, Sha'ar HaRahamim's front façade offers three arched entry portals, both symbolizing the liturgical division of Jews into Kohayn, Levi, and Yisrael and recalling the threefold courtyard of the ancient Temple in Jerusalem.[29] Currently, the main doorway is surmounted by a six-pointed star—a Star of David, in this context. The irony, here and on other Jewish structures, is that this symbol cannot automatically be used to identify a given edifice as Jewish—although obviously in this case that is the distinct intention of using it as a decorative element—since the intertwined pair of triangles that comprise such a star-form has a long history in and beyond India, apart from its gradual emergence as a specifically Jewish symbol in the 19th and early 20th centuries.[30]

As with most of the Bene Israel synagogues, that façade and its entry portals are accessed by way of a courtyard entered through a handsome doorway in a low outer wall—and the edifice itself is flanked by peripheral buildings used for diverse social and educational purposes. A generic relationship to synagogues in other parts of the world may be seen in its interior configuration: the *aron/heikhal*—Holy Ark, in which the Torah scrolls are housed (currently with a pair of doors of intricately carved dark wood, suggesting an indigenous style)—is located on the wall opposite from where one enters the sanctuary, which is to say: the western wall, facing Jerusalem. The readers' platform/pulpit (the *bimah/teva*) is placed close to the center of the space (which is longer than it is wide by an approximately 2:1 measurement ratio) surrounded by a railing made

---

[29] As this feature entered into church architecture, it offered a triune symbolism for Christians. Whether the structure of this synagogue deliberately follows a reclaimed Jewish symbolic path or merely imitates its Christian neighbors is open to speculation.

[30] See Gunther Plaut, *The Magen David: How the Six-Pointed Star Became an Emblem for the Jewish People* (New York: B'nai B'rith Publishing, 1991); and Soltes, *Tradition and Transformation: Three Millennia of Jewish Art & Architecture* (New York: Canal Street Studios, 2016), pp. 60–61.

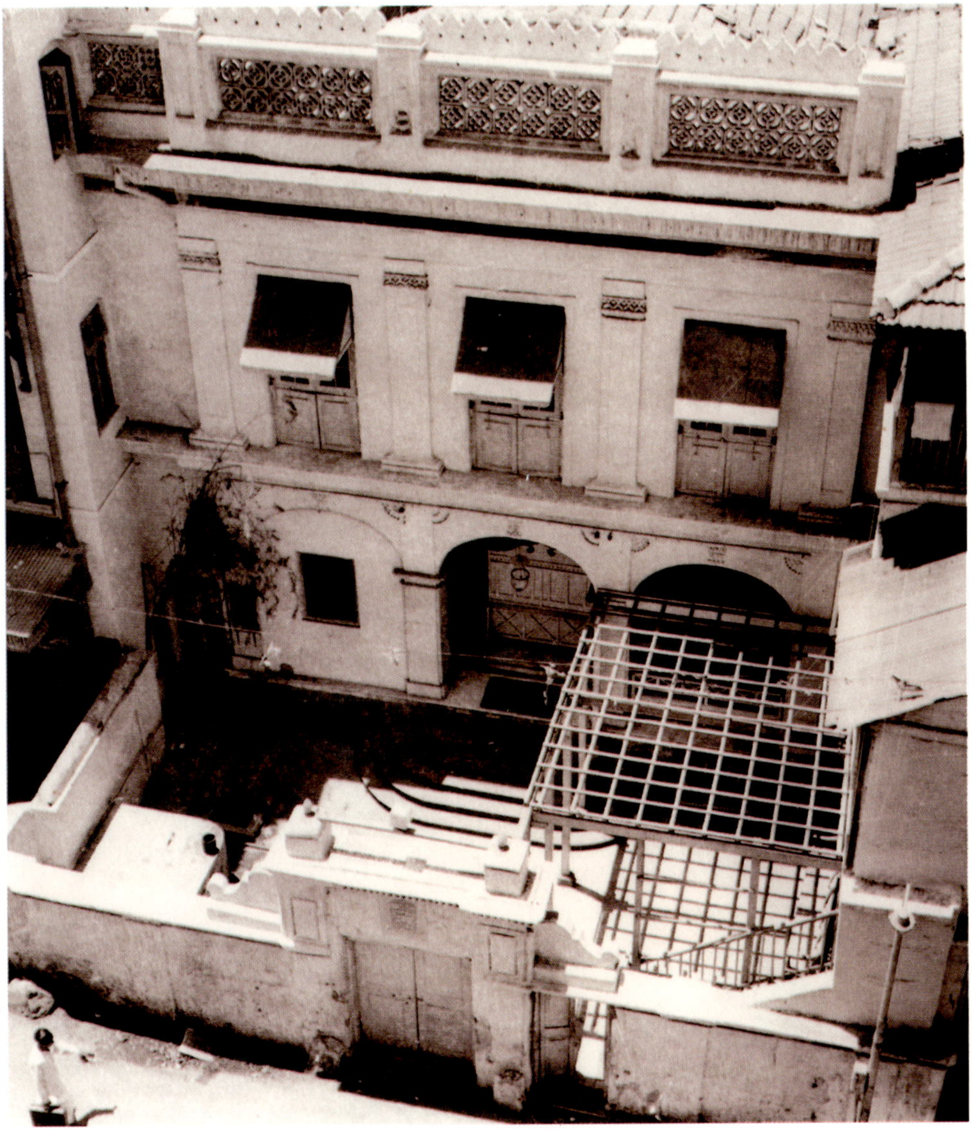

Fig. 3. Sha'ar HaRahamim, the first Bene Israel synagogue, built in 1796

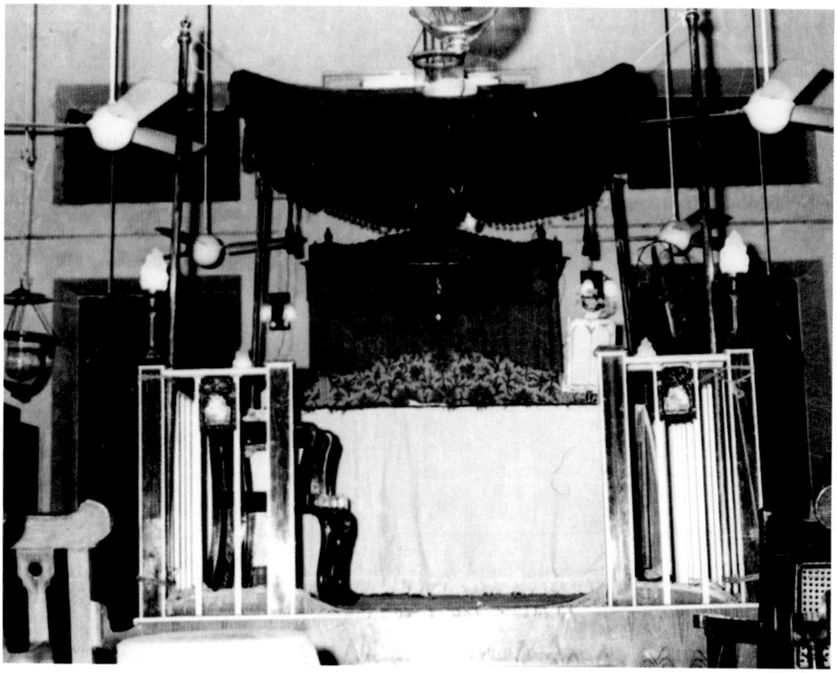

Fig. 4. Sha'ar HaRahamim interior towards the *aron/heikhal*

of wooden latticework, and by benches along the side and western walls (Fig. 4).[31]

The symbolic response to the Talmudic dictum calling for the elevation of the sanctuary above the community—which throughout most of Christendom and the Muslim world was virtually impossible until the 19th century—led to this sort of internal elevation of the two focal points: where the Torah is stored and where it is read and interpreted

[31] The rail, consistent with the pattern found in many synagogues all over the world—as there is sometimes a railing leading up to the *heikhal/aron*, as well—fulfills the rabbinic injunction to 'build a fence around the Torah' (Pirkei Avot 1:1) in a literal way.

three times per week. Thus, in spite of the not infrequent two or three-story height comfortably achieved by many of these synagogues, they follow aspects of the internal pattern traditional elsewhere in the Jewish world—indeed, on the one hand, the configuration, with the *bimah/teva* in the center, rather than on the wall opposite the *aron/heikhal*, echoes that of the traditional Ashkenazi configuration—but also typical of Cochini synagogues, from whom we might suppose the inspiration for this configuration was most directly received.

On the other hand, the vocabulary referring to these two primary components of the sanctuary is Sephardic. The splendid array of low-hanging oil lamps (mostly now electrified)—aside from the Eternal Lamp (*Ner Tamid*) hanging before the *heikhal* as a symbol of God's eternal presence, found in virtually every synagogue of whatever sort across the world—that are kindled on the Sabbath and festival eves is closer in feel to that sort of proliferation across the Muslim world (in both mosques and synagogues) than per se in the Ashkenazi or Sephardi worlds (Figs 5a, b and c).

These aspects of internal configuration are reflected in subsequent Bene Israel (and non-Bene Israel) synagogues. For other such synagogue structures followed in due course: thus Sha'ar Ratzon (Gate of [Divine] Will/Desire) was dedicated in 1839 (or perhaps 1843); and Tiferet Israel (Beauty of Israel) in 1886—and refurbished in 1923; Etz Hayim (Tree of Life), was established, albeit as a prayer hall rather than a full-fledged synagogue, in 1888; Magen Hassidim (Shield of the Pious) was also built as a prayer hall, in 1904, and expanded and rededicated as a full synagogue in 1931; and much later, in 1946, the Kurla Bene Israel prayer hall was formally founded, although the Kurla Bene Israel community members had been praying together since 1915, first in a series of houses

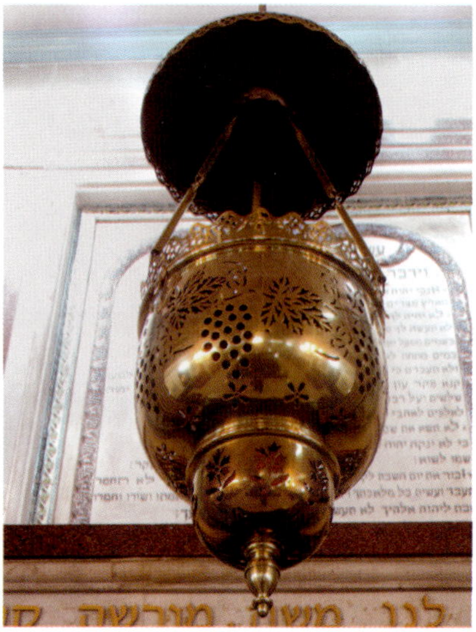

Fig. 5b. *Ner Tamid*, Magen Hasidim Synagogue, Mumbai

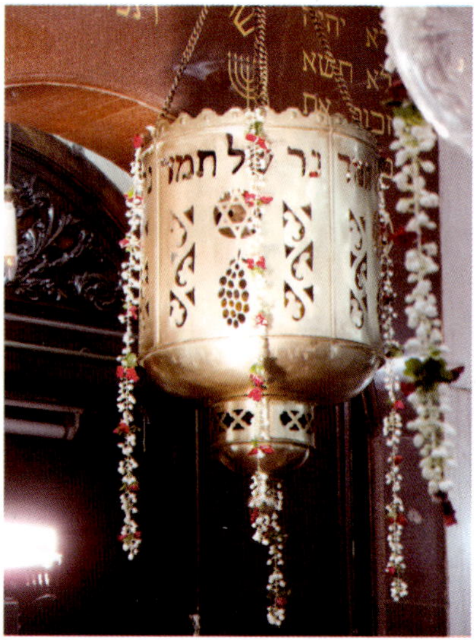

Fig. 5c. *Ner Tamid*, Tifereth Israel Synagogue, Mumbai

and then (from 1933 until 1946) in a rented structure, the so-called Old Court Building.

Other synagogues were also established during the latter part of this period in Pen, Alibag, Pune and Ahmedabad. The urban synagogues all tend to use light-colored plaster made of polished lime and sand—called *chunam*—highlighted by white or a lighter version of the main color to punctuate relief elements. They also tend to offer exterior front facades that are direct or variant versions of Western architectural styles—from neo-Romanesque and neo-Gothic to Baroque as well as Art Deco in the case of two Bene Israel structures built in the 1930s—all but eschewing elements that would be recognizable as indigenously Hindu or Muslim in aspect. Given the time period, which was an era of

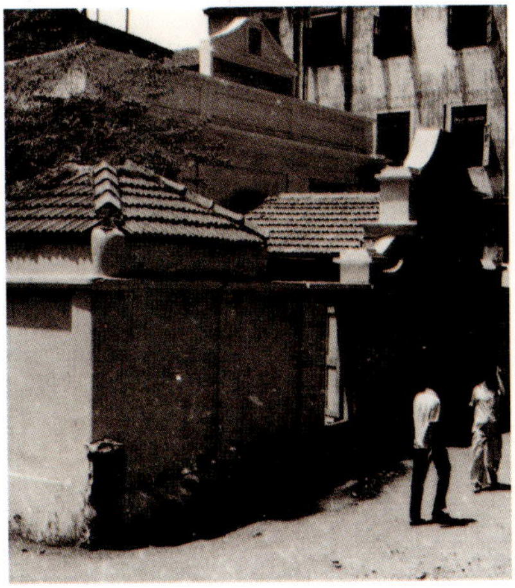

Fig. 6. Shar Ratzon, Mumbai, 1839

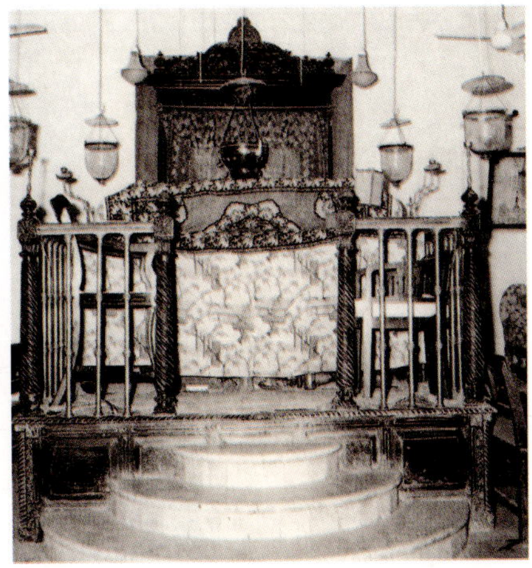

Fig. 7. Shar Ratzon interior towards the *aron/heikhal*

domination by European colonial powers—most obviously, the British—this is not altogether surprising; it is consistent with the other cultural ways in which the Bene Israel were drawn to and fitted themselves relatively well into the British system of governance.

Sha'ar Ratzon sits unobtrusively behind its protective outer wall, the not-quite-imposing monumental gate into that wall surmounted by a triangular fronton (its top levelled) echoed by an identically proportioned fronton above the façade of the building itself, and with an identifying inscription in Hebrew below a Star of David—without which one might pass by this simple building, somewhat classical in its lightly decorated rectilinearity, without recognizing it as a synagogue (Fig. 6). On the interior—configured with the *teva* toward the center, (accessed by a graceful series of three rounded stairs that become smaller as one ascends from the tiled floor) and the *heikhal* embedded in the western wall—the *teva*'s perimeter fencing is punctuated at the corners by a series of beautifully turned small pillar forms (intended to recall the pair of columns mentioned in I Kings 7:13-22 as rising before King Solomon's Temple, and referred to by name, as 'Yakhin and Boaz') and above and around the *heikhal* there runs a beautiful and intricate wood-carved decorative element (Fig. 7).

So, too, Tiferet Israel is a less-than-dominating structure, its rigorous rectilinear tan and brown façade identifiable as a synagogue only by the series of Stars of David that punctuate the upper register of its front and side faces (Fig. 8). It, too, is accessed by a series of three doorways. On the interior, the inset *heikhal* is surmounted by an arched form, echoed by the monumental arched structure of reddish wood that protrudes out from the western wall. One recognizes both an allusion to Yakhin and Boaz and to the so-called 'Syrian gable' that was a characteristic transom feature over the doorways of early Judaeo-Palestinian synagogues (Fig. 9) in the second through fourth centuries. Arguably, as a compendium, the monumental arch also recalls the kind of triumphant arches used by the Romans that find their way, slightly attenuated, into large churches by the medieval period, to separate nave from apse, connoting the victory of life over death associated with the rituals enacted at the altar within that apse. Borrowed from that Christian tradition, this Jewish usage would offer an analogous statement: that beyond the arch within the *heikhal* are the Torah scrolls regarded as 'a tree of life (*etzhayyim* in Hebrew) to them that hold fast to it' (Fig. 10).

The Etz Hayyim (Tree of Life) Synagogue—not altogether surprisingly, given that it was established merely as a prayer hall—has a simple exterior with no marks that would identify it, per se, as a

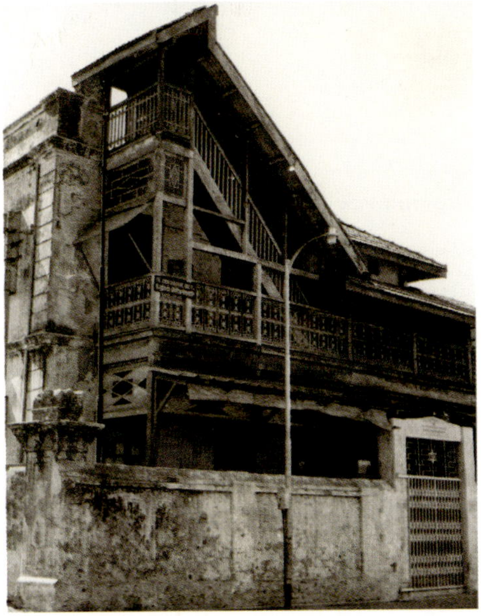

Fig. 8. Tiferet Israel Synagogue, Mumbai, built in 1886

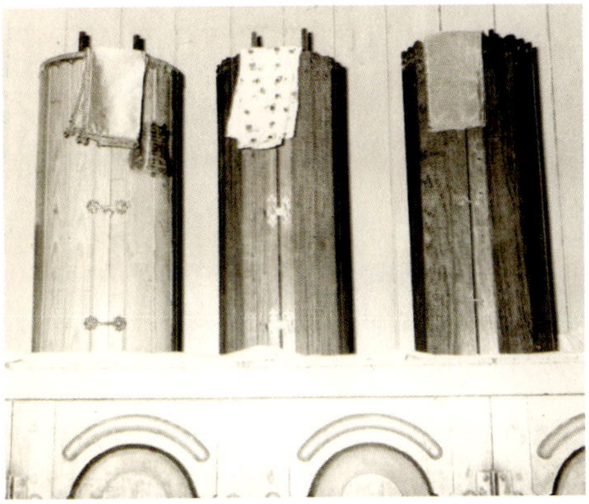

Fig. 10. Torah *tiks* (cases) in Beth Ha-Olam, *aron/heikhal*

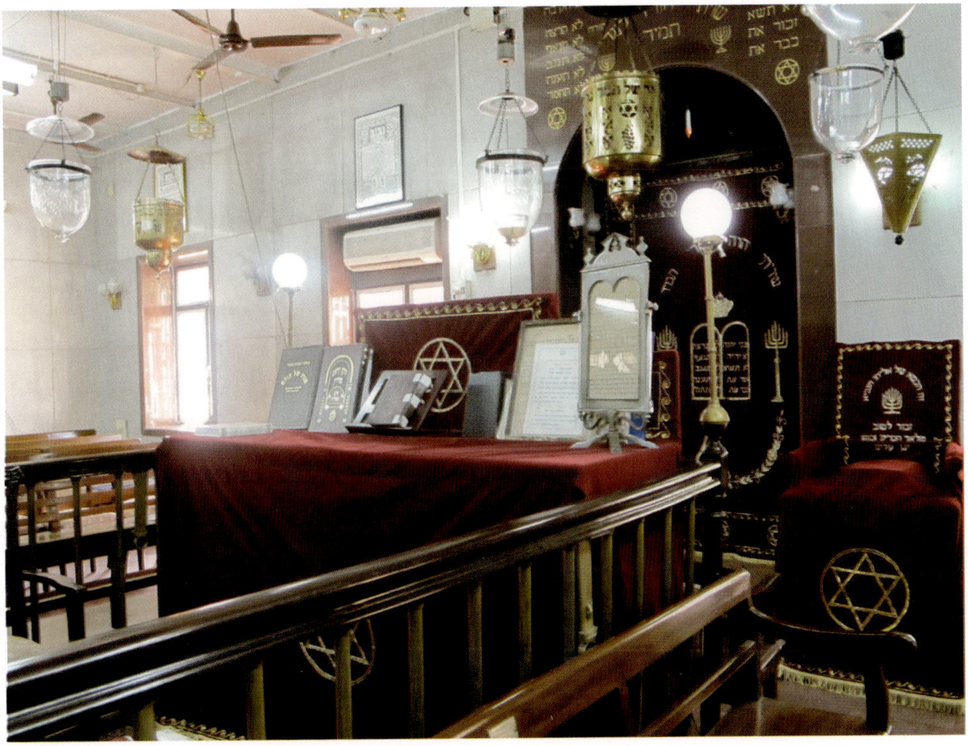

Fig. 9. Tiferet Israel Synagogue interior

Jewish edifice, except the Star of David over the doorway of the courtyard wall (Fig. 11). Magen Hassidim presents a roofline that rises from the otherwise rectilinear edifice to offer a gentle, rounded curve that repeats on a smaller scale to encompass the entry area, at the lower part of which—just below a low-relief-carved Star of David—the façade yields inward to an open porch. That opened porch is subdivided into three components by a pair of Corinthian-capped columns: once again, one might suppose that the pair of columns is intended to allude to the pair before King Solomon's Temple in Jerusalem (Fig. 12). That symbolic vocabulary is repeated on the interior, where, however, instead of columns, fluted pilasters flank the *aron/heikhal*—a smaller pair immediately to either side of it and a larger, floor-to-ceiling pair delineating the larger raised space for which the *aron/heikhal* with its *parokhet* (Torah Ark curtain) and *Ner Tamid* (Eternal Light) are the joint centerpiece: the first protecting the word of God written on the Torah scrolls and the second symbolizing God's eternal Presence (Figs 13a and b).

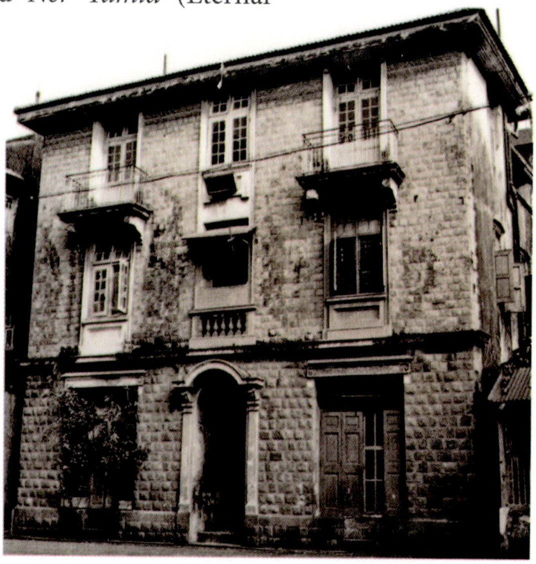

Fig. 11. Etz Hatyyim Synagogue exterior, Mumbai

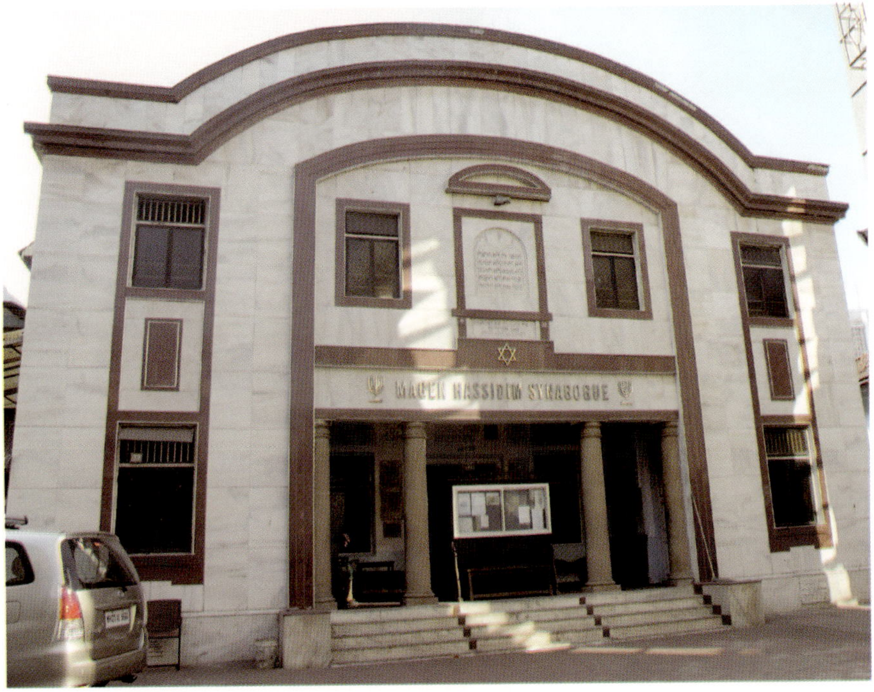

Fig. 12. Magen Hassidim Synagogue, Mumbai

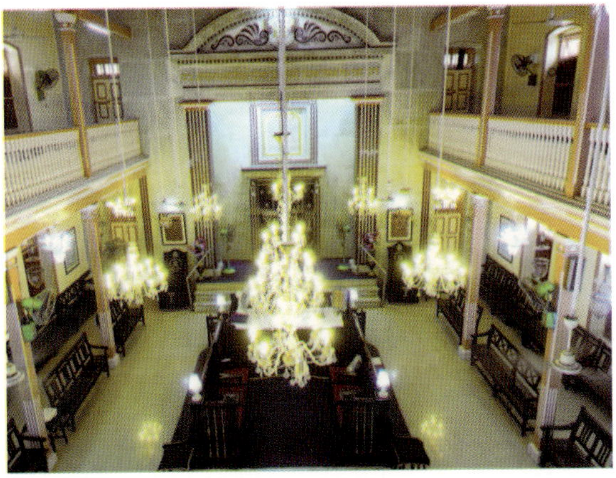

Fig. 13a. Magen Hassidim Synagogue interior

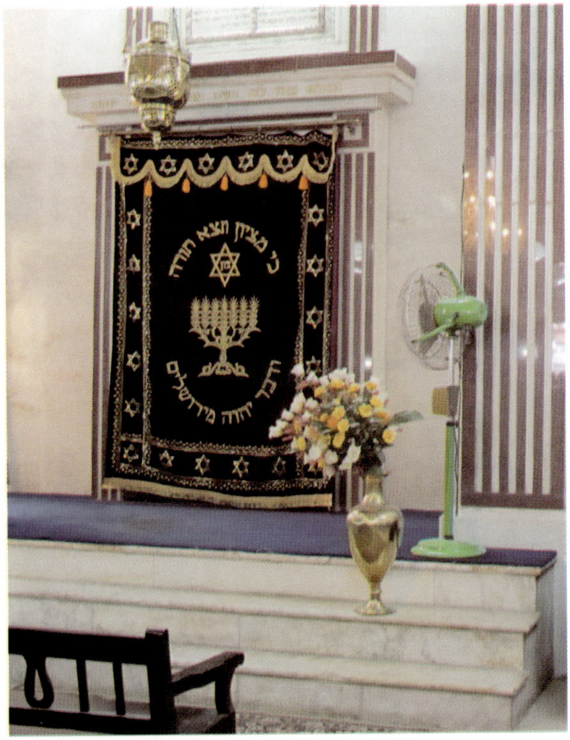

Fig. 13b. Magen Hassidim Synagogue *aron/heikhal*

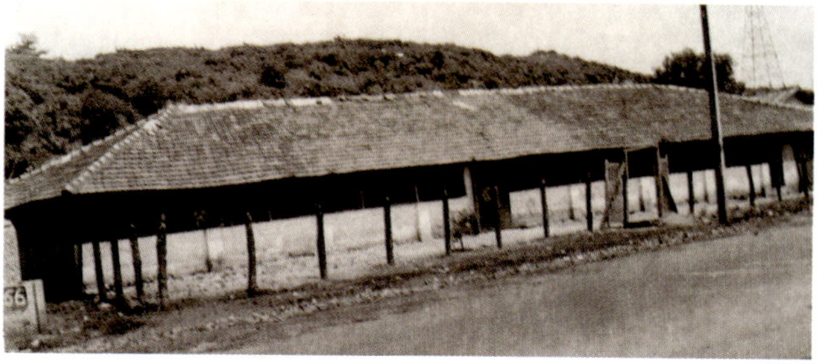

Fig. 14. Kurla prayer hall, Mumbai

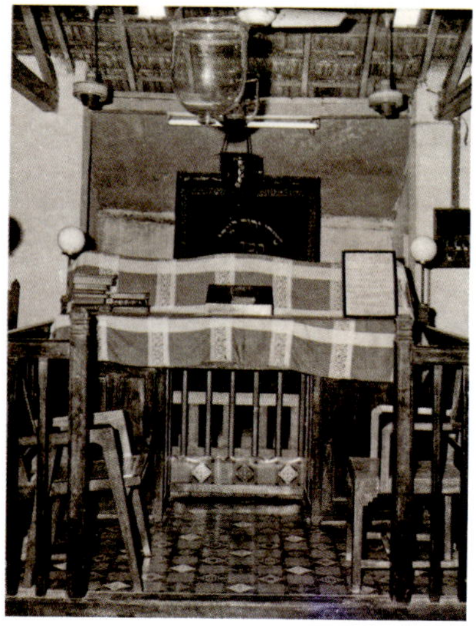

Fig. 15. Kurla prayer hall interior, *teva/ bimah*, 1948

The Kurla prayer hall is a low-lying, one-story strip building with few identifying elements on the exterior: a Star of David and a Marathi inscription identifying the hall on the small gable over the entrance (Fig. 14). On the interior, a low-relief seven-branched candelabrum—a menorah—adorns the entablature above its simple, rectilinear *heikhal*. This is one of the few instances when the image of the menorah, rather than that of a six-pointed star, is presented as a central part of Bene Israel synagogue décor. Even with its modest size, the edifice interior contains a raised *teva* and a raised *heikhal* (Fig. 15). In fact, its *heikhal* contains a number of Torah scrolls, each of which is encased in a hard carapace, a container (referred to in Sephardic-Mizrahi vocabulary as a *tik*) made of wood covered with beaten silver ornately decorated, sometimes with gilded silver or semi-precious stones as elements.

Indeed, each of the Bene Israel synagogues has (or had) a number of Torah scrolls, each encased in a *tik* within their diverse *heikhalot* (plural of *heikhal*). The *tik*s vary in terms of specifics: some are simply round and sometimes they are polygonal in configuration. The wood may be simple and unadorned, perhaps crowned with metallic decorative crenelations, or covered with velvet and/or silver and/or semi-precious stones, or simply carved up and beautifully painted with low-relief abstract—usually floral—patterns (Fig. 16). The specifics typically reflect one or more of a range of influences: from the Cochini or Baghdadi Jews or the Yemenite Jews, who were essential to the community as it was beginning to develop its new, mainstream Jewish sense of self, in the 18th and 19th centuries. The first Torah scroll to arrive as a permanent part of the Bene Israel community in Bombay, in fact, came there in 1844, apparently sent as a gift from the Bene Israel community that had established itself in Aden five years earlier.

Other Bene Israel synagogues are found outside Mumbai—for example, and chronologically speaking, the earliest: Beth El (House of the Lord) synagogue, in Revdanda. It was first constructed in 1842 and rebuilt in 1876—and renovated in 2008 (Fig. 17). Typical of a small-town rather than urban

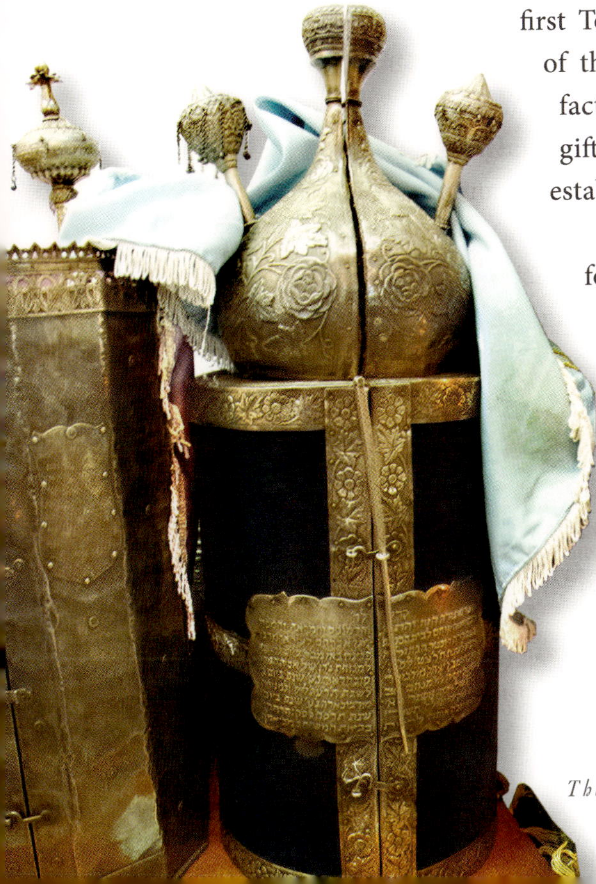

Fig. 16. Sepher Torah, Magen Abraham Synagogue, Ahmedabad

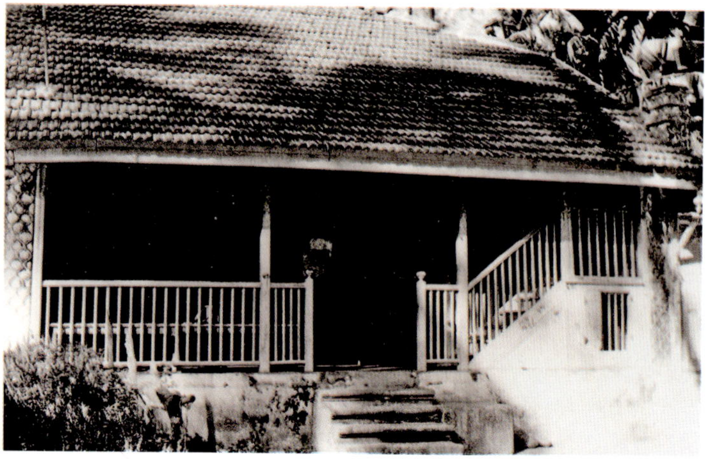

Fig 17. Beth El Synagogue, Revdanda, exterior

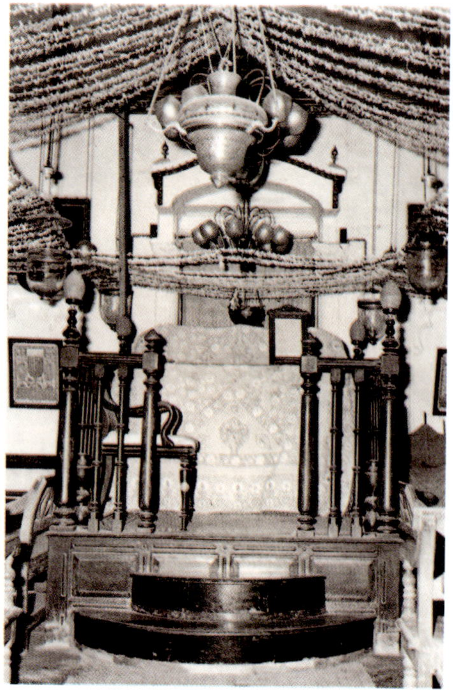

Fig. 18b. Beth El Synagogue, Revdanda, *teva/bimah*

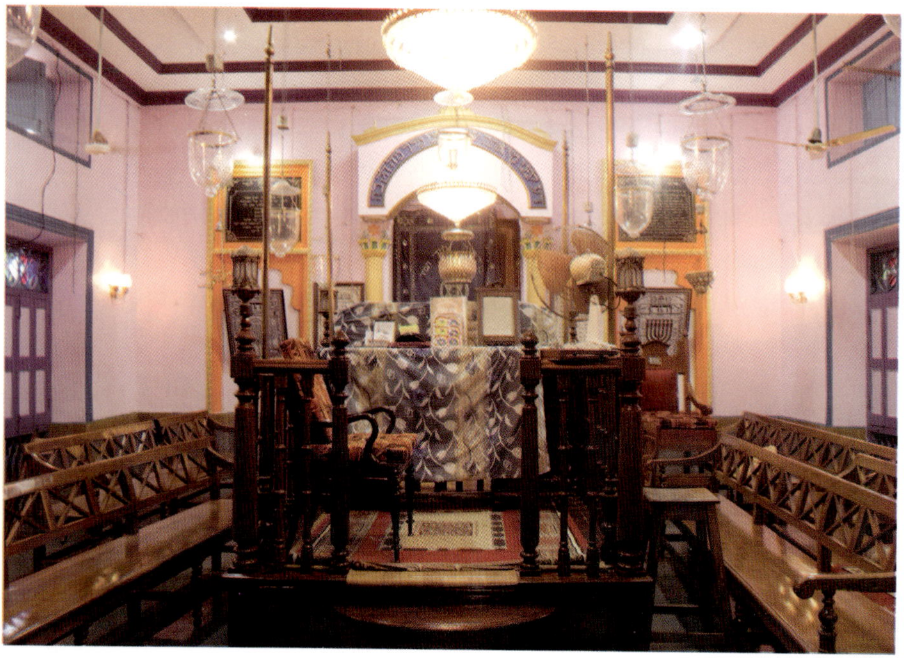

Fig. 18a. Beth El Synagogue, Revdanda, interior

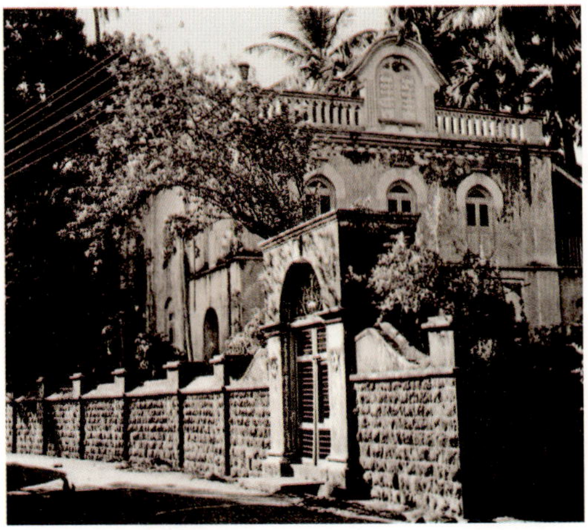

Fig. 19. Magen Aboth Synagogue, Alibag

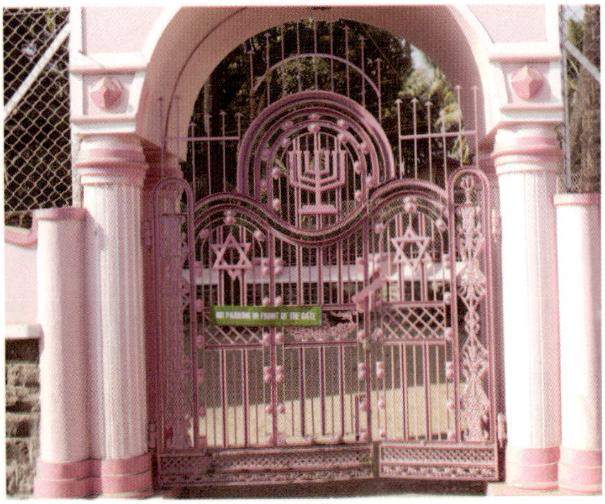

Fig. 20. Magen Aboth Synagogue outer gate, Alibag

synagogue, it is very modestly scaled, and would hardly be noticed from the outside; the interior is almost all salmon pink in color, with highlights in red and blue (Figs 18a and b). The Magen Aboth (Shield of [Our] Fathers) synagogue, in Alibag, was founded shortly after Beth El, in 1843, by a group of Bene Israel who had retired from the military and were led by the Hakham Shelomo Sharabi (Fig. 19). The edifice was rebuilt in 1910 and rededicated after renovations recently, in 2003; the new outer gate is boldly embellished with two stars of David and a Menorah (Fig. 20). The first thing that catches one's eye is its color—from that bright, pink gate to the renovated building façade, where a bright, light blue punctuated by darker blue detailing around the arched trio of upper-story windows that echo the doorways below, and along the edges of the rectilinear pilasters that mark the corners of the front façade. That same dark blue highlights the line

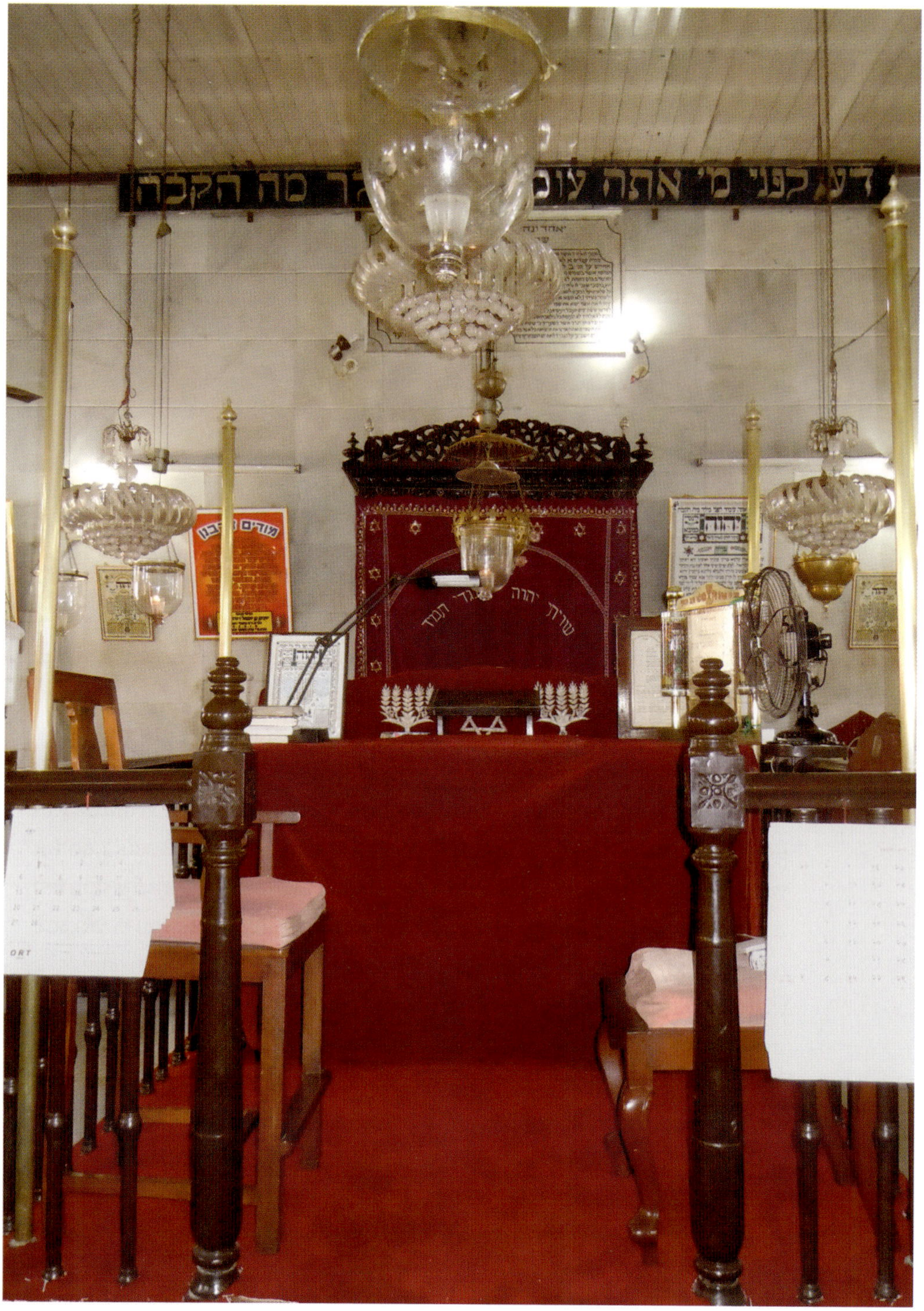

Fig. 21. Beth El Synagogue, Panvel

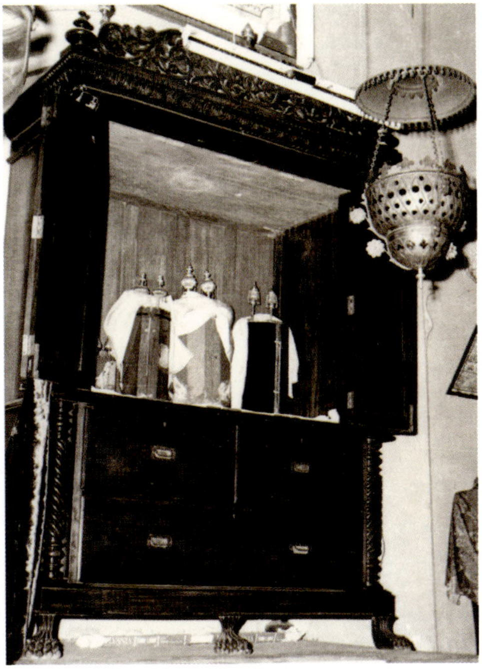

Fig. 22. Beth El Synagogue, interior, Panvel

separating the top of the main façade from the double curved, broken fronton above it, and also the black squared forms that add more decoration to that upper part of the building, as well as the two Stars of David that flank a well-lit inset white central area embellished with a decalogue.

A second Beth El Synagogue was founded in Panvel in 1849, making it one of the oldest along the Konkan coast. It is wonderfully non-descript on its exterior, but with the requisite, handsomely contrived elements expected of a sanctuary on its interior: white walls and against them the dramatic dark wood of the benches around the periphery, the *teva* that dominates the center, and the large *heikhal* on the western wall (Figs 21 and 22).

Panvel also serves as a particularly picturesque symbol of how diminished in size the Bene Israel—and general—Jewish community in India has become during the past 70 years or so—most of it, to repeat, having moved to Israel. The poignant landscape of the Jewish cemetery offers grasses and other vegetation gradually overwhelming the scattered gravestones, the latter slowly tilting and sinking into the earth of Mother India (Fig 23).

In Pen, the Beth Ha Elohim (House of the Lord) Synagogue, built in 1861 by Hannahbai Haeem Divekar (and rebuilt in 1893) currently presents a delightful salmon-colored exterior—lighter pink highlighted by decorative elements of a deeper pink (Figs 24a and b). Rising within its modest courtyard from above the outer perimeter wall, it presents three large doorways: a pair of rectangles flanking a central portal over which a gentle arched form is surmounted by large fanning bricolation, somewhat neo-baroque in style. The more flamboyant—no doubt because it is more visible from the street—second story extends above a layered entablature. There the bold embellishments include pairs of

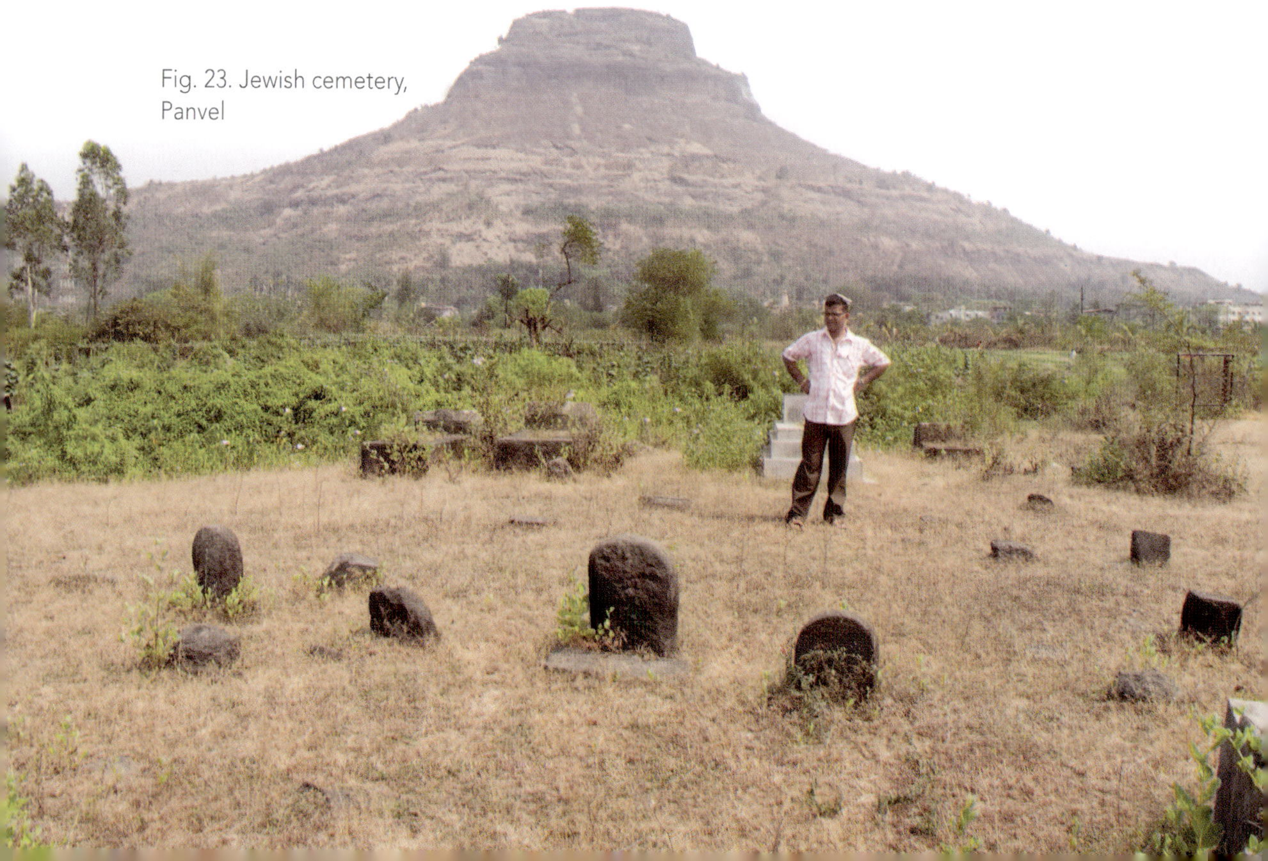

Fig. 23. Jewish cemetery, Panvel

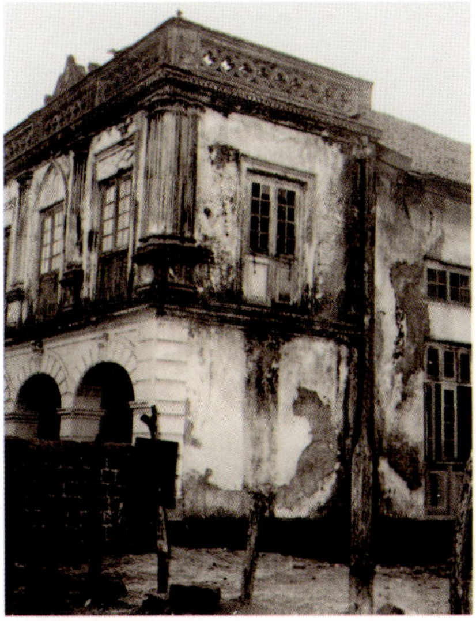

Fig. 24a. Beth Ha Elohim Synagogue exterior, Pen

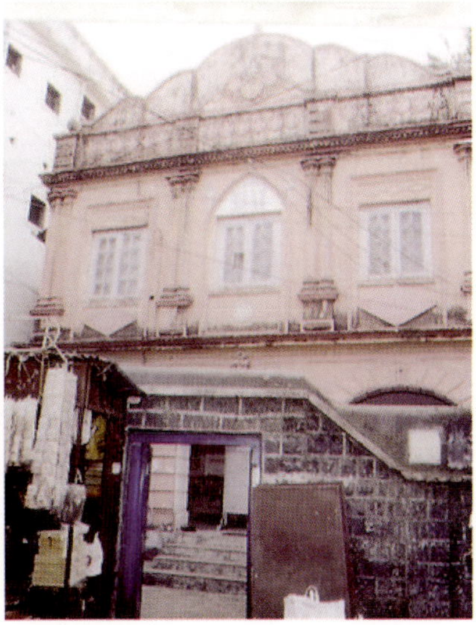

Fig. 24b. Beth Ha Elohim Synagogue, front view, Pen

curvy-fluted pilasters flanking the central window and another four wrapping around each of the two corners of the front façade and sides. The two flanking windows are rectilinear, with decorative diamond-shaped motifs, whereas the decor of the central window rises in a kind of ogive arch. The upper entablature outcropping continues the horizontal subdivision of the façade into three parts; each of these parts on the upper entablature is decorated with six stylized lotus florets within circles—giving 18 in all, which is the symbol of life in Jewish numerological thought.[32]

[32] Every consonant in the Hebrew alphabet has a numerical value, and the two consonants comprising the root of the word for 'life'—'*het*' and '*yud*'—represent 'eight' and 'ten' respectively. Thus 18 symbolizes '*hai*' meaning 'life'.

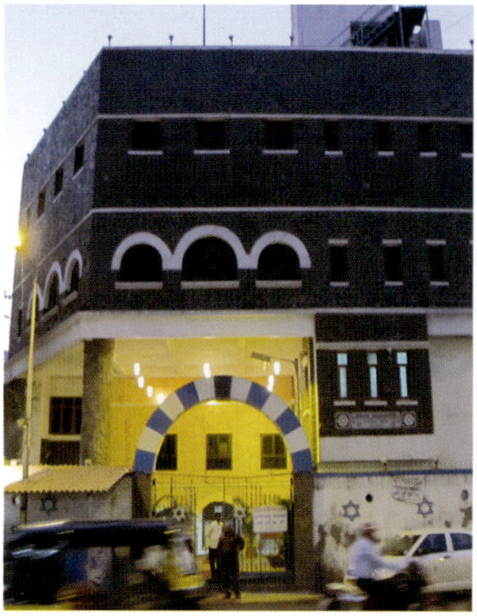

Fig. 26a. Shar HaShamayim Synagogue exterior

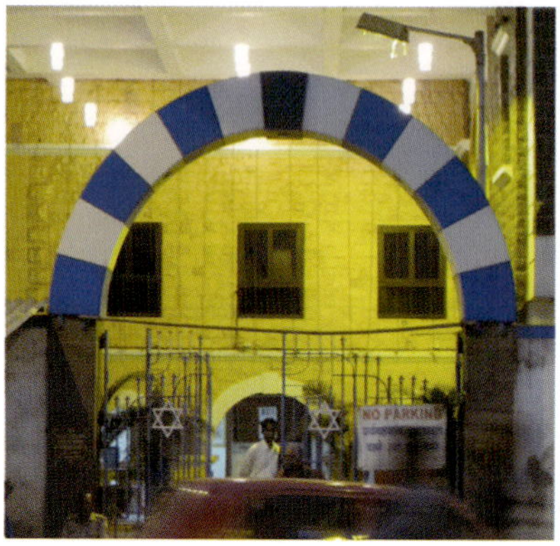

Fig. 26b. Shar HaShamayim Synagogue outer gate

The Shar HaShamayim (Gate of Heaven) synagogue in Thane (virtually a suburb of Mumbai), with its three-fold arched doorways, was built in 1879, but radically renovated—and expanded—in 2009 (Fig. 25). That expansion echoes the three-arched form on both the front and one side of the box-like structure rising up and around the original edifice (Fig. 26a)—as well as bright yellow pigment covering the original facade, which has become the inner entry area, and the refurbishment of an outer gate, adding a blue-and-white archway (Fig. 26b). The upper walls of the interior echo the exterior hue. A sparkling white marble floor supports the sort of arrangement seen elsewhere: a slightly raised, fenced-in *bimah/teva* in the middle, oriented toward an arched form in which the *aron/hekhal* is embedded. The mahogany

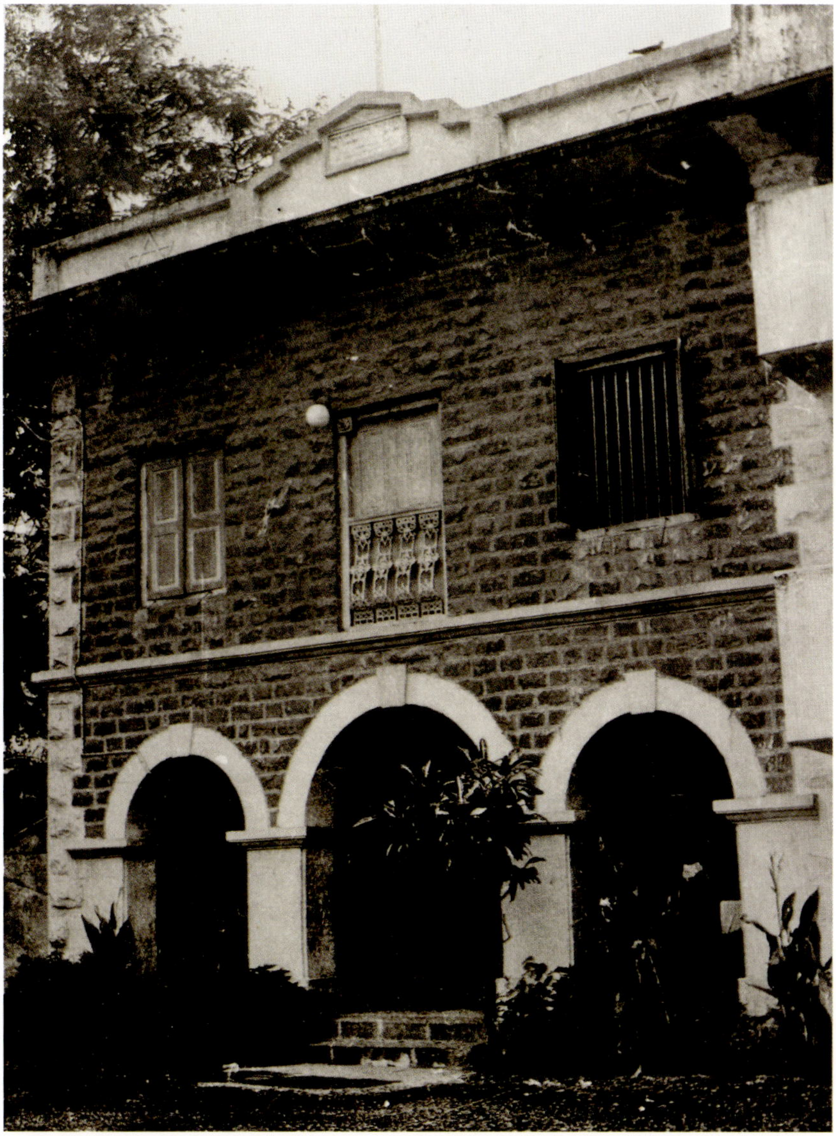

Fig. 25. Shar HaShamayim Synagogue, Thane

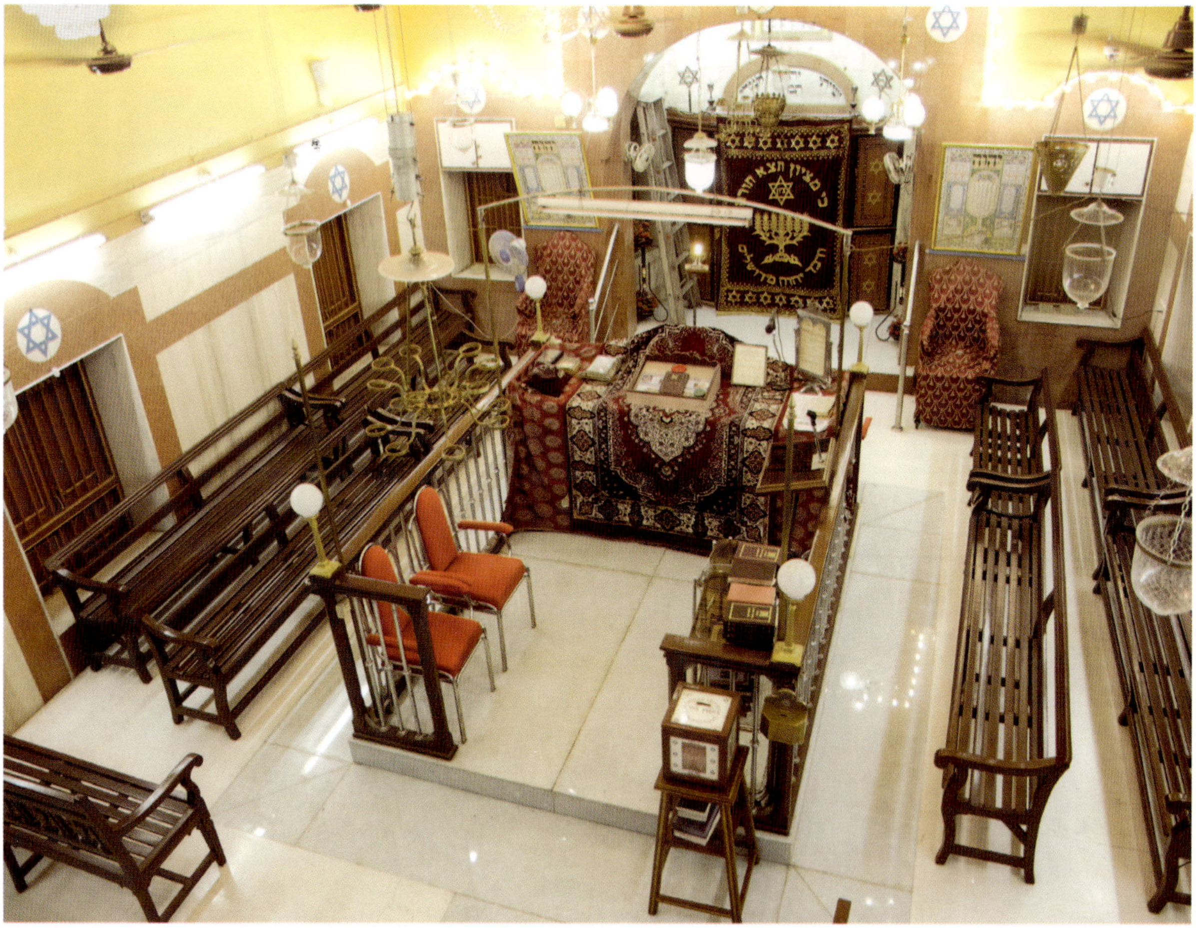

Fig. 27. Shar HaShamayim Synagogue interior

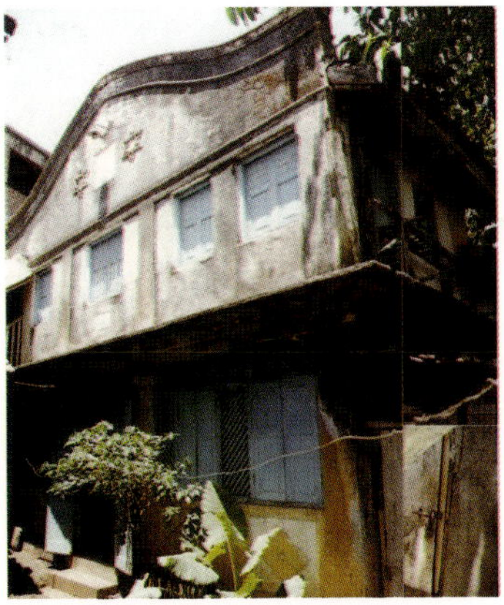

Fig. 28. Shaar HaTefilah Synagogue, Mhasla

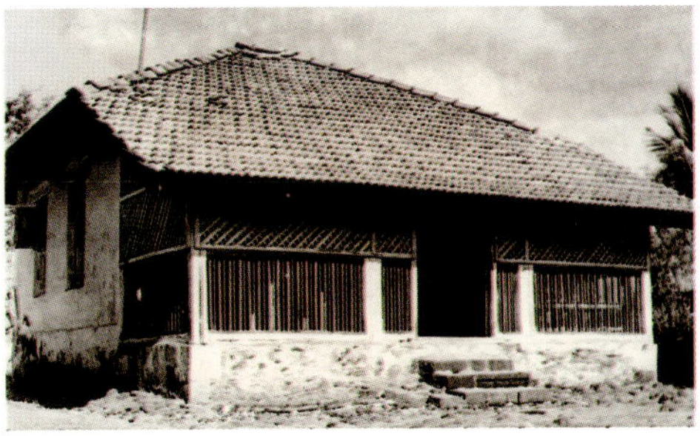

Fig. 29. Beth El Synagogue, Ashtami

benched seating around the periphery offers a handsome contrast to the diverse elements that embellish the walls and ceiling (Fig 27).

Mhasla's Shaar HaTefilah (Gate of Prayer)—with its bright blue treble doors, each with a basket-weave wooden slat screening around it, its pigment-echoing small upper-story windows, and a pair of Stars of David flanking a decalogue toward the peak of its curved fronton—was originally built in 1886, rebuilt and rededicated in 1921, and renovated in 2015 (Fig. 28).

Mention might also be made of the Beth El synagogue in Ashtami, built in 1882—because it is so different from the larger, more ornate urban structures and also different from the more modest village synagogues (Fig. 29). This particular Beth El resembles an everyday village house, with a tiled roof, front porch (originally serving as the women's section), and its sanctuary presents a portable reader's desk rather than a permanent *teva/bimah*.

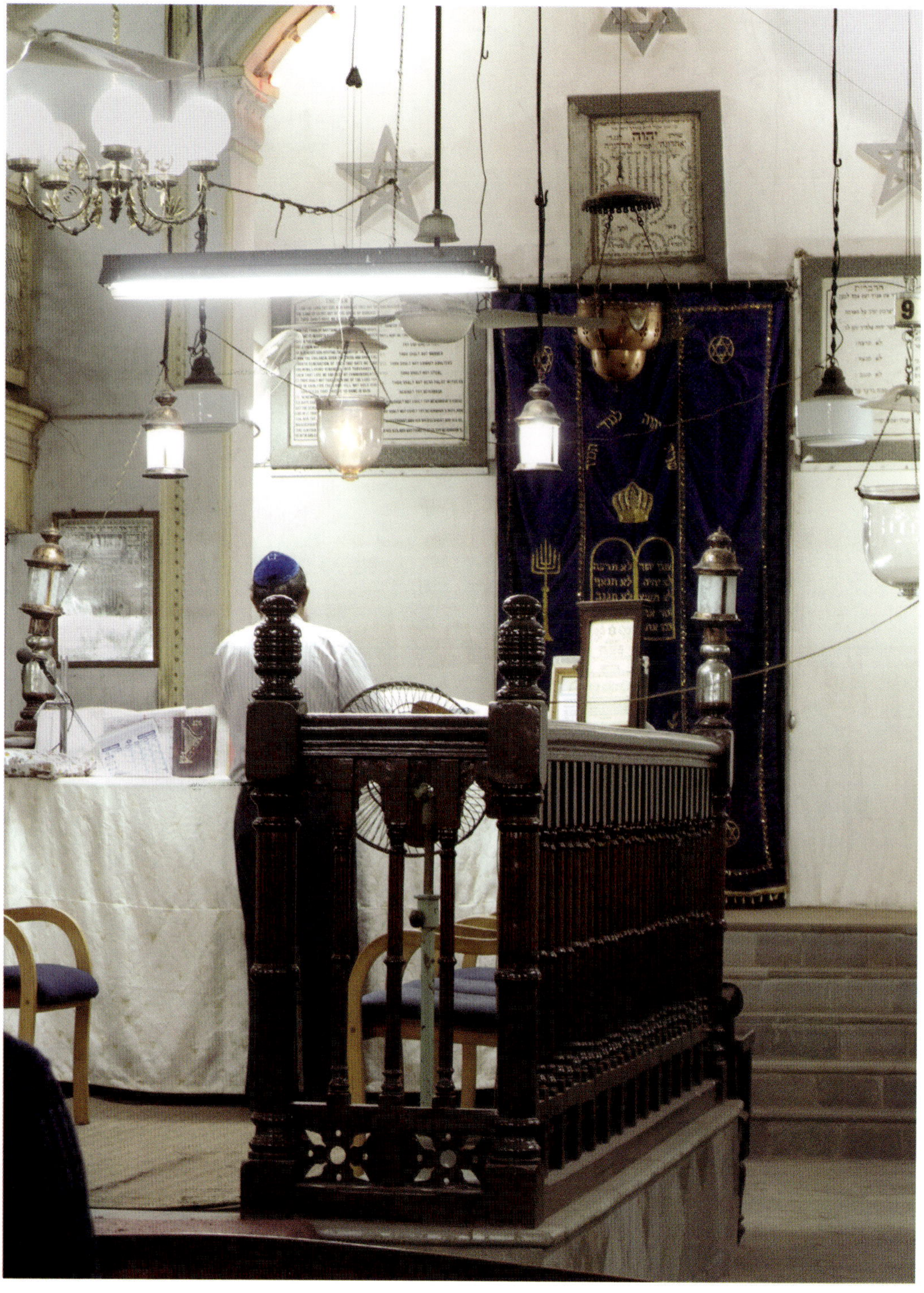

Fig. 30b. Succat Shelomo Synagogue interior detail

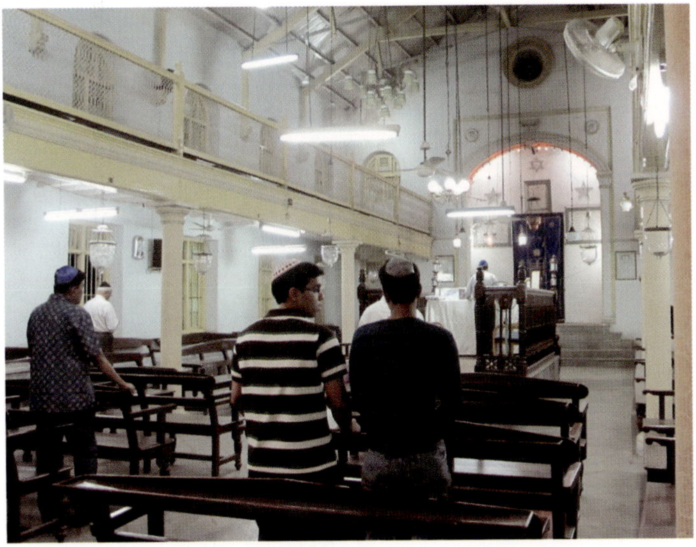

Fig. 30a. Succat Shelomo Synagogue interior, Pune

Not far from Mumbai, somewhat inland, in Pune, the second largest city in Maharashtra, stands the imposing Succath Shelomo (Shelter of Solomon) Synagogue, built in 1921. Its scintillating pale blue—nearly white—interior is highlighted by a creamy color for the pillars that hold up the women's gallery and the entablature and railing of the gallery itself. The *heikhal* presents a straightforward rectangular opening, but it is set within a larger arched form and decorated by three stars within and two outside that inset. Four of these are five-pointed stars—thus twice offering the number that, in Jewish terms, symbolizes the contents of the *heikhal*: the Torah: the five books of Moses (Figs 30a and b).

In Ahmedabad, the Magen Abraham (Shield of Abraham) Synagogue began as a prayer hall in 1906 and was consecrated as a full synagogue in September, 1934. The front façade of the edifice is

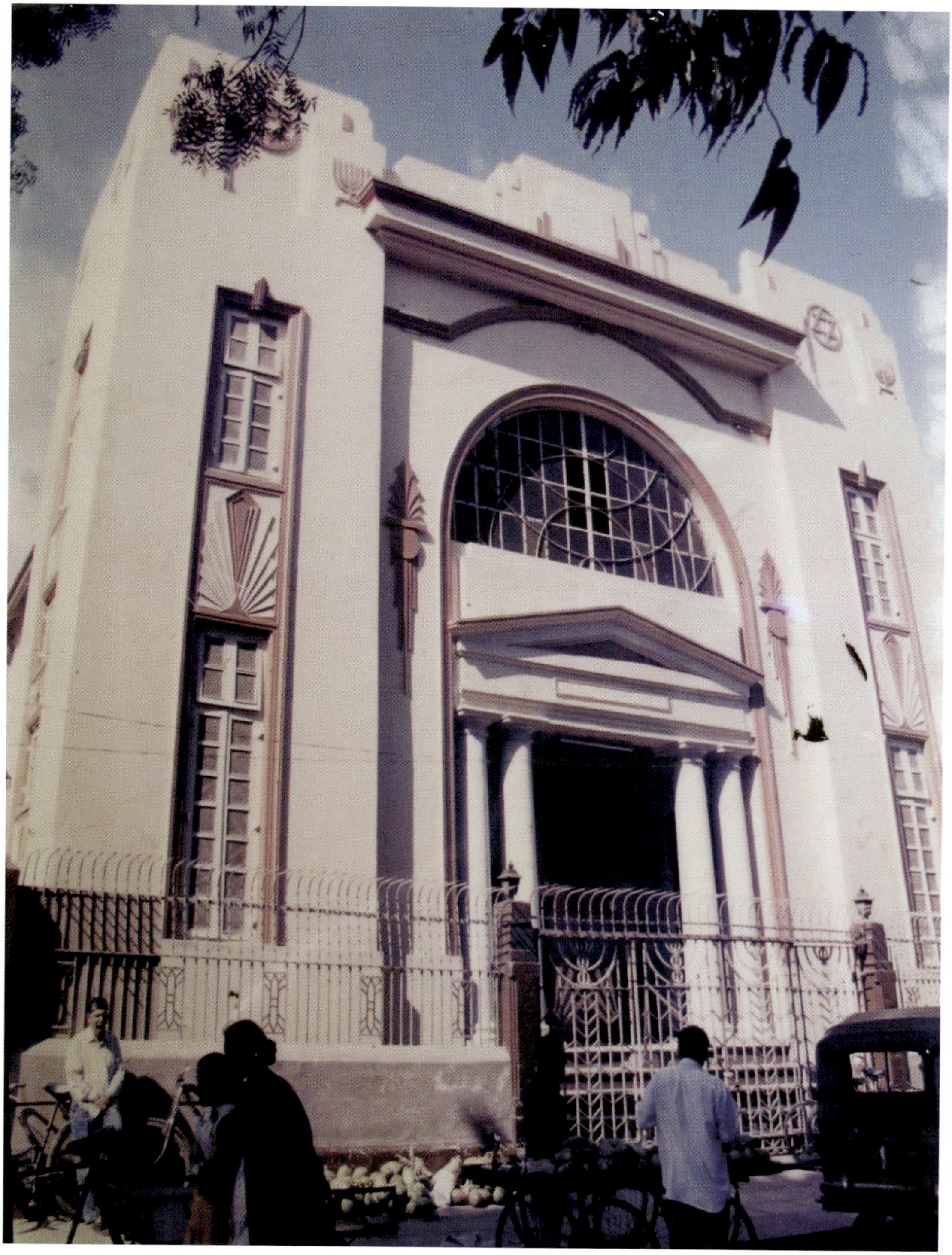

Fig. 31. Magen Abraham Synagogue exterior, Ahmedabad

distinctly Art Deco in style, particularly the two high windows within the thick, tower-like walls flanking the inset center of the façade with its own deco embellishments (Fig. 31). On the upper register of each of these side 'towers' a Star of David is incised in low relief in a circle and flanked by a low-relief-carved pair of seven-branched *menorot*; this trio of symbols is also repeated around the outer sides of the 'towers'. The inset center of the façade offers a neo-classical doorway, flanked by double columns and surmounted by a flat, triangular fronton, the entirety in turn encased by a soaring arched form with a multi-colored window suggesting a Syrian gable-style transom. Above that arch is a low-relief, lower-angled decorative arch—like the other relief elements, painted a reddish brown against the cream color of the building—and above it an entablature outcropping surmounted by a decalogue.

On the interior, among the more interesting and unique features is the towering extrusion—a stylized mountain of large stone blocks, a contrastively curved seven-branched menorah near its apogee—that rises above the *heikhal*. That bold construction is highlighted by dark-and-light art deco fan motifs that are repeated in off-white in the corners of the ceiling above, and resonate with the triangular-toothed cornice decorations that accentuate the meeting between walls and ceiling (Fig. 32).

More recently and further afield is the 1956 Judah Hyam Synagogue in New Delhi, built in the clean-lined international style, not uncommon in Europe and the United States at that time. One might also mention the Magen Shalom (Shield of Peace) Synagogue constructed in Karachi—in what is now Pakistan—in 1892 and rebuilt in 1912. A fairly nondescript rectangular two-story box from the outside, on the inside it boasted a particularly dramatic *heikhal*, its arched form embedded within a deep-

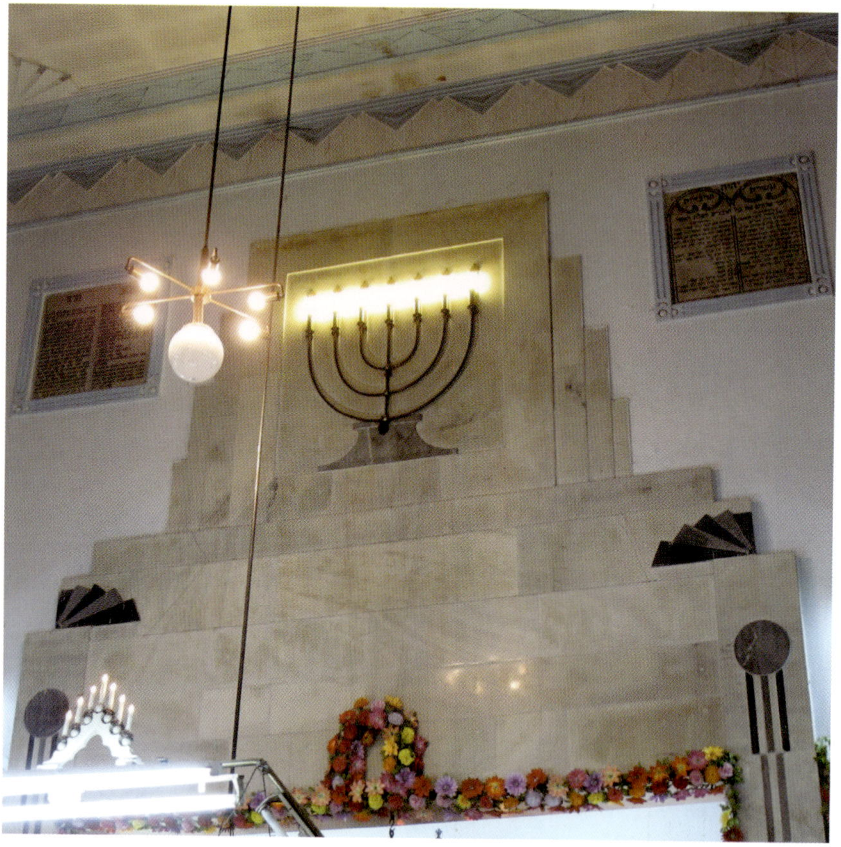

Fig. 32. Magen Abraham Synagogue interior

set, wide, and high niche embellished with beautifully carved plaster floral motifs and the entire arch broken up by scallops in a style familiar from Islamic decor. Shortly after the reshaping of the subcontinent into India and two Pakistans through the post-colonial partition of 1947, this synagogue was demolished at the order of Pakistan's autocratic president at that time, General Zia ul Haq.

V. Mumbai Beyond the Bene Israel: Three Synagogues as Epilogues

Among the important crevasses within the variegated surface of the dynamic and diverse story of the Bene Israel and its array of synagogues, one must add a significant detail that underscores the larger complexity of Jewish history in India. While one tends, for strong demographic reasons, to associate Mumbai and its environs with the Bene Israel community and its synagogues, and to think of the Baghdadi Jewish community and its synagogues, primarily in association with Calcutta,[33] it should be noted that—as mentioned in passing at the beginning of the previous section of this essay—two of the more architecturally dominant synagogue buildings in the Mumbai area were originally built to serve the Baghdadi—Iraqi—community. I bring them into the discussion here for completeness' sake, since Jael Silliman's focus on the Baghdadi community and its synagogues is devoted to Calcutta.

The Magen David (Shield/Star of David) Synagogue, in the Mumbai neighborhood of Byculla, was erected in 1864 with funding from the renowned Elias David Sassoon. Designed to serve the expanding Baghdadi Jewish community whose members had fled the persecution enacted by the governor (*wali*) of Baghdad, Da'ud Pasha, it was substantially expanded—as the community had grown significantly—in 1910, largely through funds from Jacob Sassoon, David's son. The synagogue is one of the largest in Asia outside of Israel, and currently serves Indian Jews of all backgrounds and denominations—in fact offering programs to all Indians, Jewish and otherwise. The exterior—a

[33] See Chapter Three.

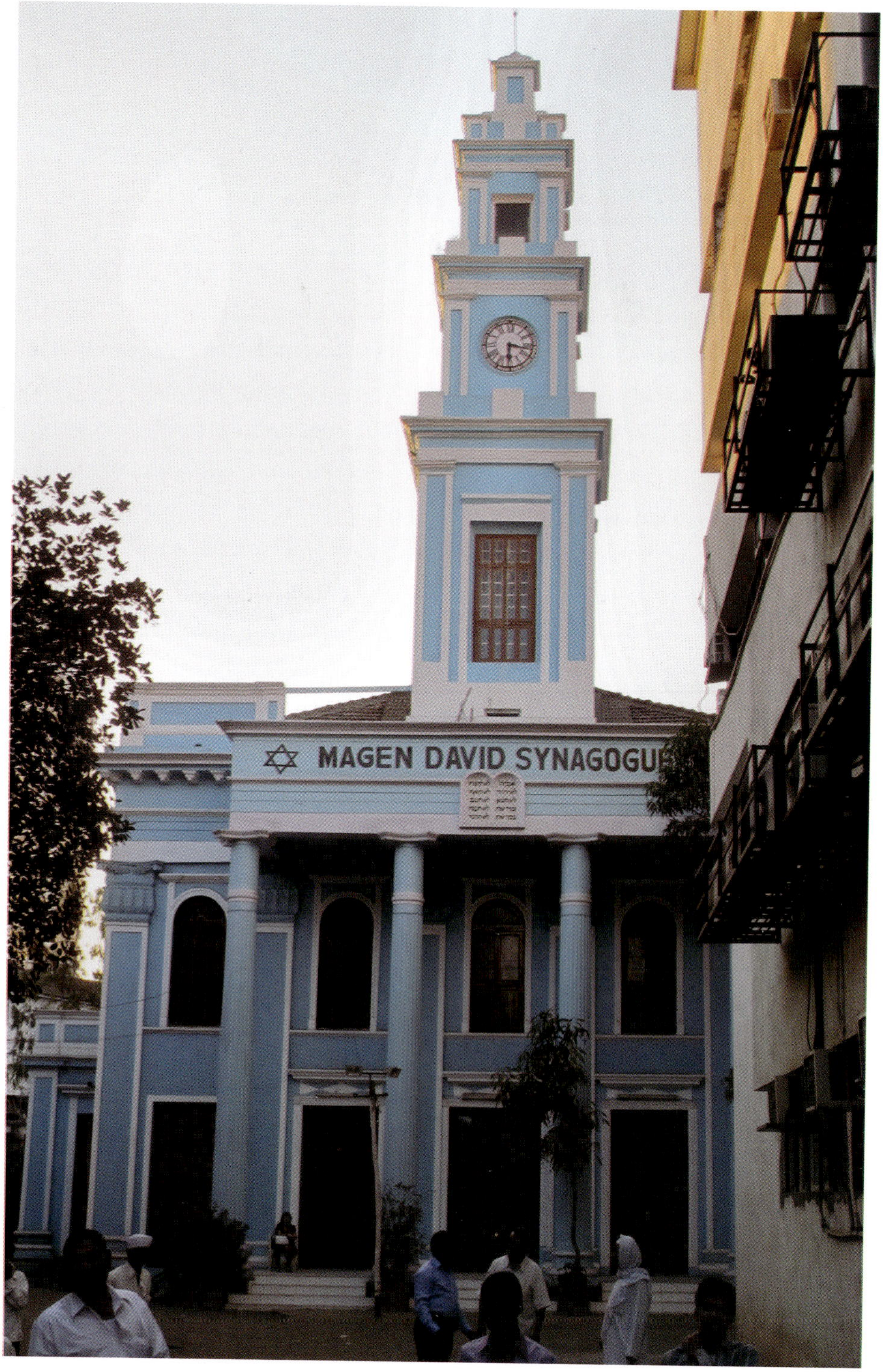

Fig. 33. Magen David Synagogue exterior, Mumbai

stunning light blue color now, highlighted by white (it is not clear as to what the original color was)—could hardly be more Anglo-Victorian in style, its fairly austere rectilinearity relieved by its second-story arched windows—their forms echoing that of the small, white affix offering the Ten Commandments that dominates the central fronton—and its tall, yet somewhat slender frontal columns. The windows are made of splendid stained-glass windows and the structure is surmounted by a soaring, four-layered clock tower that would be at home atop an English church or town hall (Fig. 33).

The impressive blue-and-white interior is broadly configured, in spite of the community's origin, in the Ashkenazi style: the *teva/bimah* is toward the center of the space. The rectilinearity of that island contrasts with the soaring curved arch, leading in almost like a church-style apse, to the *heikhal/aron*, with its interior, curved wall subdivided into three rectilinearly-decorated elements—reminding the viewer in symbolic terms of the dictum that the world stands on three things: Torah, Service, and Good Works. Both of these focal elements of the sanctuary follow a pattern familiar across the Jewish world of being elevated; they are accessed by steps—and are enhanced by substantive lighting patterns. The *teva/bimah* is further surrounded by the railing that literalizes the dictum to 'build a fence around the Torah'.[34] Wooden benches shape a rectangular horseshoe around the ground-floor periphery, and the women's section—the second-floor balcony—is shaped by arches that echo the apse arch (Fig. 34).

The interior of the Knesset Eliyahoo (Gathering/Congregation of Elijah) Synagogue—built in 1884 in the Colaba district of Mumbai through the funding of Jacob Sassoon, David's son—has a light blue-

[34] See fn. 31, p. 78.

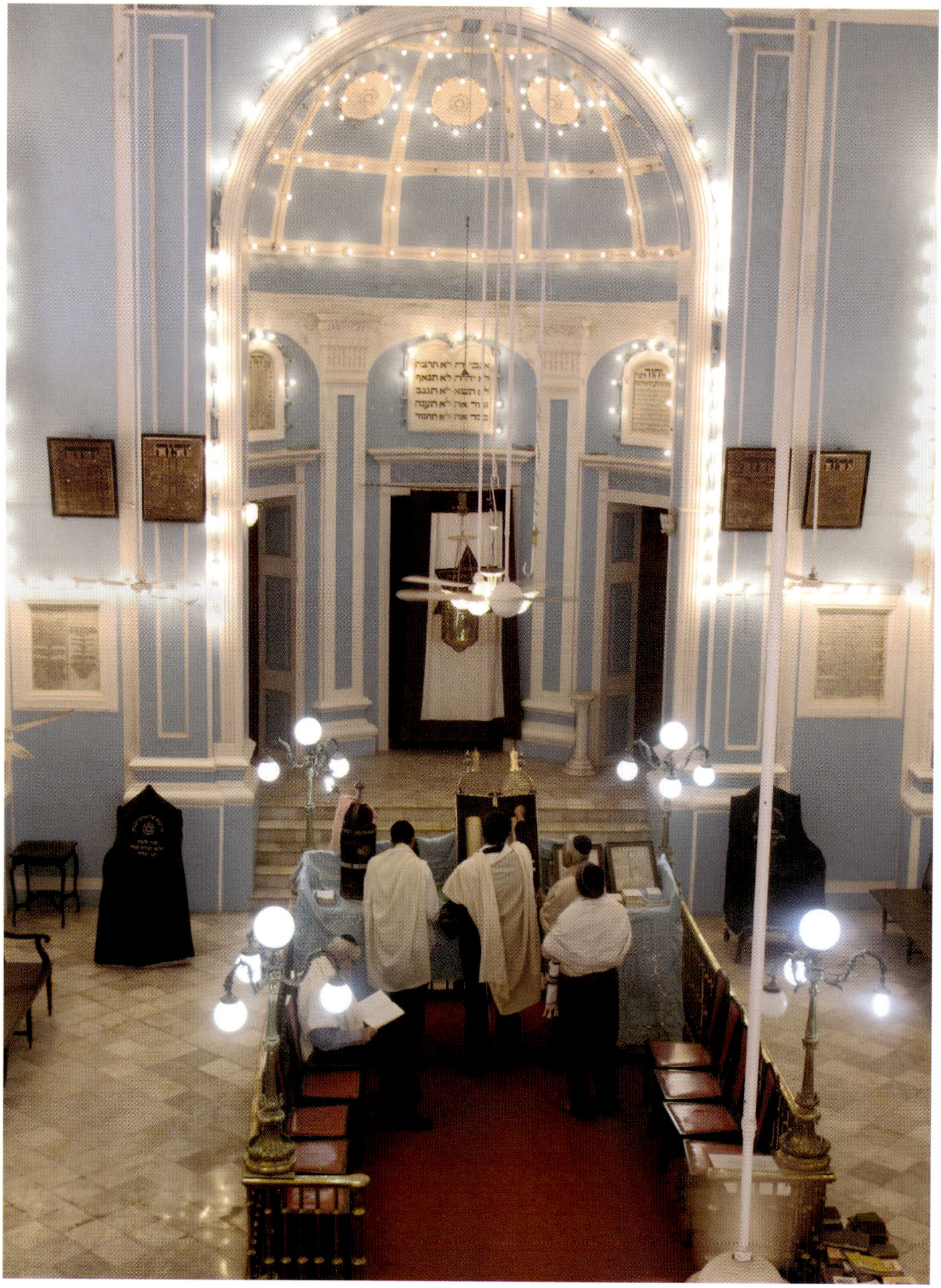

Fig. 34. Magen David Synagogue interior, Mumbai

and-white color scheme virtually identical to that of Magen David. The British connection is even more literal here: the synagogue was designed by the British architectural firm Gostling & Morris (situated, however, in Bombay). This centrally-placed, elevated *teva/bimah*—the four corners of its railing punctuated by large, handsome brass lights each with a single globe—orients one toward the west (the direction of Jerusalem) and toward the significantly elevated *heikhal/aron*, accessed by six flowing steps; over the *aron/heikhal* itself an enormous stained-glass window, with three subset components, rises, creating an overall soaring arch setting for the place where the Torah scrolls rest when they are not out, being read (Fig. 35).

The exterior of Knesset Eliyahoo, unlike most of the Indian synagogues, is built directly out on the street, rather than within a courtyard accessed by a gate. The façade is festooned with a symphony of rectilinear pilasters alternating with the upper two stories of high, arching windows, the ground-floor array—separated by a decorative cornice from the upper stories—is instead punctuated by large bricolated outcroppings. The main synagogue entrance is rather modest, but marked by a triangular fronton, pushing out from the façade, over the doorway. That small fronton echoes the gargantuan upper fronton that forms the peak of the rectilinear central outcropping of the structure's face. All of these sharp, squared off edges encompass the delightfully contrastive interior curves of the stained-glass window and its relief-carved framing (Fig. 36). Until recently, the entire outer carapace of the building had been, like its interior and like the Magen David synagogue facade, colored light-blue with white high lights, but the renovation of 2019 changed the primary color to a deep turquoise.

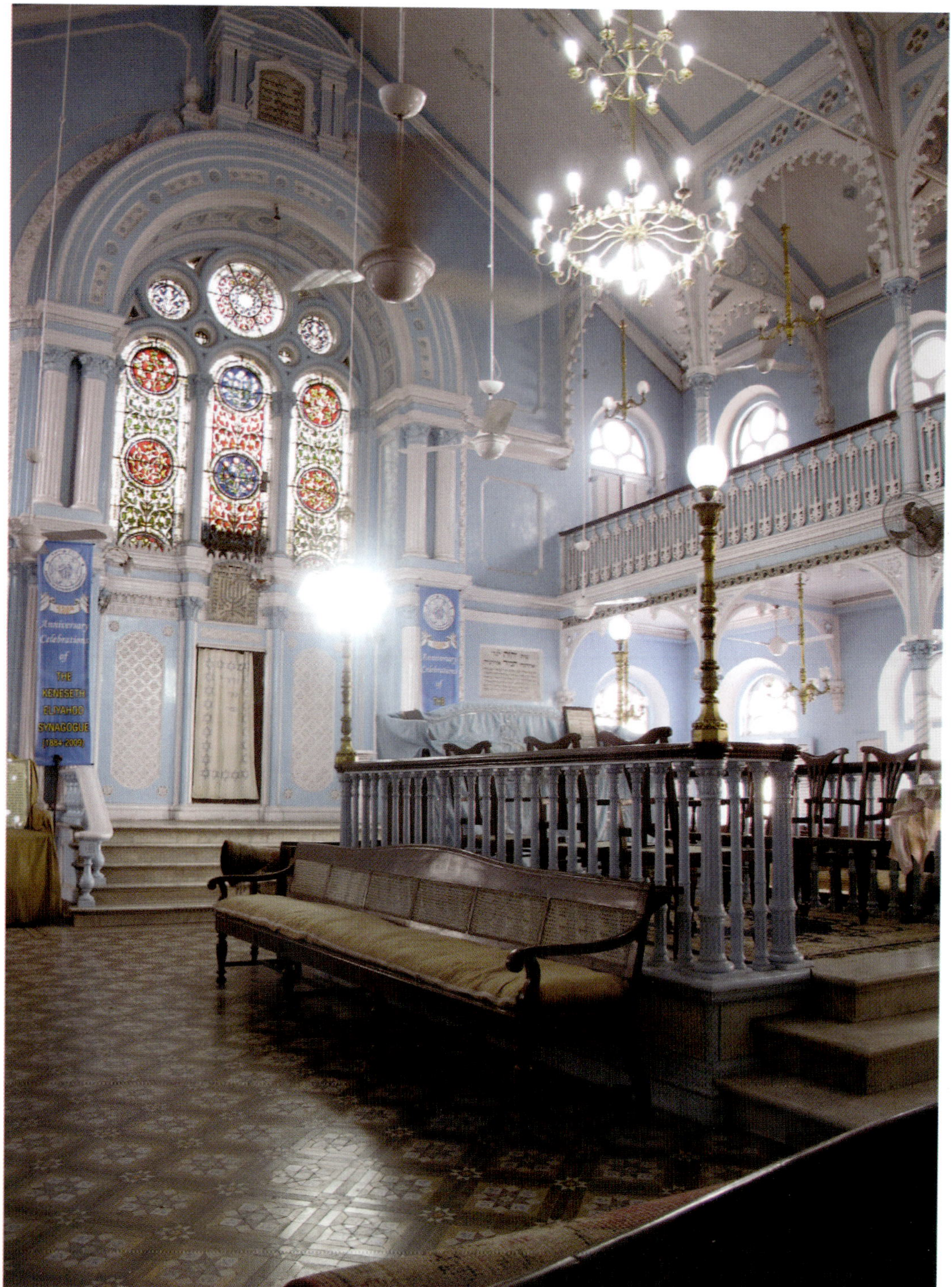

Fig. 35. Knesset Eliyahoo Synagogue interior, Mumbai

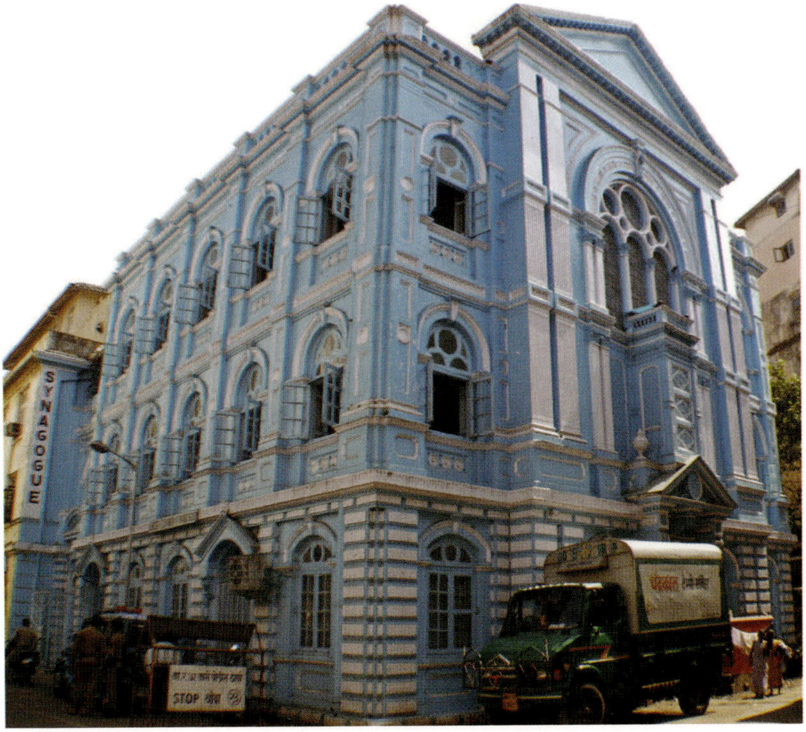

Fig. 36. Knesset Eliyahoo Synagogue exterior, Mumbai

We must turn this wonderfully complicated narrative screw one further twist, for in Pune there is also a Baghdadi synagogue, built by Elias David Sassoon in 1867, just a few years after he had constructed the Magen David Synagogue in Byculla. Called Lal Dewal (Red Walls) in Marathi, or Ohel David (Tent of David) in Hebrew—punning between the name of the first king of united ancient Israel and Sassoon's own name—this renowned red-brick edifice is the largest synagogue in India; it is arguably the largest in Asia. With its pointed 90-foot high spire (its clock imported from London), tall, attenuated ogive-arched windows, and oculus—and even with the virtually Moghul-style *jali*-like balustrade surmounting the narthex structure—it could hardly be more reminiscent of neo-Gothic British ecclesiastical architecture (Fig. 37). Given that most of the small community of Bene Israel in Pune were British army personnel who arrived when the British established an army headquarters there in 1856, the style of this Baghdadi synagogue connects these two Indian Jewish communities from a unique sort of angle.

The Iraqi Jewish population of Mumbai and its environs (including Pune) increased in the aftermath of the *Farhud* (pogrom)

Fig. 37.
Ohel David Synagogue, Pune

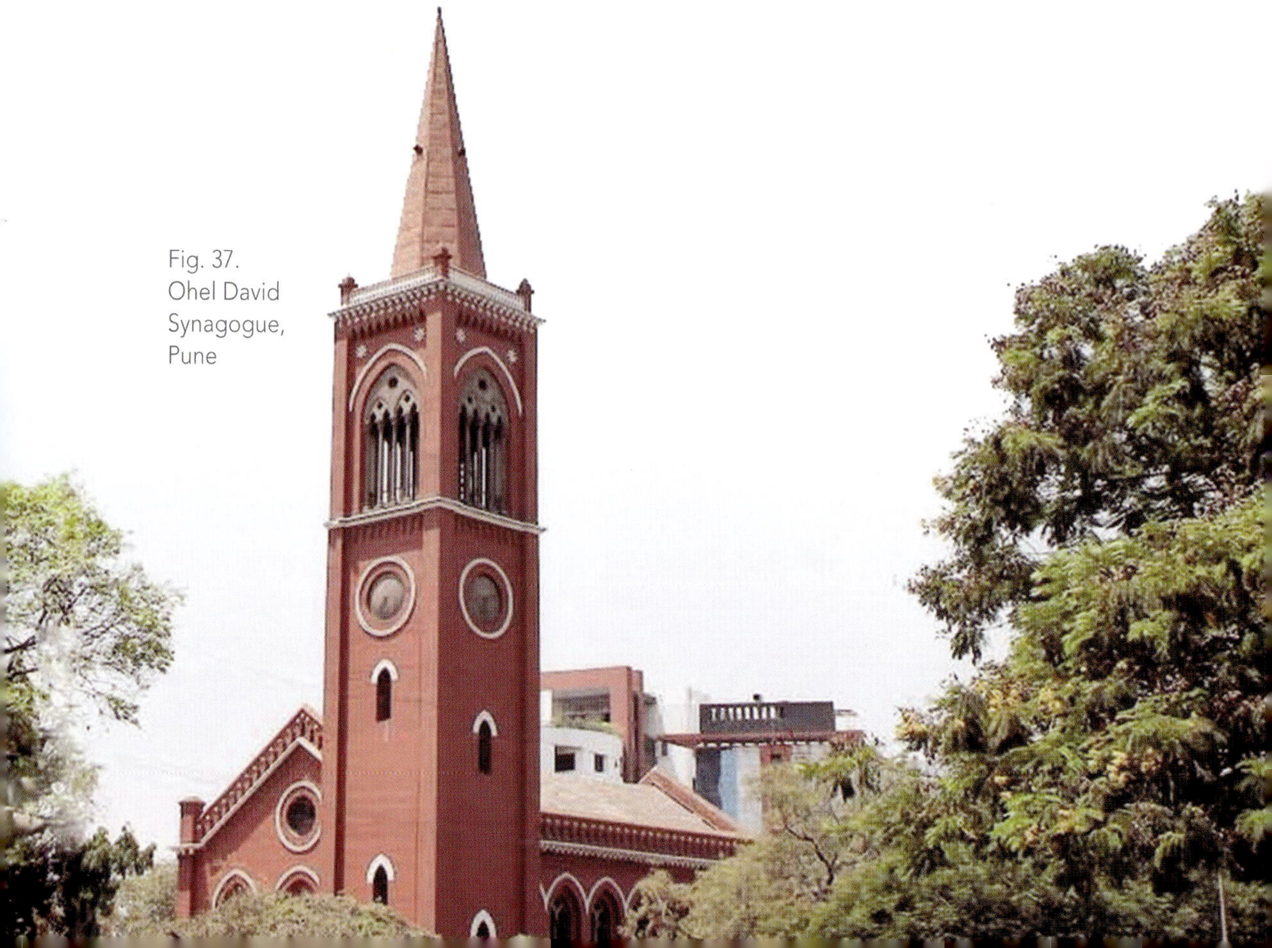

of 1941 (in the midst of World War II), swelling the congregation of Knesset Eliyahoo, in particular. Conversely, the unprecedented attack on Jews in Mumbai on 26 November 2008—a function not of internal Indian realities as much as of the complexities of the Israel-Palestine relationship and its world-wide repercussions during the past 50 years—included among its victims the young Rabbi Gavriel Holzberg, who had conducted services the previous day in this synagogue, together with his wife and four other Jews from Israel, Mexico, and the United States. The slaughter at Chabad-run Nariman House, among other consequences, helped to forge a closer bond between the small populations of Baghdadi and Bene Israel Jews in Mumbai.[35]Indeed, with partition and the coming into existence of the state of Israel in 1948, to repeat, a substantial migration of Bene Israel (and Baghdadi, Cochini, and other Jews) from India began to find its way toward Israel. In the decades since then, the Bene Israel community, relocated and variously distributed through different parts of Israel, from Dimona to Ashdod, has grown to a community of more than 60,000 individuals, and built several dozen synagogues in its new home, even more diverse in architectural style than those in India, in part reflecting the eclectic diversity of architectural styles and tastes in Israel in general. Or rather, it has built synagogues in the homeland to which it has returned—somewhere between 14 and 28 centuries after it left, during which time it arrived, settled and grew prosperous in India.

---

[35] See later in this volume, Chapter Five, p. 288, for a slightly fuller reference and the brief discussion of the effect of this massacre on the work of Siona Benjamin. Also see later in this volume, Chapter Six, pp. 304–8, for a brief discussion of the emerging Indian Jewish Center in Israel that reflects participation of all of the Indian Jewish communities residing there.

To put this in the specific terms of Bene Israel vocabulary: India remains the motherland of the community, while Israel is the fatherland. If Indian Jews are, as noted in the introduction, both Indian and Jewish, the Bene Israel in Israel are both devoted to India and enamored of Israel. The younger generation, born in Israel, is increasingly interested in reconnecting to its roots in India. The paths of dispersion move back and forth in opposite directions as time and space spread their tendrils outward.

Selected Bibliography

Bhende, Asha A., and Ralphy E. Jhirad. *Demographic and Socio-Economic Characteristics of Jews in India*. Mumbai: ORT India, 1997.

Fischel,Walter, J. *Unknown Jews in Unknown Lands: the Travels of Rabbi David D'Beth Hillel, 1824–1832*. New York: Ktar Publishing House, 1973.

Hodes, Joseph. *From India to Israel: Identity, Immigration, and the Struggle for Religious Equality*. Montreal: McGill-Queen's Press, 2014.

Israel, Benjamin J. *The Jews of India*. New Delhi: Mosaic Books, 2001.

Katz, Nathan. *Who Are the Jews of India?* Los Angeles: California University Press, 2000.

Kushner, Gilbert. *Immigrants from India in Israel*. Tucson: The University of Arizona Press, 1973.

Moses, Nissim, comp. and ed. *Bene Israel of India: Heritage and Customs*. Mumbai: Ralphy Jhirad and the Bene Israel Heritage Museum & Genealogical Research Centre, 2015.

Samuel, Shellim. *A Treatise on the Origin and Early History of the Bene Israel of Maharashtra State*. Bombay: Distributors Iyer and Iyer, 1963.

Sapphir, Jacob. *Eben Sappir* (2 vols); Vol I, Lyck: Mekize Nirdamim, 1866; Vol II: Mainz, 1874.

Slapak, Orpa, ed. *The Jews of India: A Story of Three Communities*. Jerusalem: The

Israel Museum (Distributed by University Press of New England), 1995.

Sohoni, Pushkar, and Kenneth X. Robbins. *Jewish Heritage of the Deccan: Mumbai, the Northern Konkan, Pune*. Mumbai: Deccan Heritage Foundation; Jaico, 2017.

Strizower, Schifra. *The Children of Israel; the Bene Israel of Bombay*. Oxford: Basil Blackwell, 1971.

Timberg, Thomas A., ed. *Jews in India*. New York: Advent Books, 1986.

Toledano, Dayan Dr Pinchas. *The Bene Israel of India*. London: Society of Heshaim, Spanish & Portuguese Jews' Congregation, 2002.

Weil, Shalva, ed. *India's Jewish Heritage: Ritual, Art, & Life-Cycle*. Mumbai: Marg Publications, 2002.

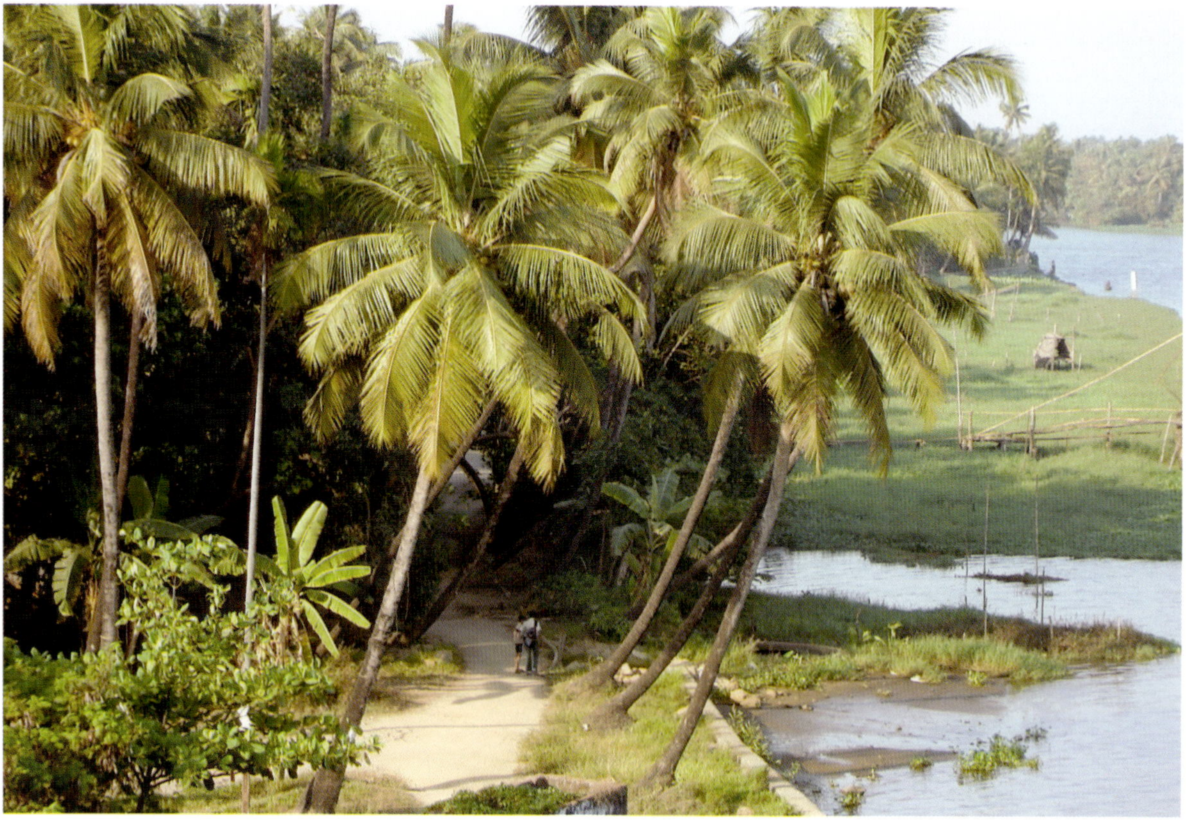

Kerala landscape by the Periyar river

CHAPTER TWO

The Kerala Synagogues

HERITAGE OF THE COCHIN JEWS

Orna Eliyahu-Oron and Barbara C. Johnson

Introduction

When most of the 'Cochin' Jews from Kerala moved to Israel in the mid-1950s they left behind their eight beloved synagogues.[1] Each was the center of religious and social life for one of the eight Kerala Jewish communities, five located in the harbor metropolis of Kochi-Ernakulam and three in the countryside further north. This article will focus on the buildings themselves, discussing shared and unique features of their architecture and contents, along with what is known of their history.

[1] A note on place names and spellings: Kerala is an Indian state created in 1956 by combining the Malayalam-speaking regions on the southwest coast, including the kingdoms formerly called Cochin and Travancore. In 1996 the English spelling of Cochin was officially changed to Kochi. For centuries the Jews of the region were called 'Cochin Jews' because most of them lived in the kingdom of Cochin—though only three of their communities were located in the city of Kochi. When most of them arrived in Israel during the 1950s they were called 'Cochinim' in Hebrew—a collective ethnic label that they now use themselves.

As of early 2020, seven of the eight Kerala synagogues remain standing, though Kadavumbhagam in Kochi has partially collapsed during a recent storm. The eighth, Thekkumbhagam in Kochi, was dismantled in 1957. Tourists are welcome at the well-preserved Paradesi synagogue in Kochi and at one of the two synagogues in downtown Ernakulam. The Ernakulam synagogues have the same names—Kadavumbhagam and Thekkumbhagam—as two of those in Kochi. About two hours to the north, visitors can easily access the two synagogues in Parur and Chendamangalam; both have been restored and renovated as part of the Kerala Government's Muziris Heritage Project to promote Kerala tourism. Special arrangements must be made to see the northernmost standing synagogue, located in nearby Mala.

One of the eight synagogues, Thekkumbhagam in downtown Ernakulam, is a relatively new structure, built to replace an older one that was demolished in 1939 for an ambitious reconstruction project that was never completed. The rich heritage of this previous Ernakulam synagogue and also of the demolished Thekkumbhagam synagogue in Kochi had remained hidden until recently. We will provide new information and some visual evidence about both in order to perpetuate their memory.

This article depends on documentary research and photographic evidence, interviews, material from Malayalam-language Jewish songs, the work of other scholars,[2] and personal observation through our

[2] We offer particular thanks to Paul Laju for permission to use his photographs in this article, and for the thoroughly researched and frequently updated information he posts in his online blog 'Jewish Monuments of Kerala'. We also thank Thoufeek Zakriya for his well-researched online blog and for his help with this article; and we appreciate Jay Waronker for his M.A. thesis (2010) and his ongoing involvement with Kerala synagogues.

own visits to Kerala. After Orna Eliyahu-Oron first travelled to Kerala in 1993 to explore her roots as the daughter of Cochini immigrants to Israel, she decided to concentrate her graduate studies at Hebrew University on the Kerala synagogues. She returned in 1995 as a member of a team from the university's Center for Jewish Art (CJA) to document the synagogues, and then went back again in 1996 to concentrate on her own research project. During the 1960s Barbara Johnson lived for four years in Tamil Nadu, the Indian state directly east of Kerala, where she taught English in a women's college. She first visited Kerala in 1968, meeting Jews in Kochi and Ernakulam, and she has devoted much of her academic research since then to Kerala Jewish history and culture. We began working together in 1999 on the intersection of Malayalam Jewish songs and synagogues.

Historical and Cultural Context

Ancestors of today's Israeli Cochinim lived in peace and security on the tropical coast of southwest India—an area traditionally called Kerala, land of the kera or coconut tree, and known to many outsiders as the Malabar Coast. Jewish merchants from West Asia participated in the active sea trade linking the Mediterranean with Kerala, probably in the early centuries CE and certainly later on, especially as part of the commerce in pepper and other spices.[3] Some of them settled down there, marrying and converting local residents and forming Jewish communities; copper plate inscriptions in old Malayalam testify to the

[3] Chakravarti (2007).

presence of Jewish trade guilds at least as early as the eighth century. Their continued involvement in the Indian Ocean trade made it possible to maintain contact with Jews in other lands, ordering Hebrew books and observing orthodox religious practices at home and in their synagogues.

In recent centuries Kerala Jews followed the Sephardic ritual tradition practiced across the Middle East and the Mediterranean basin, and they also maintained contact with Jewish communities in Europe. They were proud and religiously observant Jews who also identified with the general local culture of Kerala, enjoying good relationships with their Hindu, Christian, and Muslim neighbors. A number of their synagogues were built on land donated by local Hindu rulers, whose custom it was to give land and other support for religious buildings, whether Hindu, Muslim, Christian, or Jewish. There are large Muslim and Christian minority populations in Kerala, many descended (like the Jews) from early immigrants by sea.

There is evidence of a long-standing Jewish community in the city of Cranganore (present-day Kodungallur), identified with Muziris, which was an important medieval port. [4] It was the capital of the powerful Chera kingdom in 1000 CE, the year in which an inscription was engraved there on copper tablets, recording a set of privileges granted to Joseph Rabban, leader of a Jewish trade guild.[5] Cranganore remained a center

[4] There is also evidence of an earlier Jewish presence in Kerala north of Cranganore, but this article concentrates on the eight synagogues and communities that prospered and endured down to the 20th century. See Gamliel (2018a).

[5] See Narayanan (2003) for analysis of the inscription and its historical context. See Johnson (1982) for a discussion of folk traditions about Joseph Rabban and Cranganore (also referred to as 'Shingly'), which are featured in many scholarly and popular accounts of Kerala Jewish history and culture. They are associated primarily with the Paradesi synagogue community, just one of the eight to be discussed in this article.

of international commerce until 1341, when a catastrophic flood silted up its harbor and opened a large harbor at Kochi, about 30km to the south. Kochi then grew to be a major trade center, attracting many Jews to settle there. Some remained in Cranganore until the 16th century when Portuguese troops took over the city; and others stayed in three nearby Jewish communities where synagogues are still found today (see Fig. 1a, the map).

Kerala Jewish history was strongly influenced by European colonialism, beginning with Portuguese dominance from 1498 to 1663. After the naval power of Portugal prevailed over Arab competition for the India trade, Portuguese colonies were established in key port cities, including Cranganore and Kochi. Early in the 16th century a Hindu ruler of Cranganore moved to Kochi, where he maintained a strong protective relationship with the Jewish communities there.

In 1663 the Portuguese were defeated by Dutch naval power, and the Jews fared quite well under Dutch rule until 1795, when British colonial rule was established, lasting until Indian Independence in 1947. While the English concentrated on developing commercial and then industrial centers in the larger port cities of Bombay and Calcutta, they exercised 'indirect' rule over many small Indian kingdoms, including Cochin, where the Raja maintained considerable control over internal affairs. When the economic prosperity of Kerala declined in the 19th and early 20th centuries, some Cochin Jews moved to Bombay, Calcutta, or even Rangoon for work, but almost all maintained connections with their home communities and rejoined them in the 1950s, emigrating to Israel as Cochinim.

As noted, the synagogues were central to Kerala Jewish life. Each of the eight communities was called by the name of its synagogue, and

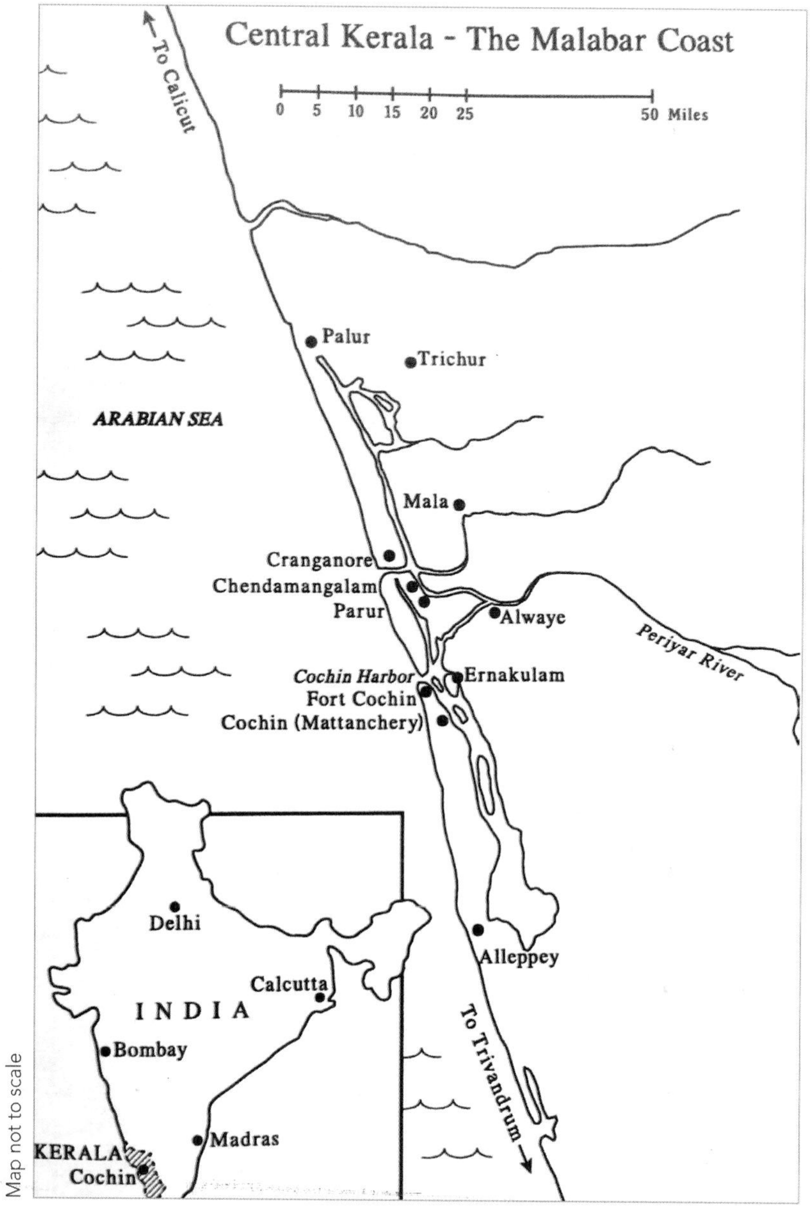

Fig. 1a. Map of Jewish settlements in Kerala
Fred Estabrook, in Ruby Daniel and Barbara C. Johnson, *Ruby of Cochin: An Indian Jewish Woman Remembers* (Philadelphia: Jewish Publication Society, 1995), p. 5.

each was constituted as a *yogam*—a legal body with economic, religious and social responsibilities, run by elected trustees and recognized by the secular government. Membership was hereditary, with a married woman joining her husband's community. The *yogam* was responsible for managing the income and expenses of its communally owned lands and for the upkeep and staffing of its synagogue, which was the place for community meetings as well as worship. A council of elders—the seven oldest male *yogam* members—had authority to call for a *yogam* assembly in the synagogue to settle disputes within the community.[6] The building itself was a source of pride and social identity to community members, and Malayalam-language songs honoring six of the eight synagogues have been preserved and sung by Kerala Jewish women.

Shared Building Style and Layout

In the local Malayalam language *palli* is the word for a synagogue, a church or a mosque: a place for monotheistic congregational worship, in contrast to Hindu temples, where multiple deities are worshipped, often through individual rather than collective rituals. In cosmopolitan Kerala it was not surprising that synagogues would share some traditional architectural elements with other places of worship. Building materials included laterite, a local stone used to construct the thick walls and covered with a white plaster called *chunam*. Some synagogues also featured the use of granite, a stronger and more expensive stone, in their foundations and columns. Another important building

6 Johnson and Hacco (2010); Bar-Giora (1958).

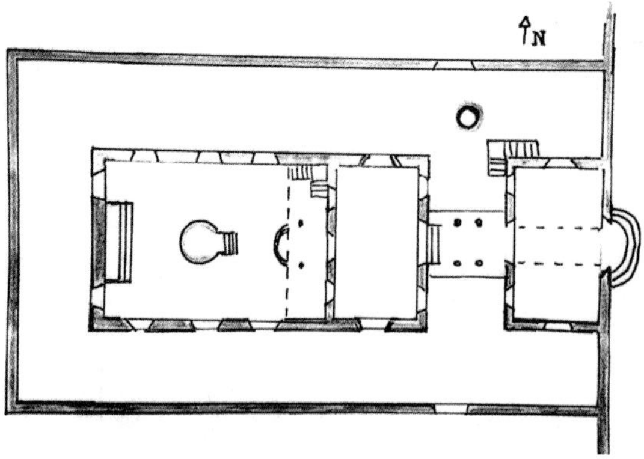

Fig. 1b. Sketch of the layout of a synagogue; Orna Eliyahu-Oron, 2020

material was teak—a costly wood used for building beams as well as decorative carvings. Teak was sometimes donated by local rulers for the construction of religious buildings.

In considering the Juta*palli* (Jewish *palli*) building style in general, we speculate that each Kerala synagogue was originally part of a walled complex containing at least three structures: the gatehouse or entrance building and the main synagogue building, connected by a breezeway (Fig. 1b). At least six of the synagogues built since the 16th century shared this architectural layout, resembling in some ways the old Kerala churches and mosques surviving from earlier times. Though two of the eight were rebuilt in the early 20th century as stand-alone buildings, their individual architectural features incorporate the social functions which were associated with a gatehouse in the other six, and perhaps in their own earlier versions.

Both the gatehouse and the synagogue building are entered from the east, so that the worshippers move gradually from the outside public space into the sanctuary, where the *heikhal* (Torah Ark) is situated on the western wall, closest to Jerusalem. The entrance building is connected to the upper story of the synagogue by a breezeway with a roof and open or latticed sides, over which women can walk to enter their seating section on the upper level of the prayer hall (Fig. 17).

Male worshippers enter the synagogue building on the ground floor passing first through the courtyard beneath the breezeway and then (after removing their sandals) into the *azarah*, an entrance room serving as an overflow space—then finally into the sanctuary. Taking up most of the main building, the sanctuary is a lofty rectangular hall with a teak wood ceiling, tall windows, and usually a tiled floor. In most cases the ceiling is covered with ornately carved floral designs. Hanging over the hall are numerous oil lamps and candelabras. On the western wall is the *heikhal* (Fig. 22), a monumental, elaborately carved wooden cabinet housing the Torah scrolls in Torah cases often covered with silver. The scrolls themselves are made of parchment, on which the first five books of the Hebrew Bible have been hand-written by a learned scribe.

Prayers are conducted from the harp-shaped *tebah* (reader's desk) located in the center of the room, as is common in Sephardic synagogues worldwide (Fig. 13).The *tebah,* made of wooden frames and multiple brass columns, is built on an elevated platform accessed by stairs from the east side.

An architectural feature unique to Kerala synagogues is a second *tebah.*[7] It is located in the center of a balcony which stretches the width of the building at the eastern end of the hall, supported by two columns made of brass or wood, referred to as 'Yachin and Boaz' in memory of the two pillars by that name in the Biblical description of the First Temple in Jerusalem.[8]The balcony rim and the ceiling under it may be painted or decorated with wood carvings. The 'Torah service' and readings from the Torah on weekdays are conducted from the central *tebah*, but on

[7] *Tebah* is the Kerala pronunciation of the Sephardi Hebrew term *tevah.* In Ashkenazi synagogues the reader's desk is called a *bimah.* Several old Sephardi synagogues have a second *tevah* but not of the same design.

[8] I Kings, 7:21.

Shabbat or a festival day, prayer leaders ascend from the hall to this upper *tebah* by a set of stairs in the northeast corner of the room, carrying the encased Torah scroll from which the weekly or festival portion of the scriptures will be chanted (Figs 6 and 21).

Male worshippers sit on benches toward the back of the sanctuary, along the side walls, and around the *tebah* in the center of the room. Though seated separately from the men, as throughout the orthodox Jewish world, the women in Kerala uniquely sit right behind the upper *tebah*, in a room called the *ezrat nashim* (women's section) separated only by a partition of open lattice work, through which they can view the opened Torah scroll and hear every word of the reading and the service. This architectural feature contributes to their educated and lively participation in the singing of Hebrew liturgical responses and songs along with the men of the community. Most of the women would have learned as children to read Hebrew and to follow the service in their prayer books, in contrast to orthodox Jewish women in many other places, where girls are not necessarily educated in Hebrew and men at prayer are forbidden to hear the voices of women singing.

The Three Synagogues of Kochi

Three of the eight Kerala synagogues that remained standing until the mid-1950s were located in the area of Kochi known as Jewtown. Jewtown is part of Mattancherry, currently a municipal ward of the Kochi Corporation. All three synagogues faced on Jew Street, the major north-south thoroughfare on the eastern side of Kochi Island, paralleling the harbor.

Just south of Mattancherry is the municipal ward known as Kochangadi. According to local tradition, a much earlier synagogue (not included here as one of the eight) was built in that area, associated with an inscription from the 14th century. Though there is no verifiable information about this *palli*, it is believed to have been built about a kilometer to the south of Jewtown on what is still officially called Kochangadi Street—an extension of Jew Street on the current map of the neighborhood. Tradition also holds that it served as a place of Jewish worship until the late 18th or early 19th century. According to the inscription, a synagogue was erected in 1344—just three years after the flood of 1341 opened up the harbor at Kochi to Jewish commerce. The inscribed stone slab was kept for some time in the Kadavumbhagam *Palli*, and in 1818 it was moved to the Paradesi *Palli* courtyard, where it can still be viewed on a wall of the courtyard (Fig. 2).[9] The memory of its traditional location continued into the 20th century, as eminent members of the Jewish community Ruby Daniel (b. 1912) and Samuel

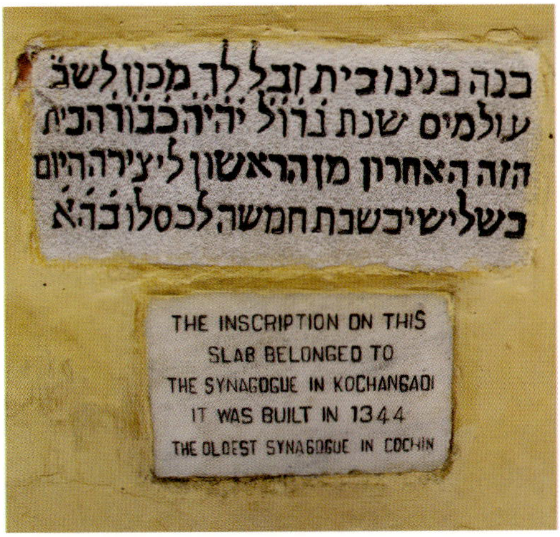

Fig. 2. Kochangadi Synagogue inscription; Siona Benjamin, 2011

[9] The text of the inscription is found in Sassoon (1932, 577, Ms 13). Gamliel (2018, 45–46) suggests that it was the original inscription for the Kadavumbhagam Synagogue in Jewtown.

Hallegua (b. 1931) both remembered the place. Daniel recalled seeing a piece of its wall still preserved and kept clean by a Muslim woman; and she also recounted a legend about its miraculous construction.[10]

Kadavumbhagam-Kochi Synagogue

The first synagogue to be built in Jewtown, Mattancherry, was Kadavumbhagam *Palli*, erected in 1544. It seems likely that it was built because the earlier synagogue or synagogues were not large enough to accommodate a new influx of Jews, who were coming to Kochi as merchants and some perhaps as direct or indirect refugees from persecution in Spain or Portugal. By this time the Portuguese had established political control of the western and north-western part of Kochi Island (now called Fort Kochi), but the Hindu Maharaja controlled Mattancherry. Both the Portuguese and the Raja were eager to deal with the Jewish merchants. Though the attitude of the Portuguese colonial rulers varied, the Raja's territory remained a safe and welcoming place for the Jews, even when the Portuguese turned against them.

The founding date of 1544 is inscribed on another stone tablet, also preserved today on a wall of the Paradesi *Palli* courtyard. It seems clear that Kadavumbhagam was the synagogue mentioned in records from the 1555–58 Portuguese Inquisition trials in India, which refer to the recent building of a 'New Synagogue' in Cochin with accusations that certain Portuguese New Christians (forced converts from Judaism) had attended this synagogue and even contributed funds to its construction.[11]

---

[10] Daniel and Johnson (1995, 128). Tavim (1996, 70) reported that Hallegua remembered the site.

[11] Tavim (1996, 70–74).

True to its name, Kadavumbhagam *Palli* (synagogue by the side of the landing place) is located close to the harbor, opposite a former boat jetty that would have been convenient for Jewish merchants involved in the export trade. Before the 1950s emigration to Israel, Jewish houses lined both sides of the street in this neighborhood. Ruby Daniel's family lived nearby, with neighbors belonging to both the Kadavumbhagam and Thekkumbhagam communities. In addition to relating various stories of miraculous events associated with the synagogue, as did other Jews and non-Jewish neighbors, Daniel wrote that when the Cochin Maharaja's boat used to pass by this site, the Jews of the synagogue would be requested in advance to open its doors and the doors of the Ark, so that the Maharaja could stop and prostrate himself in respect.[12]

Kadavumbhagam *Palli* was constructed on the same model as the other Kerala synagogues, with a gatehouse opening eastward onto the street, a bridge connecting to the second floor of the main building, and a surrounding walled courtyard. We can speculate that the structures were originally surrounded by a compound much larger than what is indicated by the remnants of a perimeter wall no more than 6 meters from the synagogue building on its north, east and south sides.[13]

Photographs from the mid-20th century show the two-storey gatehouse, which was removed sometime after 1957 to make room for the road to be widened. In the front view (Fig. 3) we see that this gatehouse was entered from the street by way of a small open portico with a tiled roof. The side view (Fig. 4) reveals that the gatehouse stood separate from but very close to the synagogue itself, leaving room only

---

[12] Daniel and Johnson (1995, 129).

[13] Waronker (2010, 217).

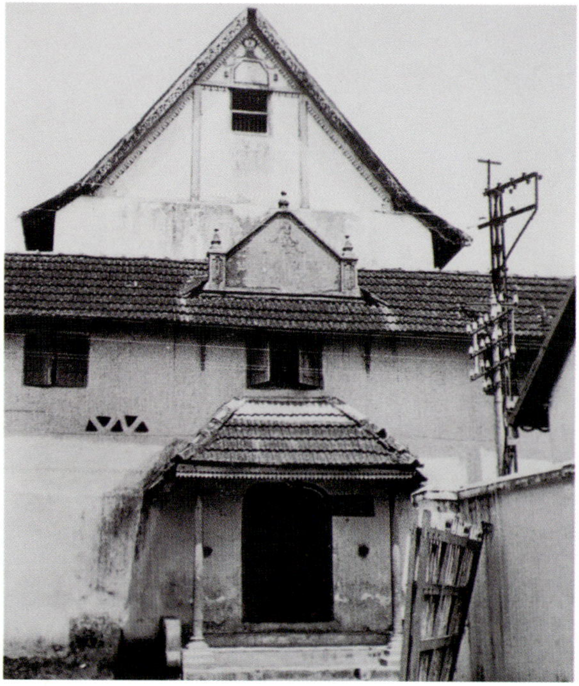

Fig. 3. Kadavumbhagam-Kochi Synagogue façade;
Elias Madai, 1957; courtesy of Israel Museum

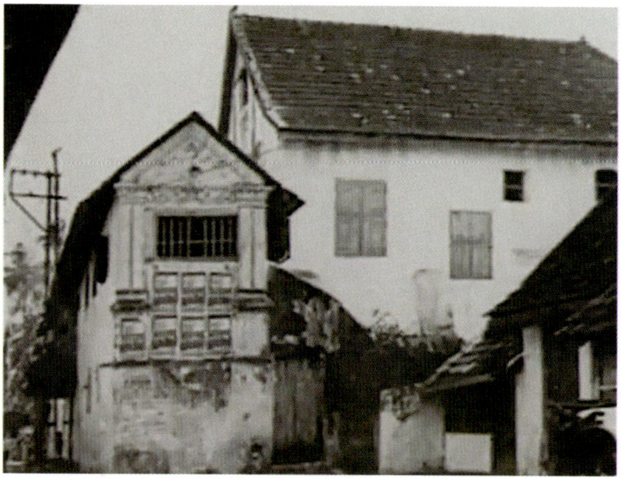

Fig. 4. Kadavumbhagam-Kochi Synagogue gatehouse from the side; https://www.youtube.com/watch?v=IdKevt83qH8. Video קלח - ןיצוקתודהי 1, 2 min. 2 sec. Accessed 26 April, 2020

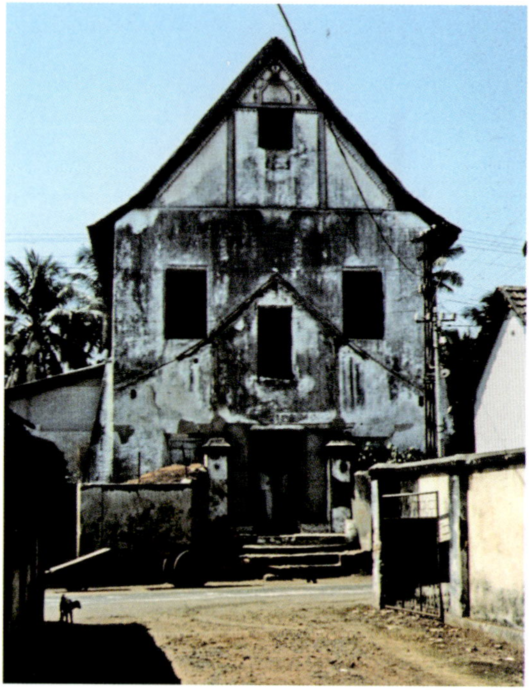

Fig. 5. Kadavumbhagam-Kochi Synagogue façade;
Barbara C. Johnson, 1977

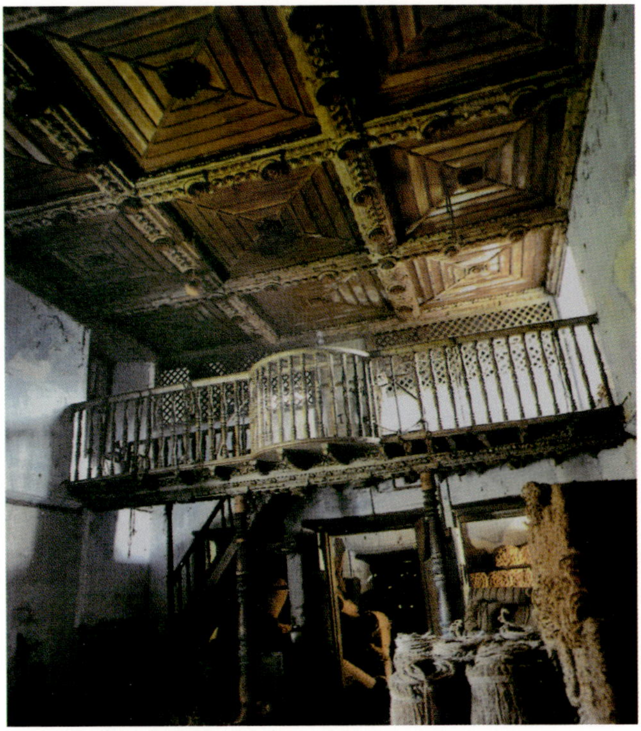

Fig. 6. Kadavumbhagam-Kochi Synagogue interior; Jörg Drechsel, 1990, courtesy of Israel Museum

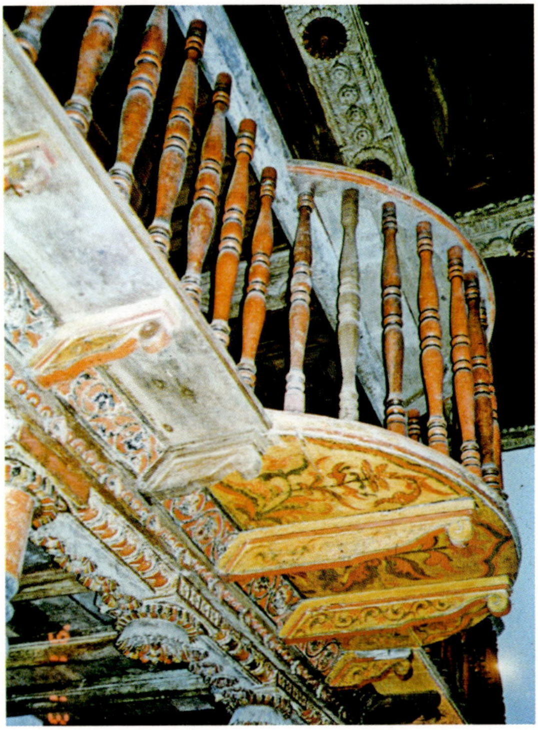

Fig. 7. Kadavumbhagam-Kochi Synagogue renovation; Barbara C. Johnson, 1995, Israel Museum

for a short connection between the two buildings. A 1977 photo (Fig. 5) clearly shows remnants of the roof of a breezeway and of a wooden door opening into the upstairs of the synagogue, by which the women could pass through the study room and enter the *ezrat nashim*.

With its gatehouse and breezeway removed and its congregation departed for Israel, the Kadavumbhagam building was used as a commercial warehouse by a series of non-Jewish owners (Fig. 6). In 1991, the Israel Museum was able to purchase and transport to Jerusalem almost all of its wooden interior, including its heavy teakwood beams. Over the next several years the intricately carved ceiling, the doors, the upper *tebah* (Fig 7) and its staircase all underwent an intensive and complex process of renovation. A section of the Museum roof was raised to accommodate the five-and-a-half meter height required to install the entire Kadavumbhagam interior as a permanent exhibition, which opened in 1995.[14] Carbon dating commissioned by the Israel Museum provided convincing evidence that this *palli* from Kochi was indeed the original 16th century building, in which the elaborate wooden details had been periodically renovated throughout the centuries.[15]

The furnishings of the *Palli*—its *heikhal*, *tebah* and Torah ark curtains— could not be brought to the Israel Museum because they were no longer in Kochi. In the 1950s the Kadavumbhagam elders had arranged to send them to Israel ahead of their own emigration. But members of the Kadavumbhagam congregation in Israel were not aware of the shipment, and it remained in Israeli customs until people from Moshav Nehalim, an Orthodox Ashkenazi community in central Israel, bought it at auction. Though the cloth curtains and the wooden parts of the *tebah* didn't survive the shipment, the *heikhal* is still in good condition. It is one of the newest Kerala Torah Arks, built in 1937–1940 after the previous one had suffered severe weather damage. It is made of teak wood, carved and painted in red, blue and gold, and its shape is patterned after older *heikhalot* from Kochi and Ernakulam.[16]

Sadly, after 1991 there was no one left in Kochi to maintain the empty shell of Kerala's oldest synagogue, until the Kerala Government Archaeology Department gave it a 'Protected Monument' status in 2016 and began to plan for its restoration. During the Muziris-Kochi Biennale

---

[14] The entire project was made possible by a large donation from Fred and Della Worms, Jewish benefactors from London. For details see Slapak (1995) and Fishof (1995).

[15] Dr. Israel Carmi, Weizmann Institute, Letter to Israel Museum, 5 June 1996. Copy provided by Orpah Slapak.

[16] Eliyahu-Oron (2004, 6769, 11–116).

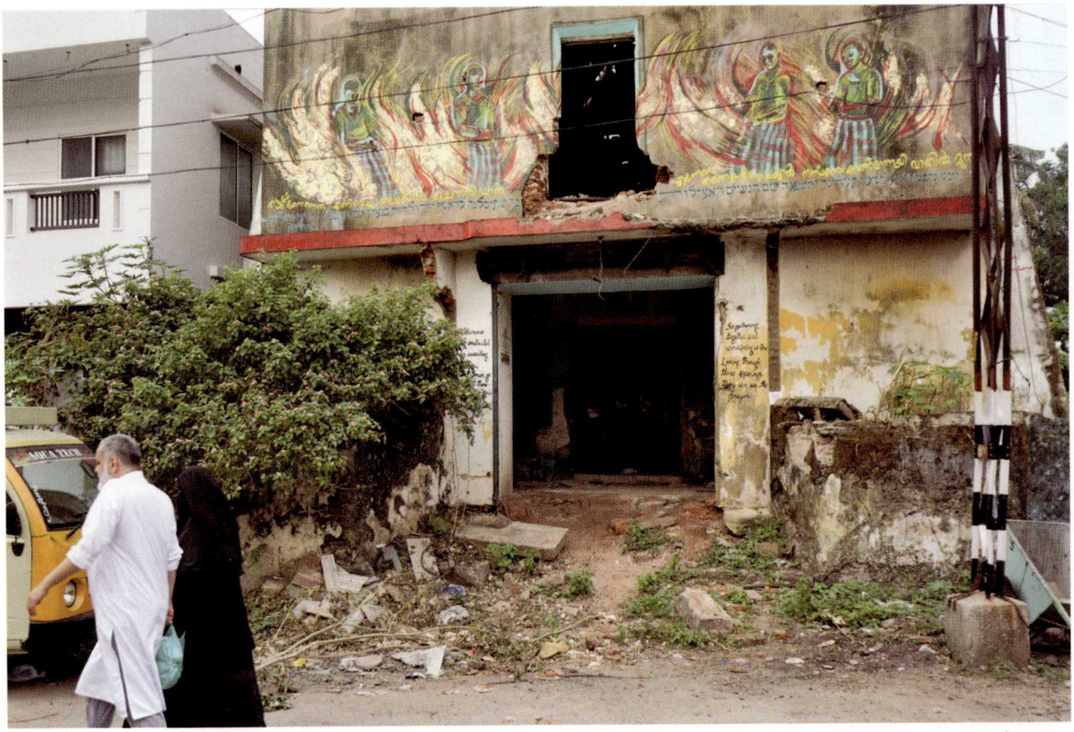

Fig. 8. Kadavumbhagam-Kochi Synagogue façade mural—'Red Crown Green Parrot', public art project by Meydad Eliyahu and Thoufeek Zakriya; Kashi Art Gallery collateral project as part of the Kochi Muziris Biennale 2018

of December 2018, the synagogue was honored for the last time by two young men. Meydad Eliyahu, an Israeli Cochini artist, and Thoufeek Zakriya, a Muslim calligrapher and researcher from Kochi, teamed up to paint a mural on its façade, as part of their ambitious project entitled 'Red Crown, Green Parrot' (see Fig. 8).[17]

[17] See the video at https://www.youtube.com/watch?v=0gIBjv44KvI. Accessed 25 February 2020.

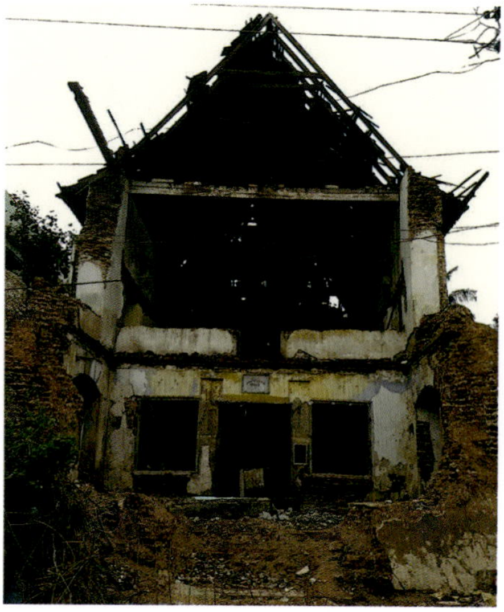

Fig. 9. Kadavumbhagam-Kochi Synagogue collapsed; Paul Laju, 2019

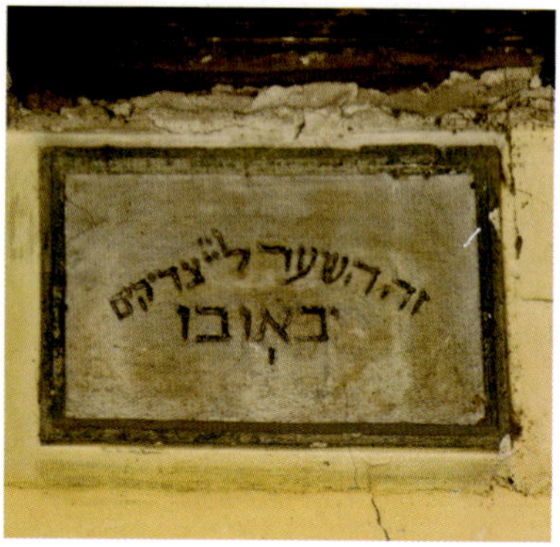

Fig. 10. Kadavumbhagam-Kochi Synagogue inscription, after the collapse; Paul Laju, 2019

However, the government restoration plans had been delayed too long, and on 10 September 2019 its front portion (the former *azarah*) completely collapsed in a monsoon storm (Figs 9 and 10),[18] exposing the Hebrew inscription above the entrance to the sanctuary: 'This is the gate of the Lord; the righteous shall enter in' (Psalm 118:20).[19]

Paradesi Synagogue

In 1568, not long after the construction of the Kadavumbhagam *Palli*, the Paradesi synagogue was built at the northern end of Jewtown Road (see Fig. 11). Perhaps more room was already needed to accommodate

---

[18] https://www.newindianexpress.com/cities/kochi/2019/sep/11/kadavumbagam-synagogue-a-heritage-structure-collapses-2031908.html. Accessed 25 February 2020.

[19] This verse was also inscribed above the entrance to Kochi's Thekkumbhagam *Palli*.

the continuing influx of Jewish merchants from the Mediterranean and from Western Asia—or perhaps the new arrivals wanted to establish a community of their own. Like Muslims from overseas, Jewish newcomers to Kerala were called *paradesi*s ('foreigners') in the Malayalam language. As noted, early 15th century newcomers to Kochi worshipped in the old Kochangadi synagogue and then helped build the Kadavumbhagam *Palli*. In the long run their descendants acculturated thoroughly to the much older Jewish culture of Kerala, adopting its language and customs. They continued to welcome Jewish immigrants, who brought Sephardi, Yemenite, and Iraqi elements into the Hebrew liturgy and music of all the Kerala Jewish communities; but the designation of this new synagogue in 1568 as the Paradesi *Palli* may be taken as marking establishment of a community apart from the rest.

The Paradesi Synagogue was built on a plot of land donated by the Kochi Raja, who had recently moved into a new palace right next to it. According to Paradesi tradition, the ruler's gift of this land was a compassionate response to welcome a large group of Jews fleeing from Cranganore because of a 1565 Portuguese attack on them there. Though there is no historical evidence of a mass Jewish exodus from Cranganore at that time, the story emphasizes the well-documented relationship of mutual respect between their ancestors and the Raja.[20]

A century later the Portuguese were battling with the Dutch for control of the Malabar Coast and the Indian Ocean trade. In 1662, the Paradesi Synagogue was set afire and partially destroyed by Portuguese troops retaliating for the Jewish support of Dutch military efforts to overthrow Portuguese rule.[21] The Dutch did defeat the Portuguese the

---

20 Johnson (1982).

21 Segal (1993, 38).

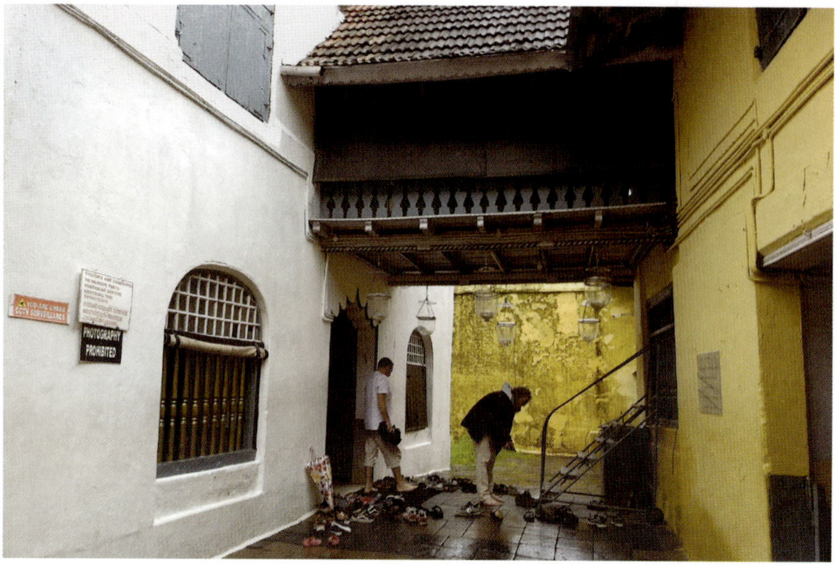

Fig. 11. Paradesi Synagogue breezeway; Paul Laju, 2011

following year; and the Jews rebuilt their synagogue and continued to prosper during Dutch political and economic rule of Kerala (1663–1795).

The new Paradesi Synagogue, re-built after the fire, was constructed according to the pattern exemplified in Kadavumbhagam. The *Palli* complex includes a large gatehouse opening onto the street, a large rectangular synagogue building and a relatively short breezeway connecting the second story of the gatehouse to the *ezrat nashim*. Around the synagogue is a narrow surrounding courtyard and a long wall facing the street.

The gatehouse of Paradesi *Palli* is much larger than others. As seen in Figure 12, it extends the full width of the compound's front wall. Entering through the outside door, a room on the left contains the

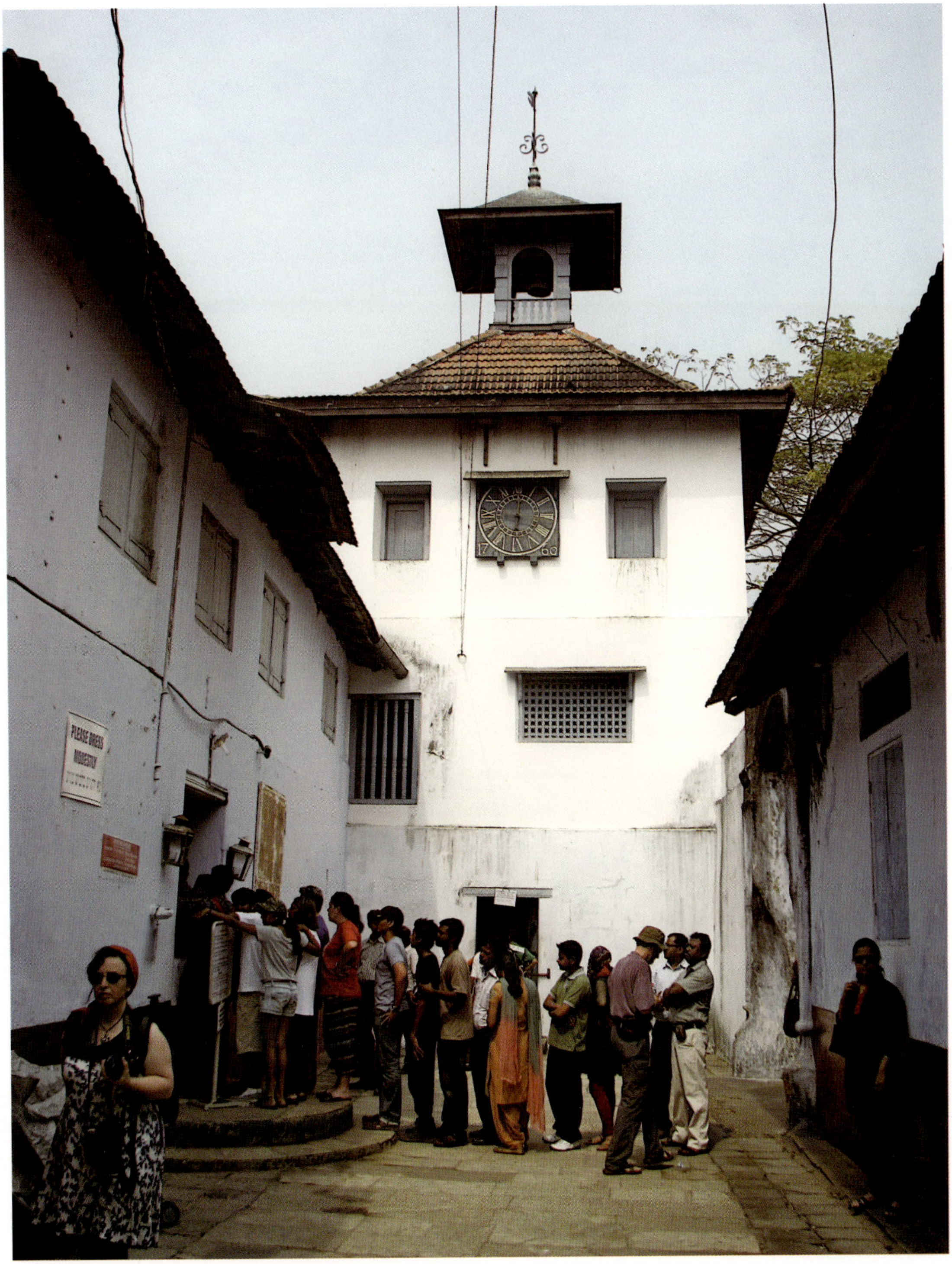

Fig. 12. Paradesi Synagogue entrance; Paul Laju, 2011

stairway leading upstairs, by which women could access the *ezrat nashim* through a breezeway much shorter than those of other synagogues (Fig. 11). Other rooms on the second floor were formerly used for Torah study and for meetings of community elders. One of the three downstairs rooms now houses a set of 10 paintings that portray the legendary past of the Paradesi community and the construction of its synagogue.

The interior of the Paradesi sanctuary resembles in its layout those of the other Kerala synagogues, in particular the neighboring Thekkumbhagam *Palli* (no longer standing), as will be discussed later. Its Torah Ark is similar in age and style,[22] and so is its central *tebah*, pictured in Figure 13.[23] In addition to the *tebah*, this photograph shows a brilliant yellow, red and gold parochet covering the doors of the *heikhal*. The *heikhal* curtains of Kerala were typically made of silk with a central panel embroidered with silver or gold thread. In some cases the panel was a piece of an intricately embroidered wedding skirt, donated in memory of a family member.

There are several architectural elements unique to the Paradesi *Palli*. As seen in Figure 14, the top of the outer door to the *azarah* is fashioned with six architectural cusps—a pattern featured in medieval Spanish synagogues.[24] Both Figures 13 and 14 also show parts of the world-famous floor of the Paradesi sanctuary, uniquely paved with

[22] Eliyahu-Oron (2004, 72–79). Dating to 1662 (Paradesi) and circa 1647 (Thekkumbhagam), both were built as an architectural façade following a scheme found in Italian Torah Arks from the late 16th to 17th centuries. After the initial Italian influence, other Torah Arks in Kerala were copied from one synagogue to the other.

[23] Compare with Figure 18 later in this chapter.

[24] This feature was pointed out and discussed by Waronker (2010, 194). There was a wooden door pediment in that same shape above the entrance of Thekkumbhagam-Kochi Synagogue.

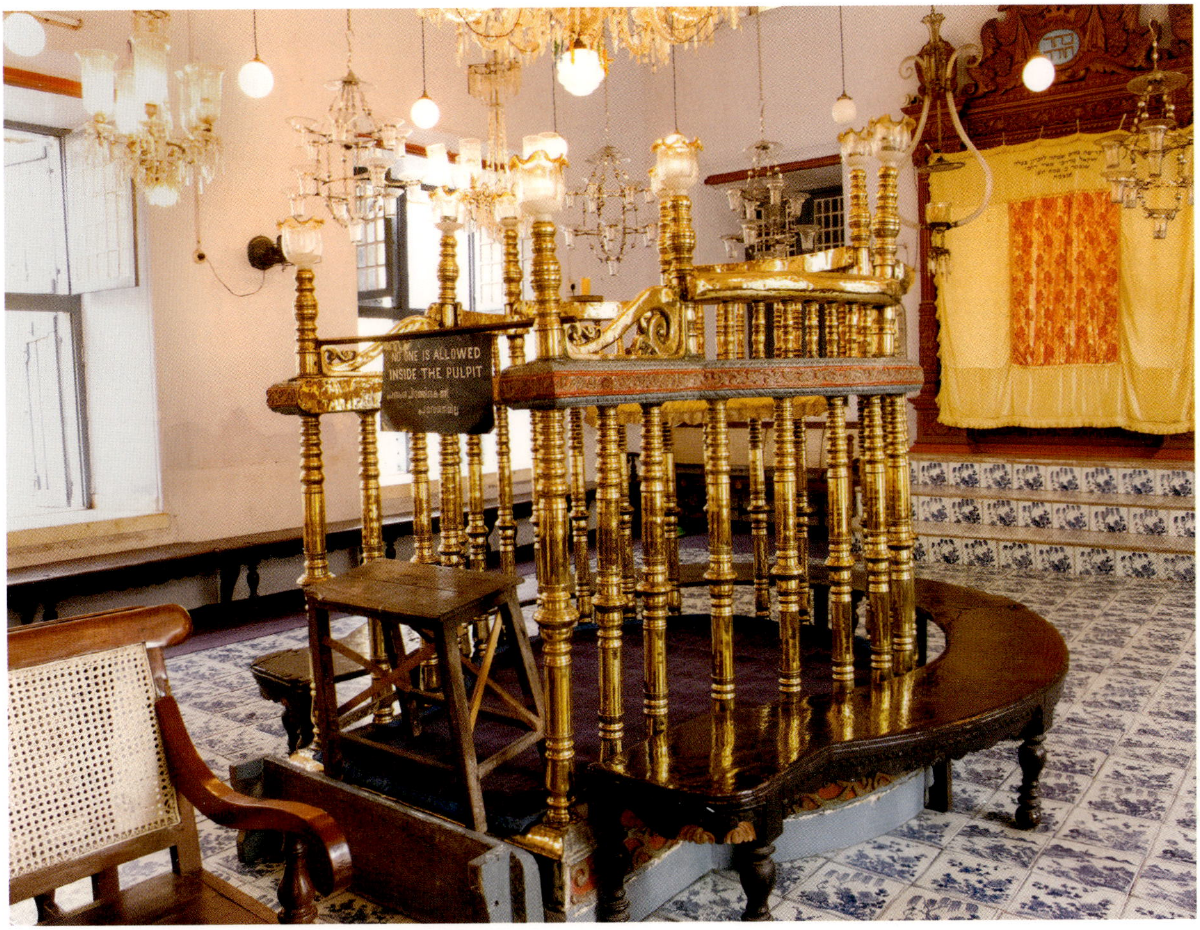

Fig. 13. Paradesi Synagogue interior; Siona Benjamin, 2011

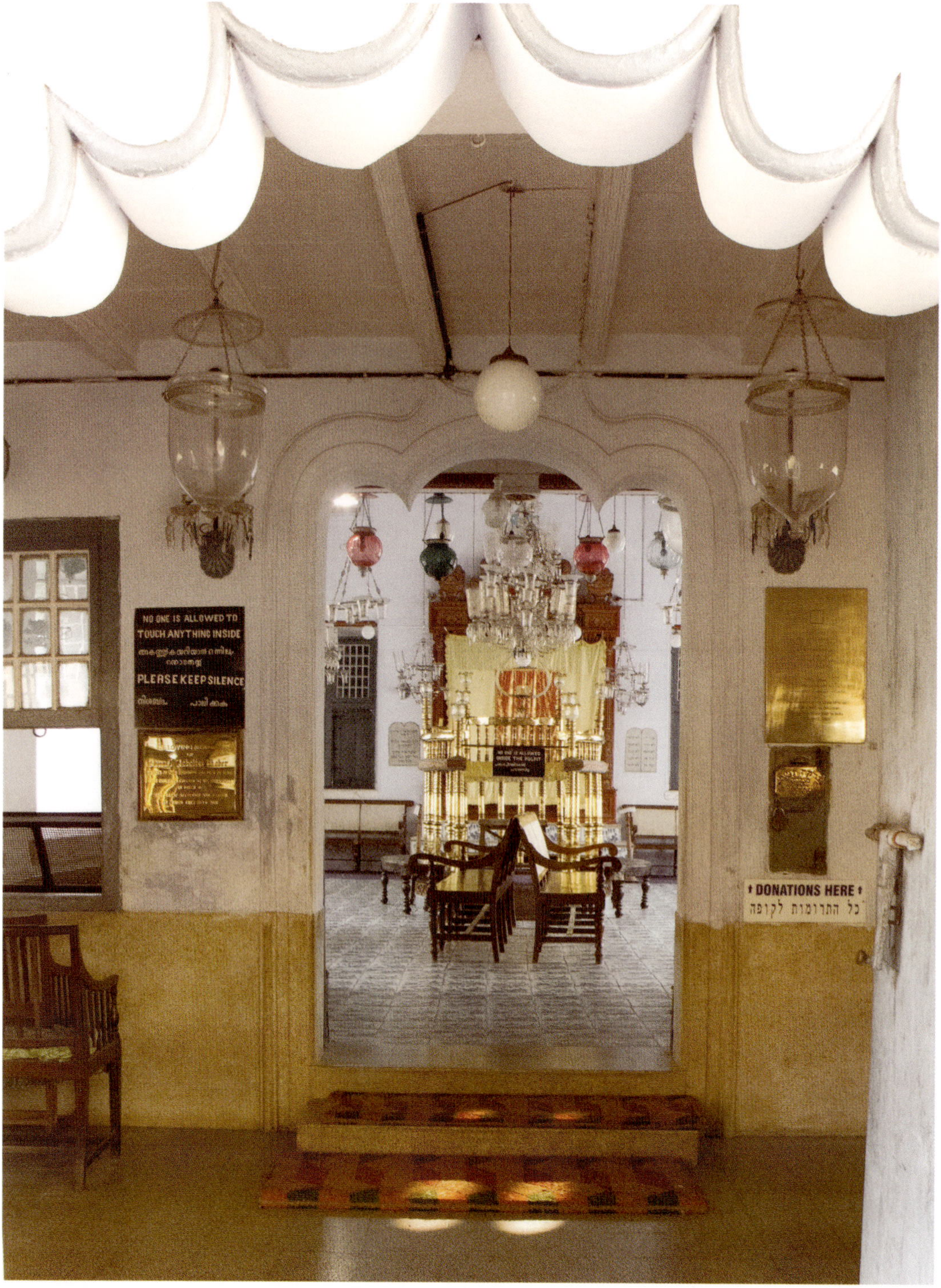

Fig. 14. Paradesi Synagogue sanctuary entrance; Siona Benjamin, 2011

approximately 1,100 blue and white Chinese porcelain tiles arranged in alternating horizontal rows. The floor was created in 1762 on the initiative of Ezekiel Rahaby, a wealthy and powerful merchant, who was a close associate of the Raja and also the official representative of the Dutch East India Company.

Another unique feature of the Paradesi *Palli* is its three-story clock tower with a cupola on top. As is clear in Figure 11, the tower is immediately visible to anyone walking north on Synagogue Lane, because the street dead-ends at its façade. The building of this structure in 1761 was also financed by Ezekiel Rahaby. Though free-standing, the square building is incorporated into the *Palli* compound. The clock in the tower has three dials: one with Roman numerals facing south to the Jewtown street, another with Hebrew letters facing west to the synagogue, and one with Malayalam letters facing north to the Raja's palace. The bell was cleaned and re-hung when the entire clock tower was renovated, between 2001 and 2006, with help from the World Monuments Fund.[25]

During the mass emigration of Kerala Jews to Israel in the 1950s, most of the Paradesi community stayed behind in Jewtown, Kochi. In 1968 they celebrated the 400th anniversary of their synagogue's founding with a week-long celebration, highlighted by an academic conference and a visit from Prime Minister Indira Gandhi.[26] In a gradual but escalating movement, almost all the remaining Paradesi Jews departed from India during the 1970s and early 1980s. By 1985 there were only 50 left in Kerala, compared to about 165 Paradesi Cochinim in Israel,

---

[25] https://www.wmf.org/project/paradesi-synagogue (Accessed 25 February 2020). Ilana Weil's article is useful for information about the Paradesi *Palli*, in particular its clock tower and gatehouse, (Weil 2002).

[26] Velayudhan (1958) was the commemoration volume for this series of events.

where they continued to maintain a strong sense of community identity.[27] Though scattered, their community has grown in numbers since then, and in December 2018 more than 150 traveled from Israel and other countries back to Kochi, to celebrate the Synagogue's 450th anniversary, with several days of worship services, meetings and reunions with old friends.[28]

Today the *Palli* is administered and maintained by an international Paradesi Synagogue Trust, with a board made up of members in India, Israel, and North America.[29] Though only occasionally used for worship, it continues to be a popular tourist destination.

Thekkumbhagam-Kochi Synagogue

The Thekkumbhagam (Southside) *Palli*, which was located near the Paradesi *Palli* at the northern end of Jew Street, was demolished in the 1950s by a few of its members who stayed in India after the others had left for Israel.[30] Fortunately the *heikhal* was first dis-assembled, along with a Hebrew-inscribed door pediment, and stored at the Kadavumbhagam Synagogue in Ernakulam. In 1967 these treasures were brought to the Judah Magnes Museum in Berkeley, California, but we are not aware of anything else that was saved from this synagogue.

---

[27] Johnson (1985).

[28] https://timesofindia.indiatimes.com/city/kochi/200-jews-arrive-in-kochi-to-mark-450th-anniversary-of-paradesi-synagogue/articleshow/66979476.cms. Accessed 25 February 2020.

[29] We thank Kenny Salem in Toronto, Canada, a member of the Paradesi Synagogue Trust Board for this information.

[30] Eliyahu Barmouth (2001,18–19) describes the demolishing of the synagogue. In an April 2014 interview with Orna Eliyahu-Oron he explained that his father, the former synagogue manager, dis-assembled the *heikhal* and stored it in Ernakulam.

There is some uncertainty about when Thekkumbhagam-Kochi was built. Manuscript #880 in the Sassoon collection—which gives building dates for all the Kerala synagogues without supporting documentation—lists the date as 1624.[31] But an actual inscription copied in the Sassoon catalogue and labeled as 'a record of the Thekkumbhagam Synagogue' states that a synagogue (unnamed) was built by Yaakov Castiel in 1489—i.e. 55 years before Kadavumbhagam.[32] Ophira Gamliel's linguistic and historical research provides convincing support for the inscription's earlier date.[33] Because the inscription tablet was not saved when Thekkumbhagam was torn down, it is no longer available for scholarly analysis unless a photograph of it can be found.

In considering the earlier date of the inscription, it seems unlikely that a 15th century synagogue founded after Kochangadi and before Kadavumbhagam would have been constructed so far north of those Jewish communities, especially a *palli* named 'Southside'. It seems more likely that members of the 15th century community associated with the inscription needed to build a new *palli* 200 years later and that they moved north to build it in Jewtown, where land was then available, taking with them the foundation inscription from the

[31] Sassoon (1932, 1056, Ms.#880). A.I.Simon (1947, 40) gave a different date, stating that the mural slabs of Thekkumbhagam and Kadavumbhagam were 'meddled with' during a legal contest between the two communities in 1881, when each claimed to be the oldest. Simon himself was a partisan in the matter, eager to prove that his own Paradesi Synagogue was older than Thekkumbhagam.

[32] The inscription is found in Sassoon (1932, 57, Ms. #13).

[33] Gamliel (2018b, 46–48). She presents her analysis as evidence of a Spanish Jewish commercial presence in Kerala before the final Jewish expulsions from Iberia and before the Portuguese arrival on the Malabar Coast.

original building and preserving their community identity with the name Thekkumbhagam.[34]

This theory fits with an explanation of the 'Southside' name by several members of Thekkumbhagam-Kochi, who told us that the name was handed down because their long-ago ancestors lived south of Jewtown, or in Kochangadi.[35] Also the Malayalam-language 'Thekkumbhagam-Kochi *Palli* Song' begins by praising 'God Most High …Who gave us the *Palli* from before' and relates how the 'southside people' came together and requested permission from their assembly elders to build a *palli*. The elders encouraged them to build without delay. After laying a solid foundation, they had a grand celebration, and the Paradesi elders took up a collection to help their efforts.[36]

Whenever the *palli* in Jewtown was built, we know that after it was demolished, the land on which it had stood was purchased by a Paradesi community member, who built a modern-style house on it, and after his death it was purchased by a non-Jew.

The first substantial information about the structure of the lost synagogue was collected in 2011 by researcher Thoufeek Zakriya of Kochi. When he interviewed elderly Jews in the neighborhood they described Thekkumbhagam as 'like the Paradesi *Palli*' in terms of its

[34] Paradesi sources have maintained that the Thekkumbhagam and Kadavumbhagam synagogues in Kochi were named for two synagogues in medieval Cranganore—a tradition supporting the narrative that their own collective ancestors migrated from medieval 'Shingly'. There is no verifiable evidence about the names or locations of any synagogues in Cranganore.

[35] Interviews were with Eliyahu Barmouth and members of the Japheth-Madai family in Jerusalem.

[36] Sung in 1972 by Leah Eliavoo; recording in Johnson (2005), Track 15. The Malayalam text is in Zacharia and Gamliel (2005, 44–45), Hebrew translation, pp. 36–38.

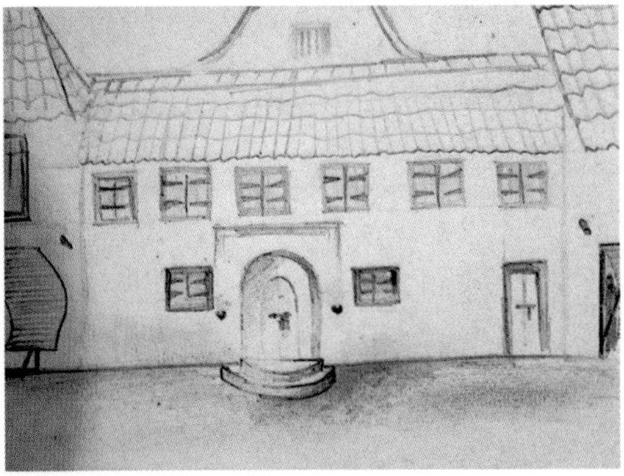

Fig. 15. Sketch of the Thekkumbhagam-Kochi Synagogue façade; Thoufeek Zakriya, 2011

structure and layout. He made a sketch of its facade, based on their description and on old photographs collected by the owner of the property at that time (Fig. 15).[37] The accuracy of their description and of his sketch is confirmed by several photographs from anthropologist David Mandelbaum's 1937 trip to Kochi.

First, Zakriya's sketch of the façade shows three curved steps leading up to the arched doorway which was the main gatehouse entrance. This arched doorway frames the young boys in Figure 16. Behind the boys we get a glimpse of the courtyard beyond the gatehouse and the southeast corner of the Synagogue building.

Second, if his informants were right that the old *Palli* followed the typical Kerala layout it would have had a breezeway connecting the upstairs of the gatehouse with the upstairs room of the sanctuary building. Figure 17 and another 1937 photo[38] show this breezeway with a tiled

[37] The residents were Sarah Cohen (who lived opposite the synagogue), Isaac Ashkenazy (whose family home was just to the north of it) and Gamliel Salem. All are no longer living. We thank Thoufeek Zakriya for contributing the sketch to this article and for further information in personal e-mails, 21 March 2014 and 2 February 2020. Unfortunately he no longer has access to the photos he mentioned.

[38] David Goodman Mandelbaum papers, Bancroft Library, University of California, Berkeley. BANC PIC 1989.072-PIC, photo CJ-65.

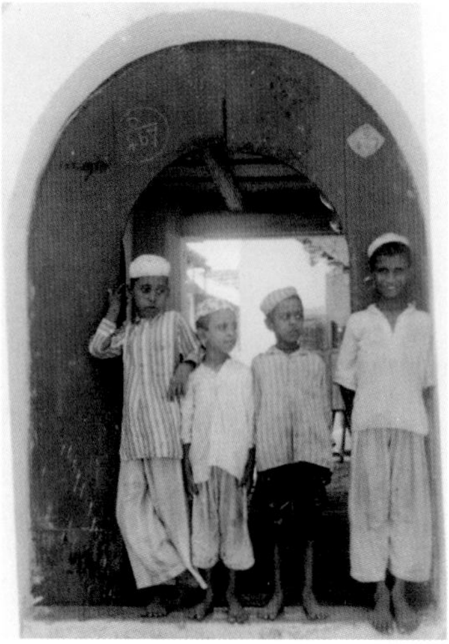

Fig. 16. Thekkumbhagam-Kochi Synagogue entrance; David G. Mandelbaum papers, Bancroft #CJ31, 1937

roof and a carved wooden railing—similar to the Paradesi breezeway but considerably longer and supported by at least two pillars. Visible beneath the breezeway are many hanging glass lamps and globes. Some were brightly colored according to Ruby Daniel and her sister Rahel Kala, who remembered them many years later in Israel. As in the Paradesi complex, the courtyard was paved with stone tiles, though in 1937 many of the Thekkumbhagam tiles were in disrepair.

Also visible in Figure 17 is the exterior wall of a room in the northeast corner of the courtyard. The other 1937 photo of the breezeway shows that this corner room was connected with the gatehouse. Looking again at Zakriya's sketch, we can see a second door in the wall, smaller than the arched door of the main entrance. According to his informants, the second door was used as a

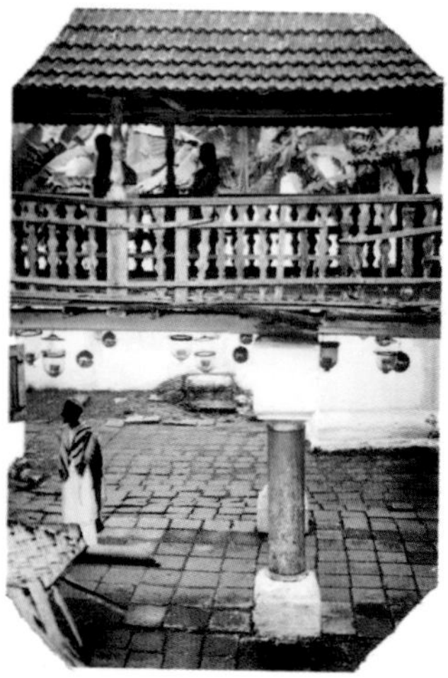

Fig. 17. Thekkumbhagam-Kochi Synagogue breezeway; David G. Mandelbaum papers, Bancroft # CJ69, 1937

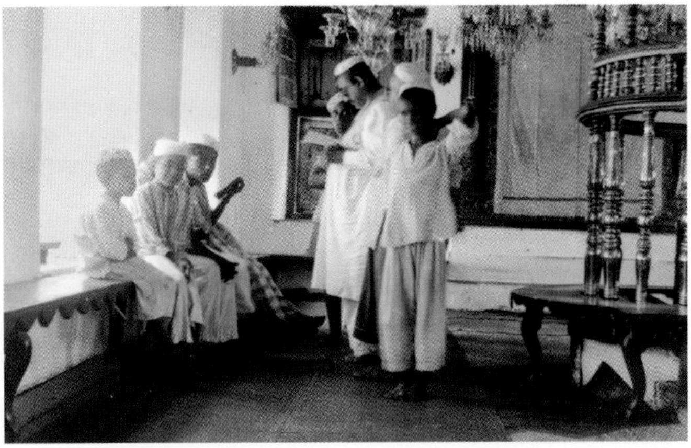

Fig. 18. Thekkumbhagam-Kochi Synagogue interior
David G. Mandelbaum papers, Bancroft #CJ30, 1937

women's entrance, and they told him that in the past there was a similar women's entrance into the Paradesi Synagogue courtyard. Zakriya suggests that if there was such a Paradesi Synagogue door, it would have been lost when the Clock Tower was renovated.

One more 1937 photograph gives a glimpse of the Thekkumbhagam Synagogue interior. Figure 18 shows the southwest corner of the sanctuary, with bright light from two tall open windows shining on the Torah teacher Elias Shlomo Madai and his students, who have gathered inside for special prayers before Yom Kippur. Here we can see many other similarities with the Paradesi Synagogue. On the right is the harp-shaped *tebah* made of wood and shiny brass. In the back on a raised podium is the *heikhal* with a white *parokhet* (curtain). Also visible are the wooden benches around the walls and *tebah*, and the hanging glass oil lamps and chandeliers. The floors are covered with mats, as was customary in most of the synagogues, except for the Paradesi *Palli*.

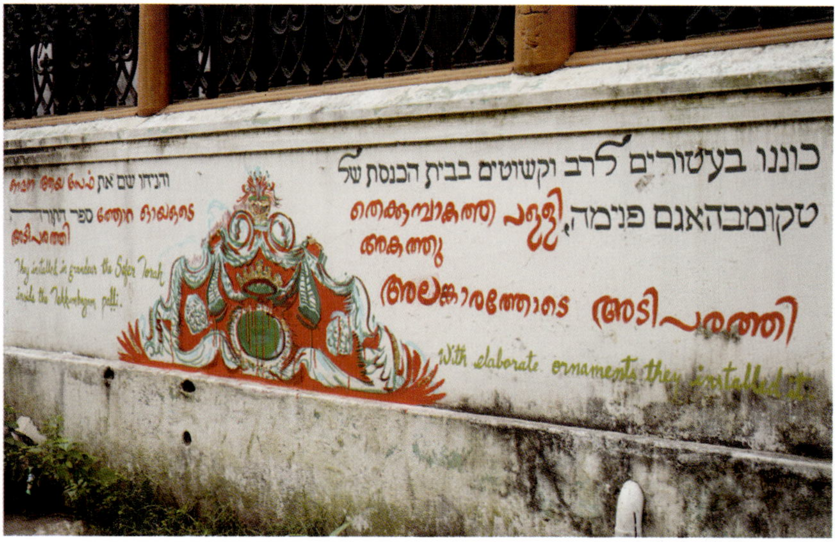

Fig. 19. Thekkumbhagam-Kochi mural 'Red Crown Green Parrot', public art project by Meydad Eliyahu and Thoufeek Zakriya; Kashi Art Gallery collateral project as part of the Kochi Muziris Biennale 2018

The Thekkumbhagam *heikhal* itself is still stored today in Berkeley at the Magnes Collection of Jewish Art and Life, where there is no room tall enough to display it intact. In 2013 some of its pieces were at the center of the exhibition 'Global India: Kerala, Israel, Berkeley'.[39]

During the 2018 Muziris Biennale in Kochi, Thoufeek Zakriya joined with Meydad Eliyahu to keep alive the memory of Thekkumbhagam *Palli* by painting a 'red crown' mural of its *heikhal* pediment on the half-wall in front of the building where the synagogue used to stand (Fig. 19).

[39] For a photo of the entire *heikhal* see https://magnes.berkeley.edu/digital-programs/media-resources/images/magnes-holdings-jews-india. Accessed 25 February 2020.

The Synagogues of Ernakulam

There are two synagogues across the harbor from the island city of Kochi, in the large mainland city of Ernakulam. Until the early 20th century Ernakulam was a smaller city than Kochi, though the district offices and courts of the British colonial government and a second palace of the Kochi Raja were located there. Only after the modern harbor was created, between 1920 and 1940, did Ernakulam begin developing into the busy commercial and residential city that it remains today, eclipsing Kochi in size. An earlier name for the Ernakulam area was Anjikaimal, referring to the *Anchi* (five) *Kaimals* (Nair chieftains) who ruled different parts of the territory before it was consolidated under the rule of the Kochi Raja.[40]

We have inconclusive information about when the two Ernakulam synagogues were built. The undated Sassoon Ms. #880, mentioned earlier, lists their founding dates as 1200 CE for Kadavumbhagam (long before the 1341 flood that precipitated the opening up of a harbor there) and 1580 CE for Thekkumbhagam.[41] According to interviews with community members from Thekkumbhagam *Palli*, their synagogue was established after the community grew too big for Kadavumbhagam.[42] This must have been considerably before 1686, when a delegation of four Jews was sent by the Portuguese Jewish community in Amsterdam to inquire about 'the manner in which our brethren living in Cochin govern themselves'. Their report, written by Mosseh Pereyra de Paiva, provides the oldest published record of two Jewish communities in Ernakulam.[43]

[40] Sreedhara Menon (1967, 195).

[41] Sassoon (1932, 1056, Ms.#880).

[42] Eliyahu-Oron (2004, 26).

[43] Pereyra De Paiva in Timberg (1986, 126–134).

The Amsterdam Jews undertook a voyage of more than a year, visiting Kochi for six days in November 1686. Though they spent most of their limited time with the Paradesi community in Jewtown, on 25 November they went by boat to visit two synagogues in 'Angicaymal on the other side of the river'; and Pereyra de Paiva's report provides lively details about their visit. In the middle of the harbor they were greeted by a boat with instrumental music and escorted to the shore. There a large crowd had gathered, including learned men and a *hazan* (prayer leader) who escorted them to one synagogue, where they recited the afternoon prayer service. Next they 'ascended a gallery in the *azarah*' where they were served food and drink. After two hours at the table they were led to the other synagogue 'through illuminated streets with music' and there they recited the evening prayer service.

Pereyra de Paiva did not indicate whether he saw a compound wall or a gatehouse entrance building associated with either synagogue, but his mention of a 'gallery in the azarah' of the first *palli* suggests that there was a fairly spacious upstairs room in its sanctuary building, reached by a staircase in the entrance room. Nor did he give the name of either synagogue; but he did mention elsewhere in his report that there were 150 families in Angicaymal with two synagogues, compared to 120 families with three synagogues in Kochi, and that they were 'poor people' compared to the Jews in Parur and Chenot (Chendamangalam).

The Ernakulam synagogues have the same names as two of those in Kochi: Kadavumbhagam and Thekkumbhagam. But in contrast to Kochi, these two *palli* names are not geographically significant in Ernakulam. Both buildings are situated in the very busy downtown commercial area. Kadavumbhagam ('by the boat landing place') *Palli* is on Market Road, not even near the water, and Ernakulam's Thekkumbhagam ('southside')

Synagogue, which is accessible from Jew Street, is not south of—but northwest of—the other *palli*. We speculate that both synagogues were formerly accessible from Jew Street, which runs west to east between them, from near the harbor to Market Street. There is also an Ernakulam oral tradition that the names Kadavumbhagam and Thekkumbhagam were given in memory of two synagogues with those names in ancient Cranganore.

Both synagogues have been kept in fairly good condition, though they ceased to function as regular places of worship many decades ago, after almost all their members left for Israel. Before the mass emigration of the 1950s there were more than 900 Jews living in Ernakulam.[44]

Kadavumbhagam-Ernakulam Synagogue

Kadavumbhagam *Palli* is a free-standing two-story building with a unique façade, and with no recorded tradition of ever having been connected to a gatehouse or other entrance building. Its two front corners are angled so that it appears half-octagonal from the front. The present building includes two sections almost equal in size. The sanctuary with its *azarah* is in the back on the western side, and a two-story section is connected in the front, not separate like the entrance buildings of most Kerala synagogues. Waronker was told that the front section was added to the 'original' building, perhaps as early as the 17th century,[45] but he was given no evidence for that. As noted above, there certainly were two Ernakulam synagogues before 1686, but it is possible that a different one was built in 1711, when the Kadavumbhagam Jews of Ernakulam

[44] Kushner (1973, 15).

[45] Waronker (2010, 250).

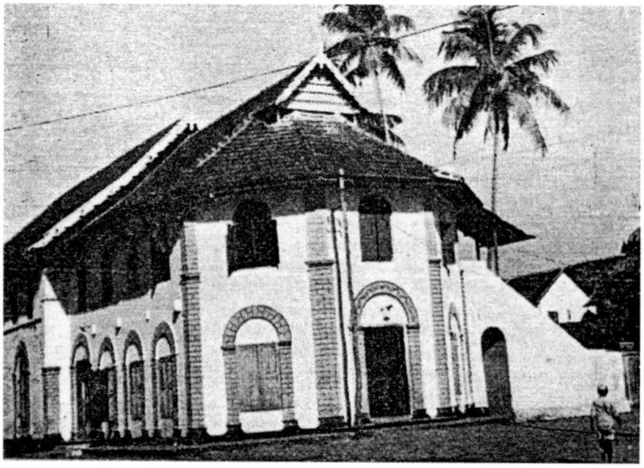

Fig. 20. Kadavumbhagam-Ernakulam Synagogue façade, 1952 or 1955; Naftali Bar Giora, 'Sources for the History of the Relations between the White and the Black Jews in Kochin.' *Sefunot*, vol. 1 (1957), photo #5

received a grant of land from the Kochi Raja.[46] Based on community information, long-time Ernakulam resident Eliya ben Eliyahu wrote that the *Palli* was 'rebuilt' in 1916.[47]

In the early 1950s Naftali Bar-Giora was told that 'the new building was established on the ruins of a former building'.[48] The photo he published (Fig. 20) shows an addition on the northern side of the front section (no longer standing), which probably was an outside staircase by which women could ascend to the upper floor.[49]

When the Synagogue was in regular use, the social functions of the front section were similar to those associated with an entrance building or gatehouse in other synagogues. The downstairs hall was used for

---

[46] Reported by Lord (1907, 78, 86, 100). Thanks to Paul Laju for the citation.

[47] Ben Eliyahu (1978, 77).

[48] Waronker (2010, 250). Bar-Giora (1958, 223). Naftali Bar-Giora was an emissary of the Israeli government, who spent 1952 and some of 1955 in Kerala arranging for the immigration. Johnson and Hacco (2009, 102).

[49] Illustration from Bar-Giora (1957, following p. 246).

overflow seating during holidays, weddings and other special occasions. Waronker noted a wooden staircase in the northeast corner of the room, leading to a large upstairs room. This upper space was used as a *beit midrash* (religious school) where the children learned Hebrew and the men studied Talmud.

A pair of doors still leads from the upstairs room of the front section into the women's space, which is directly above the *azarah*. As in all Kerala synagogues, this *ezrat nashim* is right behind the upper *tebah* from which the Sefer Torah is read on Shabbat and holidays. In this *Palli* the separation is minimal, consisting of a low dividing wall with wooden uprights through which the women could see and hear clearly all that was happening on the upper *tebah* and in the sanctuary below (Fig. 21).

As is typical, the *azarah* downstairs leads directly into the sanctuary. The sanctuary interior is still well-preserved, with beautifully carved ornamentation in the profusion of lotus flowers portrayed beneath the upper *tebah* and in the large recessed ceiling panel, made up of hundreds of small panels, each with its own lotus in the center. The wood-carved *heikhal*, probably constructed in 1916 when the synagogue was rebuilt, is painted in red and white and gilded (Fig. 22, placed as the frontispiece of this book, see p. 2). In 1996, pieces of carved wood were discovered in the attic, resembling in style the 16th century *heikhal* from Ernakulam-Thekkumbhagam *Palli* (see later in this chapter). Most likely they were part of an earlier Kadavumbhagam building and *heikhal*.[50]

Once most of its community had gone to Israel, Ernakulam-Kadavumbhagam *Palli* became a hidden treasure, rarely visited by

[50] Eliyahu-Oron (2004, 50–53).

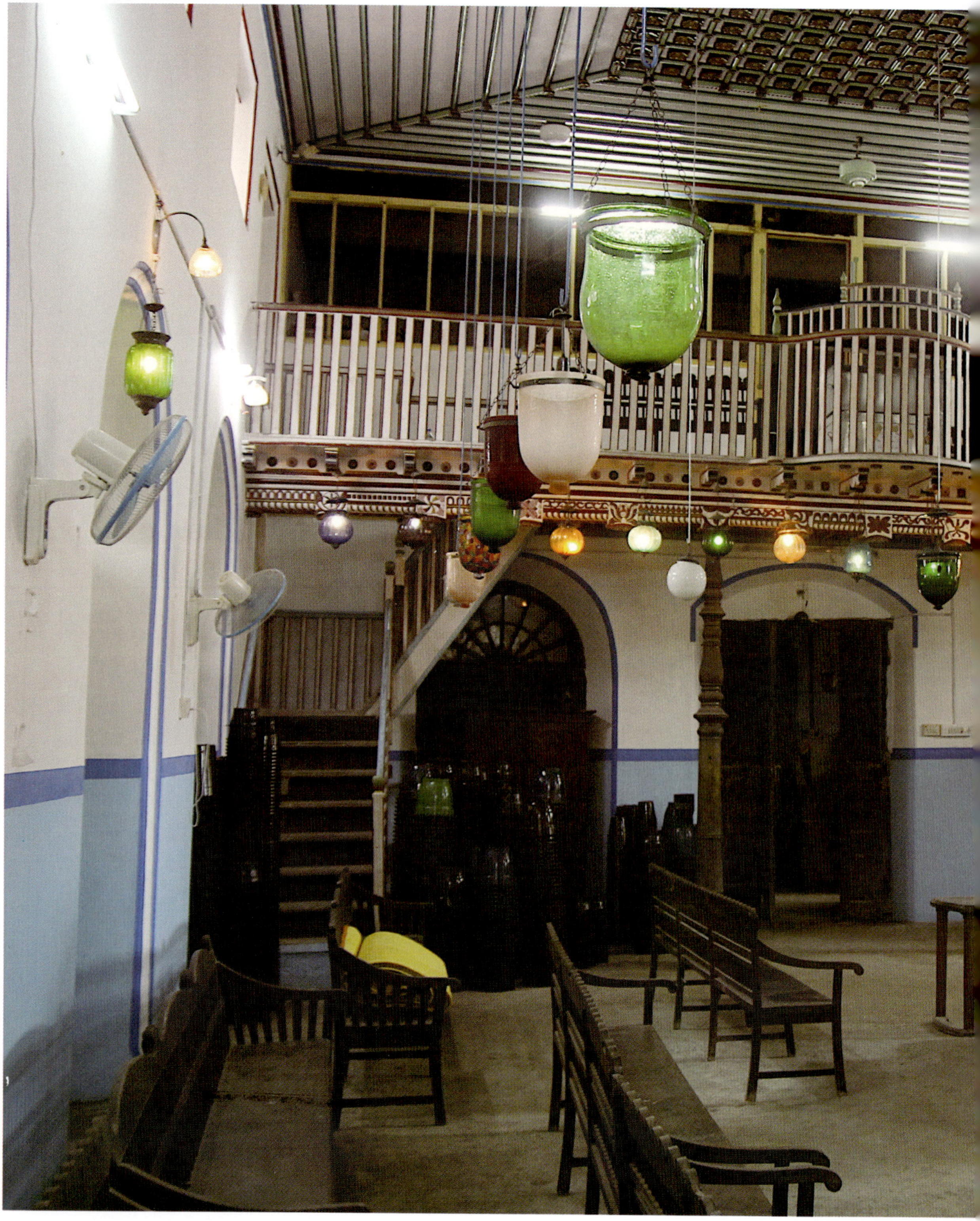

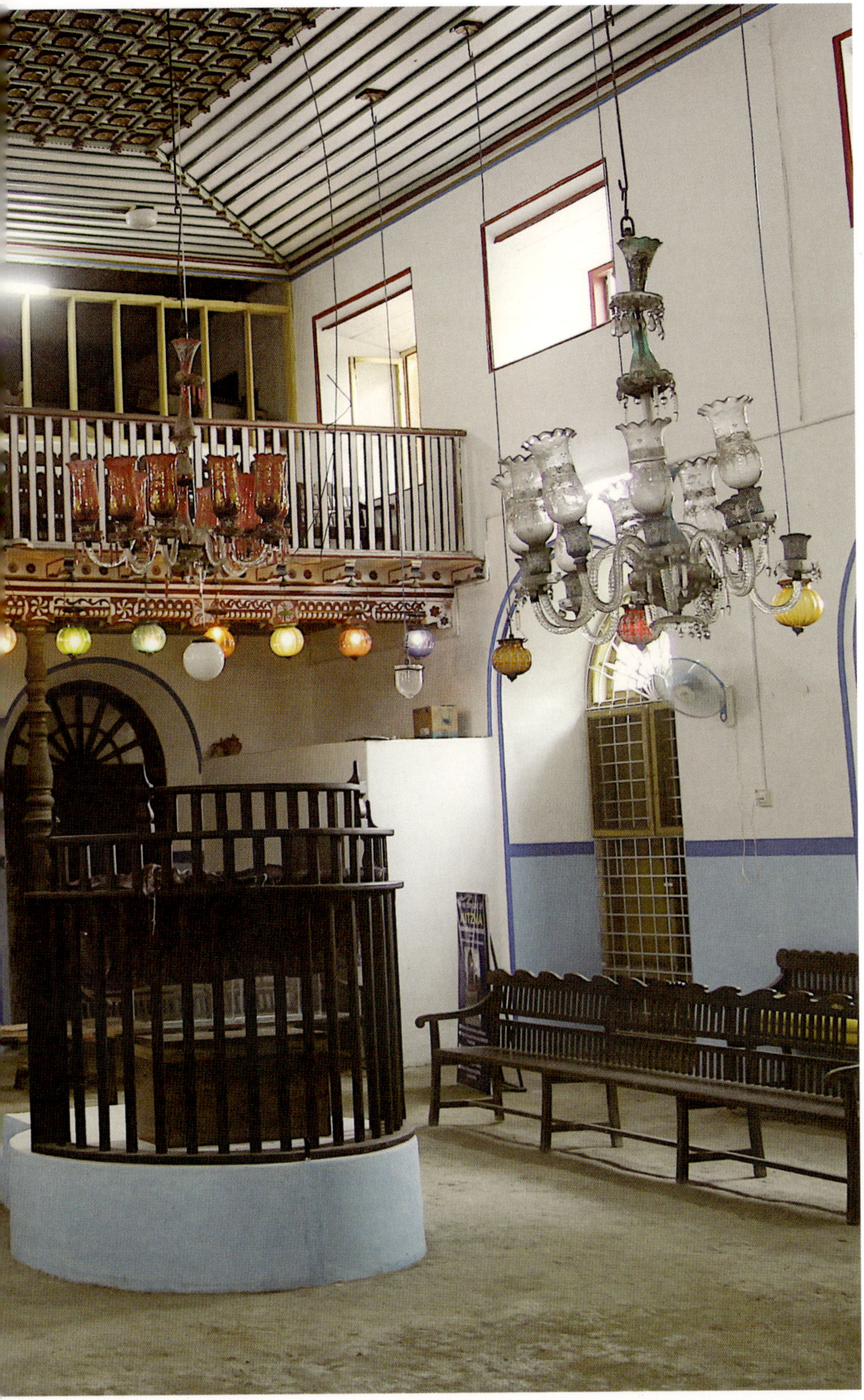

Fig. 21. Kadavumbhagam-Ernakulam Synagogue interior; Paul Laju, 2016

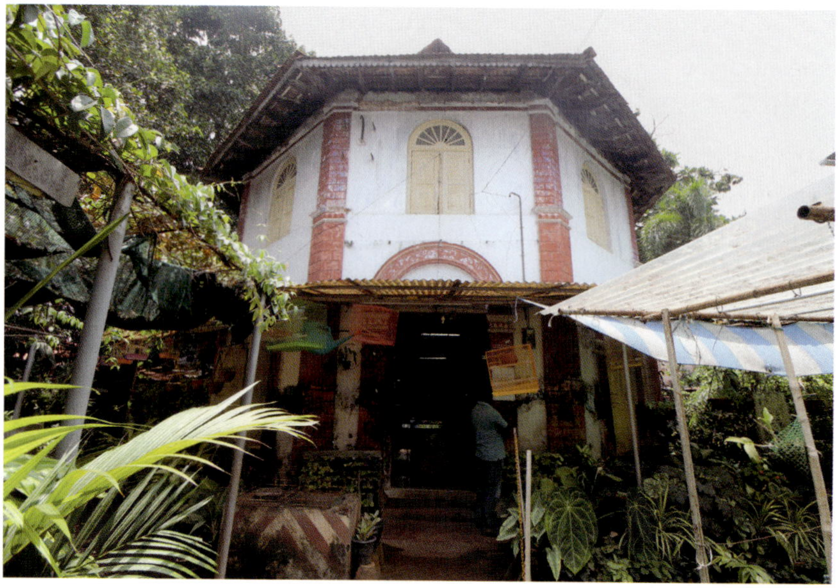

Fig. 23. Kadavumbhagam-Ernakulam Synagogue entrance; Paul Laju, 2016

outsiders until recently. A remnant of its congregation continued to use the *Palli* until it was closed in 1972. Between 1975 and 1979 the synagogue suffered from neglect and theft. Finally, in 1979 the remaining community transferred guardianship of the *Palli* to one of its members, Elias 'Babu' Josephai, who then used the building and courtyard to establish 'Cochin Blossoms', his current plant and tropical fish sales business.[51] Over the years he has used the front room for sales and some other parts of the building and courtyard for equipment and storage (Fig. 23).

[51] In 1975 the building was damaged in a monsoon storm, including its roof, walls and foundation, so that the entire structure had to be hydraulically lifted. In 1978 thieves broke in and stole some of the contents. Waronker obtained this chronology from interviews with Josephai in 2007 and 2009.

In recent years Mr. Josephai has become proactive in overseeing renovations to the sanctuary, and in welcoming a growing number of Indian and international tourists to visit Kadavumbhagam. Religious services have been held there by visiting Jews, and in December 2018 a group of Israeli Cochinim brought a Torah Scroll to be installed in its beautifully preserved *heikhal*. A lively celebration of this public event included a procession through the streets, accompanied by traditional Kerala drummers, and tributes to the Israeli visitors.[52]

A visit to this *palli* is now included in 'Jewish Heritage' tours of Kerala. It is accessed from Market Street through a gate labeled 'Cochin Blossoms' as well as 'Kadavumbhagam Synagogue'.

Thekkumbhagam-Ernakulam Synagogue

The Thekkumbhagam *Palli* in Ernakulam is the newest of the Kerala synagogue structures, built in 1939–1940 to replace an older building. Its interior was never completed. Work on the building stopped with the advent of World War II, and shortly after the war most members of its congregation began plans to move to Israel. The synagogue is not in use any more nor is it open to visitors, but its basic structure seems sound. It stands in a walled compound, entered from two directions, from the south through a narrow, gated passageway accessed from Jew Street and from the north through another narrow alley.

Contemporary photos show a large stand-alone building painted yellow with a white trim (Fig. 25). Its front door entrance is flanked by

[52] For a YouTube recording of this event, see: https://www.youtube.com/watch?v=QdOq39Agp4E&feature=youtu.be&fbclid=IwAR1pTzxWNrE9iDYMCHdMpMp2oP2LjS33HloRzw7ap4F8Uz_JY9indVUlLes. Accessed 25 February 2020.

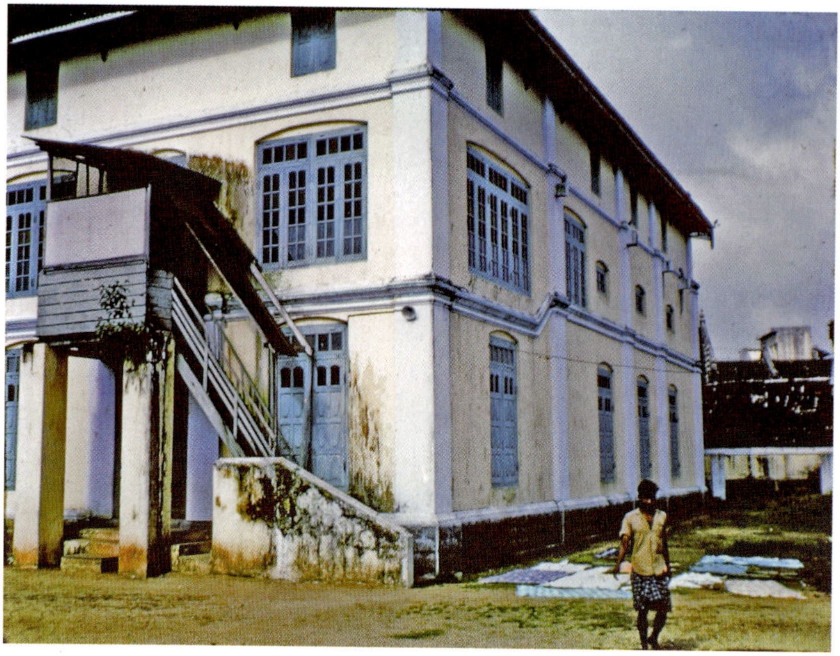
Fig. 24. Thekkumbhagam-Ernakulam Synagogue exterior; Barbara C. Johnson, 1968

two large pillars supporting an open porch with a door opening to the second floor level. An earlier photo shows that in 1968 the porch could be reached by an outside staircase, giving the women direct and separate access to the *ezrat nashim* (Fig. 24).

In 1973 the *heikhal* from this synagogue found a new home, when a delegation of Thekkumbhagam community members came back to Ernakulam from Moshav Nevatim in the south of Israel. They arranged to transport the *heikhal*, the *tebah*, Torah scrolls and other ritual objects to their new synagogue there. The majority population of this agricultural settlement had come from Thekkumbhagam-Ernakulam. Inspired by the Kerala synagogues, the Nevatim Synagogue was built

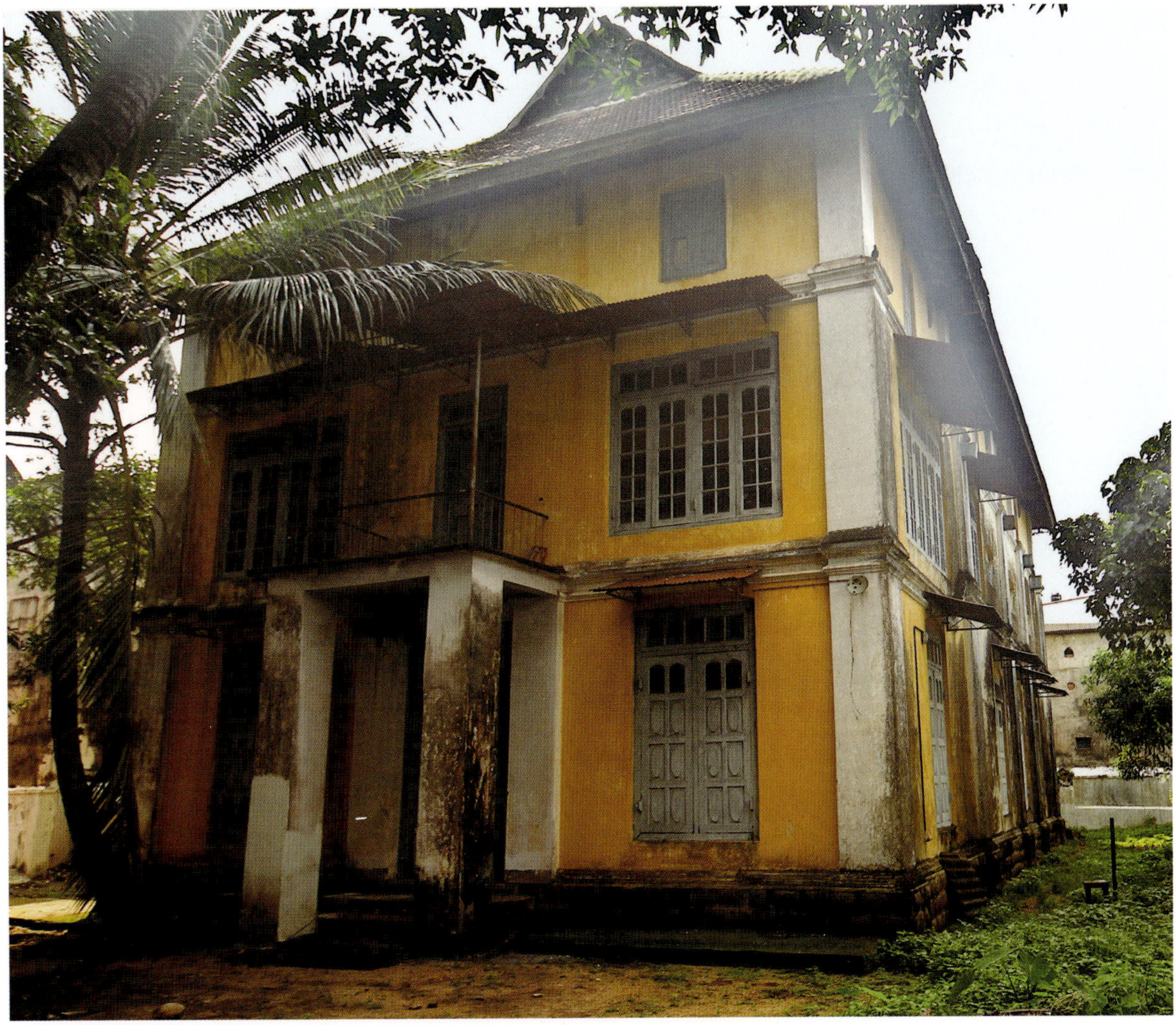

Fig. 25. Thekkumbhagam-Ernakulam Synagogue exterior; Paul Laju, 2019

with two *tebahs*, and to this day all religious services there are conducted according to Kerala traditions. Meanwhile, the *palli* in Ernakulam was left as an almost empty shell.

When Orna Eliyahu-Oron visited Ernakulam in 1995 with a research group from the Center for Jewish Art they documented the building and the sparse contents of its interior but did not inquire about the old synagogue, which had been torn down in 1939. It was only during her return research trip in 1996 that she began to learn about the earlier *palli*. Barbara Johnson began to investigate the former *palli* in 1999, using references from a Malayalam Jewish women's song.

To learn about the old synagogue we relied on information from community members who were alive while it was still in use and who witnessed the construction of the new one.[53] It became clear that the architectural layout of the old Thekkumbhagam *Palli* followed the standard pattern for Kerala synagogues—a walled compound with a large sanctuary building two storys in height, connected by a breezeway to a smaller entrance building. The courtyard used to be much larger, accessed directly from Jew Street. At some point most of the land fronting on Jew Street was sold and a new wall was built around the now smaller compound, leaving only the narrow passages through which it is accessed today. Rather than being paved, the surface of the entire compound used to be covered in *charal*, the fine white riverbed sand.

The entrance building was free-standing, not connected to a compound wall and not opening onto the street like a gatehouse. However it fulfilled many of the same functions as the gatehouse in other Kerala

---

[53] Our informants in Ernakulam were Isaac Joshua, Abraham (Avramai) Eliyahu and Sara Elias, and in Israel Haim Yefet in Nevatim and Bezalel Eliyahu in Shachar.

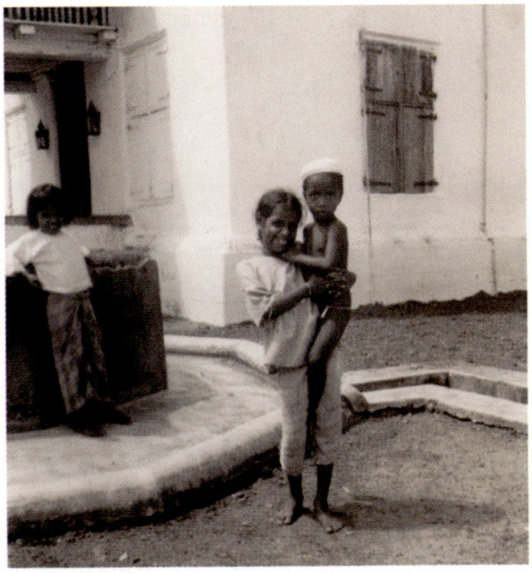

Fig. 26. Thekkumbhagam-Ernakulam Synagogue exterior; David G. Mandelbaum papers, Bancroft #CJ10, 1937

synagogues. Women climbed the stairs in the 'staircase room' in order to access the breezeway leading them to the *ezrat nashim* overlooking the upper *tebah*.

A 1937 photograph provides tangible evidence for the existence of this breezeway, which can be seen in the background in the upper left corner, behind the well and the children in the foreground (Fig. 26). There was a finished path under the breezeway, raised about a foot above the sand of the courtyard. Close to the sanctuary building there were cement benches on each side of the path, which provided overflow seating for men who were studying in the *azarah*. Another 1937 photo shows children sitting on one of the benches, which were similar to those under the breezeway in Parur.[54]

Isaac Joshua, a Thekkumbhagam member and president of the Association of Kerala Jews, had a good memory for architectural and decorative details, mentioning that there were wood carvings underneath the tiled roof of the breezeway. While showing the interior of the new synagogue he recalled that the railing of the upper *tebah* in the old synagogue was painted red and orange, and the ceiling beneath

[54] David Goodman Mandelbaum papers, Bancroft Library, University of California, Berkeley. BANC PIC 1989.072-PIC, Photo CJ2.

the *tebah* was painted green, with flower designs.[55] The interior of the new synagogue has no such decorative features.

The most exciting discovery about the old Thekkumbhagam Synagogue occurred during Orna Eliyahu-Oron's 1996 research trip when she and Professor Ehud Netzer explored the attic of the new building, following information from community members who knew that remnants were stored there. In the attic they found the façade of a very early *heikhal* (Fig. 27). Unlike any of the other surviving Kerala *heikhalot*, this one was built as a rectangular armoire, free-standing against the wall. The *heikhal* has two sets of doors, as in all the other *heikhalot*, but no pillars. The façade is intricately carved but not painted. Its design consists of 42 small square panels decorated with floral motifs. On the top part of the upper door there is an ornamental arch. This *heikhal* shape and basic surface decoration of small squares resembles Italian Torah Arks from the late 15th century, but since it was made by local artists the motifs and the style are typical to Kerala.[56]

After the old *heikhal* was discovered, the late Dr. Basil Elias, then president of the Kerala Jews Association, arranged for its reconstruction and placed it in the sanctuary on the empty podium that had been left with the removal of the newer *heikhal* in 1973 (Fig. 28).

In addition to restoration of the old *heikhal* to its former condition and to the place where it belongs in the sanctuary, memory of the old synagogue is also preserved today in a Malayalam Jewish song that is still remembered by a few Cochini women in Israel. In 1999, when Barbara

---

[55] Note the similarity with the original floral paintings in Kadavumbhagam-KochiSynagogue, uncovered by the restoration process at the Israel Museum (Fig. 7).

[56] Eliyahu-Oron (2004, 50–51, 54–58).

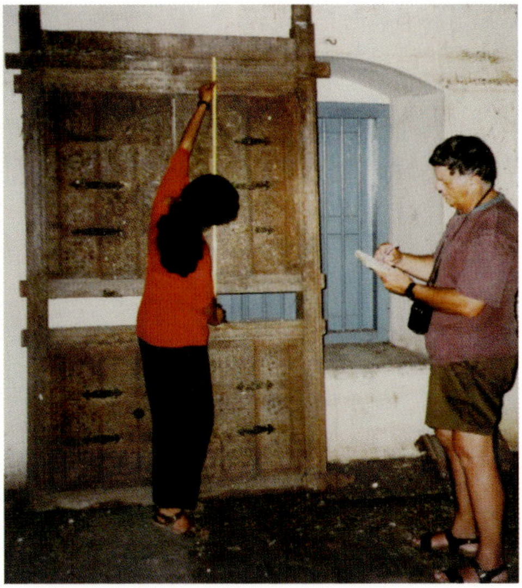

Fig. 27. Thekkumbhagam-Ernakulam Synagogue's old *heikhal* discovery; Assaf Oron, 1996

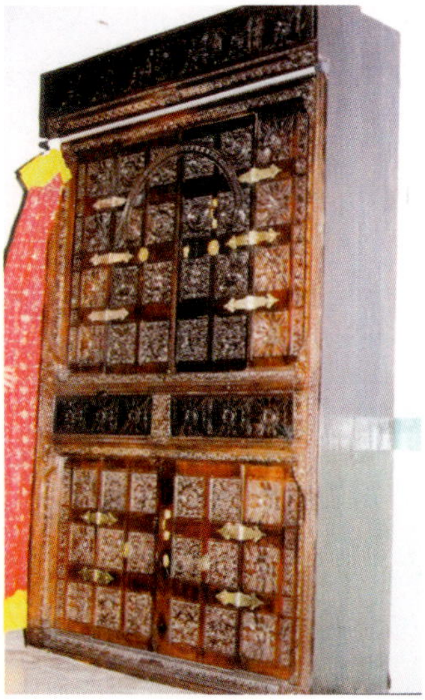

Fig. 28. Thekkumbhagam-Ernakulam Synagogue's old *heikhal* restored; Barbara C. Johnson, 1999

Johnson was studying these Jewish women's songs with Professor Scaria Zacharia of Calicut University, they took Orna Eliyahu-Oron's advice and consulted Isaac Joshua about the 'Thekkumbhagam-Ernakulam *Palli* Song'. He took them to the synagogue and identified several poetic references—to the place in front of the *Palli* (the entrance building), the *charal* sand, the upper floor 'where heaven's beauty descends' (the *ezrat nashim*) and also the black floor of the sanctuary. Explaining that the floor was special and different from the other Kerala synagogues in that it was shiny and black, being made of lime mortar regularly polished with carbon charcoal—a type of floor traditionally found in homes of the wealthy and royalty—he illuminated the song's final stanza:

In its golden essence Juta *Palli* is pure.
Of golden black its floor doth shine,
So bright it rings out like bells that chime.
Like a treasure box is our Thekkumbhagam!
Here in this *palli*, the joy of our life,
Waken our hearts to praise you, Lord.[57]

Three Synagogues near Kodungallur

The synagogues of Parur, Chendamangalam, and Mala are located within 10 km of the modern city of Kodungallur, with which they share a historical connection. Formerly called Cranganore, the city is located on the Kerala coast about 38km north of Ernakulam by road. In the past it was easiest for Jews in Kochi/Ernakulam to reach their relatives and friends in all three villages by boat, travelling on the network of inland waterways that still reaches all the way to Kodungallur. Now the drive can be made on National Highway 66, which passes through North Paravur, just south of the Jewish Synagogue and then, 5 km further on, through Chendamangalam. Mala is further inland from Kodungallur, travelling by road on State Highway 51.

As noted, ancient and medieval Cranganore played an important role in Kerala Jewish history—both legendary and verifiable. Even after the flood of 1341 had silted up its harbor many Jews stayed in the area. When Pereyra de Paiva visited Kochi in 1685 he was told there

[57] Sung by Miriam Daniel, Johnson (2004: Track 15). Malayalam text in Zacharia and Gamliel (2005, 51–52), Hebrew translation pp. 46–47. English translation by Tziporah Lane and Barbara Johnson.

were Jewish communities in Chendamangalam and Parur. During field research in 1968 Kerala scholar Thankappan Nair was told that all three Jewish communities had received generous grants of land from local chieftains, and that their synagogues were also endowed with land for keeping perpetually lit lamps.[58]

We have not found much specific information about how these three communities were affected by political changes and turmoil in Kerala during the 16th and 17th centuries, though the Malayalam language 'Parur *Palli* song' narrates how some Portuguese shot at the Parur synagogue and were reprimanded by a local 'justice-loving' boatman.[59] At the beginning of British colonial rule the Anglo-Mysore war of 1789–90 brought an invasion from the north by Muslim troops under the leadership of Tipu Sultan—an invasion that profoundly affected Jewish lives and synagogues. In 1817 or 1818 an English missionary named Thomas Dawson visited Parur, Chendamangalam, and Mala, where he found that the Jews in each place had been 'victims of Tipu's ferocity' and that their synagogues were 'in ruins'.[60] All were rebuilt later in the 19th century and two were rebuilt again in the early 20th century.

When most of the Jews in this area departed for Israel in the 1950s they left each *palli* in good condition, but by the end of the century the future of each synagogue was uncertain. For all three an unexpected rescue emerged in the creation of the Muziris Heritage Project, celebrating Kerala's rich history and cultural diversity. The project was developed by the state's Tourism Department in response to public

58 Nair (1975, 493–494, 496).

59 The Malayalam text of the song is found in Zacharia and Gamliel (2005, 42–43), Hebrew translation pp. 34–35.

60 Hunt (1920, 153).

enthusiasm about an archaeological excavation at what was thought to be the site of the ancient harbor of Muziris, located between Kodungallur and North Paravur.[61] The Chendamangalam *Palli* was one of the first historic buildings in the area to be chosen for renovation, followed by the Parur *Palli*, a palace, a fort and many buildings. Tourists can now enjoy hop-on hop-off boat tours featuring the archaeological site, churches, mosques, Hindu temples and other attractions, in addition to the synagogues.[62] Very recently the geographic area of the project has expanded to include Mala.

The Muziris Project now attracts tens of thousands of tourists each year from all over India and from many other countries—including Israeli families with roots in Chendamangalam, Mala, and Parur.

Parur Synagogue

Parur Synagogue is located on Jews Street in the small city of North Paravur, an administrative center with many educational and religious institutions. In 1974 Jews Street was a dead-end lane in a quiet part of town, running south to north and ending at a footpath and canal where small and medium-sized boats could dock to take on and unload passengers and produce. Two *chunam* pillars stood on either side of the street near its entrance to form an *eruv*—marking the territory within which Jewish law permitted the carrying of needed items in public on the Sabbath and certain holidays.[63] Only Jewish homes were found beyond

[61] Pattanam was thought to be a possible location of the ancient seaport that the Romans called Muziris. Nine seasons of excavation and research were sponsored by the Kerala Council for Historical Research (KCHR).

[62] https://www.muzirisheritage.org/muziris-project.php. Accessed 25 February 2020.

[63] Another explanation for the two pillars is that they were erected in 1887 to prevent Christian religious processions from entering the street. Nair (1975, 496).

the pillars, with the *Palli* about midway on the left. Today National Highway 66 runs just south of Jews Street, but the two pillars still mark its entrance and the old *Palli* has been renovated and transformed into a tourist attraction on the Muziris Heritage route.

Now there is a paved street at the north end, separating Jews Street from the canal, with a boat jetty on the canal to the east. Just to the west the Municipal Vegetable Market is a Muziris Heritage site. According to Parur Jews interviewed in 1968, the whole of Jews Street and the vegetable market west of it were originally part of a 48-acre piece of land given to the Jews rent-free by the local raja.[64] Paravur was a small principality governed by a Brahmin ruler who owed allegiance to the Kochi Raja until 1764, when his territory was annexed by the Raja of Travancore, south of Kochi.[65]

According to the list of synagogues in Sassoon manuscript #880, the Parur *Palli* was built in 1164,[66] but 1616 is the earliest confirmed date. It is found in an inscription on a stone tablet affixed to a wall in the current *palli* complex honoring David, son of Yaakov Castiel, with the implication that he financed the building.[67]

In 1685 Pereyra De Paiva, the Dutch visitor to Kochi, was told that there were 100 'well-provided' families in Parur. When Rev. Dawson visited Parur in 1817 or 1818, he found that Jewish worship services were being held on the synagogue's 'porch' because the rest of the *palli* had

---

[64] Nair (1975, 494).

[65] Sreedhara Menon (1967, 196f).

[66] Sassoon (1932, 1056,Ms. #880, p. 1).

[67] Sassoon (1932, 578,Ms #13). Members of the Castiel family were prominent in the Paradesi community of Kochi, and David ben Yaakov Castiel's connection with Parur is not known. The inscription honoring him is a Hebrew poem by Eliya Ha-Adeni from Kochi.

been destroyed by the troops of Tipu Sultan.[68] It was rebuilt sometime later in the 19th century, and when a new *heikhal* was created in 1891 it incorporated remnants from an older *heikhal* that showed burn marks from a fire.[69]

Of all eight Kerala synagogue complexes, Parur is the only one with three separate buildings: first a traditional gatehouse and then an intermediate structure connected by a breezeway to the synagogue building itself. The 'Parur *Palli* Song' mentioned above describes how 'four good *palli* structures were built, fitting together in just the right way', and its description of 'a fine and delicate stone' that was cut and 'fixed in the corner, to be seen' may be a reference to the 1616 inscription.

The two-story gatehouse (Fig. 29) opening onto the street is a handsome building with an upstairs porch, which has a waist-high wooden railing and a tiled roof supported by four pairs of pillars. The gatehouse measures almost 10m across—the same width as the synagogue building—and about 6.5 m in depth. There are two rooms inside the gatehouse, on either side of a central open area. In 1974 Barbara Johnson was told that these rooms traditionally served as storerooms for the year's supply of paddy rice for the entire community.[70]

Passing through the gatehouse one enters a long courtyard area leading to the middle building, which is almost as wide as the gatehouse but only half as deep. The 1616 dedication tablet mentioned above is mounted on the wall to the right of its arched entry (Fig. 30). On the ground floor of this intermediate structure another central foyer

---

[68] Hunt (1929, 153).

[69] Eliyahu-Oron (2004, 52–53, 106–107).

[70] Later Waronker was told they had been used as meeting rooms and then as living quarters for community members who had not yet left for Israel (2010, 115).

is flanked by two small rooms formerly used for storage. Upstairs is a room accessed by an exterior staircase attached to the northwest corner of the building.

Exiting the first floor of the middle building through another arched doorway provides a view of the open area under the breezeway bridge—a view that matches the verbal description of the old Thekkumbhagam-Ernakulam *Palli* which is no longer standing (Fig. 31). The bridge is supported by three pairs of sturdy *chunam* columns, creating an elegant 14m long passageway leading into the Synagogue building.[71] Built-in benches between the last two sets of columns provide a seating area that was used in the past for overflow crowds or for casual socializing. This is the pathway by which men and boys would enter the *azarah*.

Jewish women entered the synagogue building from the second story of the middle building, walking inside the breezeway bridge directly to their section overlooking the upper *tebah* (Fig. 32). This bridge has a tall tiled roof. Its slatted wooden sides—slanted outward—create a well-ventilated space that is larger, darker, more private and perhaps cooler than the comparatively open breezeways of the synagogues in Kochi.[72]

On the ground level the sanctuary building is entered through a 'double' wooden door—a door with an arched top set into a larger rectangular door—and the entrance from the *azarah* into the sanctuary is through a similar double door. The sanctuary interior is notable for

[71] This architectural arrangement has a striking resemblance to the Paliam Palace in nearby Chendamangalam. https://www.muzirisheritage.org/kerala-history-museum.php. Accessed 15 Feb., 2020.

[72] In the renovated Parur complex, access from the middle building to the bridge is blocked off, but it can be entered from the *ezrat nashim* in the Synagogue building.

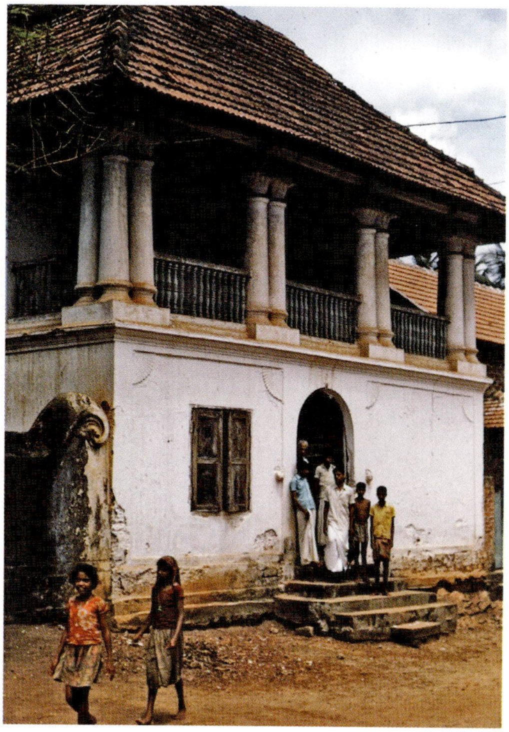

Fig. 29. Parur Synagogue gatehouse; Barbara C. Johnson, 1974

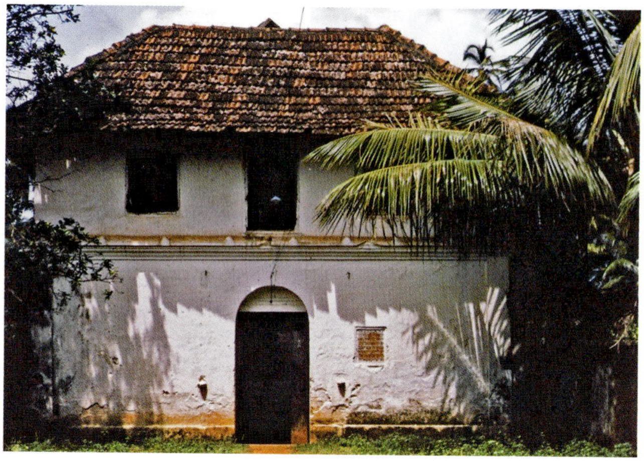

Fig. 30. Parur Synagogue middle building; Barbara C. Johnson, 1974

its decorations. The surface under the upper *tebah* is highly decorated with carvings of typical lotus flowers and panels with unusual images of parrots and vases with floral designs. At the time of the 1995 survey these carvings were painted in red, and other colors visible under the gallery were green, black, and gold. The sanctuary floor is paved with terracotta tiles and the recessed ceiling is made up of multiple small square panels of carved wood, with a flower in the center of each square.

The monumental *heikhal* was built in 1891. It is the tallest of the Kerala *heikhal*ot (487 cm high) and is intricately carved but not painted—unlike most of the others, which are painted and gilded. This *heikhal* has an extra decorative panel between the main body and the

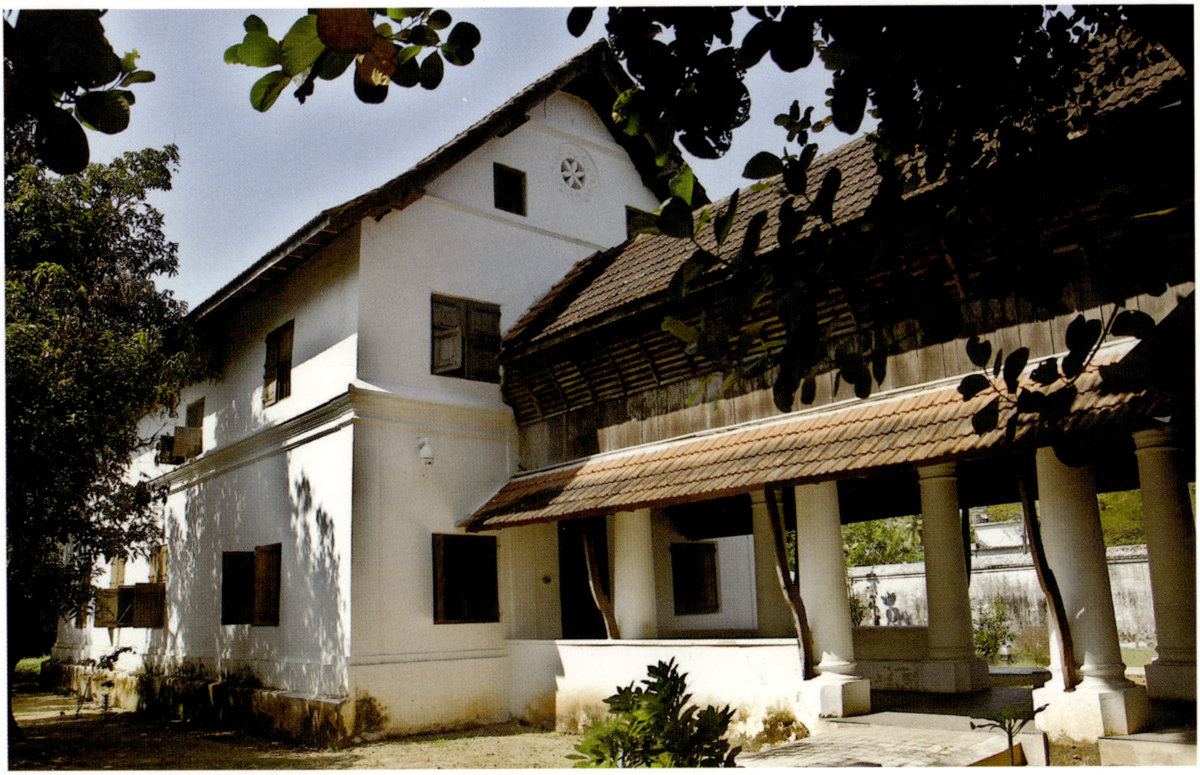

Fig. 31. Parur Synagogue breezeway and *Palli* building; Paul Laju, 2015

pediment, and on top is a three-dimensional crown (Fig. 33). Other unique details include a Hebrew dedication inscription, a depiction of the priestly breastplate, and the image of a seven-branched menorah with grape vines (in lieu of olive branches) on either side, with a Hebrew quote from Zechariah 4:2-3 arched above the image. These elements may reflect Messianic thinking among the Jews of Parur in the late 19th century, influenced by emissaries from the land of Israel.[73]

The central *heikhal*, lower *tebah*, Torah cases and chandeliers from Parur were purchased and sent to the Israel Museum in Jerusalem in 1995, to be incorporated into the Kadavumbhagam-Kochi sanctuary

[73] Eliyahu-Oron (2004, 86–90).

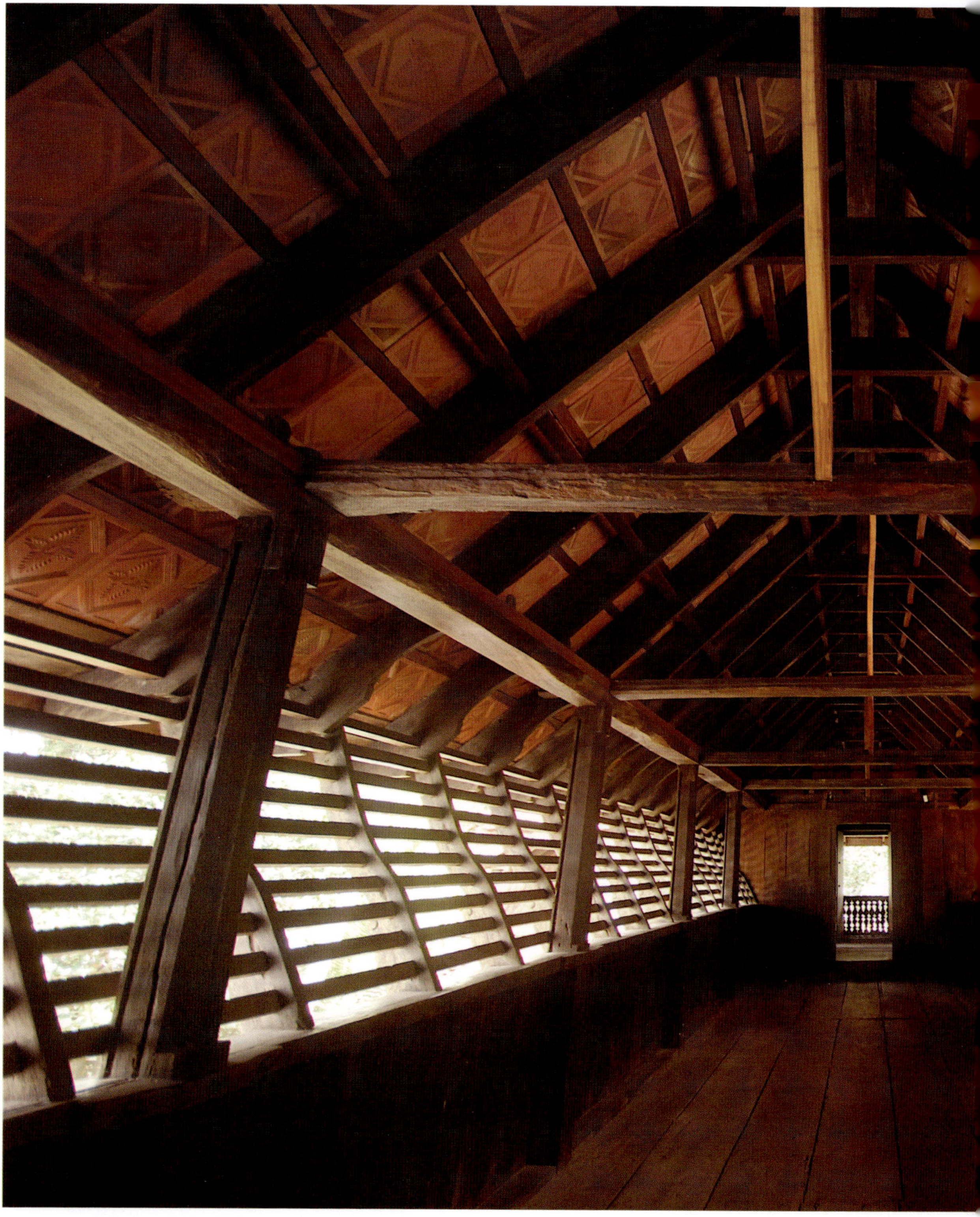

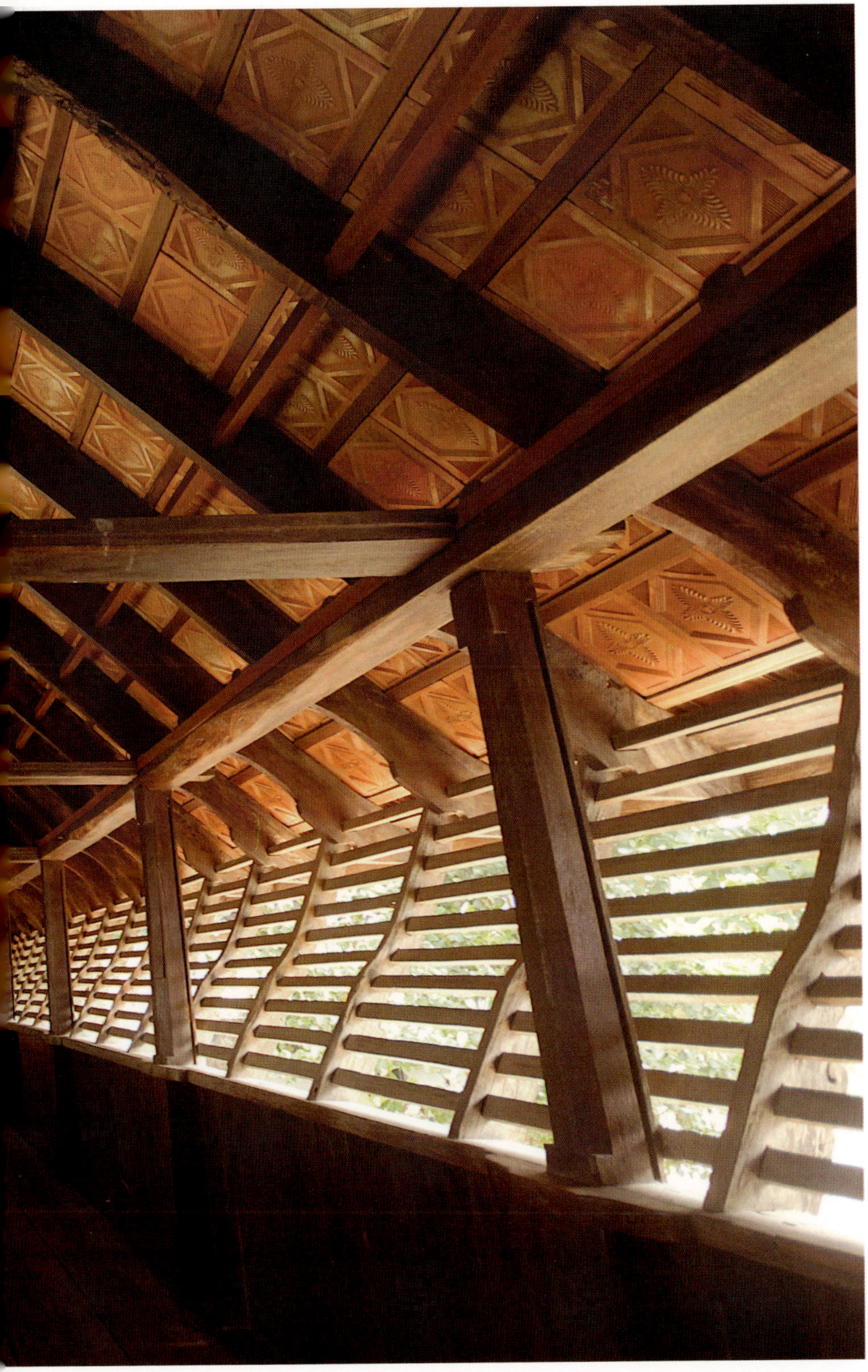

Fig. 32. Parur Synagogue breezeway interior; Paul Laju, 2016

interior on permanent display there. When the Synagogue's renovation was undertaken in Kerala, skilled craftsmen were employed to make copies of the central *tebah* and *heikhal*, both of which were installed in their proper places and are on view for visitors today.

Chendamangalam Synagogue

Chendamangalam is a small town located in the countryside 23 km north of Ernakulam and a few km east of North Paravur at the conjunction of three rivers. It is the historical home of the Paliam family, led by the eldest male, titled Paliat Achan, who was hereditary commander-in-chief and prime minister under the Raja of Cochin during the 17th and 18th centuries. Today Chendamangalam is a featured stop on the Muziris Heritage Project tours because of its two recently restored monuments, the Paliam Palace and the synagogue.

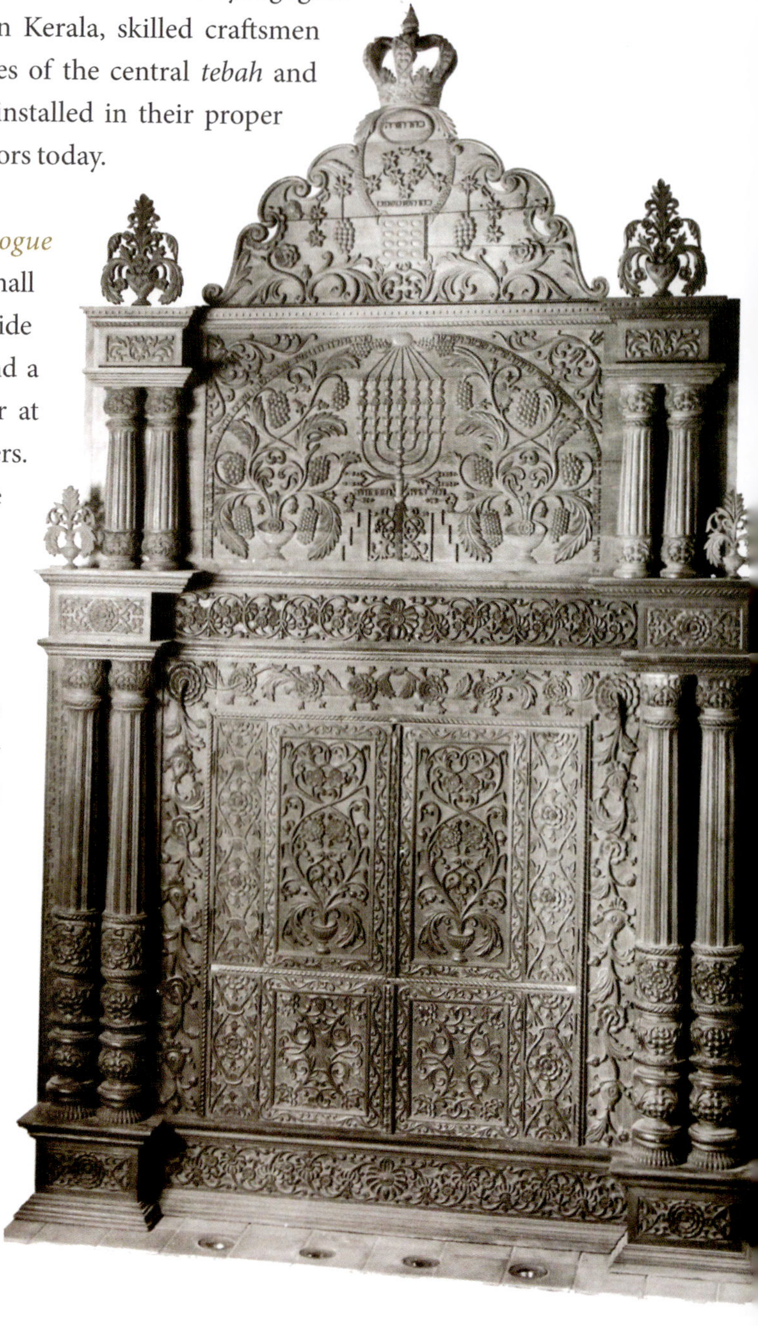

Fig. 33. Parur Synagogue *heikhal*; Courtesy of Israel Museum, 1995

The synagogue is on the eastern outskirts of town, in a quiet area close to the water. Evidence for a 13th-century Jewish presence in the Chendamangalam area is found in a monument now installed in front of the synagogue, to the right of the entrance. It is a tombstone inscribed in Hebrew, recording the death in 1268 of a woman named Sarah bat Israel (Sarah daughter of Israel).[74]

According to members of the Paliam family interviewed in 1968, the Chendamangalam Jews were originally given extensive rent-free lands by the local chieftain called Villarvattam Raja, predecessor of the Paliat Achan.[75] Sassoon Ms #880 lists 1614 as the date of its building, and Kerala Government archaeologists responsible for its renovations believe that the *palli* was built in 1565 and repaired in 1621.[76] Pereyra de Paiva, the Dutch visitor to Kochi in 1685, was told that Chendamangalam had 50 'well-provided' Jewish families.[77] After their *palli* was destroyed in the Anglo-Mysore war it took some time to replace it. Chendamangalam Jews petitioned the Diwan (Prime Minister) of Kochi in 1837, asking for 50 logs of teak wood to rebuild their synagogue, 'which was destroyed in the late conflagration at that place'.[78]

---

[74] See Gamliel (2018b, 45) for details about the inscription and interesting speculation about the identity of Sarah bat Israel.

[75] Nair (1975, 494). He reported that this information was corroborated by the long-term manager of the Paliam Estate Office and by Jewish elders in Parur.

[76] Sassoon (1932, 1056). Waronker (2010,141, 146) cites 2006 interviews with Dr.V.M. Nair, head of the Kerala Department of Archaeology and Deepa V., conservation engineer of the Chendamangalam restoration project, for dating and related information.

[77] Pereyra de Paiva, in Timberg (1986, 126).

[78] 'A Collection of Historical Records,' copied from Diwan's Diary. Selected Papers 1826–1835 (Book No. 133), S.S. Koder papers, Vol. 3. Notes taken by Barbara Johnson in Cochin, 1974.

The new synagogue did not last through the 19th century. According to interviews with community members in Israel who were born in Chendamangalam, it had to be rebuilt again after yet another fire.[79] One informant reported that years after the synagogue was gone, local non-Jews were seen digging in the site in hopes of finding gold. The new synagogue was built near the site of the old one but not on top of it, limiting the amount of available space for a new *palli*.

After most of the Jewish population left Chendamangalam in the 1950s, its remaining community members moved to Alwaye, Parur, or Kochi,[80] and the synagogue building fell into disrepair. In 1981 Barbara Johnson found it encroached by vegetation, with cracks in the exterior and its interior damaged by vandals (Fig. 34). In 1995 when Orna Eliyahu-Oron visited with the CJA survey team they found that the damage had continued, but they succeeded in documenting the building and its remaining ritual objects (Fig. 35).

By the first years of the 21st century, given that portions of its roof and floor had collapsed and its structural integrity was severely compromised, the Association of Kerala Jews agreed to transfer ownership of the *Palli* to the Indian Department of Archaeology's Kerala office. An ambitious restoration project costing about $80,000 was carried out by a team of highly trained craftsmen and carpenters, funded by the Kerala government.[81] A 'Kerala Jews Lifestyle Museum' was created inside the renovated *Palli*, and the building renovation was completed in time for a

[79] Interviews in Israel: Orna with Menahem Kadvil (Rechasim), on 11 April, 2002 and Bezalel Eliyahu (Shahar), on 2 August, 2002; Barbara with Galia Hacco (Modi'in), summer 2000.

[80] Yehudi (1989, 102–103).

[81] Waronker (2010,142–143).

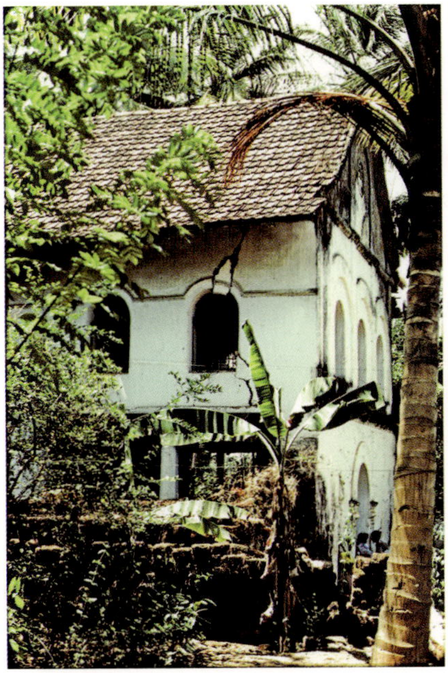

Fig. 34. Chendamangalam Synagogue exterior; Barbara C. Johnson, 1981

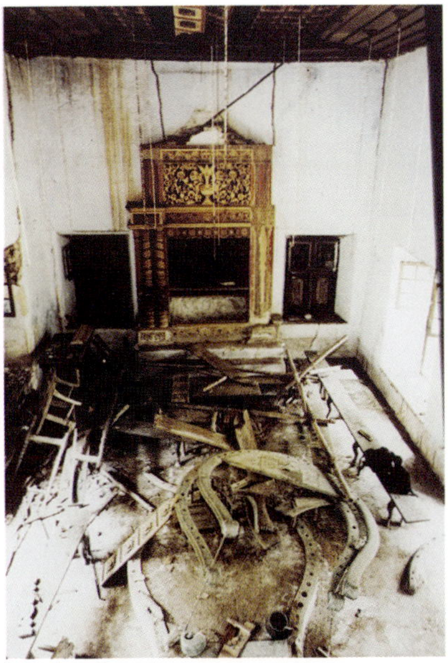

Fig. 35. Chendamangalam Synagogue interior, 1995; Zev Radovan, 1995, CJA#242435

grand opening of the museum in February 2006, attended by the Israeli consul general and many Cochini Jews from Israel.[82]

Among the eight synagogues of Kerala, Chendamangalam has a unique spatial layout (Fig. 36). Unlike six of the others, it has no separate gatehouse or breezeway, probably because of the land constraints when it

[82] The Museum was created in 2005–2006 by Waronker in cooperation with Atty. Marian S. Sofaer of Palo Alto, California and Dr. Shalva Weil from Hebrew University in Jerusalem and funded by the Koret Foundation. It contains historical information about the Jewish community of Chendamangalam, including reproductions of many old documents and photographs.

was built. The double doors at its entrance lead from the outside directly into a small open area which Waronker describes as a recessed porch, paved with granite and terracotta tiles (Fig. 37). It is open on the north and south sides, with built-in benches on its eastern wall, and two prominent granite pillars.[83] Directly above this open area and supported by the granite pillars is an upstairs room, which was used for classes and study.

[83] Waronker 2010: 146–147.

Fig. 36. Chendamangalam Synagogue exterior; Paul Laju, 2016

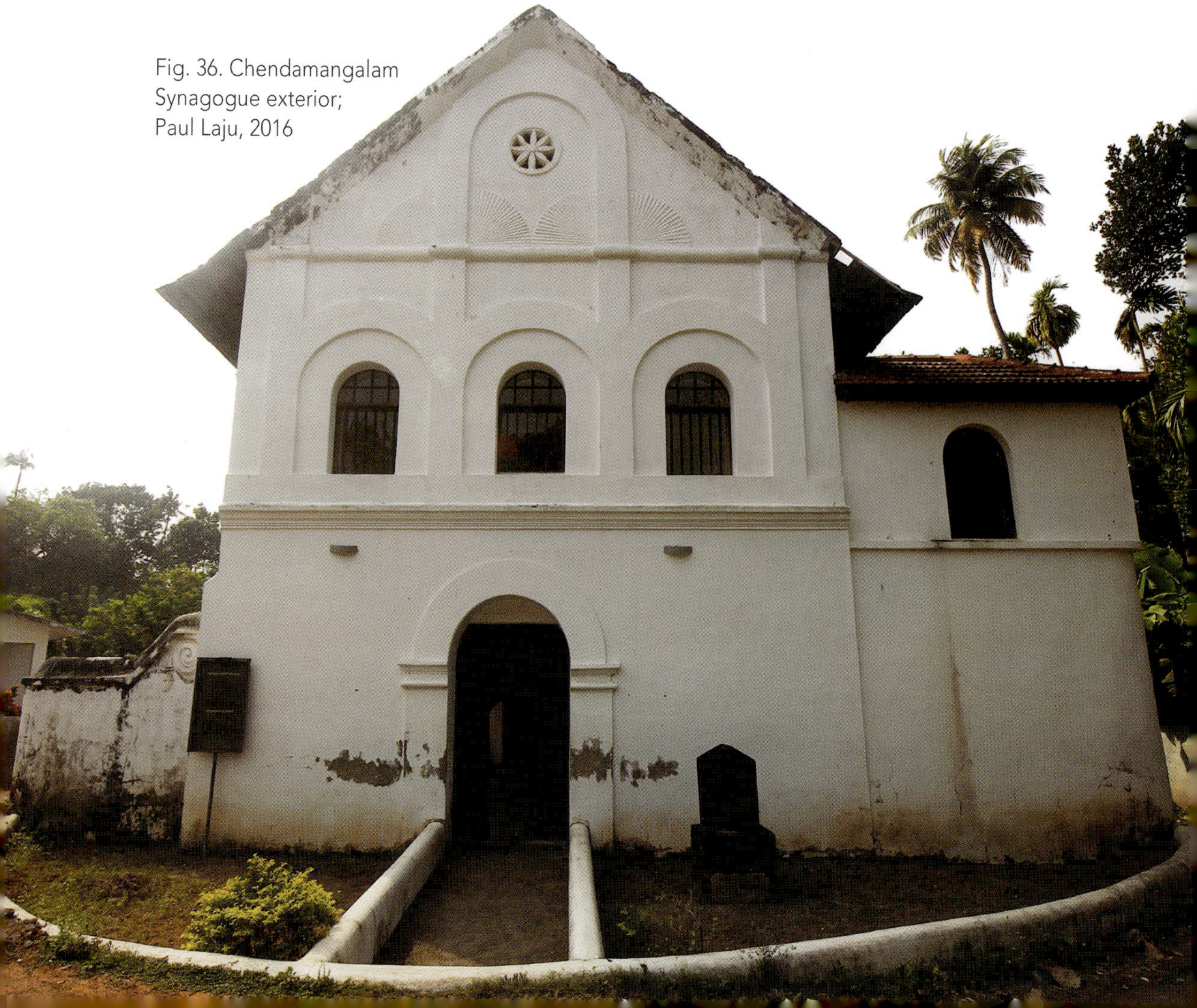

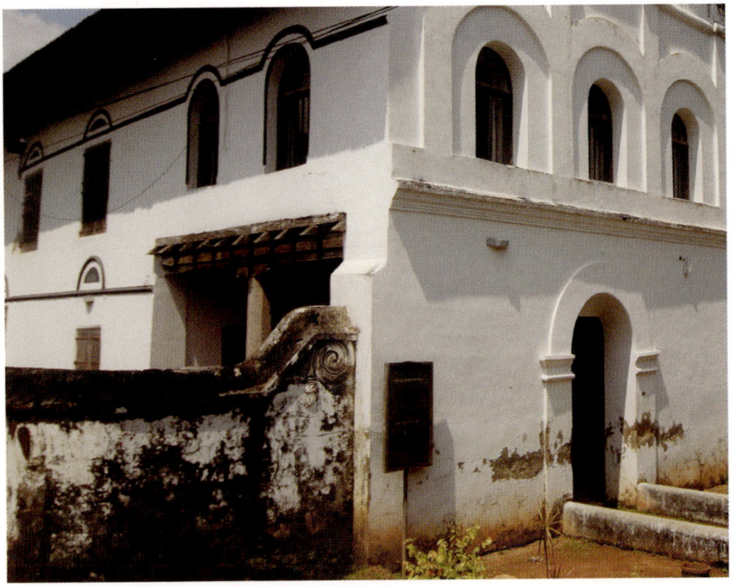

Fig. 37. Chendamangalam Synagogue recessed porch with pillars, seen within the outer wall; Paul Laju, 2019

On the west side of the porch area there are three stone steps leading up to a pair of doors that open to the *azarah*, which has the same proportions and transitional function as the anteroom in each of the eight synagogues. This *azarah* has a special doorway into the sanctuary, its doorframe decorated with painted floral designs. An ornately carved and painted wooden panel above the door portrays the seven-branch menorah with olive trees, a reference to the prophetic vision of Zechariah alluded to on the top panel of the Parur synagogue *heikhal*. The Chendamangalam doorframe and panel are now painted in deep green, red and gold colors to match the colors of the *heikhal*, replacing the colors from before the renovation,which are seen in Figure 38.

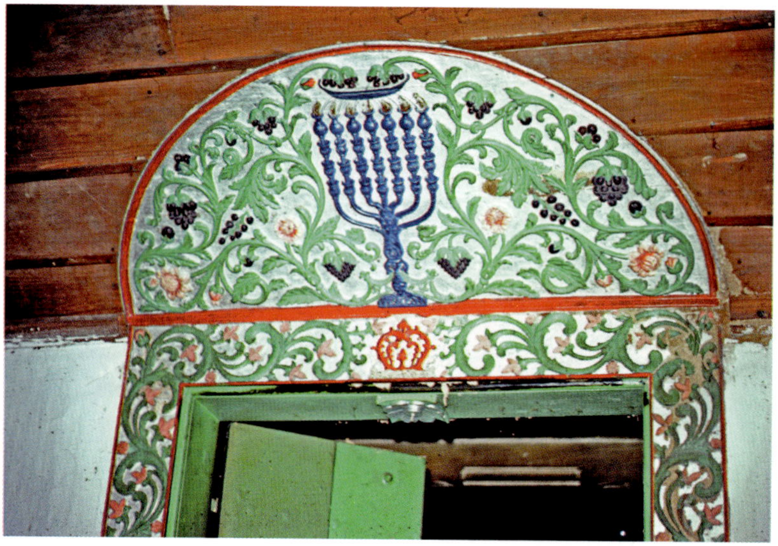

Fig. 38. Chendamangalam Synagogue, panel above the doorway; Barbara C. Johnson, 1981

The sanctuary measures 11 m by 6.2 m—comparable in size to Kadavumbhagam-Kochi but small in comparison with all the others. It has the same upper *tevah* structure on the east side. In the center of the renovated sanctuary (Fig. 39)a traditional central horseshoe-shaped *tebah* has been reconstructed of wood, gilded to resemble the brass parts of the original *tebah* that were stolen. The *heikhal* is relatively large and is decorated with floral and ornamental designs. Its three-tiered structure resembles the Parur *heikhal*, but in contrast it is painted in green, red, yellow, orange, and gilt, rendering it the most colorful among known Kerala *heikhalot*.

A feature unique to the Chendamangalam *Palli* is its 'stair tower', a square two-story structure attached to the north side of the synagogue building, seen on the right in Figure 36. It encloses a spiral staircase, climbing up to a door in the northeast corner of the upstairs room where classes used to be held. This staircase was the women's direct access to the *ezrat nashim* immediately above the downstairs *azarah* and behind the upper *tebah* overlooking the prayer hall.[84]

Mala Synagogue

Today Mala is a large town in the Thrissur district, east of Kodungallur. The old synagogue stands in its busy commercial center, facing the main east-west road running through the town, which is now designated as State Highway 51. According to local tradition in Mala, Jews began to settle there after the 1341 flood, and large tracts of land were granted to them by the feudal chieftains known as Kodasseri Karthas.[85] A Malayalam folk song preserved by Kerala Jewish women recounts a legendary origin story in which the ruler of Kodungallur invited a group of Jews to settle in Mala and build a synagogue there because he wanted more religious diversity in his kingdom. In typical royal fashion he contributed wood for them to build the synagogue, and the song describes their adventures in going up to the hills to cut down the trees. It also mentions the Kodasseri ruler, who donated a Torah scroll for the *Palli*.[86]

---

[84] It is possible that this arrangement for an enclosed external staircase was the prototype for the former addition to the Kadavumbhagam-Ernakulam *Palli*— the only other synagogue to lack a gatehouse or entrance building and breezeway from which women could reach the *ezrat nashim* (See Fig. 20).

[85] Nair 1975, 493–494. While doing historical research on Jewish communities in the area, Nair was told in the Mala municipal office that the original grant was recorded on an *ola* (palm leaf manuscript) which was destroyed by the passage of time.

[86] Zacharia and Gamliel (2005). Malayalam text, pp.46–48; Hebrew translation, pp. 39–42.

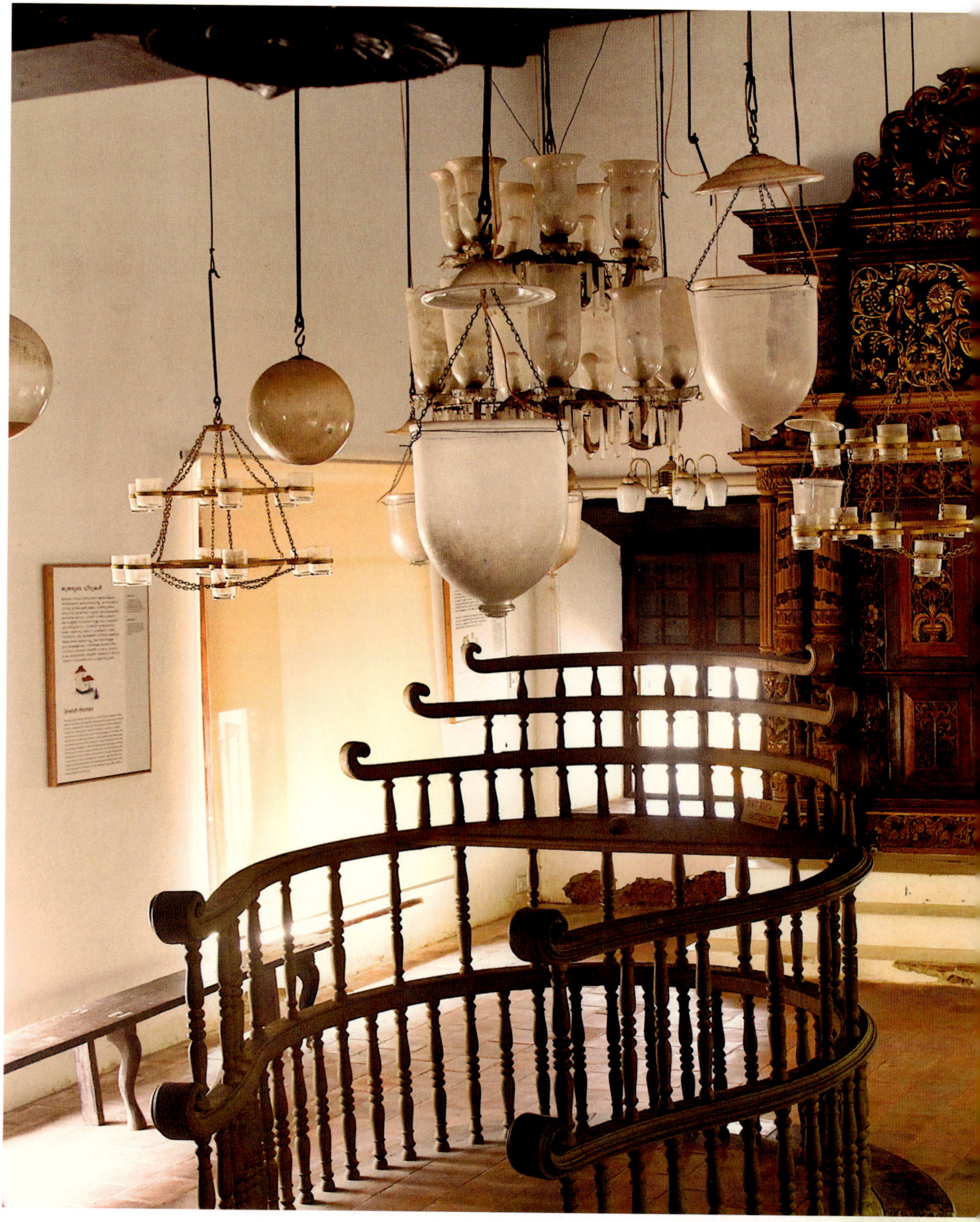

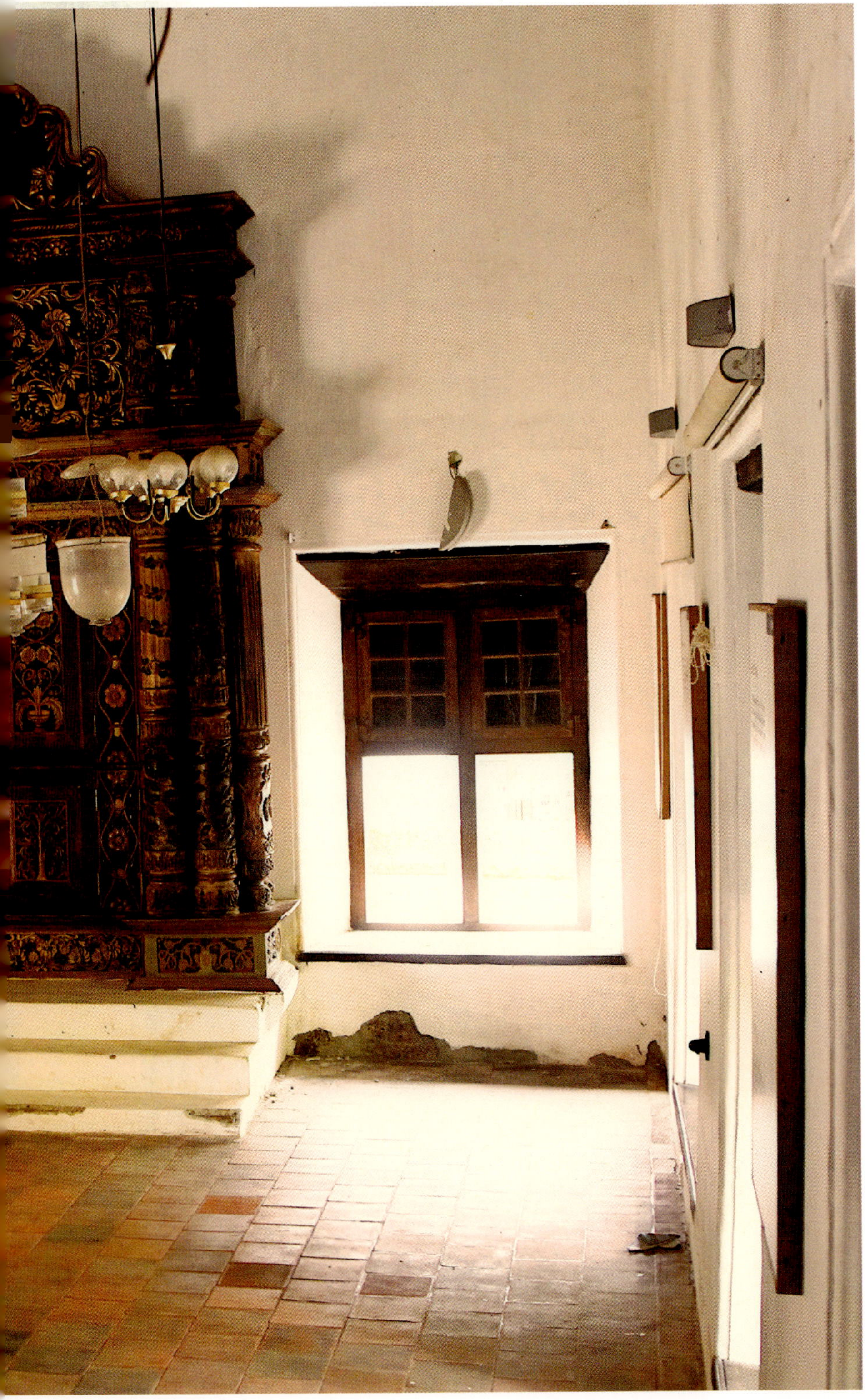

Fig. 39. Chendamangalam synagogue, interior with *heikhal*; Paul Laju, 2019

There is no firm evidence for when a *palli* was first built in Mala, but the list in Sassoon Ms. #880 dates it to 1597.[87] In 1768, 50 Jewish families were living in Mala, according to a Hebrew letter written from Kochi to the Netherlands that year.[88] As reported by Rev. Dawson, their synagogue was destroyed or badly damaged during the Anglo-Mysore war of 1789–90, and it is not known when the next one was built.

When Waronker was doing his research in Mala before 2010, people living near the *Palli* told him that their former Jewish neighbors had been productive shop-owners, traders and agricultural workers, who owned much of the property around the synagogue.[89] In the 1950s an apparently good relationship between Mala Jews and their neighbors was demonstrated in the unique long-term arrangement they made for their synagogue as they were leaving for Israel. Before the entire community departed in 1955, the synagogue trustees donated the building and its property to Mala's Gram Panchayat (municipal council) (Fig. 40). They stipulated that it should not be used as a slaughterhouse or as a meeting place for non-Jewish religious services, and that the council would be responsible for maintaining the building and grounds, as well as the nearby Jewish cemetery.[90]

When donated in 1955, the *Palli* had three structures; a gatehouse, a breezeway bridge and the synagogue prayer hall. The synagogue building was subsequently used for municipal government offices and community events, and for a while the second floor of its gatehouse,

---

87 Sassoon (1932, p. 1056, Ms. # 880).

88 Koder (1949).

89 Waronker (2010, 158).

90 The text of the deed is found in Yehudi (1990, 93–96). Figure 38 was published in Koder, et. al. (1968, facing p. 51).

where the Hebrew school had been held, was used as classroom space for Mala children who awaited the building of a new public school.

Then within a short time the council transformed the two-story gatehouse and connecting breezeway into commercial rental property facing the busy street. These structures were expanded and occupied by small shops, and at some point they were literally cut off from the main building, leaving a five-foot gap between the sanctuary and the former breezeway, as in Figure 41 from 1995.

Figure 42 is a photograph taken from the street in 2015, showing the upper storey of the former gatehouse, which featured a narrow balcony with a railing in front of shuttered windows and a central door, similar in style to the balcony of the Parur gatehouse.

During the first decade of the 21st century Jay Waronker was able to gain access to the upstairs of the former gatehouse and breezeway, documenting them with detailed analyses and photographs.[91] Both the former gatehouse and breezeway structures were completely demolished in 2017 in order to widen Highway 15 as it passes through Mala, so the second story and roof of the synagogue building can be seen from the highway (Fig. 43).

Today the *Palli* compound is accessed from a side street. The current entrance to the building is through a new door on the south side leading into the former sanctuary, replacing one of its large windows and bypassing the *azarah*. Figure 44 shows this new side entrance, with a partial view of the former gatehouse and breezeway roofs before they were destroyed.

---

[91] Waronker (2010, 179–81).

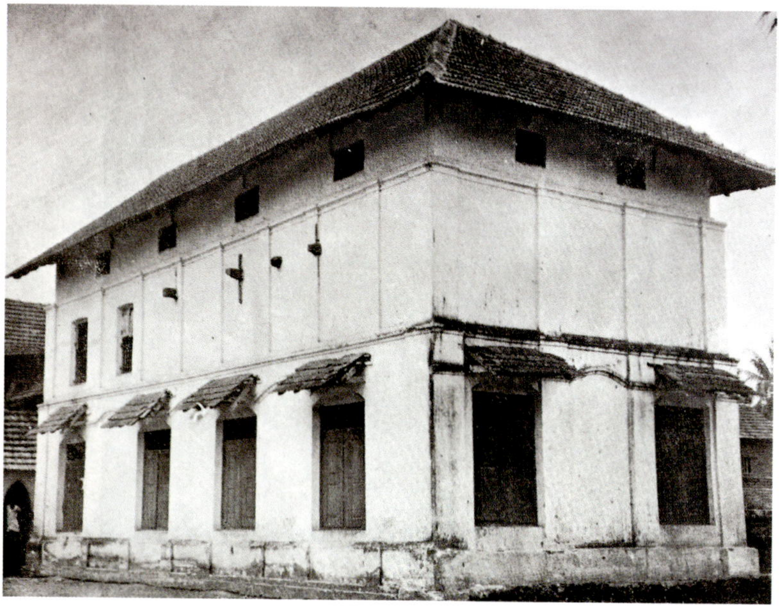

Fig. 40. Mala Synagogue 1950s, *Cochin Synagogue Quarter Centenary Souvenir;* Ernakulam: Thilakam Press, 1958. Photo facing p. 51.

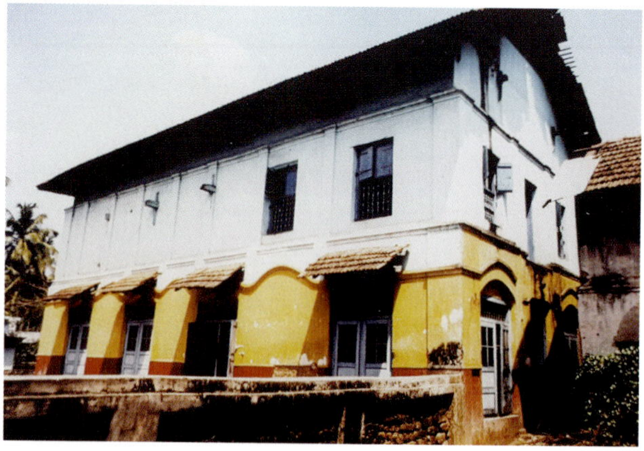

Fig. 41. Mala Synagogue, gap between synagogue and breezeway; Zev Radovan, 1995 CJA #244982

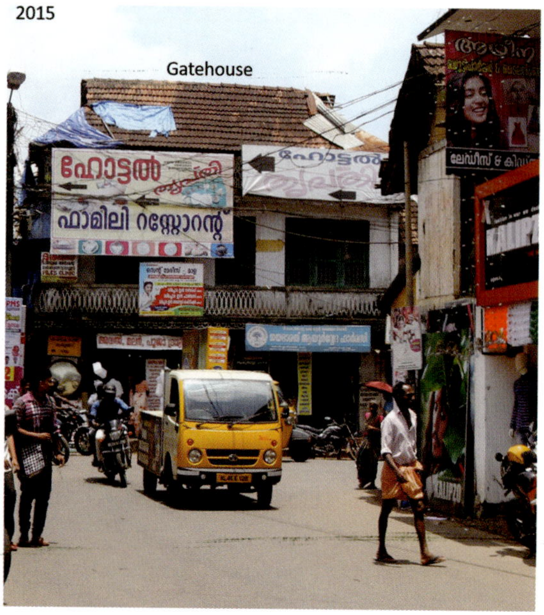

Fig. 42. Mala Synagogue, former gatehouse from the street; Paul Laju, 2015

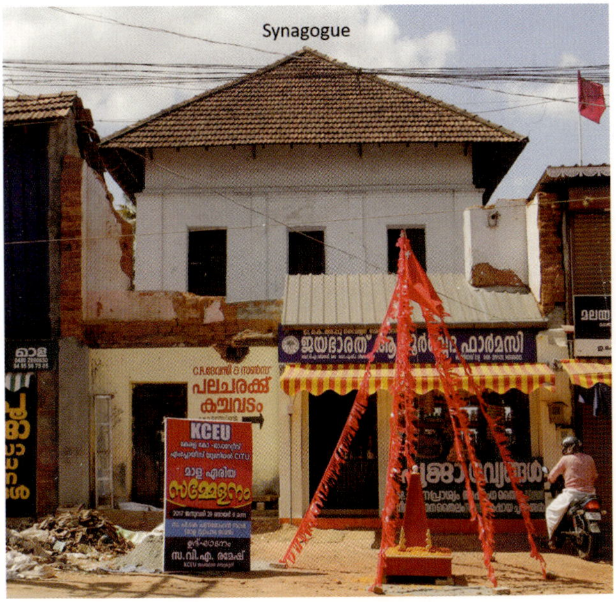

Fig. 43. Mala Synagogue, after the gatehouse was demolished; Paul Laju, 2017

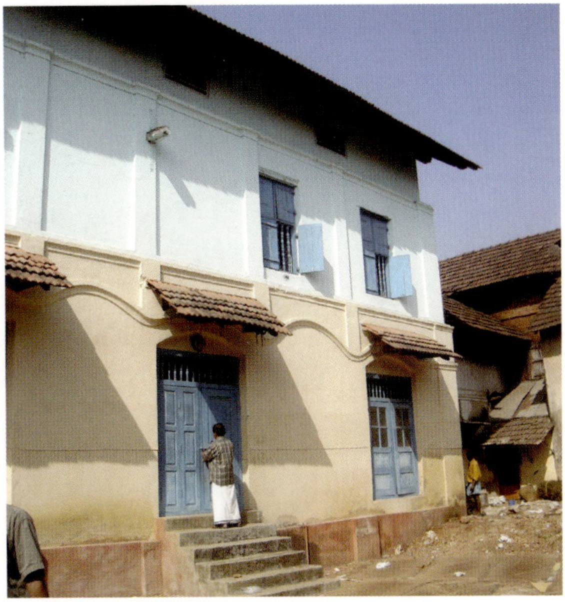

Fig. 44. Mala Synagogue, new entrance; Barbara C. Johnson, 2006

According to an inscription in Hebrew and Malayalam on the balcony frieze of its upper *tebah*, the Mala synagogue building was constructed in 1909 on the site of an earlier building; but there is no evidence of whether or not the old gatehouse and breezeway were also replaced. The sanctuary interior (Fig. 45) has the basic structure found in other Kerala synagogues, except that its wooden ceiling is constructed of wide wood planks and beams rather than being paneled, recessed, or decorated with carvings. The only example of decorative art is found beneath the frieze of the upper *tebah* (Fig. 46), where there are 26 elegantly carved lotus flowers, each lotus unique in shape and arrangement. In contrast to Figures 45 and 46 from 1995, today the lotus carvings are painted a dark brown color, along with the ceiling and all the interior woodwork, while the walls are all white.

It is not known what became of the *heikhal*, the central *tebah*, or other movable contents of Mala *Palli*. When interviewed, former

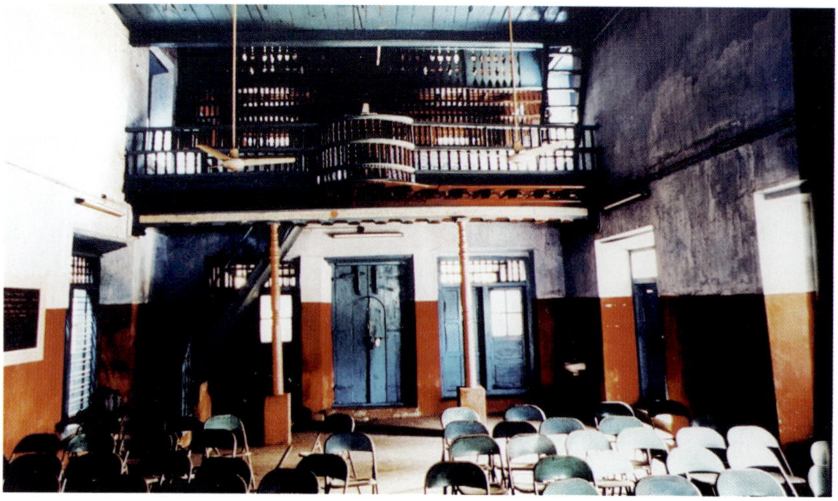

Fig. 45. Mala Synagogue interior; Zev Radovan, 1995 CJA #17161

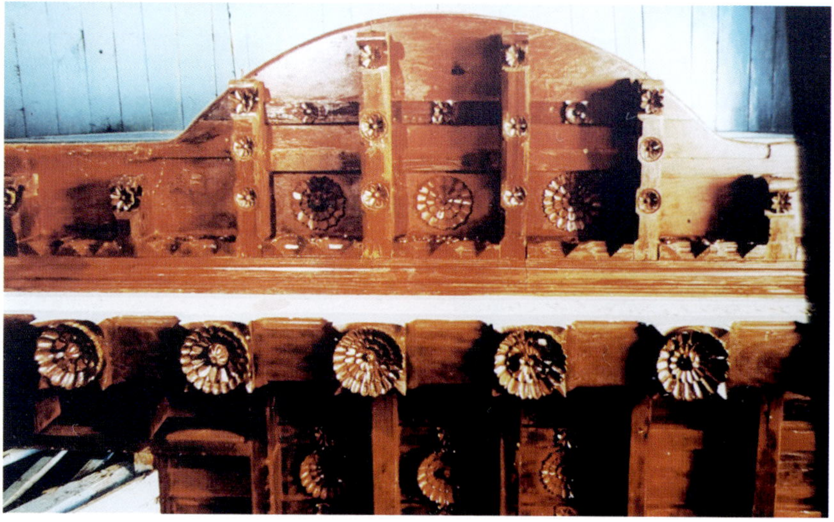

Fig. 46. Mala Synagogue upper *tebah*; Zev Radovan, 1995 CJA# 242854

synagogue members said that the *heikhal* was similar to the one in Parur, in its shape and in that it was also carved but unpainted.

Over the years the Mala Synagogue building and grounds have become quite decrepit. The cemetery was not maintained, and only three of the tombstones there remain standing. In 2014 there was an effort to take over half the cemetery acreage with the intent of creating a park with a sports stadium, but a long protest campaign was successfully waged through the efforts of a local Hindu historian, Professor C. Karmachandran, and other intellectuals and activists who formed the Mala Heritage Conservation Society. In 2017 the Kerala Government declared the synagogue and Jewish cemetery in Mala to be 'protected monuments'.[92] Responsibility for them has now been taken over by the Muziris Heritage Project.

To celebrate the 65th anniversary of the Jewish agreement to donate their synagogue and cemetery to the people of Mala, on 4 January 2020 the Muziris Heritage Project and the Mala Panchayat co-sponsored a one-day International Seminar on the Jewish Heritage in Kerala and a 'Mala-Muziris Heritage Walk'.[93] Many young people were involved in the march through town to the synagogue, beginning at Malakadavu ('Mala landing place'), which will also be developed as a Muziris Heritage site.[94]

In addition to his years of advocacy for preservation of the building and cemetery, Prof. Karmachandran has made contact with many Israeli

---

92 http://www.newindianexpress.com/states/kerala/2018/jan/22/mala-synagogue-cemetery-declared-protected-monuments-1760746.html. Accessed 25 February 2020.

93 https://www.facebook.com/permalink.php?id=647758395332488&story_fbid=2471645249610451. Accessed 25 February 2020.

94 https://www.thehindu.com/news/national/kerala/malakadavu-waterway-gets-fresh-lease-of-life/article26235184.ece. Accessed 25 February 2020.

families who used to live in Mala. With their help he has identified 43 buildings in Mala that were formerly occupied by Jewish residents.[95] His active 'Mala Jewish Monuments' Facebook page has a large following, and includes postings by members of the Mala families now in Israel, who have come back to visit in the past few years. [96]

Conclusion

Our research for this article began with the desire to discover and document as much as possible about the history and architecture of eight synagogues. Recognizing that these buildings had been central to the community lives of Kerala Jews who left them behind when they moved to Israel, we value the opportunity to preserve and publish what we have learned.

While the search sometimes took us wandering far into the past, it has also opened new windows to the present. We are relieved to report on the rescue and restoration of buildings that were in danger of destruction, through official Kerala government support for the Muziris project. We are grateful to learn about the personal commitment of Kerala activists who are protecting historical Jewish sites. And we appreciate the enthusiastic commitment of new Kerala researchers—Muslim, Christian, and Hindu—who are devoted to protecting the memory of the synagogues. It is heartening to know that Kerala's

[95] Paul Laju, personal communication, January 2020.

[96] https://www.facebook.com/MALA-Jewish-Monuments-647758395332488/. Accessed 25 January 2020.

longstanding reputation still prevails—as a meeting place of cultures, a haven of inter-religious tolerance, and a consistent place of safety for Jews.

Finally, we celebrate the recent increase in visits to Kerala and involvement in its cultural life by Israeli Cochinim. May a new generation grow in enthusiasm to visit the home and synagogues of their ancestors, to learn more about what it was like 'Growing up Jewish in Kerala'.

Bibliography

Bar Giora, Naftali. 'Sources for the History of the Relations between the White and the Black Jews in Kochin.' *Sefunot*, vol. 1 (1957): 242–278. Hebrew.

———. 'History of the Synagogues in Kochin.' *Sefunot*, vol. 2 (1958): 214–245. Hebrew.

Barmouth, Eliyahu. *The Jews of Cochin: In Search of Roots*. Jerusalem: 2001.

Ben Eliahu, Eliya. *The Synagogues in India*. Kiryat Motzkin, Israel: 1978.

Chakravarti, Ranabir. 'Reaching Out to Distant Shores: Indo-Judaic Trade Contacts (Up to CD 1300).'In *Indo-Judaic Studies in the Twenty-First Century: A View from the Margin*, edited by Nathan Katz, pp.19–43. New York: Palgrave Macmillan. 2007.

Daniel, Ruby, and Barbara C. Johnson. *Ruby of Cochin: A Jewish Woman Remembers*. Philadelphia: The Jewish Publication Society, 1995.

Eliyahu-Oron, Orna. 'Heichalot (Torah Arks) from the Synagogues of Cochin Jews in India.' MA Thesis, Department of Art History, The Hebrew University of Jerusalem: 2004. Hebrew.

Fishof, Iris. 'Moving the Cochin Synagogue from India to the Israel Museum: A Curator's Perspective.' *The Israel Museum Journal*, vol. 13 (1995):19–28. Jerusalem.

Gamliel, Ophira. 'Back from Shingly: Revisiting the Premodern History of the Jews in Kerala.' *The Indian Economic and Social History Review*, vol. 55 (1) (2018a): 53–76.

———. 'Textual Crossroads and Transregional Encounters: Jewish Networks in

Kerala, 900–1600s.' *Social Orbit*, vol. 4 (1) (2018b): 41–73. Farook University, Kozhikode, Kerala.

Hunt, W.S. *The Anglican Church in Travancore and Cochin, 1816–1916*. Kottayam: Church Missionary Society Press, 1920. Reprint 1968.

Johnson, Barbara C. 'Cranganore, Joseph Rabban and Cheraman Perumal: An Origin Theme in Cochin Jewish Folklore.' *Pe'amim (Quarterly Journal of the Ben-Zvi Institute)*, vol. 13 (1982): 71–83. Jerusalem, Hebrew. English version in Timberg 1986, 161–176.

———. 'Our Community.'I In *Two Worlds: the Cochin Paradesi Jews in India and Israel*. Ph.D. Dissertation, Department of Anthropology, University of Massachusetts, 1985.

Johnson, Barbara C. ed. *Oh, Lovely Parrot: Jewish Women's Songs from Kerala*. (CD and book). Jerusalem: The Jewish Music Research Center, The Hebrew University of Jerusalem. 2004.

Johnson, Barbara C., and Galia Hacco. 'Juta*palli* Yogam in Kerala Jewish Communal Organization: Some Hebrew Sources Translated.' *Tapasam: A Quarterly Journal for Kerala Studies*, vol. 6(1) (April 2009): 111–139. Association for Comparative Studies, Changanassery, Kerala..

Katz, Nathan and Ellen Goldberg. *The Last Jews of Cochin: Jewish Identity in Hindu India*. Columbia: University of South Carolina Press, 1993.

Koder, Shabdai Samuel. 'A Hebrew Letter of 1768.' *Bulletin of the Rama Varma Research Institute*, Vol.15 (April 1949): 1–7.

Koder, Shabdai Samuel, et. al., eds. *Cochin Synagogue Quarter centenary Souvenir*. Ernakulam: Thilakam Press, 1968.

Kushner, Gilbert. *Immigrants from India in Israel*. Tucson: The University of Arizona Press, 1973.

Lord, J. Henry. *The Jews in India and the Far East*. Kohlapur: Mission Press. 1907.

Menon, A. Sreedhara. *A Survey of Kerala History. Kottayam*: Sahitya Pravarthaka Co-operative Society. 1976.

Nair, P. Thankappan. 'Jews of Cennamangalam and Paravur.' *Journal of Kerala Studies*, vol.2 (Dec. 1975): 479–508.

Narayanan, M.G.S. 'Further Studies in the Jewish Copper Plates of Cochin.' *Journal of Indo-Judaic Studies*, Vol. 6 (June 2003): 19–28.

Pereyra de Paiva, Mosseh. *Notisias dos Judeos de Cochim*. Amsterdam: House of Vry Levy, 1687. (Portuguese). Transl. by F. Fegueiredo, in S.S. Koder, 'Saga of the Jews of Cochin.' In *The Cochin Synagogue Quartercentenary Souvenir*, Koder et. al., eds. Ernakulam: Thilakam Press, 1968. Reprinted in Timberg, 1986, 121–142.

Salem, Abraham Barak. *Eternal Light or Jew Town Synagogue.* Ernakulam: S.D. Printing Works, 1929.

Sassoon, David S. Ohel David: *Descriptive Catalogue of the Hebrew and Samaritan Manuscripts in the Sassoon Library.*Vol.2, London: Oxford University Press, 1932.

Segal, J.B. *A History of the Jews of Cochin.* London: Vallentine Mitchell, 1993.

Slapak, Orpa. 'The Cochin Jews: The Synagogue.' In *The Jews of India: A Story of Three Communities*, edited by Orpa Slapak,pp. 56–67. Jerusalem: The Israel Museum, 1995.

Tavim, José Alberto Rodrigues da Silva, 'Une presence portugaiseautour de la 'nouvelle synagogue' de Cochin.' In Aldina da Silva, André Myre and Tereza Pinto, eds., *Les Juifs Portugais: Exil Héritage Perspectives 1496-1996*, pp. 67–81. Montreal: Médiaspaul, 1996. French.

Timberg, Thomas A., ed. *Jews in India*. New York: Advent Books, 1986.

Velayudhan, P.S. et al., eds. *Commemoration Volume, Cochin Synagogue Quartercentenary Celebrations*. Cochin: Kerala History Association, 1971.

Waronker, Jay Arthur. 'The Synagogues of Kerala, India: Their Architecture, History, Context, and Meaning.' Unpublished M.A. Thesis, Cornell University, 2010.

Weil, Ilana. 'The Architecture of the Paradesi Cochin Synagogue.' In *India's Jewish Heritage*, edited by Shalva Weil, pp. 51–59. Mumbai: Marg Publications, 2002.

Yehudi, Prem Doss Swami Doss. *The Shingly Hebrews*. Trivandrum: Sachethana, 1990.

Zacharia, Scaria and Ophira Gamliel, translators and editors. *Karkulali - Yefefiah - Gorgeous!: Jewish Women's Songs in Malayalam with Hebrew Translations.* Jerusalem: Ben-Zvi Institute, Yad Izhak Ben-Zvi and The Hebrew University, 2005.

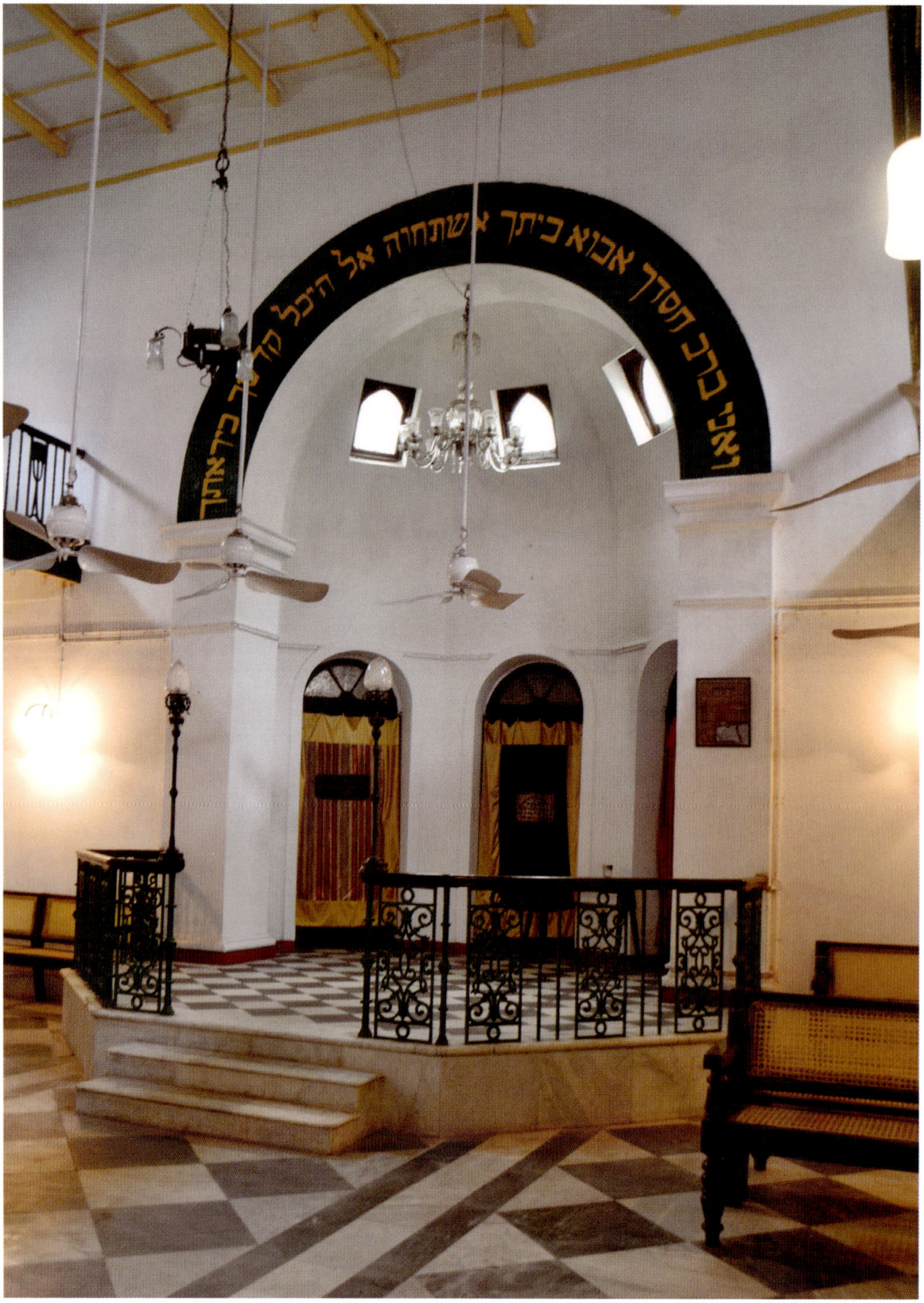

Fig. 1.Neveh Shalome Synagogue interior, toward the *heikhal*. Note the unusual multiple arched 'sub-*heikhalot*', each with its own *parokhet* (curtain).

CHAPTER THREE

Therein Lies a Tale

THE SYNAGOGUES OF THE BAGHDADI JEWS OF CALCUTTA

Jael Silliman

Introduction: The Five Synagogues of Calcutta

Today there are fewer than 20 Jews left in Calcutta[1] but there are still three impressive synagogues—Neveh Shalome, Beth El, and Magen David. They are clustered rather close together in what was once central Calcutta, home to many communities who migrated to the colonial city between the 18th and early 20th centuries to seek their fortunes. The Jews were active in all spheres of Calcutta's social, political, economic, and cultural life. These synagogues have garnered significant national and international attention for the beauty and grandeur of their architecture, and are increasingly on the tourist map as they are all well maintained

[1] The name of Calcutta was changed to Kolkata in 2001 as it is increasingly common for state, city and street names to distance themselves from the colonial legacy. For convenience I am using the earlier form of the name.

and renovated with Jewish Trust funds.[2] The most majestic and ornate of the three synagogues is the Magen David, built by the wealthy Ezra family—the city's merchant princes.[3] It is considered to be Asia's largest and most imposing synagogue. The Baghdadi Ohel David synagogue in Pune, built by David Sassoon, also lays claims to this distinction.[4]

There were once two others—although strictly speaking, they were prayer halls, rather than full synagogues: Magen Aboth and Shaare Rason—but the latter no longer stands and the former is now simply an empty room in a building with a plaque that allows visitors to know that it once was a prayer hall. As for the three extant synagogue structures, however, they have been a revelation for international media; for generations they have been served by Muslim caretakers. In today's increasingly polarized world where Jews and Muslims are all too often positioned as oppositional categories, this close relationship seems anomalous. However, Calcutta's Baghdadi Jews—so-called because they followed the liturgy of Baghdad—came from various countries of the

---

[2] The community's wealthy members were exceedingly philanthropic. They endowed schools, synagogues, and provided for the poor through numerous charities. These Trust funds are still used to run the two schools and support the synagogues. Despite considerable acrimony over the use of the Trust funds and allegations of graft and misuse, the three synagogues were renovated in 2009–2018 at considerable cost.

[3] The most prominent member of the family was David Ezra. He was appointed agent for Arab ships arriving at Calcutta and for Arab traders of Muscat and Zanzibar, importing dates and other produce and in exchange exporting rice, sugar and other commodities from India. In addition to developing trade, he had large real estate holdings; two streets were named after him—David Joseph Ezra Lane and Ezra street where he owned every property. (Musleah, *On the Banks of the Ganga*, p. 43). While the Ezras were the most prominent Jewish family, there were many other wealthy families like the Elias's, Gubbays, Arakies, Cohens, Belilios, and many more.

[4] The Sassoon family were the merchant princes of Bombay and were known for their many endowments to the Jewish community and to the City.

Middle East and were familiar with both the Islamic faith and Islamic customs, and this made their choice of Muslims as caretakers a straightforward matter. The two communities shared much in common; both, for instance are 'People of the Book', have some similar dietary traditions (Halal/Kashrut), and prohibit idolatry.

These Muslim caretakers have served the synagogues well while maintaining their own faith. Visitors today are encouraged not to visit on Friday afternoons as that is the time when the staff observe their *Namaz* (prayer). It is this mutual respect for, and acceptance of one another's faith and traditions, that made Calcutta a city where a multiplicity of religions could flourish cheek by jowl.[5] Jews, like many other traders who made the city their home in the colonial period (18th to mid-20th century),[6] were free to worship as they chose in a city that accommodated their diverse needs. For example, as Jews did not carry money on Sabbath, they were able to ride trams using a token.

As mentioned earlier, in addition to Calcutta's three existing synagogues, there was the Magen Aboth prayer hall, also known simply as the Beth Knesset ('synagogue'—literally 'House of Gathering'). It was located on Blackburn Lane, not far from the three substantive synagogues.

Magen Aboth was led by Hacham Twena, the most learned scholar from the Calcutta community, who founded it in 1897. Born in Baghdad, he is first recorded in Calcutta in 1883 in connection with the dedication

---

[5] Calcutta has a unique sacred topography; many religions built impressive edifices across the city. Religious tolerance was deeply embedded in the spiritual psyche of many of the Hindu reform leaders like Swami Vivekananda. For more information about this diverse religious space see Mala Mukerjee and Jael Silliman, *Where Gods Reside: The Sacred Places of Kolkata* (New Delhi: Niyogi Books, 2018).

[6] Calcutta was the capital of British India from 1772 to 1911.

of a Sefer Torah in the Beth El synagogue, and trained in the yeshiva Beth Zilka headed by Rabbi Abdullah Somekh. Twena was sent to Bombay (Mumbai) to serve as a Rabbi. He then moved to Calcutta. He was first employed to teach Talmud and sold religious articles as well as performed the ritual slaughter of poultry and conducted services at the Neveh Shalome and the Magen David synagogues. He then established the Magen Aboth prayer hall, where he administered primarily to the poor in the community. Though the Baghdadi Jews were known for their wealth, half of the community's members were poor and relied on Jewish charities. As many members of the community in the late 19th century still spoke Arabic, Twena preached in Arabic and ran a printing press to publish his prolific writings in Arabic and Hebrew.[7]

In 1933, as the community was still flourishing and expanding, a second prayer hall, Shaare Rason, was built in Sudder Street, then a residential area where many Jews had started to live at the turn of the century. Members of the Jewish community had first lived, worked and prayed in what was known as the 'grey area' of the city where the four synagogues are located, along with other members of such minority communities as the Armenians, Parsees, and Chinese.[8] As the Baghdadi Jews became more Anglicized in their ways, they moved to the Southern part of the colonial city, home to many of its Europeans and Anglo-Indians. A prayer hall that was more conveniently located relative to where Calcutta's Jews were residing in the 1930s was very

---

[7] Hacham Twena died in 1913 and there are many legends associated with his death. For more, see www.jewishcalcutta.in.

[8] The Northern part of the City is where the 'Natives' lived, the grey area was home to many minority communities and was the commercial area. It was centrally located. The Southern part was where the Europeans lived.

popular, especially for daily and Sabbath services. Though Anglicized, they remained very observant and would not drive on the Sabbath.

While the Jews of Calcutta embraced India as their home, they also supported Jewish charities and religious institutions in the Holy Land, especially the four cities—Jerusalem, Safed, Tiberias, and Hebron—with sacred historic associations for which charity boxes were set up in the synagogues.[9] The community also entertained Shleecheem (emissaries from Palestine), most of them Ashkenazi, who sought support. Bogus Shleecheem became a bone of contention across the Baghdadi diaspora, whose members also felt burdened by the constant stream of Palestinian visitors seeking monetary support.

The most notable and least recorded donation in the accounts of Calcutta Jewish history is that of Yosef Abraham Shalom of Calcutta (1833–1911) who built the first hospital in Jerusalem in 1900 and the Beit Hadas in Hebron in 1909. His family built a major yeshiva in Jerusalem (that still operates today!)—Porat Josef—near to the Kotel (the Western Wall; it is located on the steps coming down from the Jewish quarter to the Kotel), which bears his name. The family originally bought the site overlooking the Temple Mount with the intention of building a hospital. Ben Ish Chai of Baghdad, whose guidance was sought, thought a yeshiva should be endowed instead. The cornerstone for Porat Yosef was laid in 1914. Construction was delayed, however, because of World War I; the yeshiva was finally opened in 1923. Yosef Shalome lies buried in the large Jewish cemetery in Narkeldanga, which used to be on the outskirts of the city, but is now very much part of the sprawling metropolis.

[9] They also supported religious causes and holy sites in the countries from which they came.

Throughout the 19th and early 20th centuries the synagogues were the dominant cohesive force and served as places for religious worship as well as social gatherings and community meetings. It was at the synagogue that important events in the lives of community members were announced, among them weddings, bar mitzvahs, and *maftir*s (being called to offer the final Torah or *haftarah*—prophetic books—reading of the morning service). Registries of marriages and circumcisions were also maintained by several of the *hazan*s (cantors, prayer-leaders) and kept in the various synagogues. Synagogue politics, family rivalries, disputes over property, management and the naming of synagogues were commonplace. The synagogue management structures and investments demonstrated high levels of community organization, business acumen, philanthropy and knowledge of and outreach to Jews in other parts of the world, who were always welcomed at the synagogue and given refuge by Jewish community members in times of need.

The Synagogues

Neveh Shalome

When the first Jewish settlers came to Calcutta from Syria in the 1790s, they sought a place to pray and rented a hall from an Armenian.[10] Observant as they were, they soon purchased a large house that became Neveh Shalome. Dwek Cohen, the son-in-law of Shalome Cohen, the founder of the community, raised money through donations to pay

[10] The Armenians had come to Calcutta before the British did in the mid-18th century and were quite established by the time the first Jewish settler arrived.

for the synagogue. In 1826 the congregation gathered at the house and dedicated it as a place of worship. In 1837 there were 307 Jews in Calcutta.[11] Dwek Cohen introduced the system of auctioning privileges and religious services to augment the income from individual donations. In keeping with Middle Eastern tradition, all the synagogues maintained a separate women's section. In the three large synagogues, the women would sit upstairs; in the prayer halls they were separated from the men by a partition.

Neveh Shalome was demolished in 1884 to make way for the magnificent Magen David Synagogue that was built on the extended property of Neveh Shalome by the fabulously wealthy Sir David Ezra. The Ezra family had made its fortune in the export of indigo and silk to the Near East and opium on a large scale to Hong Kong. Sir David rapidly expanded the family business enterprise to many other lucrative concerns. Neveh Shalome was rebuilt in 1912 because a feud had developed when the Ezras changed the name of the new synagogue to Magen David. The new Neveh Shalome was built along the architectural lines of the old synagogue. It is typically Middle Eastern, with few Western architectural flourishes (Figs 1 and 1a).

The boys of the Talmud Torah, skilled readers one and all, were brought twice a day to make up the *minyan* (quorum of 10 adults) for the *shaharit* (morning) and the *arbitminha* (afternoon) services during the first 20 years of the 20th century. Ezra Arakie, the school's philanthropist, wished to inculcate a religious education through prayer services in the synagogue and thus the boys became skilled readers. The synagogue funds were also used to support poorer community members. It was estimated

[11] Musleah (1975, 32).

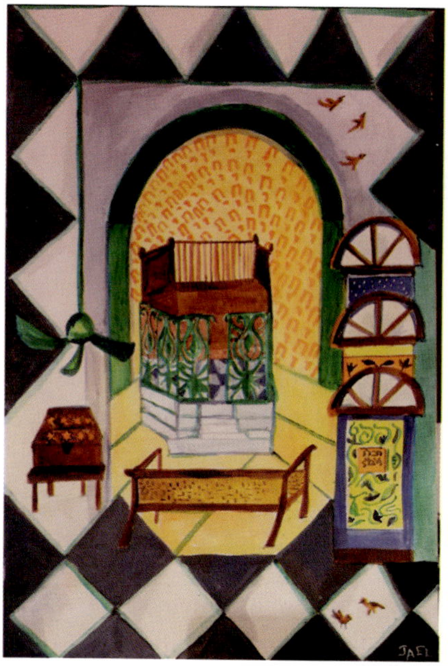

Fig. 1a. Author's impression of the interior of Neveh Shalome Synagogue

that in 1877 the expenditure of the two synagogues and public philanthropy exceeded 2,000 pounds sterling annually.[12] Thus from the establishment of the first synagogue, the city's Baghdadi Jews displayed the deeply religious and charitable impulses of the Baghdadi community.

Beth El

The Baghdadi Jews prospered through trade across Asia. In the mid-19th century trade between Iraq and India was almost entirely under Jewish control, though they did have to compete with Muslim Arabs and Persians as well as Europeans.[13] The community expanded rapidly as other Middle Eastern Jews flocked to Calcutta in search of opportunities. This made it necessary to build a larger synagogue. Also called Neveh Shalome during the lifetime of Dwek Cohen, Beth El was built by Joseph Ezra and Ezekiel Judah in 1855–56 (Fig. 2). The synagogue's entry hall displays an oil painting of one of the early members of the community dressed in Middle Eastern robes and turban, clearly

[12] Musleah (1975, 102).

[13] Musleah (1975, 48).

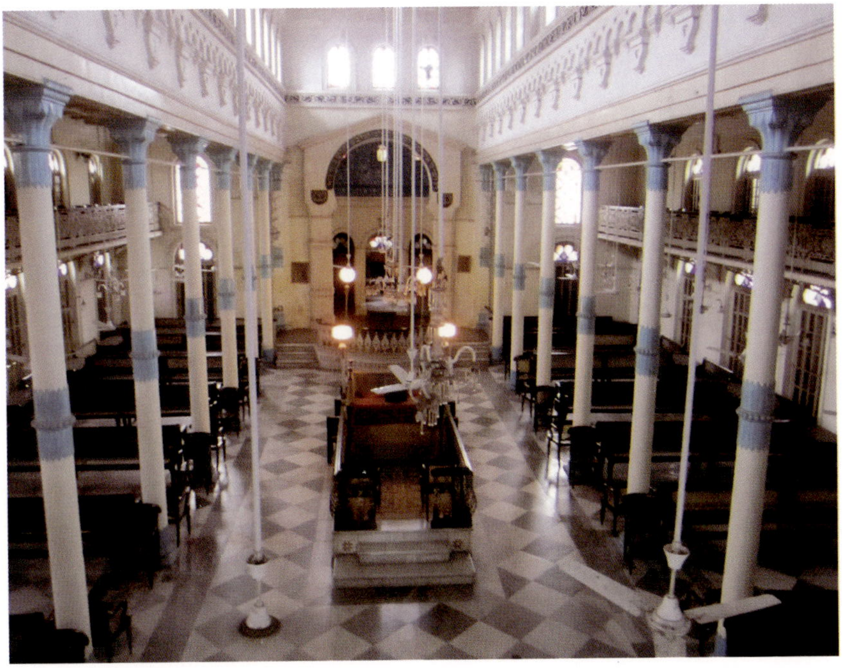

Fig. 2. Beth El Synagogue interior

denoting the strong Arab orientation of the early settlers. However, the openness to other influences is evident in the many motifs used in the synagogue, including the large blue, white, and red flowered patterned stained-glass window that towers above the entrance. As in the other two synagogues, Beth El contains old teak chairs upstairs and family benches downstairs, which still retain some of the intricately designed cane work that was woven by Chinese craftsmen.

The wine cellar in the synagogue basement holds many large clay amphorae and several brown and ochre patterned vats that hail from China. These indicate the congregants' underlying, wide trading relationships and networks. The Baghdadi community traded across Asia from Basra to Shanghai and along the way, in all the major port cities, Baghdadi Jews lived and worked to extend these family networks. Kosher red wine was made locally in Calcutta until the early 1970s when Isaac Agha Baba passed away in his 80s. By then he was the only person who knew how to make the wine and ensure that it was Kosher. The 'sacred wine' was stored and sold to Jewish community members for ritual purposes. Not just Kosher wine was made at Beth El; there is a large clay oven, a tandoor, in the synagogue's courtyard where Matzah was made. The wheat was checked from the time it was growing in the field until it was ground into flour. The making of Matzah was supervised by a non-profit Matzah Board made up of two members of each of the three major synagogues. A *mikvah* (ritual bath) was also built in the courtyard that was renovated during the 1940s to be more modern, with amenities like running water. The community was influenced by the many cultures around it, European and Chinese, for example, which is evident in the style and furnishings that they selected for the synagogue.

Magen David

Sir David Ezra built the Magen David Synagogue in 1884 in memory of his father, Elia Ezra. It was built by the British firm Mackintosh Burn and Co and designed by their architect Ormond in the Italian Renaissance style (Fig. 3). It was modeled after the old Telegraph office and other public buildings of the period.[14] It is referred to locally as *Lal Girja* (Red Church) as its façade is prominently red brick with some grey elements and it has a steeple, clock face, and bells. As the Calcutta Jews looked for

[14] Musleah (1975, 27).

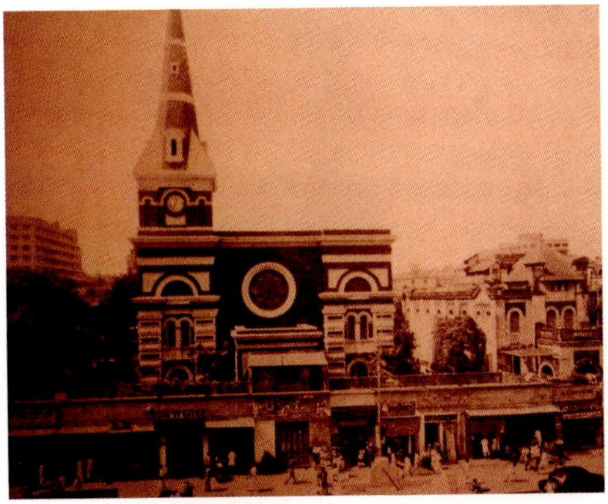

Fig. 3. Magen David Synagogue exterior

guidance to Baghdad in religious matters, they asked whether it would be *halachic* (consistent with rabbinic law) for the synagogue to have a steeple and were told that it did not go against Jewish law to have one, as long as it was higher than the others around it. The steeple is 142 feet high. A clock placed 64 feet high, imported from London, graces the fourth level of the steeple. It was then the largest of all public clocks in public spaces in Calcutta. Clearly it seemed as if the synagogue donors were both influenced by and competing with the many cathedrals and churches in the city, as they sought to make their mark on its landscape and culture.

Magen David boasts soaring ceilings, sturdy pinkish-hued Mirzapur stone pillars with their pediments imported from London, and a large round stained-glass window opposite the sanctuary (Fig. 4). There was an elaborate chandelier that burned olive oil in the middle of the large hall atop the *Tevah* (pulpit); electricity was installed in 1902. In 1918 the chandelier was a 'cut-glass thirty light electrolier' that had been in the Grand Opera House in Calcutta. It was gifted to the synagogue by E.M.D Cohen, a benefactor. High blue and white floral decorated arches with psalms in Hebrew lettering are indeed imposing. The ornate apse-like *heikhal* has a floor of Castilian

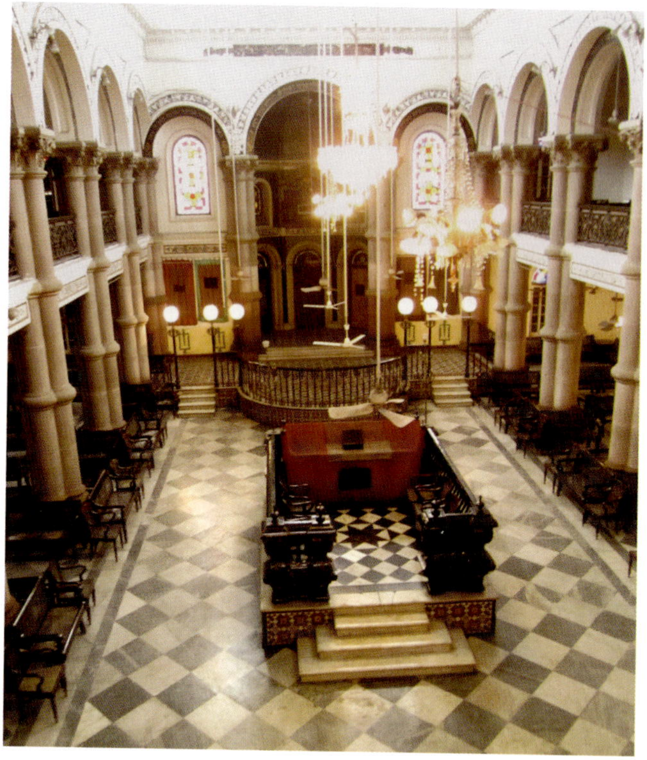

Fig. 4. Magen David Synagogue interior

tiles created by Manton Holland and Company of London (Figs 5 and 5a).The star-studded cobalt blue dome, a focal point in the house of worship, is adorned with Jewish mystical symbols.

Embedded as they are in the lifestyle of colonial Calcutta, Western architectural materials and decorations reveal the transformation of the Arab Jewish identity of the community to that of an Anglo-Jewish community. This is also clearly seen in the photographs of the founders that grace the staircase. They are dressed in Western style and differ

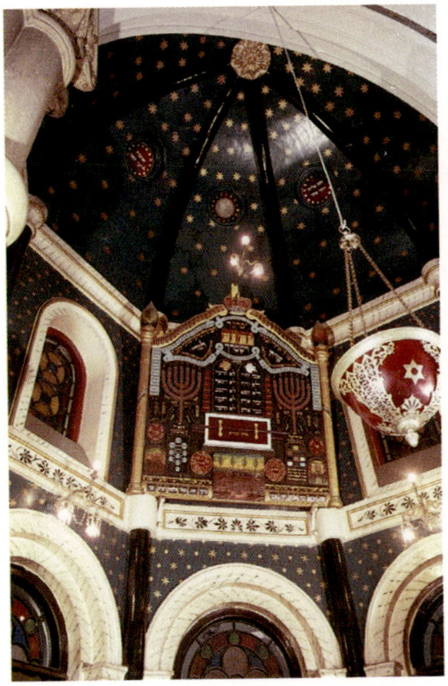

Fig. 5. Detail of the dome and arches in Magen David Synagogue

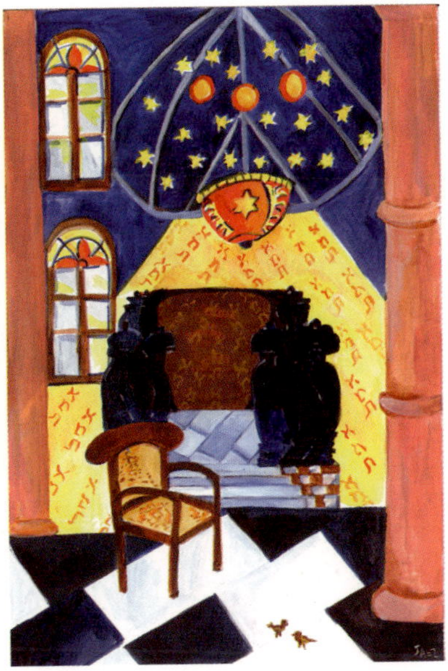

Fig. 5a. Author's impression of the interior of Magen David Synagogue

from the founder portrait at Beth El. Only the portrait of E.M.D. Cohen, who served as *hazan* of both Neveh Shalome and Magen David for 50 years, portrays him still in quasi-Middle Eastern dress.[15] A wealthy landowner, E.M.D. Cohen established the important printing press that published the *Paerah*, which was a very popular paper in the Jewish community. It was referred to as *The Jewish Gazette* and was known the world over, and was frequently quoted by the Jewish Press in Europe. The *Paerah* contained a weekly calendar with announcements of births, circumcisions and marriages as well as trade advertisements of Jewish

[15] He was also the Honorary Secretary of the Jewish Girls School and the Magen David Synagogue.

merchants and their arrival and departure dates to and from Calcutta and other cities in India and beyond. Its editorials, which commented on local Jewish news as well as items related to world Jewry, were wide-ranging, with topics of interest to the Calcutta community.

There were always some European Jews in Calcutta who engaged with the Calcutta community, and the city's Jews remained solicitous and hospitable to other Jews. For example, E.M.D. Cohen, who was deeply concerned about the religious needs of Jewish soldiers during World War I, arranged for about 70 boys from 24 units throughout India to spend the High Holidays in the traditional manner by writing to the Battalion, Brigade, and Divisional Commanding officers. He also communicated with the authorities regarding Jewish soldiers in matters such as the sick and wounded and, in cases of death, burial.[16] The numbers of such soldiers grew rapidly during World War II, when many British and American soldiers were stationed in Calcutta. Jews also fled to Calcutta from Burma and Southeast Asia. All were welcomed at the Synagogue and financial assistance and employment were afforded to them whenever possible. The Jews of Calcutta also gave refuge to European Jews fleeing the Holocaust.

The Reverend David Seligson, one of the first American chaplains to volunteer overseas during World War II, introduced the Young People's Congregation at the Beth El Synagogue. After services he would meet with the youth to discuss the prayers in English in a bid to deepen their Jewish learning. Many of the young servicemen visited Jewish homes and some married women from the community. These 'GI brides' were among the first to emigrate to the US, Canada, and England in the 1940s.

---

16 Musleah (1975, 97).

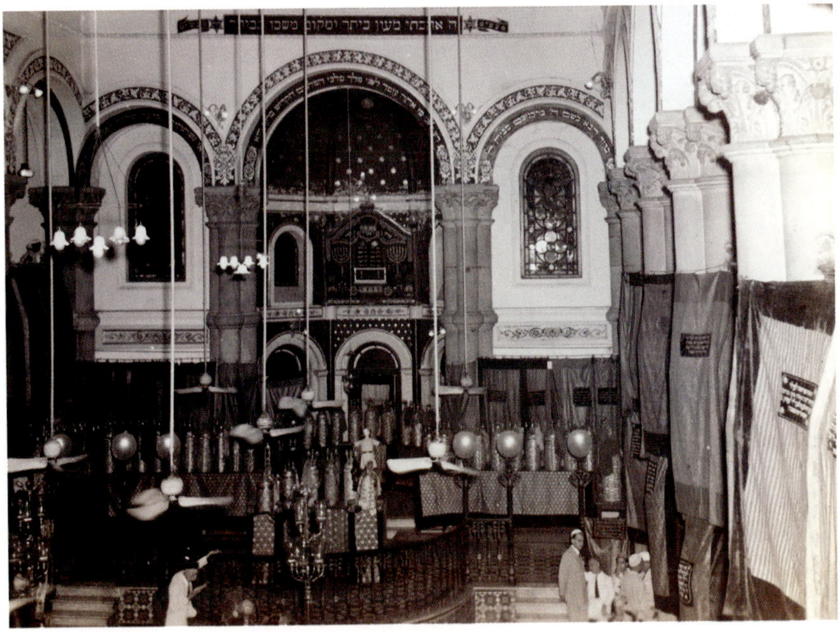

Fig. 6. Magen David sanctuary with its Torah scrolls

Calcutta's Jewish community was so wealthy that at one time each synagogue housed dozens of *sifrei Torah* (Torah scrolls) gifted by families. By the 1930s the Neveh Shalome had about 50, the Beth El had over 90, the Magen David over 80 and the two prayer halls between them had about 15 (Fig. 6).[17] Each scroll was written on parchment by dedicated scribes in Baghdad. The parchment was wrapped around a pair of spindles and encased in a *tik* (a large wood container embellished with silver that is elaborately patterned; each of these cases weighs between 10 and 15 kgs). The scrolls were taken out and read from on every Sabbath, Monday and Thursday, and displayed during the Simhat

[17] Musleah (1975, 199).

Torah Festival. Today only four old *sifrei Torah* remain in Calcutta, two of which are unfortunately spoiled by dampness.[18]

There were also elaborate *parokhot* (Holy Ark curtains or decorative hangings) gifted in memory of family members and made of expensive cashmere wool, velvet or silk with the name and blessing embossed in gold zari threads in a rectangular inset. Not only do the *sifrei Torah* and rich *parokhot* denote the enormous wealth of the community, they illustrate how this diaspora community fashioned ritual and religious objects with local jewelry, weaving, and embroidery traditions. Today these beautiful ritual items are in Baghdadi synagogues across the world and several *sifrei Torah* are in the Israel Museum in Jerusalem.

The Emigration from the City

Calcutta's synagogues are no longer used for services because of the emigration of the Jewish population. From a community of around 4,500 or so in the mid-20th century it had dwindled to about 700 or so people by the 1970s. There were several reasons for their emigration. The British were leaving India and the Baghdadi Jews who had migrated here during the Raj were unsure of their future. They had witnessed the terrible rioting that had rocked Bengal before and after Partition. Prime Minister Nehru was articulating a Socialist vision for the nation and the wealthier Jews were uncertain of their financial prospects. Meanwhile, the British offered citizenship to Indians and many, including some Jews, emigrated to Britain. Once the wealthier members of the community

---

[18] When the Synagogue was rededicated in 2018 a new Torah scroll was purchased in Israel to be housed in it.

had left, the middle-class and poorer Jews who were employed in Jewish businesses emigrated too.

At the global level, the Holocaust and Anti-Semitism in Europe, that had brought Jewish refugees to Calcutta, and the Jews fleeing persecution in Arab lands after the formation of Israel, also had an impact on the psyche of the Calcutta Jews. It made them more uncertain of their future in a changing India. Baghdadi Jews from Burma, who were often relatives of Calcutta Jews, obtained refugee status to emigrate to the United States. Some younger and more idealistic members of the community made *aliyah* to Israel as did some of the poorer community members who thought they would have a better future there. Many immigrated to Australia, Canada and the USA. As the community was small and tight-knit, family members emigrated with their kin. A fragment of the community remained. By the 1970s among the community of barely 700 remaining in the city were many elderly Jews, who did not want to start their lives anew in unknown places. Thus, though the Jewish community had always been welcomed in India and never faced any Anti-Semitism, they left India for political, economic, and familial reasons.

Although the synagogues still functioned as long as a *minyan* could be formed, the last wedding held in Magen David was in the early 1980s.[19] Today services are held when Jewish visitors from abroad attend the synagogue for special occasions, or when they visit India to pray in synagogues across the country as part of Jewish heritage tours. The Calcutta Jews were so attached to their synagogues that there was a plan to transport Magen David brick-by-brick to Jerusalem. Calcutta Jews

---

[19] The first wedding took place at the Neveh Shalome in 1815 when Moses Dwek married Luna, Shalome Cohen's eldest daughter.

living abroad had met with Teddy Kolek, then Mayor of Jerusalem, to find a suitable site in which to locate it. They felt that it was a shame that the synagogue was no longer being used as a place of worship and wanted to see it filled with prayer and devotion again. However, the few Jews left in Calcutta opposed this plan and registered the Magen David with the Archaeological Survey of India (ASI) to ensure that it could never be moved. Today both the Magen David and the Beth El synagogues are under the aegis of the ASI.

Conclusion

Calcutta's synagogues tell a complex story of the community—their origins and Judeo-Arab orientation, their rapid rise, economic success and Anglicized orientation in the late 19th and early 20th centuries, and their steep decline in number that occurred in the 1940s/50s as a result of tumultuous global and national events. The synagogues speak to the fundamentally religious nature of the members of the community, the wealth they amassed, their wide trading network, and their on-going understanding, engagement, and involvement in matters pertaining to the larger Jewish world. The synagogues also bear testimony to their very philanthropic gestures that took care of the poorer and otherwise disadvantaged members of the Jewish community in Calcutta and in the wider Jewish world. The synagogue structures and furnishings also track the cultural shift of the Baghdadi Jews of the Middle East from their Judeo-Arabic to their Anglo-Judaic identity.

The synagogues also tell us about the good relationships their congregants enjoyed with the many communities around them and shows how they adapted some of these other communities' material and cultural traditions. The Baghdadi Jews were very much an integral part of all aspects of life in the city and were accepted with open arms by both colonial and Indian rulers. The rededication of Magen David in 2018 drew in Baghdadi Jews from many parts of the world for the celebration, who were deeply moved when the predominantly Muslim girls of the Jewish Girls School sang Hebrew songs and hymns at this auspicious event.

The three synagogues today are significant heritage sites and are visited by the descendants of Calcutta Jews seeking to learn more of their past, and by both Indian and foreign tourists. As more media attention has been focused on the Jewish community in Calcutta, people of Calcutta also visit the synagogues. They are proud of this aspect of the city's history as they represent a material manifestation of Calcutta's multicultural and multireligious past. The synagogues stand testimony to Calcutta's Jewish past and India's acceptance of the Jewish community. As anti-Semitism continues to rear its ugly head around the world, the three remaining synagogues stand witness to how the city and indeed the nation have been enriched by the Jewish presence.

Selected Bibliography

Mukerjee, Mala, and Jael Silliman. *Where Gods Reside: Sacred Places of Kolkata*. New Delhi: Niyogi Books, 2018.

Musleah, Rabbi Ezekiel N. *On the Banks of the Ganga: The Sojourn of Jews in Calcutta*. North Quincy, Massachusetts: The Christopher Publishing House, 1975.

Silliman, J. *Jewish Portraits, Indian Frames: Women's Narratives from a Diaspora of Hope*. Calcutta: Seagull Press, 1999.

www.recallingjewishcalcutta.in

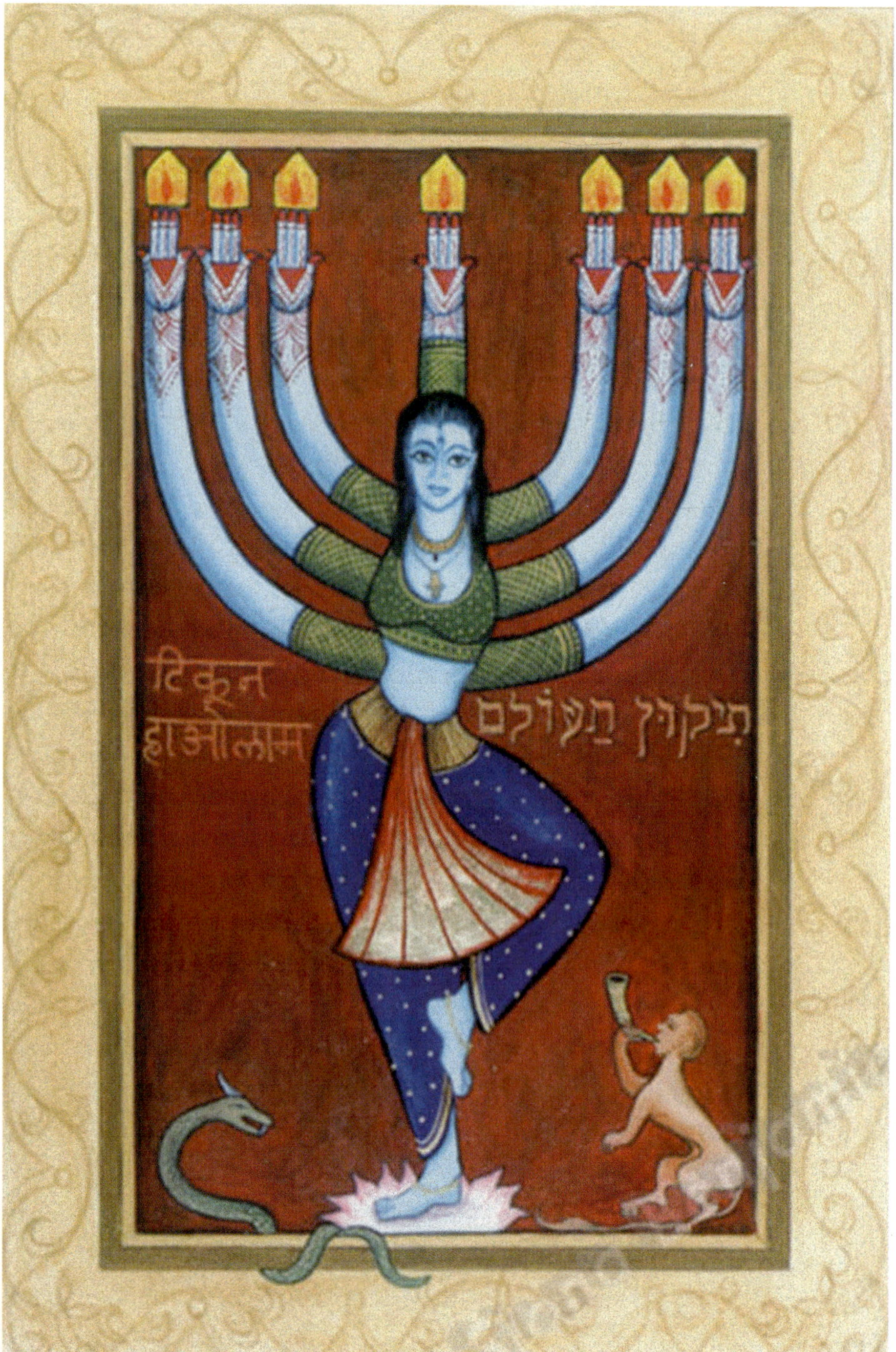

Fig. 21. Finding Home #46, Tikkun ha-Olam, Siona Benjamin, 2000

CHAPTER FOUR

How I Gradually Turned Blue and Other Stories I Remember Growing up Jewish in India

Siona Benjamin

My parents (and I) lived in what everyone called the Bollywood suburb of Bombay (now known as Mumbai), a bustling city on the west coast of India. My mother, a Bene Israel Jew from Pune (a small city near Bombay) ran a private Montessori school for 20 years and drew on mostly the children of glitzy movie stars (Bombay being the Mecca of the movie-making industry in South Asia). So quite often I had to sit through three-hour-long Bollywood movies, which—to sum up quickly—were mostly Indian versions of Rambo with the spice of some song and dance thrown in. One minute the hero was beating up the villain (whose side kick almost always was this British actor whom he called Anthony and who incidentally never said a word but just carried out the treacherous orders of the villain) and the other minute the hero would be prancing around in the middle of corn fields belting out a song with a doe-eyed damsel dressed in chiffons.

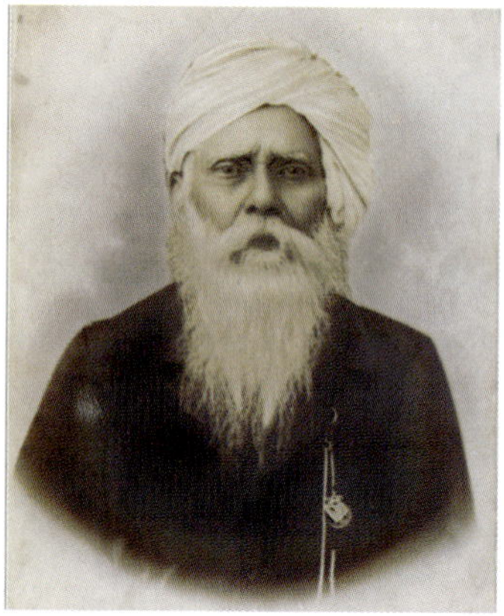

Fig. 1. Portrait of Siona Benjamin's great-great grandfather, Khan Bahadur Joseph David (Borgawker)

My parents were staunchly Jewish and proud of it (especially since India was one of the only countries where there was no anti-Semitism). So they carried out rituals and observed Jewish festivals with great fervor, and before what seemed like the exodus of the Jews from India to Israel mostly in the 1950s, 60s, and 70s, I remember preparations for the Eliyahu HaNavi prayer (invoking the prophet either to help or in thanksgiving)—recited at circumcision and baby girl-naming ceremonies, before engagements and weddings, and during certain holidays—and the Malida service, the Sabbath and large pots of Jewish halwa (sweets) made out of coconut milk for the Rosh Hashanah and Yom Kippur festivals (Figs 1, 2, 3, 4, 4a, 5, 6, and 6a).[1]

Like every group, Indian Jews have unique stories, rituals and authentic melodies in their prayers. Centuries of living in India made them blend together different influences from their surroundings. When someone asks me—especially here in America—why we Indian Jews eat

[1] The ubiquitous Eliyahu HaNavi prayer is also recited typically when a vow is made—or as a thanksgiving prayer when a vow has been fulfilled—at *Tu B'Shvat* (festival of the first fruits; around mid-February), and at the end of the festival of *Sukkot*, when fruits that have been hanging in the *sukkah* (a booth or temporary hut) are removed, and also at the end of the *Simhat Torah* ('Rejoicing the Torah') service that follows *Sukkot*. The prayer is often recited in the community at the time of dedicating or rededicating a synagogue, or in the family when something unusual and good has transpired, such as a job promotion. (ed.)

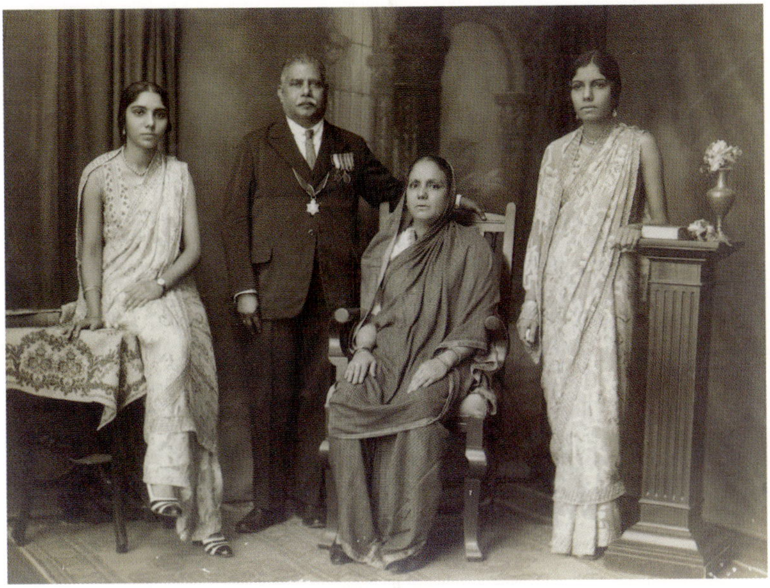

Fig. 2. Siona Benjamin's great-grand parents—Mordecai (Borgawker), his wife Simha, and their daughters Ruth and Sheba

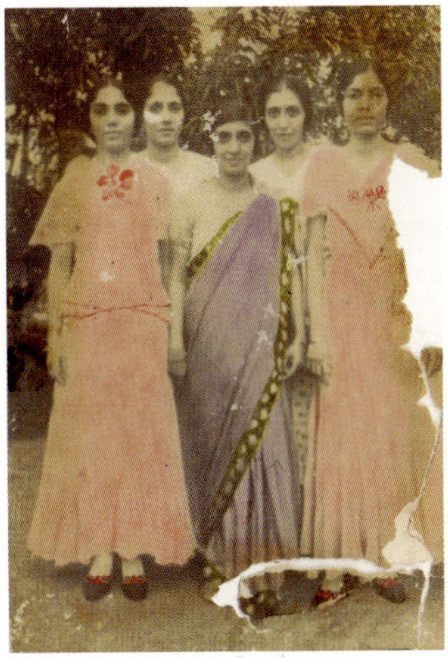

Fig. 3. Grandmother Elizabeth David Joseph with her 2 sisters-in-law Ruth and Sheba (beside her) and other members of the family behind them

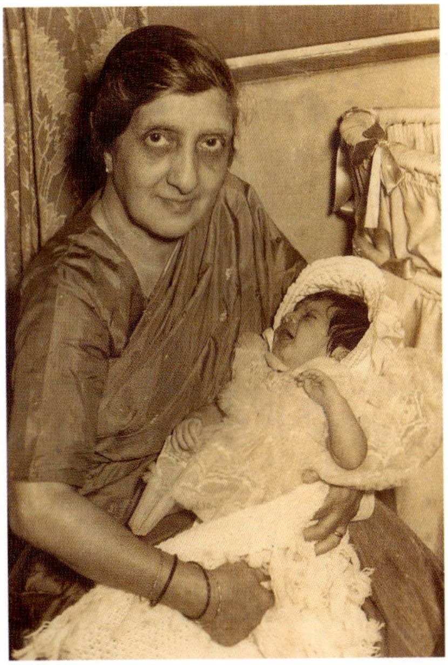

Fig. 4. Grandmother Elizabeth at Siona Benjamin's naming ceremony

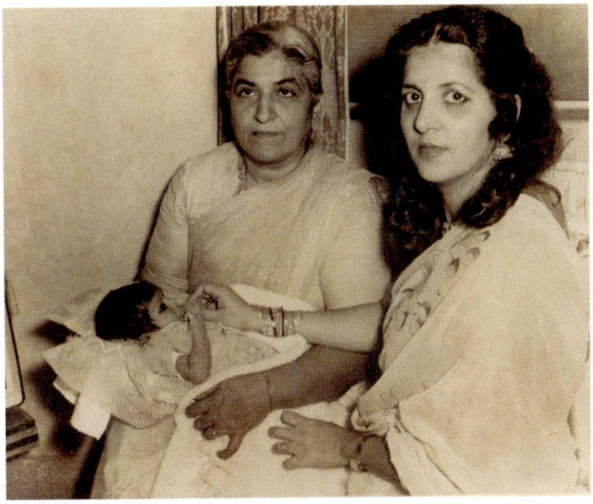

Fig. 4a. Grandmother Rebecca with mother Sophie and baby Siona

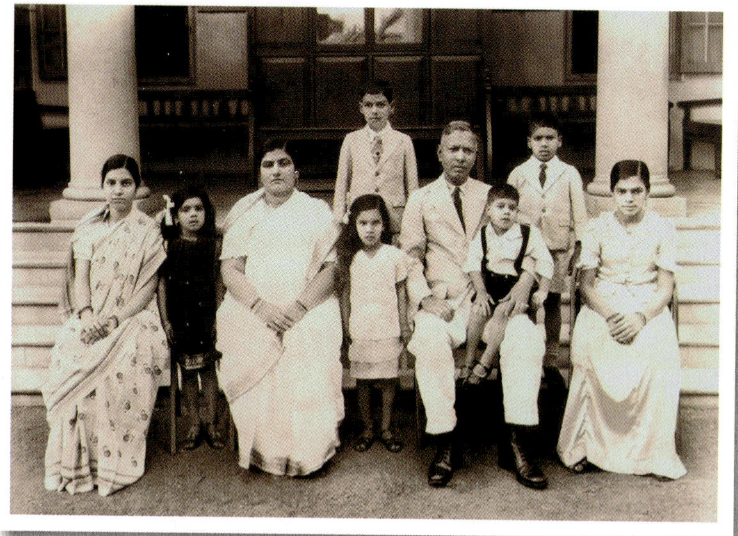

Fig. 5. Benjamin Abraham Kasookar (Siona Benjamin's paternal grandfather) with his family
Front row, left to right: Erusha Isaac; Diana Benjamin, Siona's father's sister; Rebecca Benjamin (paternal grandmother), Rosy Isaac; Benjamin Kasooker (paternal grandfather); Abraham Isaac, Siona's grand uncle; and Shoshanna, Siona's father's eldest sister
Back row, left to right: Judah Benjamin (Siona's father as a young boy) and his brotherJoseph Benjamin

Indian food or why we have a henna ceremony for our weddings, or why Indian Jews speak Marathi and not Yiddish, I remind them that Jews in every part of the world have been influenced by their own surroundings. So why can't Indian Jews make spicy curries or Indian Jewish brides have henna decoration on their hands?!

The Eliyahu HaNavi prayer is unique to the Indian Jews, particularly to the Bene Israel Jews from the Konkan coast of West India (Fig.7). I recall going with my parents, grandmother and all my family to the small towns of Alibag, Revdanda, and Khandala (south of Bombay city in the Konkan region) where my father's

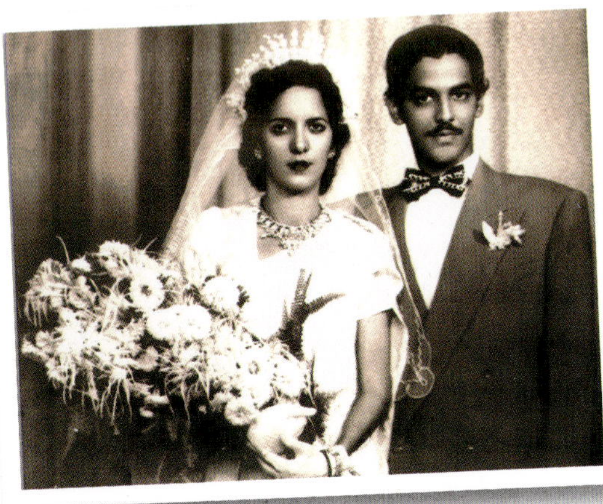

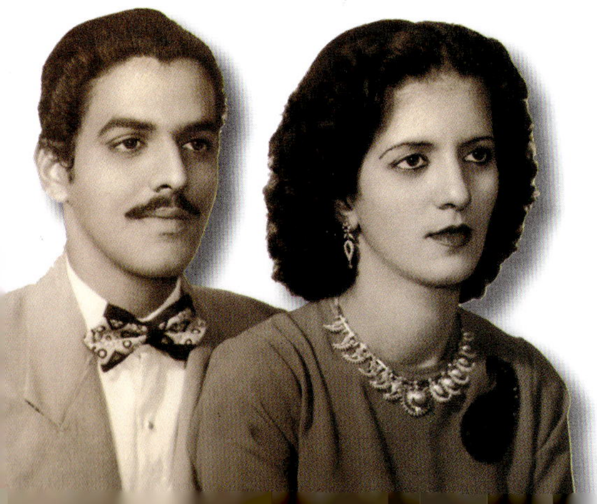

Fig. 6. Siona's parents Judah and Sophie's wedding portrait
Fig. 6a. Siona's parents in the 1950s

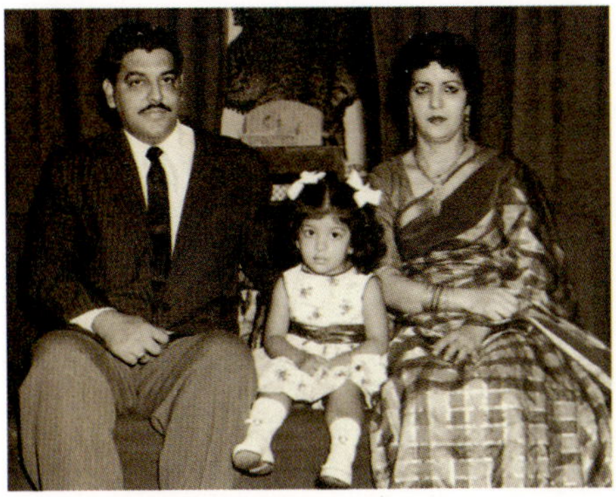

Fig. 7. Siona Benjamin with her parents in their Bombay home, 1963

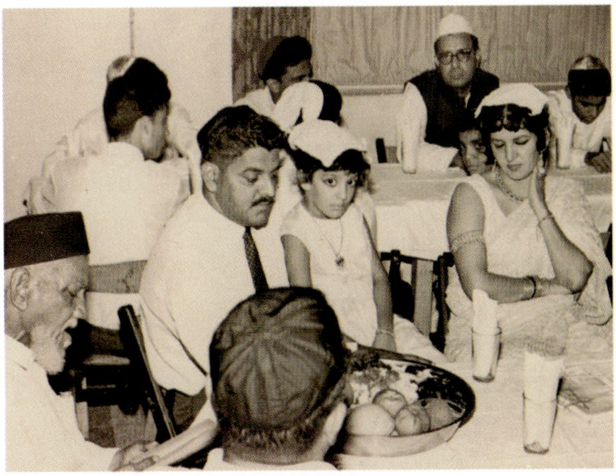

Fig. 8. Siona Benjamin and her parents at an Eliyahu HaNavi *Malida* prayer meeting

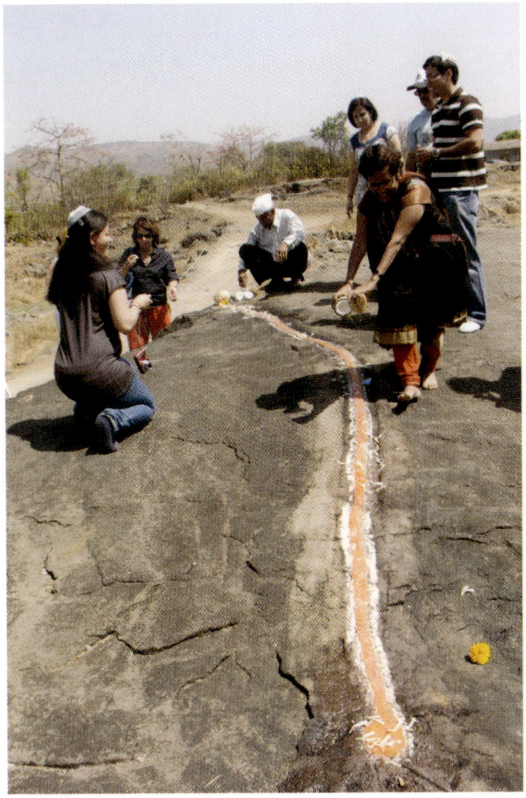

Fig 9. The tracks of the Prophet Elijah's chariot on the Elijah Rock at Khandala

family owned some farm land (Fig. 8). There the Elijah Rock is believed, in the Bene Israel tradition, to be the location where Elijah the Prophet (Eliyahu HaNavi) left to go up to heaven. I was taught to believe that the marks on this rock were the marks of the prophet's chariot wheels just before he ascended. It is still considered sacred by all Bene Israel Jews and people come from far and wide to worship at this place (Figs 9 and 9a).

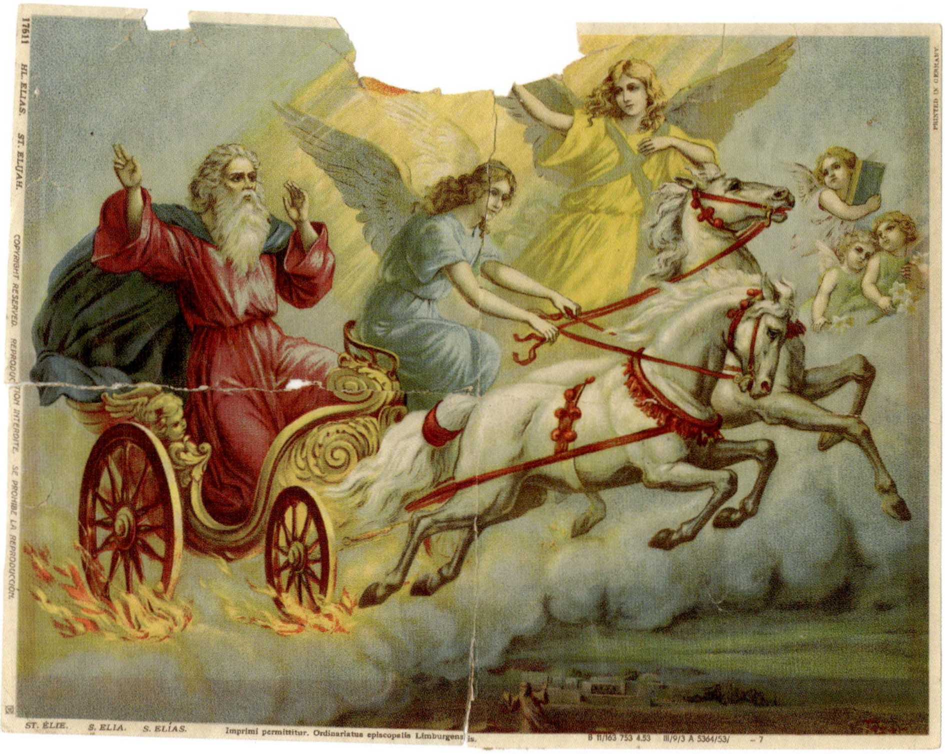

Fig. 9a. Picture of Eliyahu HaNavi from Siona's grandmother's home

My family would also congregate and often conduct prayers to the prophet and have a *Malida* ceremony. *Malida* particularly linked to the traditions of my Bene Israel community and was special to me and to all of my family. I still recall the fragrant smell of the *Malida* platter, made from flattened sweetened rice and dried fruits. As the prayers advanced there were special rituals, like the smelling of cloves that were part of the ceremony (Figs 10 and 11). Cloves are the aromatic flower buds of a tree in the family *Myrtaceae*, *Syzygium aromaticum*. They are warm and spicy to smell and I remember their fragrance so very distinctly.

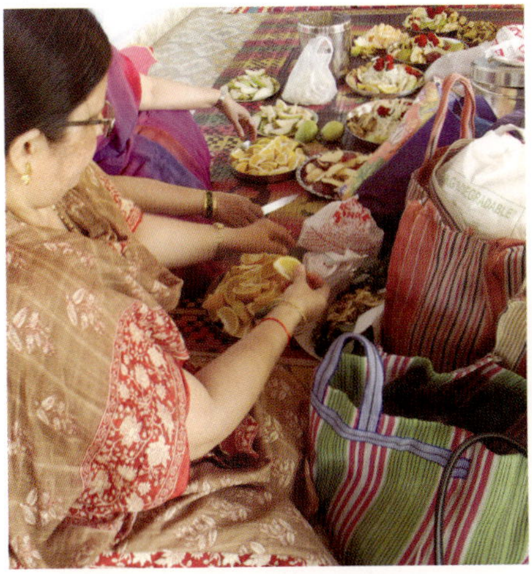

Fig. 10. Women preparing *Malida* platters

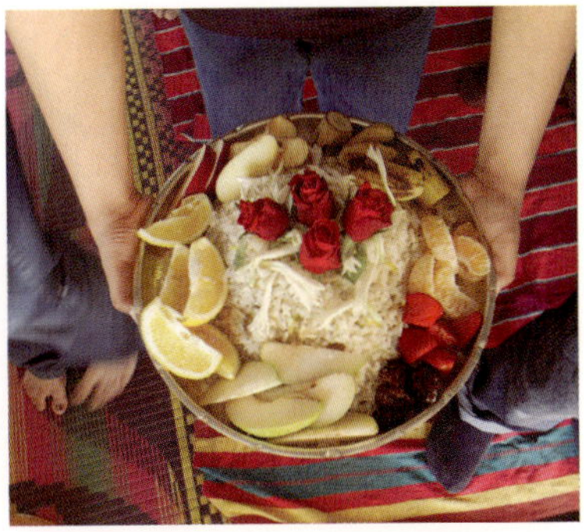

Fig. 11. A *Malida* platter of sweet flattened rice, fruits and flowers

Instead of the spice box for *Havdalah* (the ceremony to mark the end of the Sabbath), with a numerous blend of spices that I have sometimes experienced in Jewish homes in the US, Indian Jews just used cloves—in fact, one single large clove was handed to each participant in the prayer and after the prayer was recited. I recall and I still associate the smell of cloves with my childhood. Coconuts and dates were also part of the *Malida* platter as they are fruits of the desert, making us remember the land of Israel. Other fruits also decorated the platter and after the prayers the womenfolk in my family would serve us this delicious *Malida*.[2]

I also recall an old synagogue in this area and very near my grandmother's family farm. There were several synagogues in the Konkan area south of Bombay, but the Revdanda Synagogue was the one I recall

[2] '*Malida*' is apparently a borrowing from Farsi; the ceremony is also drawn from the Parsi festive meal of *Jashan*, and the term means 'peace offering'. (ed.)

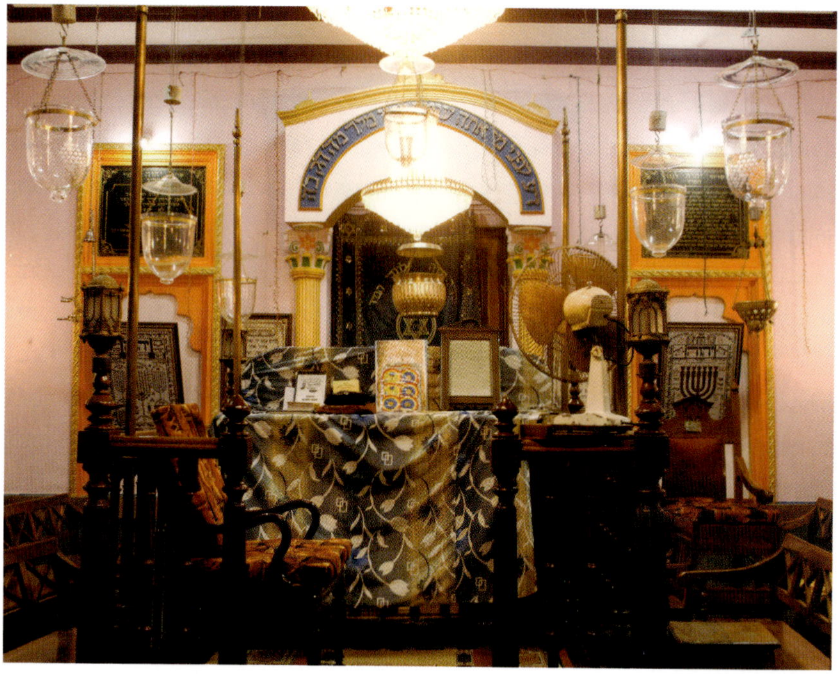

Fig. 12. Revdanda Synagogue

the most. Always brightly painted, it stood out in the Indian landscape with its bright pink gates with menorah symbols on them. Inside, the synagogue was colorful, too, with velvet curtains that covered the Torah Ark. Wooden benches arranged in a semi-circle surrounded the central *bimah (tevah)* where the *hazan* reciting the prayers would be facing the Torah Ark. Later, when I came to live in America, I remember finding it different where the congregation in Ashkenazi synagogues faced the Torah ark but the person at the *bimah* had his back to the Ark. Indian synagogues are all like theaters in the round and people sat around the centrally located *bimah*.

Other little memories are so unforgettable, like the large Bene Israeli style mezuzah at the door of our home; my father kissing it when he left to go to work and when he entered our home upon his return (Fig. 13). My mother lighting the shabbat lamp every Friday; she made her shabbat lamp in a glass bowl with oil and water, the oil floating on top of the bowl and the wick staying lit almost all night long! My mother taught me some prayers, particularly the *shema*, which I recited every night before falling asleep. Later on, this was important to share with my daughter and she had her Indian-Jewish Bat Mitzvah inspired by her grandmother's stories and her visits to Jewish India. Yet another amazing full circle achieved! I designed a tree of life for my daughter's Bat Mitzvah *tallit* (prayer shawl), my mother got it embroidered in India and she then hand sewed 613 red beads on it—their number symbolizing the 613 *mitzvot* (commandments, but the term comes to refer to good deeds, as well) in the Torah and their color symbolizing pomegranate seeds with their connotation of fertility and thus of good fortune—as a special blessing for her granddaughter. These little memories are the inspiration for, and the basis of, my version of a prayer that I offer through my art-making.

My schooling…well, I started off in a private Catholic convent school run by British, Swedish, and Indian nuns and I ended up doing my high school in a Zoroastrian (Parsi) school. These schools somewhat remind me now of parts of the Harry Potter movie…no, we did not have changing stairs and flying brooms, but we did have thick stone walls and nuns in white who seemed to glide down the stairs in a very Harry Potterish

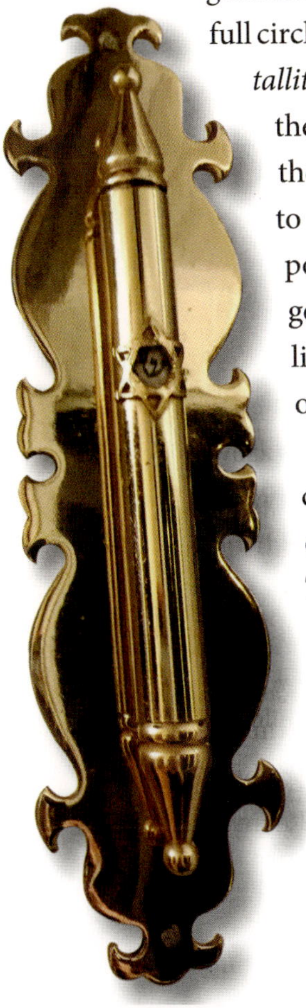

Fig. 13. Indian mezuzah

way. So, to give you a snapshot, Sister John of the Cross and Sister Mary Magdeline would conduct the daily Hail Mary prayers and then we stood in pinafored rows in our separate houses to be taken to gym or to our respective classes. I belonged to the Green House, otherwise known at the House of Scott—Sir Walter Scott that is—other houses were: Red, which was Shakespeare; Blue was Tennyson, and Yellow, Dickens. The high school was just as formidable—the same thick stone walls (which, by the way did little to stop the interaction with the boys' school next door, which was run by the priests), and the large open fields that looked onto the Arabian Sea. So here we were, girls with names as diverse as Radhika Verma, Zehra Mahmood, Kawaljeet Singh, Yevonne Aptekar and Miriam Abraham (the other two Jewish girls in the class) and others like my friends Lorraine DeSouza, Annabel Fernandez, Mohini Char and Nuzhath Iraqi.

My two best friends in school—and I have remained close friends with them throughout these many years—were Sunita Pinto, from a Portuguese Christian family and Tina Tejani, who is from a Muslim family; in high school, I added a third best friend, Varsha Desai, who is Hindu. I remember feeling no differences between our families and in our friendships. I ate and spent time in their homes and we celebrated all our respective festivals together. I remember getting plates of sweets made in our Muslim friends' homes and sending platters of Jewish coconut milk halwa to all these friends during Rosh Hashanah. I remember receiving plates of almond marzipan and Christmas plum cake from our Christian friends and sending good wishes and Jewish recipes back to these families during Passover and other Jewish festivals.

My mother ran a private primary school for over 20 years and I watched it grow into a bigger business through my childhood. My

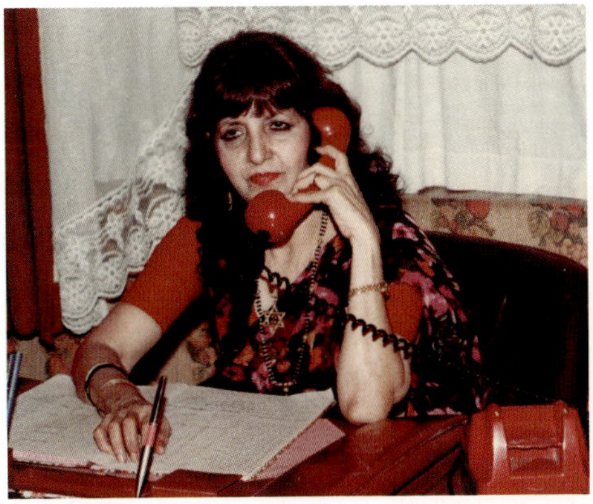

Figure 14. Sophie Benjamin in her Sofia school. She owned a kindergarten through primary school for 20 years (1970 to 1991) in Mumbai

parents proudly owned a 'bungalow'—a one-story house—and as my mother's school grew, I remember them adding two more floors to our home to accommodate the growing needs of her school. My mother always dressed well, ready to greet her school kids and parents and executing the duties of being the proprietress of the school all day long (Fig. 14). So she did not have time to cook and clean like some other mothers I knew. Only during the Jewish festivals did she don her apron and then took charge of stirring the coconut milk halva pot for hours on end! The halwa was poured out into flat plates and decorated with an array of dried fruits! On cooling, the halwa was ready to be sliced and arranged in decorative plates to be sent to our friends, neighbors and relatives. I remember this flurry of activity during the Jewish festival time with great fondness.

We had servants who cooked and cleaned and even a driver who fetched and ferried me to school and back. This driver doubled sometimes as a cook, when my parents had parties and they sure did love to have them! Lack of education in countries like India causes a class system that feeds on itself. My American friends have sometimes been suspicious of the fact that Indians grew up with servants who cooked and cleaned for

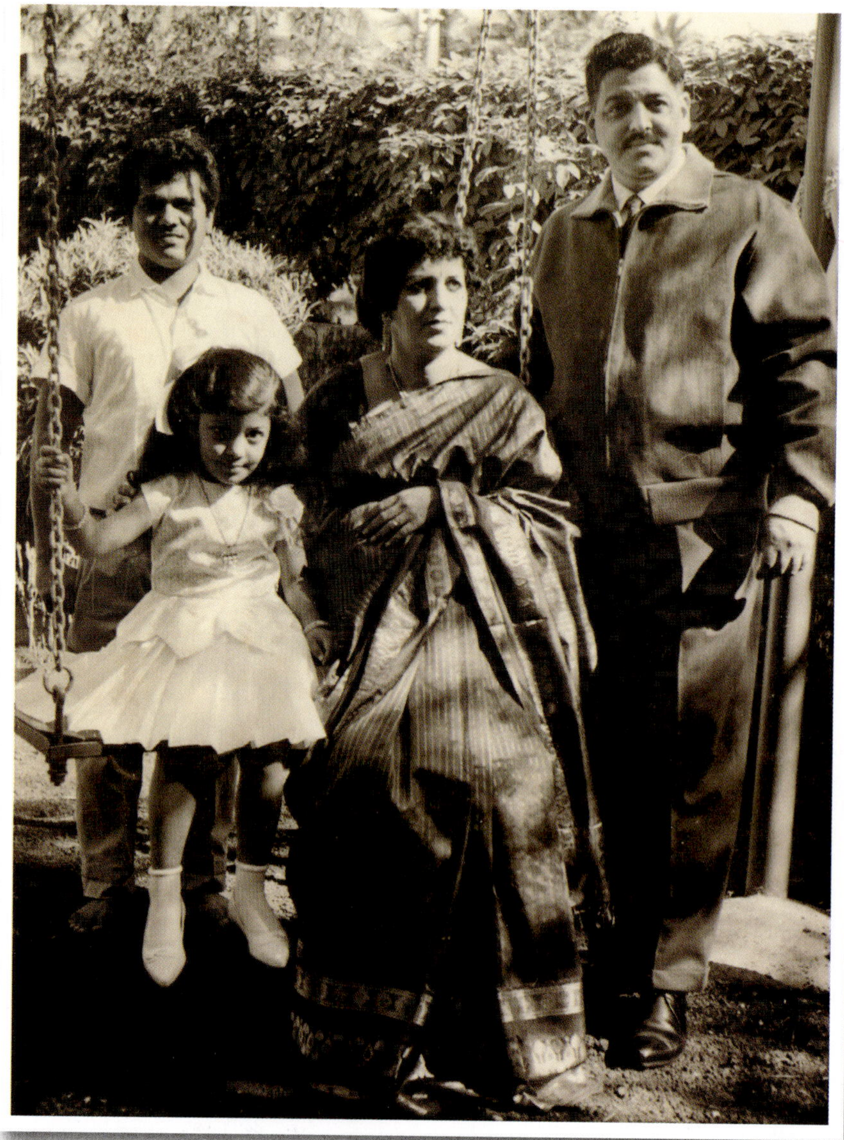

Fig. 15. Raghu with Siona Benjamin and her parents

us. It is easy to surmise that these people were somewhat like slaves and were used and abused. There is, of course, some truth in this, as indeed the lack of resources makes people poorer and so lack opportunities in a country of well over a billion people. But is this not a problem many countries face even today? Race is still an issue here in America too and it is therefore inappropriate to point fingers at others.

Raghu came from South India at a very young age, barely educated and looking for work in the big city of Mumbai. He got a job at my home as he was an amazing cook and later also became the driver of the busses for my mother's private school. This Hindu, south Indian man became part of our family. Raghu stayed with and worked for my family for over 55 years and when my father passed away, he looked after my mother just like a son would. My parents cared for him like a family member and even though he was free to leave this job at any time, he chose to be a part of my family for decades. My mother later on brought him to America to visit me in my home a few times, and he was in great wonder at being able to travel across the world (Fig. 15).

This aspect of my childhood was deeply etched into my being. Raghu was family, not a servant, although technically he was, but then he must have felt like he was our family to have stayed with us for so long. Later, when he fell ill, my mother cared for him and made sure that he got the best possible medical treatment. When Raghu passed away, I mourned like I had lost a very precious family member. I did not see Raghu as anything else but that.

I recall so vividly how all kinds of people came over to my parents' home. The diversity in our house during those times resonates with me till today, making me bring that essence into my work. My parents had Muslim, Hindu, Parsi, Buddhist, and Christian (as well as Jewish)

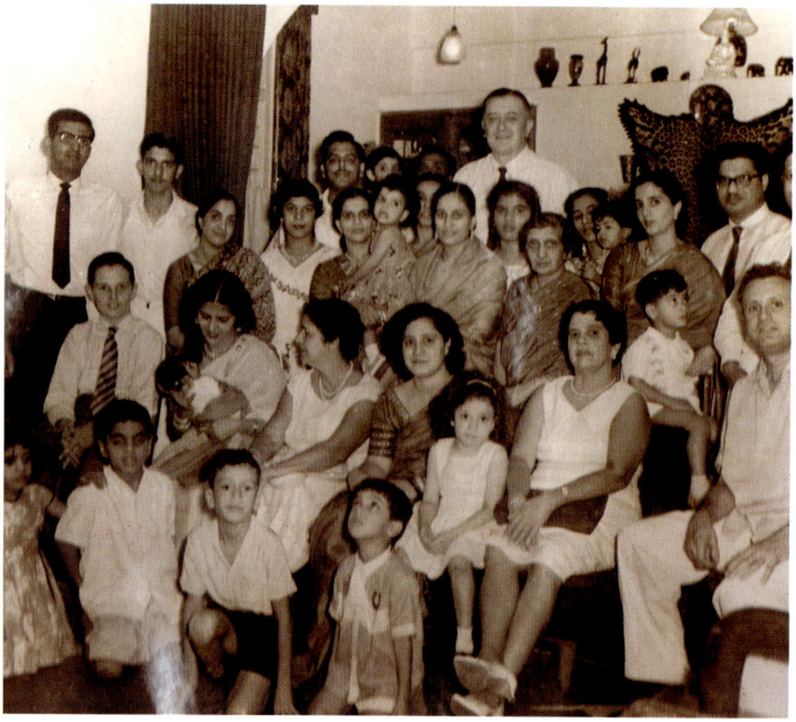

Fig. 16. Diversity at Siona's baby naming ceremony

friends! Not once was I made to feel that any of them were any different or that I had to treat them in a different way (Figs 16 and 16a). We also had my Jewish family, my cousins, over during these times and I loved playing with them. I was very sad later on when they mostly all left for Israel. I felt a bit abandoned and lonely and it was then, very early on, that this feeling of questioning what and where home really is started, even without me acknowledging or realizing it.

My mother and father lit the Shabbat lamp every Friday evening and we had special foods made with coconut milk to maintain the level of

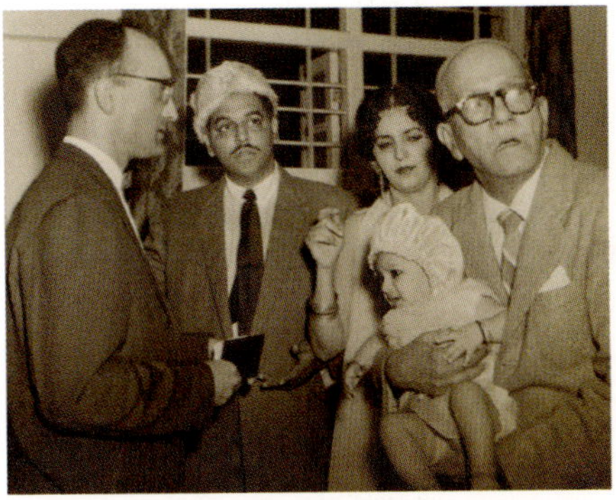

Fig. 16a. Baby Siona in the arms of her grandfather David Joseph (Borgawker) at her naming ceremony

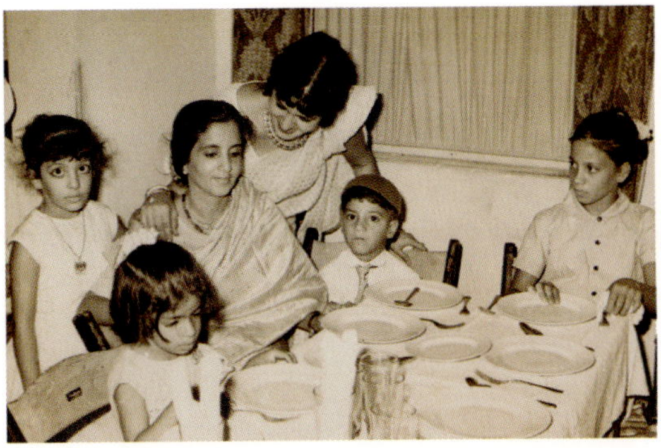

Fig. 17. Shabbat at Siona's parents' home

kashrut that keeps meat separate from milk (Fig. 17). Traditional Indian food and curries were mostly made by mixing milk and meat and since *kashrut* was to be observed, Indian Jews used delicious coconut milk or freshly grated coconut in most of their cooking. We had a garden with guava, mango and some coconut trees and very often during the season we ate the fruit from these very trees. During Yom Kippur I remember my mother making *karanje* (folded wheat dough stuffed with sweet freshly grated coconut cooked with some sugar and dry fruits).These *karanje*, otherwise also known as coconut puris, were consumed for days as my mother made them in large batches to send to friends and family.

My paternal grandmother lived in the central part of Bombay city and often we went to her home for the Jewish festivals. She made delicious Indian Jewish food as well and we ate this food in time to go for prayers and festivities at the Magen Hassidim Synagogue. My grandmother lived right opposite this synagogue, making it easy to run back and forth from the synagogue to her home!

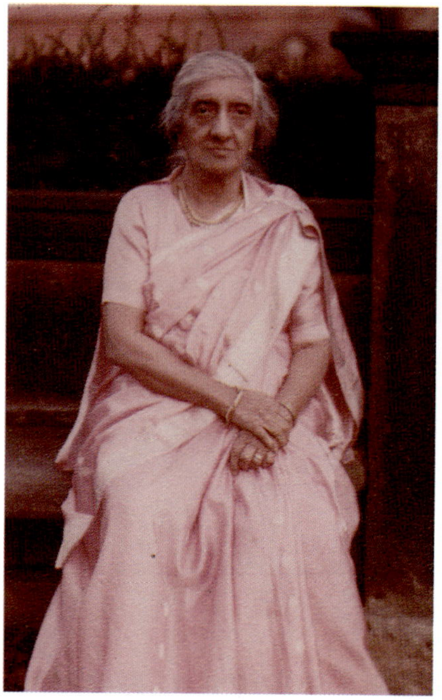

Fig. 18. Grandmother Elizabeth in Cleveland, 1970s

My maternal grandparents lived in the city of Pune and we often went to visit them as well. After my grandfather passed away, in the 1970s, my grandmother immigrated to Cleveland, Ohio, where my uncle lived and later I would visit her there too (Fig. 18). It was during one of these visits that I decided that someday I would come to the US to study art, which I later did, not knowing then that I would never return to India nor go to live in Israel like most of my family already had done. My grandmother Elizabeth's life journey had been a long and rather interesting one; she was a Jew born in Quetta, Pakistan, and later her family came to live on the west coast of India. There she was married to my grandfather David and had 10 children. These children of hers dispersed to three different continents—Asia, Africa, and North America—and made their lives in all these diverse places, perpetuating the idea of the 'Diasporic Jew' in a personal way.

This diasporic distance seemed to widen as the years went on, my parents in India, most of the family in Israel, a few relatives in the US and Canada and even an aunt in Africa. My parents visited me very often when I came to study and later on when I decided to live permanently in the US. I did not exactly plan to live here but I feel that my lack of being grounded and my sense of rootlessness in so many ways gave me license to live just anywhere—pitching my tent first and wondering later how I got there and why I stayed. I grew so used to being rootless that it seemed it was the only way to be. I did not always like it and I often secretly envied people who had hordes of family members around them and were grounded in one solid place. I had not experienced this, making me long for a permanent home, one in which I could say that I had lived my whole life.

Only later in life did I learn the true meaning and value of making all these transcultural friends, who became my family in so many ways. This rootlessness taught me to absorb and search for diversity and uniqueness and I realized I often felt bored when put in homogeneous situations. This diasporic, almost schizophrenic life gradually became alluring and inviting and I grew to like it, to love it actually—thus always seeking something different from what or where I was. Now I realize that seeking something different was seeded in me from the very beginning, that diversity was already in my childhood home, and that I have known no other way and no other kind of life.

When I think back, what I thought was the norm then, now seems unique and such a different experience. Although India always promoted hybridity and welcomed the stranger, it was the uniqueness of my parents' thinking and upbringing that sealed the deal, so to speak, in really living the experience and truly understanding the meaning of accepting diversity. Today's younger generation does not feel that much of a racial difference in America: my 24-year-old daughter has a truly multicultural group of friends living in New York City. That being said,

I must re-emphasize that still these young people are sheltered by living in America and do not often meet people with really different speaking accents, lifestyles, and experiences. India taught me to sit on the floor with some of my Hindu friends and eat delicious vegetarian food with my hands, learning to break the *chappati* bread and how to neatly wrap it around the vegetables and to enjoy the experience of tasting the food on my fingers. It taught me how to talk to a person who has a very different accent and not to feel like he is weird, but rather that you yourself are different, because you are the minority in his or her land. This experience was not parallel to any other, as it was not just about accepting the diversity within America but understanding more about the diversity in the world.

My mother ran a primary school, as I mentioned earlier, and she was brave enough to do things like have a few seats for very poor kids in every classroom. I say brave enough because she earned her living through this school and I remember how, a couple of times, the parents of an affluent family or of a wealthy film star did not approve of having their kids sit in the same classroom with their poor chauffeur's kid, for example. This was a socio-economic class-difference attitude that was not just in India but even here in the US, lest one forget! I believe that there are unspoken and unacknowledged race and class injustices in many parts of the world even today, which causes many wars and violence. My mother, however, made it very clear that these were the rules of her school, where she admitted children of all backgrounds, religions and wealth stature, and that the issue was not up for debate. She politely told the wealthy parents that they were welcome to take their kids to another school if this did not suit them. I recall that the wealthy parents did not remove their kids from the school and did not make an issue of this anymore. This was a lesson for me in accepting diversity, in also fighting for it and, therefore, in trying to make a difference.

I remember my mother guiding a very poor family who lived in a tiny hutment dwelling near our home and her school, gently pushing them to make sure that their two daughters got an education. Not only did she give them a free education in her school but she helped them to go to middle and high schools. These two sisters graduated college later on, too, and I recall their father bringing small gifts like fresh fish from the Bombay fish market as a token of his gratitude to my mother. This family was from a lower Hindu caste and although the Indian government had put out a ban on any caste discrimination, there was still an unspoken stigma and my mother was aware of that. India had for centuries possessed caste discrimination from within the Hindu religion, but now, of course, it has diminished. Many Jewish women were teachers and in the education field and having that advantage gave my mother the strength to do something for people different from herself. I now recall these stories and again I am taught the meaning of understanding the importance of accepting 'the other'. As small and insignificant as this particular part of my tale might be, there is a strong, unspoken effect that it still has on me.

The fact that my father's mother lived in a part of Bombay where Jews and Muslims lived closely together, as they shared similar monotheistic religions, seems unbelievable to most people here and now in America, whenever I tell this story. But this was how it was, a utopia that is unbelievable to most people now who are suspicious of 'the other', and yet seem to live in a globalized and more interconnected world. When my grandmother decided to immigrate to Israel, all of her Muslim neighbors and friends came to say a tear-filled goodbye to her, telling her that they would miss her like a sister. The mosque and the synagogue were right next to each other, you see, and my father knew the Muslim call to prayer by heart as he had heard it every day growing up in that neighborhood. Precisely across the narrow street was the Magen Hassidim Synagogue where he prayed with his Jewish family, and I would take my own daughter there years later to tell her many of these stories. I learned of all this too and although it did not mean much to me then, now, in the context of what has happened as the history of the world goes forward, I gather that these were indeed important experiences.

One story particularly stands out in my memory regarding the embrace of all kinds of people—in the context of a negative and dramatic experience. It took place over a span of about seven years in the mid-1990s and early 2000s. (Yes, seven years sounds like a comparison to the story of Joseph—the one with the technicolor dream coat, who interpreted the seven ears of healthy and unhealthy corn, and seven healthy and unhealthy cattle from the Egyptian pharaoh's dreams.)

By the early 1990s my mother had run her school for over 20 years. Although it had been faring well and she had built a nice reputation in our suburb of Bandra, my father's health was declining, as he had developed heart problems. At that time one of the wealthy parents from my mother's school approached them and asked if they had thought about their plans for retiring, and if they had, these people would gladly rent the first and second floors of my parents' large home. This family owned a well-known commercial airline company and they said that they would love to rent the two floors of my home so as to make one of their many offices in our space. My parents thought about it and decided to take this opportunity and indeed retire. They travelled to visit me often in the US and this would make it easier to do just that! Within months

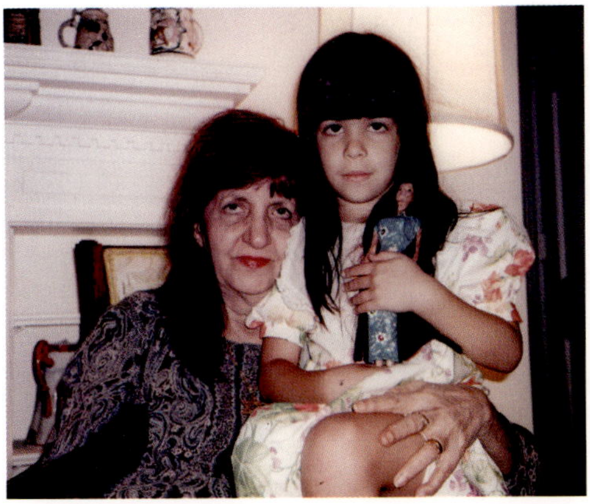

Fig. 19. Grandmother and granddaughter—Sophie Benjamin with Rachel

the school closed down (sadly) but my parents hoped to start a (joyful) retirement phase of their lives.

A few years passed and these new tenants (now having their office in my parents' home) settled into their new space and my parents enjoyed the rent and rest after many years of hard work. My father had worked for a large cargo shipping company for over 30 years and was also retired now because of his health. In early 1995, a few months pregnant with my daughter Rachel, I had a lovely visit to India together with my husband; we returned in late January and in February my father suddenly passed away. I was very sad I that could not make it back in time for his funeral, as we do the funeral rites the next day in the Jewish tradition and besides, I was heavily pregnant by then and could not endure a long plane ride back to India. To this day I am sad when I think of not having made it back home when my father passed away, but I also recognize this as the plight of many diasporic immigrants.

My mother came to be with us a month or so later, and although she was very sad with the demise of my father, on 5 July 1995, the birth of my beautiful daughter Rachel brightened up her world and she was thrilled to become a grandmother and was with me for several months after the baby was born (Fig. 19). A few months after the birth of my child, we were at home one day and Raghu, our trusted employee, called us from India and with bated breath told us that the owner of the airline company had been shot and killed! Apparently, he had left our home—also his office—that evening and had driven down our street only to be shot and killed at the end of the street! This had never ever happened in my safe neighborhood!...And this shocking news was indeed very, very disturbing to hear! My mother was distraught and tried calling several friends, only to learn from the breaking news that the airline company was known to be connected to a dubious underworld network and that the murder had been simply an act of retaliation directed from one gang to the member of another gang!

My mother was really distraught, and now hearing this news it made her feel that she had to return home as soon as possible. When she did return, my mother suffered for over seven years with the process of trying to get these tenants out of her home. They seemed to have taken over her home, her property, and her life security! I could not travel to India as she did not want us involved and endangered and so she bravely fought in the courts to get her home back from her tenants. I remember having many, many phone calls with her and now these seven or so years seem like a blur of tension and stress for all of us.

I feel that this particular story is important because, although my parents decided to sign on these tenants into their home, they were totally unaware of the dubious associations this business had and the consequences of it. I also must mention that this airline company was owned by a Muslim family, but I remember now vividly that my mother never ever brought up religion as a factor for any problems with them. Now when I think back, I am struck by this attitude, this open-mindedness, so to speak, about not regarding religion or race as a blameworthy factor for the problems my parents had with these people. Not once do I recall my mother ever saying that this family was Muslim and therefore against Jews.

Not once did she refer to that being the reason why she could not get these tenants out of her home. After over seven years she did manage to get them out of her home; she subsequently sold her home and downsized to a smaller apartment. I visited her later and I asked her why she never blamed religion, like most people would? She said in her crystal-clear way to me: 'I don't think religion or different nationalities has anything to do with people not getting along. People are the same all over the world, and there are just good and not-so-good people, that's all, it's just about how you encounter them.' I will remember this story for the difficulties my mother faced in getting back her home, but mainly for what she told me about people, about us being similar and that one should never judge them because of religion, or race, or nationality.

There are many other stories that I recall—like the pride both my parents had when they befriended an Arab family who chose to send their children to their school. When the Arab man came to admit his child, he could not help asking my mother where she was from. Was she middle-eastern, too? Was she from Iran? (Fig 20). My mother recalls telling this man that he might not want to know who she was, given world politics, and that she was a Jew. This amazing Arab man said in return that then she was indeed his sister, his Jewish sister, and he and his wife would invite my parents to many birthday parties and to their home, thereafter.

Whenever people I encounter tell me to judge because of race or religion, or they feel the need to make blanket statements because of

Fig. 20. Sophie Benjamin's portrait, taken during one of her visits to the US, 2009

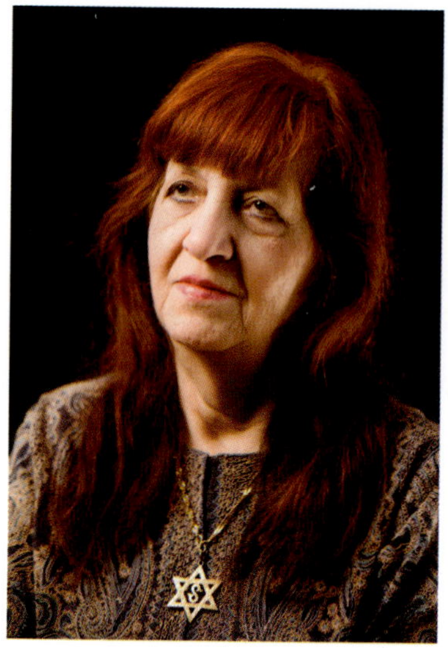

who or what the other person is, I feel very disheartened. How does one imagine one's self able to make preconceived statements about people who are different, or people about whom one doesn't know much—but should definitely spend time learning about!—before making any kind of judgement at all?! Writing down my memories for this volume has helped me to encapsulate these experiences, to reason with them, to examine them yet again: thinking over how all this has affected my mission in life through my art making. Time and time again I return to the notion of being a story teller thorough my art. To make art that becomes a time capsule for these stories and a drop in the vast ocean towards *Tikkun* and repair.

Tikkun olam (Hebrew for 'repairing the world') has come to connote social action and the pursuit of social justice. The phrase has origins in classical rabbinic literature—the phrase is found in the Mishnah, a body of classical rabbinic teachings—and emphasized in Lurianic kabbalah, a major strand in the tapestry of Jewish mysticism, originating with the work of the 16th-century kabbalist, Isaac Luria. *Tikkun olam* is thus a Jewish concept defined by acts of kindness performed to repair and perfect the world. It is often used when discussing issues of social policy, insuring safeguards for those who may be at a disadvantage.

Being able to use this concept has been a very important part of my work now—mostly because of the seeds that were already sown in my childhood, and later on, encountering the concept of *Tikkun* has given me a positive sense of power and purpose for my work.

I have made images like Finding Home #46 'Tikkun ha-Olam' ('Repairing the world') that are directly inspired by this concept (Fig. 21, p. 212). In one kabbalistic tradition, the world is compared to a pot or vessel that contains all the divinely-created virtues. However, the cosmos was unable to contain this divine energy and the pot shattered, but the broken shards retained the divine light or energy as they scattered throughout reality. It is humanity's task to reconstruct this vessel, which is done through various ethical, spiritual, intellectual, and aesthetic acts that re-establish values in our world. By making images that contribute to this *Tikkun* I am participating in my own small way in this process of 'repair'. In this particular painting, my Indian-ness and my Jewish-ness are combined in a perfect union. The figure's skin is painted the turquoise color of the sky and the ocean and stands for the strength of her diversity, her struggle to make things unite within her. The blue skin reinforces that she belongs everywhere and nowhere at the same time, as she pitches her tent in places that she has learned eventually to call home.[3]

Art school, which came after high school, it was a slightly different experience…it was a mixed bag of students from English-speaking and vernacular schools. I got a chance to brush up my Marathi-speaking skills. Marathi was the language spoken by the locals and also the Bene Israel Jews in and around Bombay and they even had the Hebrew prayers

[3] See Ori Z. Soltes, 'Finding Home: The Transcultural Worlds of Siona Benjamin,' *Feminist Studies*, 38, 3 (Fall 2012): 689–719.

transliterated into Marathi. The art school campus was a haven away from the bustle of the Bombay bazaars, with its Indo-British architecture and stories of Rudyard Kipling walking the shaded pathways of the school. We sat in these very shaded lawns and munched on spicy Indian snacks and discussed the painting class, where we had just finished an Impressionist-style painting and had pored over books of Rembrandt drawings.

So, while in India I got called everything from Parsi to Punjabi and even occasionally was called a 'cocktail' since my mother was too non-Indian-looking and apparently more Iranian-looking. And here in America a similar question is often asked: 'Where are you from?'—and now anything from Puerto Rican to Persian is a good guess. So, not surprisingly, in my paintings, I also raise questions about what and where is 'home', while evoking issues such as identity, immigration, motherhood, and the role of art in social change.

* * * * *

I remember the ornate synagogues of my childhood, the oil lamps, the velvet- and silver-covered Torah scrolls, a chair left vacant for the prophet Elijah in the synagogue. Having grown up in a predominantly Hindu and Muslim society, having been educated in Catholic and Zoroastrian schools, being raised Jewish, and now living in America, I have always had to reflect upon the cultural boundary zones in which I have lived. The feeling I have of never being able to set deep roots no matter where I am is unnerving, but on the other hand, there is something seductive about the spiritual borderland in which I seem to find myself.

In this multicultural America, I feel compelled to create art that speaks of shared similarities with my audience, not differences. My intent for my viewers is to re-evaluate their notions and concepts about identity and race, thus dispelling misconceptions that result in racism, hate, and war. In making images that question issues like identity, I feel that I can contribute to a much-needed repair to culture and society.

As a Bene Israel Jewish descendant, my recent work reflects my background and the transition between my old and new worlds. Using the rich colors of gouache, I apply layers literally with the paint and metaphorically with the content. I am inspired by the traditional styles of Indian/Persian miniature painting and Christian and Jewish illuminated manuscripts. I blend these ancient forms with contemporary pop cultural elements to create my own vocabulary. I also take inspiration from Jewish and Indian myths, in particular the stories of the goddess Kali, and the famous blue god Krishna, making them come alive to enact their stories from a mythological past. These blue-skinned characters tell (or mostly retell) stories that are divine in nature but very human in drama.

A bluish hue to skin in many stories and cultures often means sickness, death or something alien, for example in Japanese ukiyo-e prints. The turquoise blue skin of my characters portrays quite the opposite, a confidence in their difference, health and radiance, and a definite will to survive. In the process of recycling, rejuvenating and even redirecting, I am reminded of Joseph Campbell's book *The Power of Myth*, in which he eloquently states that myth-making is cyclical, timeless, and universal.

Recently I have been studying the Torah (the five books of Moses that are the first part of the Hebrew Bible) and the Talmud and Midrash (rabbinical discussion and interpretations). While growing up in India

I recall being surrounded by idols and iconography that were taboo in my Jewish world. I eyed these figures from a distance, captivated by their radiance and richness. Since Judaism stressed monotheism and iconoclasm, I somehow resisted the lure of figurative drawing for years. Initially making abstract work and then later, if I did venture to depict the forbidden fruit, my figures were shrouded with darkened faces. Now my work is filled with graven (blue) images, as suddenly it became clear during my years of studying and designing sets for theater that figurative images are not forbidden; it is forbidden to worship them—and it became clear that I liked the narrative, the theatrical, the decorative lyrical line; I carried this ornateness with me all along. These figures have thus become characters in my paintings that act out their parts, recording, balancing, rectifying, restoring, and absorbing. It is through all this that I understand how I can dip into my own personal specifics and universalize, thus playing the role of an artist/activist.

Very often I look down at my skin and it has turned blue. It tends to do that when I face certain situations of people stereotyping and categorizing other people who are unlike themselves. I have therefore over the years developed many blue-skinned characters in my paintings; this blue self-portrait of sorts takes on many roles and forms and theatrically enacts many ancient and contemporary dilemmas.

My work is celebratory of my womanhood, my abilities, my strengths, and my ambitions. After having struggled long with my own hybrid background and experience, I am beginning to see more clearly now that this blend can be humorous, enlightening and revealing. The ornate culture from which I came once seemed difficult and unnecessary to apply in my work. Now I have found a way to use it, to be able to weave current issues and parts of my life in its intricacies, thus making this ornateness strong and meaningful. In this way, I attempt to create a dialogue between the ancient and the modern, forcing a confrontation of unresolved issues.

In my series of paintings entitled 'Finding Home', I question the 'what' and 'where' of home. The desire to 'find home', spiritually and literally, has always preoccupied me—a concern to which many Americans can relate, as this comparatively younger nation is largely formed by immigrants and their descendants.

I have been repeatedly asked over the years, 'How was it growing up a girl in India? Were you oppressed? Dominated? Treated not too well?'...I always reply that women can be treated badly anywhere in the world. While there seem to be more stories of women's oppression in countries like India, I grew up empowered and was taught strength in my womanhood. While I did see and experience some stories of women's oppression growing up, it was no more than I have experienced living here in America for over 30 years! I could also say that I have experienced ignorant and somewhat racist questions more here in the west, compared to my years in India.

I grew up with Mrs Indira Gandhi as our Prime Minister and I proudly looked up to her. I was and still am proud to say that India has had a woman prime minister. I even had an opportunity to meet Mrs Gandhi with my parents in 1978 during one of our trips to Delhi (Fig. 22). That day has been one of the highlights of my life as I stood proudly beside this strong woman who had been Prime Minister and would be so again, and ever have a photo to seal the memory! I remember Mrs Gandhi inquiring about our community of Jews in India, while she was speaking to my parents, and that struck me as one more example India can boast about....being inclusive of all kinds of people over the ages.

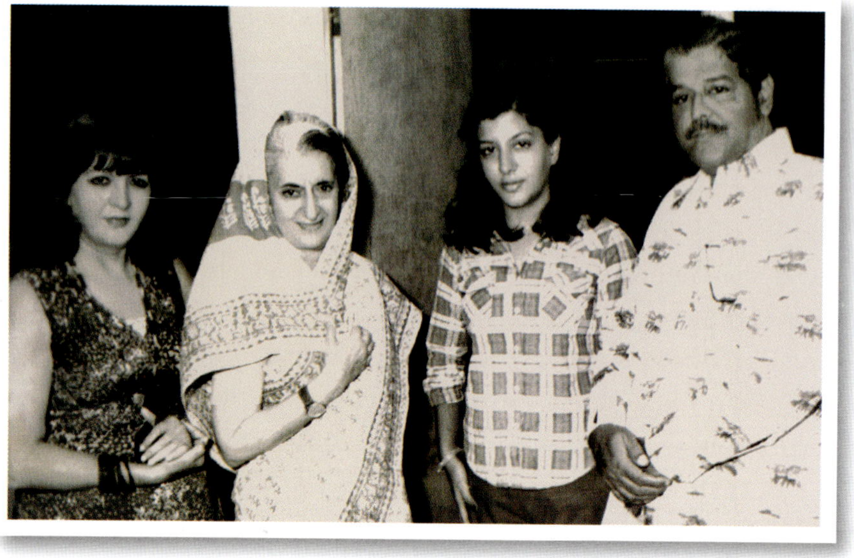

Fig. 22. Siona Benjamin with her parents and Indira Gandhi, 1978

My undergraduate study at J.J. School of Art in Bombay was solidly planted in both western and eastern painting techniques and art history studies. I took inspiration from the religious icons of many cultures, the gold leaf and gaunt figures of Byzantium and the colors and mythology of Hindustan. The study of Indian miniature paintings rooted me in the belief that contemporary artists are only seeking what has already been present and available in these paintings from long ago, the sense of discovery and history. My first Master of Fine Arts is in painting and the second MFA is in theater set design, where I immersed myself for several years in productions as a set designer and set painter for various plays, operas and musicals. This study in theater, learning the importance of storytelling, later informed my art-making process in a unique and innovative way.

I have been fortunate to have had the opportunity to study both western and eastern art and techniques. I desperately searched for my artistic voice earlier on during my many years of studying art, often trying to ape the styles of western painters and trying to find my identity in my art. Some of my western professors (during graduate school in the US) told me to paint large abstract paintings as that was the only style that would work. But I found out later on that this prescribed formula did not work for me. I liked to make small, feminine, delicate paintings with lyrical lines to tell and retell mythology. I found my voice by acknowledging that I was indeed a storyteller through my art.

However, I would never have found my purpose if I had not had the opportunity to experience making the large abstract paintings and thus learning from them. Earlier on when studying art in my undergraduate years in India, my teachers there were ironically experts who were painting in Impressionist style and we were taught to draw by copying many western masters from the Renaissance. When I decided to do my undergraduate thesis researching aspects of Indian miniature painting, the teachers told me that Indian miniature style was now a tourist art and to concentrate on real art, which was Western art. Again, my instincts told me to persevere and I did do my thesis on Indian miniatures. These sorts of cross-cultural experiences sunk in, and only later did I realize their impact on me and my art process.

My active pursuit of the Torah and rabbinic literature has resulted in the use of all this material in my work. My work is not religious but I want to stress the great importance of my culture, my religion, and the unique environments in which I grew up, which have affected everything in my life and subsequently what and how I choose to express in my work. My parents did not shove religion down my throat, nor were they strictly religious or orthodox. What they did do, perhaps without even realizing it, was to give me a strong sense of identity, belief, and hope. They introduced me to my unique culture and taught me to be proud of it.

The constant fluidity of immigrant identity is the core of my research and work. Identity is usually defined through race, ethnicity, gender, class, and religion. My art-making over the years addresses these and other important transcultural issues, which sorely need awareness and understanding during these critical times of globalization. It is through all my personal specifics that I can make sense of the world and attempt to universalize my art.

Living and making art in America now for over 32 years, it seems that I've come full circle. I have learned that people are similar all over the world. We might have different habits, food, culture, backgrounds, and different levels of education, but humanity seems to be made from one mold, seemingly diverse at first encounter but not so different at the core. My greater universal family has often been accessed through the eyes and the heart of the most unlikely individuals. I have found kinship and a feeling of family in the most diverse of people. I can say that America taught me that, and even though it seems, sometimes, that there is much more tension due to racial differences in this country, than when I grew up in India, without having to think about it, I have learned more consciously how to find oneness in this diversity.

At this mid-career stage of my life, with a fair amount of travel, experience, and work behind me, I have understood that it's not about being surrounded by people who will eliminate the loneliness and the space in one's heart that longs to be accepted or to belong. Even though my story about being brought up by loving parents, in a tolerant and accepting India, and my childhood seems a happy one, there was and

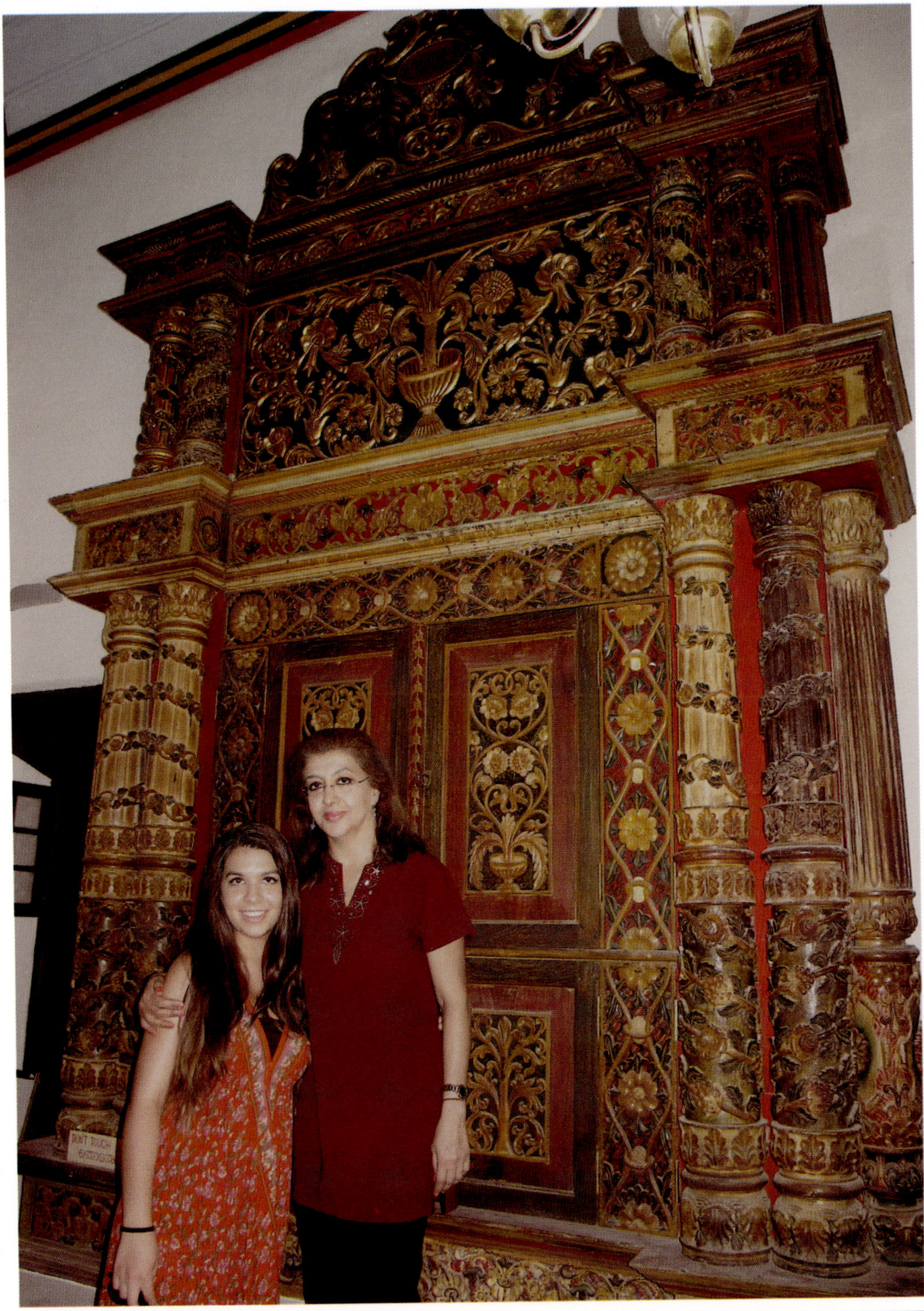

Fig. 23. Rachel and Siona at Cochin Synagogue, 2015

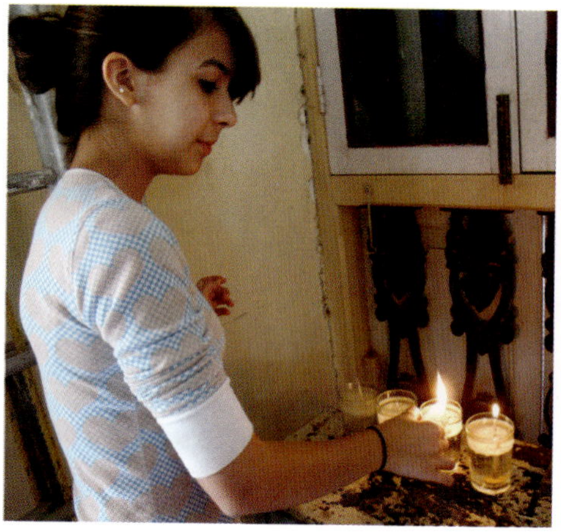

Fig. 24. Rachel kindling memorial lights in a Mumbai synagogue

still is pain in the search for belonging. I have seen many people who are just as lonely in a crowd, just as much searching within the safety of their family, community, and country. I have understood that the search for home or belonging is not out there but within us. I myself find it in memories, or in the making of my art. Others perhaps find it in something else they do. In the end it is the search that is important and it is the journey that matters.

I wish to leave these messages for my daughter, Rachel, as she is even more a transcultural being, since she is part Indian Jew, part Russian-Polish and also very American. I have tried my best, just as my parents did, to teach her to be proud of who she is. I wish her well in her journey in this world, as she finds her universe and her adventures. I wish for her to also celebrate all the uniqueness she comes with, in her own way, in her own time and in her own bountiful places (Figs 23 and 24).

The Shabbat lights that my mother and father lit every Friday evening, the *shema* prayer that they taught me to recite, the need I felt to call my mother up to tell her about anything and everything in my life and the consolation I felt after telling her, is irreplaceable and will always stay within me. Her strong sense of belief in her Jewish values

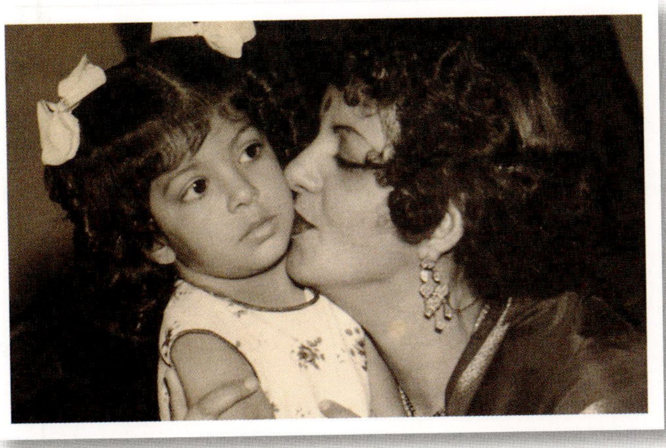

Fig. 25. Siona Benjamin as a child with her mother Sophie

taught me that it was not necessary to be strictly observant in all ways but to just carry the essence of who I was always with me (Fig. 25). In my work and life I find it important to stress not just the uniqueness of my culture but to try to cultivate the specifics of my culture, and to try to connect with a diverse universe of people. My transcultural Jewish upbringing taught me to use these specifics, but also to universalize, so anyone and everyone can hopefully identify with my work. This is what I would transmit to my own daughter; it is the gift I got growing up Jewish in India.

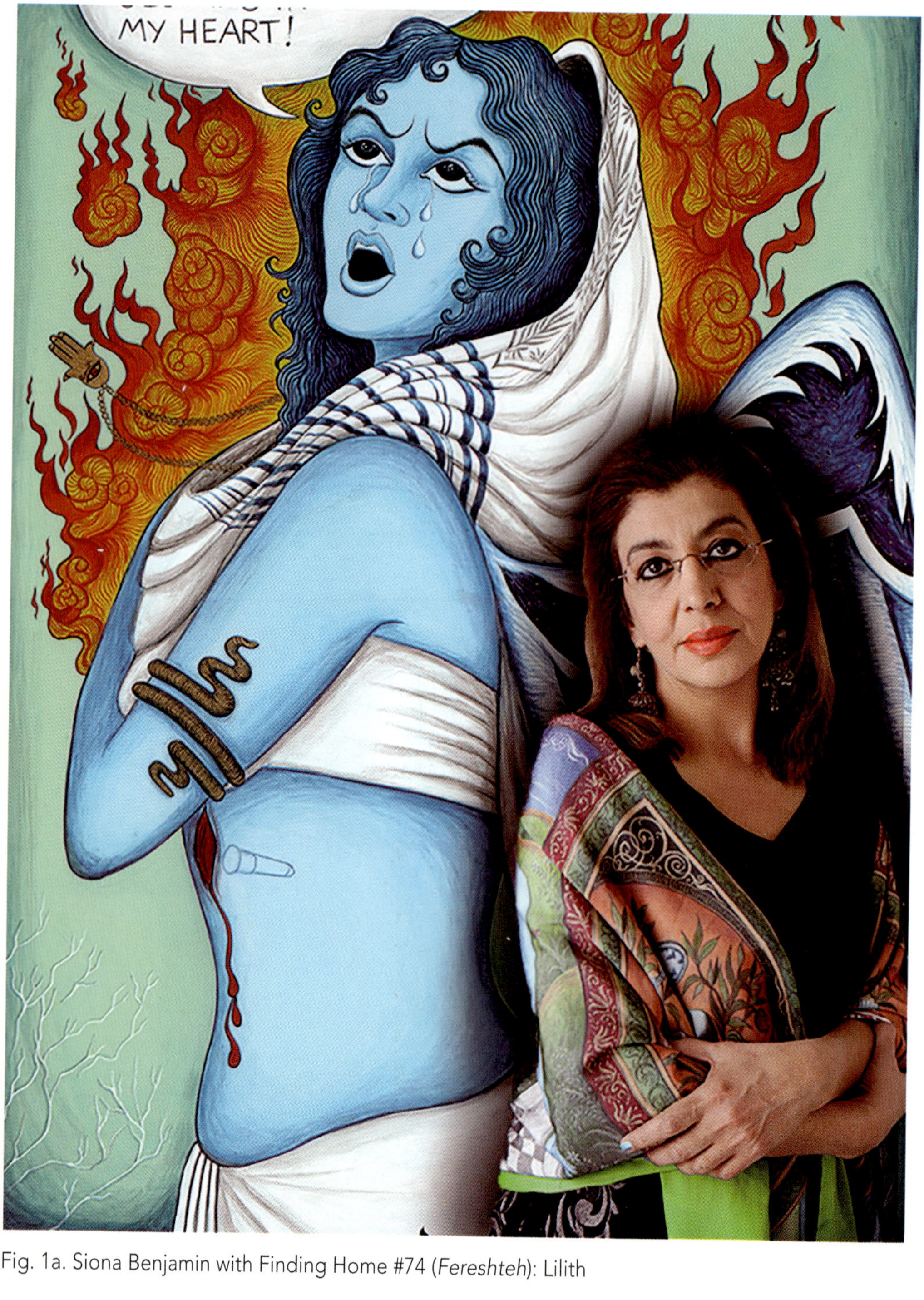

Fig. 1a. Siona Benjamin with Finding Home #74 (*Fereshteh*): Lilith

CHAPTER FIVE

Refocus and Return

SIONA BENJAMIN'S MULTI-LAYERED ART

Ori Z.Soltes

I. The transnational, multicultural, interfaith basis of Siona's art

No contemporary artist offers a more appropriate array of work to illuminate the issues under consideration in this volume than Siona Benjamin. Our arc of discussion has moved from a broad consideration of Jewish migratory patterns into eastern Asia to a general discussion of India as a country hospitable to groups and individuals from diverse religious backgrounds and the diversity of Jewish communities within India. From these broad considerations, the narrative has continued with particular focus on the three major Jewish communities in (and now outside) India—the Bene Israel, Baghdadi, and Cochini communities—considering both their histories and varied focus on their synagogues and ceremonial lives. The title of this book, *Growing Up Jewish in India*, has then found its most literal expression in the brief memoir offered up by Siona Benjamin, which carries from her childhood in Mumbai toward the present day, living in the United States—specifically in New Jersey—and from her memories of her grandparents and her parents to her aspirations for her daughter.

Not surprisingly, Siona's work—and my discussion will focus on select parts of three bodies of that work: her miniature paintings (inspired in part by illuminated manuscripts and Indian miniatures), her illuminated *Megillat Esther* (Esther Scroll), and her Fulbright combinations of manipulated photographs and painting—as it has evolved over the decades, offers a particularly rich series of reflections on her unique experience in the world, as it resonates with a determined effort to engage with, and to be part of, what improves the world through the instrumentation of applying her diversely-shaped background to the varied art that she produces. Her art is transcultural and transnational, interweaving the traditional with the modern, and it offers a range of conceptual colors that reflect her life-long experiences. To summarize what is more fully explored in her memoir, Siona grew up as a Jew in India, in Mumbai (Bombay), a region predominantly divided between Hindu and Muslim cultures—each with its own artistic sensibilities and each at times at war with the other—and attended schools that were variously Catholic and Zoroastrian.[1]

She was also a girl, of course, in a culture still finding its way with respect to healthy treatment of women—but her father consistently told her that she was as much a son as a daughter, and should never stop short of fulfilling her aspirations just because of her gender. So her childhood (and her own nature) made challenging definitions and boundaries inevitable. She came to the American Middle West and then ultimately to New Jersey, locales very different from each other

[1] I might note that, like many artists in history, Siona Benjamin typically refers to herself and is most commonly referred to simply by her first name—hence, Siona, rather than Ms. Benjamin.

and both of them parts of a larger America with its own very much still-unanswered questions of how to address religion, ethnicity, gender and race—as has become more apparent than ever in the current era.

She addresses both the divine Other addressed by religion and the human Other addressed by culture, ethnicity, gender and race. Her work falls into—and bursts the bounds of—the traditions of Indian and Pakistani miniature painting art, particularly that sponsored by the Mughals during their more than three centuries of rule (1526–1857),[2] but also reflects on the Persian miniature tradition that fed into Mughal art, as well as on the larger contours of Islamic art. Her imagery engages the delightfully unanswerable question of Jewish art and how it should be defined: through Judaism as a religion, an ethnicity, a nationality, a culture, a civilization? Through subject, style, symbol? Through the art itself or through the identity of the artist's birth or convictions? Her art encompasses feminist issues of acceptance and rejection, recognition and blindness within the male-dominated societies through which Siona has lived her life—as well as the Western-hegemonic feminist movements within those societies.

II. *Fereshteh*

Most often in her painting, Siona combines these issues, each contributing its own parts to the totality, in an unexpected manner. One group of work, begun in the late 1990s, is called *Finding Home*—a reflection of

[2] The power of the Mughal rulers began to shrink gradually by 1725 and precipitously from 1764, which latter year is typically considered the last year of the Mughal Empire. By the time the last 'emperor', Bahadur Shah II, was deposed, imprisoned and exiled by the British in 1857, he had functionally been ruling nothing more than the city of Delhi.

her ever-evolving reflections on the word 'home' and its implications, particularly for an itinerant: what are the particulars through which we shape a dwelling into a home? But there are diverse branches to that tree. One of these (a subset series of *Finding Home*, that is) is *Fereshteh*—meaning 'angels' in Urdu—and each of the primary figures in the series is overtly or covertly female. They are most often drawn from the Bible—typically either by way of the rabbinic interpretive tradition known as midrash[3] with its often phantasmagorical flights of fancy or by way of her own midrash—or by synthesizing both.

A particular sub-branch of the *Fereshteh* branch of *Finding Home* focuses on Lilith, the midrash-based first wife of Adam, who was able to fly and unwilling to be ground beneath her husband's dominating heel—for which she was not only exiled from the Garden (as Adam and Eve would be, one day) but subject to millennia of cruelty. She also came to be viewed, in more popular Jewish legend, as a seductress (particularly of pubescent boys) and as a destroyer (particularly of babies).[4]

Destruction—within the traditional rabbinic discussion—and redemption, at least in part, in Siona's re-vision, is expressed in these

[3] The term 'midrash' comes from a Hebrew-language root, d-r-sh, meaning 'to dig beneath the surface'; midrash digs beneath the surface of certain biblical texts, seeking deeper meanings.

[4] The word '*lilit*' is a hapax legomenon in the Hebrew Bible, appearing only once, in Isaiah 34:14, which makes its precise meaning less than obvious. It then appears several times in the Dead Sea Scrolls, and three times in the Gemara of the Babylonian Talmud—the third reference, (in Sabbath 1511b) offers R. Hanina noting that '...whoever sleeps alone in a house is seized by Lilith.' But it is the so-called Alphabet of Ben Sira (8th–10th c) that begins a serious elaboration of Lilith as Adam's first wife, her refusal—having been created, like him, from earth (and not, like Eve, later, from his rib)—to submit to him, and her exile and punishments. She also comes in for further discussion in the Kabbalah and later aggadic traditions. The Hebrew root of the name means 'night' (and '*lilit*' is actually one of the modern Hebrew words for 'owl').

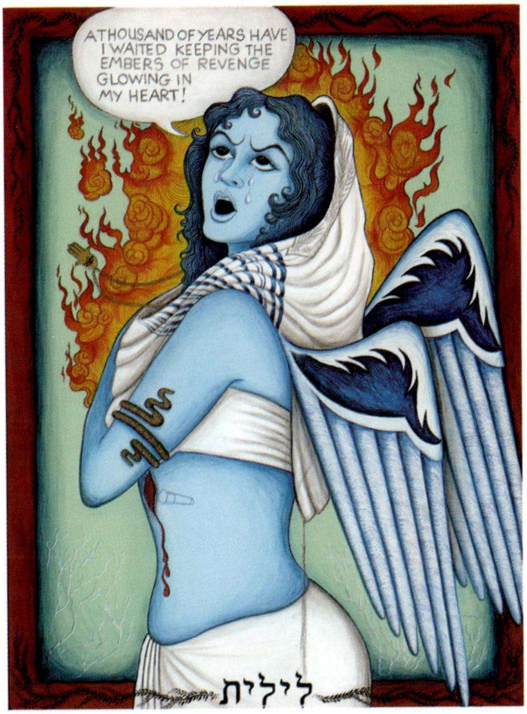

Fig. 1. Finding Home #74 (*Fereshteh*): Lilith, 2005

works. They also tend to offer the most emphatic meeting point with Bollywood on the one hand and Roy Lichtenstein's signature Pop style on the other. Her Finding Home #74 (*Fereshteh*) and #75 (*Fereshteh*) might be viewed as dark and light siblings. Siblings because they follow each other in the series (the first from 2005 and the second from 2006) and are identical in materials (gouache on wood panel) and nearly identical in size (the first 30 x 24" and the second 30 x 25"). But dark and light because they offer two different responses to the suffering to which Lilith is said to have been subject through the millennia. *Fereshteh*

#74 offers Lilith's name in Hebrew and a winged figure with a *tallit*[5] as a kerchief—one of its fringes dangling down toward the first lamed (the 'L') in her name—and a *hamseh* (a good-luck charm) with an eye in its palm dangling furiously away from her neck (Figs 1 and 1a). Such a classic Muslim amulet, frequently used also among Jews within the Muslim world, is just the sort of instrument that one might wear around one's neck to protect one from demons like Lilith, and particularly when adorned with an eye, to ward off the 'evil eye'.

So this exquisite Lilith, paradoxically, wears a protective amulet. She weeps hot tears. She has been pierced—at a point between her heart and her womb—by a bullet and she bleeds from that gaping wound. Waves of flame rise up from her—both suggesting the heat of her furious anger and also (again paradoxically) recalling the sort of flames that, in Islamic art, often rise from the head of the Prophet Muhammad to signify his connection to divinity, just as round plates of gold behind the heads of Christian saints signify that connection for them.[6] And she bellows, in a cartoon-style bubble that 'a thousand years have I waited, keeping the embers of revenge glowing in my heart!'—alluding perhaps to that part of her divinely administered punishment through which one of her children would be destroyed every day for a thousand years, and underscoring the angry aspect of those flames rising from her.

If this Lilith is vengeful (but who wouldn't be, given her multiple wounds?) her sister is protective—of us, the descendants of her husband Adam and his second wife, Eve. Her name is written in English—but

[5] A *tallit* is a Jewish prayer shawl traditionally worn only by men.

[6] The term 'halo' comes from the Greek '*helios*', meaning 'sun'. The tradition of adorning those with a divine association with some sort of stylized star/sunburst can be traced at least as far as back as ancient Mesopotamia.

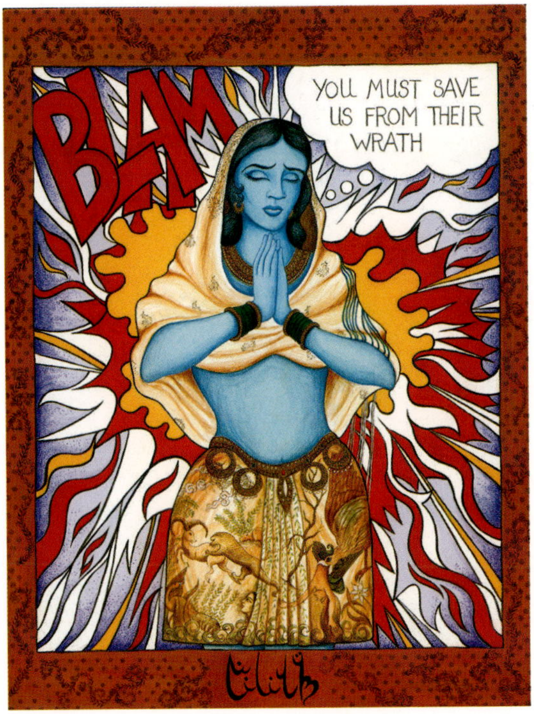

Fig. 2. Finding Home (*Fereshteh*) #75: Lilith (Blam!), 2006

stylized to create the sense of Urdu.[7] She is wrapped in a lower body garment overrun with hunting-scene figures—a lion attacking a wild mountain goat; a bird with a small woman in its beak—the tan and green pigments of which contrast sharply with her blue skin and the bright red, yellow, white, and blue colors that surround her. She raises her hands in a namaste gesture of prayer, her eyes closed, and her brows drawn up in

[7] Urdu is very close to Hindi as a language, but is typically written in Persianized Arabic letters, whereas Hindi typically uses the *Devanagari* writing system it inherited from Sanskrit.

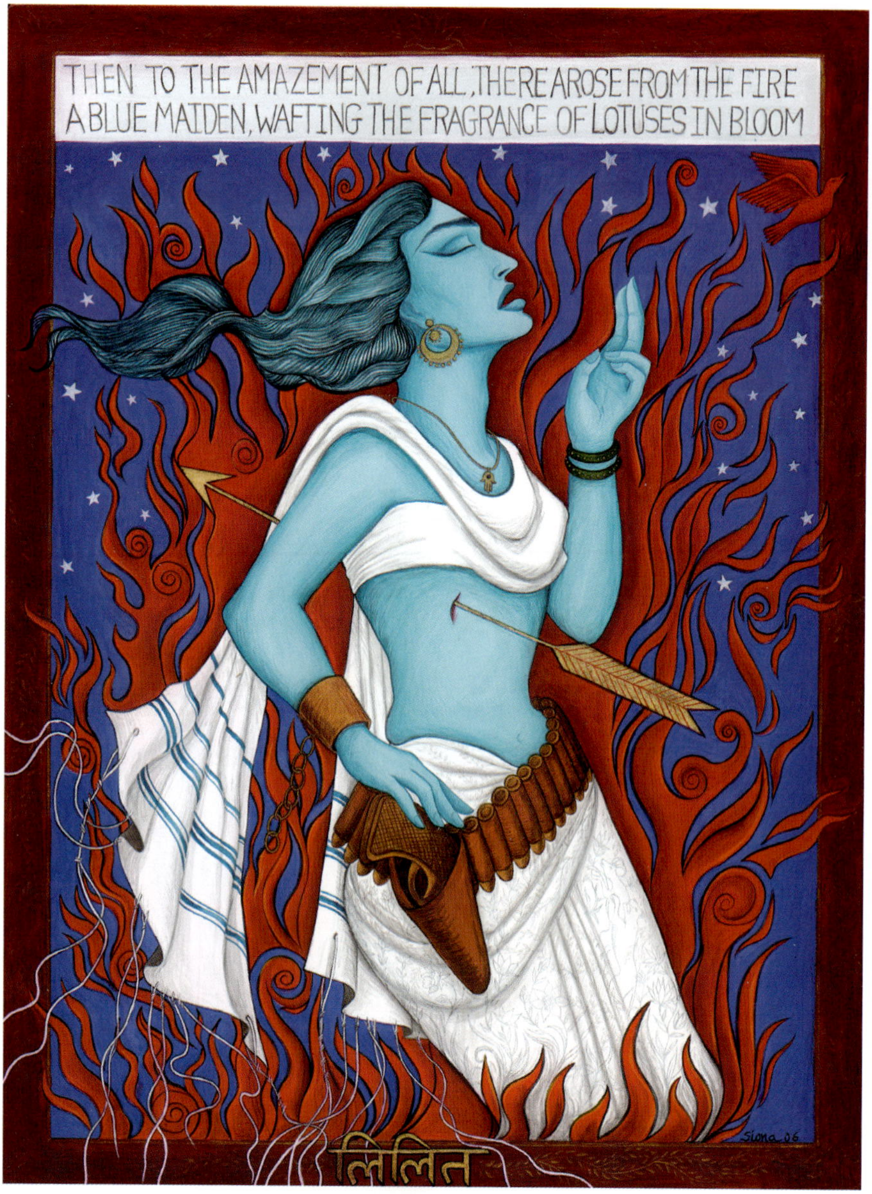

Fig. 3. Finding Home (*Fereshteh*) #80: Lilith, 2008

loving concern; the thought-bubble that rises from her head begs 'you must save us from their wrath'. Whose wrath? The wrath, surely, of the demons within us humans, of division and hostility and violence. Behind her, in pure Lichtensteinian fashion, those bright colors create an intense comic-book-style explosion, together with the bright red letters that spell out the comic-book word for an explosion: 'BLAM' (Fig. 2).

There are similarly conceived works—the 2008 Finding Home (*Fereshteh*) #80, for example, where Lilith's name is written in *Devanagari* script, and she wears a holster and gun and has been shot through with an arrow. In these three images Lilith has, one might say, become her Hindu divine counterpart, Kali / Durga: an aspect of Kali, consort of Shiva who personifies both creative and destructive forces (Fig. 3). She is both awesome and awful. She embodies both negative and positive forces, both male and female, divine and human forces. Her very Hebrew name, 'Lilit' ('night creature'), puns, by coincidence, on Sanskrit *lila*, the process through which reality is engendered.[8] In this trio of Liliths' combination of image with text, moreover, Siona not only emulates Lichtenstein but follows a path along which various contemporary

[8] Shiva is also called *Kala*, meaning 'eternal time' but also 'black' and 'death'—but 'black' also means 'deep blue', as typically associated with Krishna. Kali—often, like Krishna, blue-skinned in traditional Indian art—is named from the grammatically feminine form of the word (and name) Kala. This goddess—in the Shakti Tantric belief system, understood to encompass the totality of the gods—is associated with many other aspects of divinity, including Durga. Durga means 'invincible' and this 18-armed aspect of Kali is the warrior aspect of divinity—she embodies the combined energy of all the gods from whom she emerged, as part of divine Lila. Lila means 'play', or 'pastime' or 'sport' and refers to the notion that our world was created through the play of divine energy. It further refers to the notion that the creation of our world came about through divine self-sacrifice (i.e., destruction) and that our world, divinely derived, will be destroyed, thereby re-becoming divine (one with God)—and then the process will repeat, forever—and moreover, that the process of Lila, divine play, is a process defined by a perfect meeting of male and female opposites (in Shaivite literature this is expressed as the meeting of *lingam* and *yoni*).

Jewish artists have combined image and text as part of a challenge to the once widely-held notion that there can be no Jewish visual art because Jews are only a people of texts and not of images.[9]

Yet another Lilith (from 2006), #79 in the *Finding Home* (*Fereshteh*) series, is not actually called Lilith, but rather, 'Ishq'. The figure leaps, almost like a pinwheel before us, her head thrown back and her eyes nearly closed, as if both dancing and dying simultaneously—the wound in her side both dripping blood and sprouting foliage; the crescent moon becomes a crescent sword, its point also dripping blood toward the pretend-Urdu-formed name along the bottom of the image (Fig. 4). But the title, 'Ishq' is inscribed in the image itself, in *Devanagari*. Ishq is a word meaning 'divine love'—or particularly powerful love, even outside a divinely sourced context. It's a word that Siona uses as part of the instrumentation through which she connects tradition to modernity not in terms of art but in terms of human issues.

> Yesterday's wars are still fought today, recycling the same problems, the same anxieties and dilemmas. Nothing seems to have progressed, just the weapons of war have become more advanced in their ferocity. Therefore, these heroines of yesteryear are resurrected in my work and have become warriors of today, questioning our measure for love, for passion, for Ishq.[10]

---

[9] The #80 image is less Lichtensteinian than the others, the form and content of its text pure Benjamin redemptive midrash: the figure is surrounded by bright red flames and across the top of the image we read: 'and then to the amazement of all, there arose from the fire a blue maiden, wafting the fragrance of lotuses in bloom'.

[10] This passage comes from Siona Benjamin's remarks written in conjunction with the exhibition, 'ISHQ: Paintings by Siona Benjamin', in the Bernstein Gallery of the Woodrow Wilson School at Princeton University (October–December, 2011).

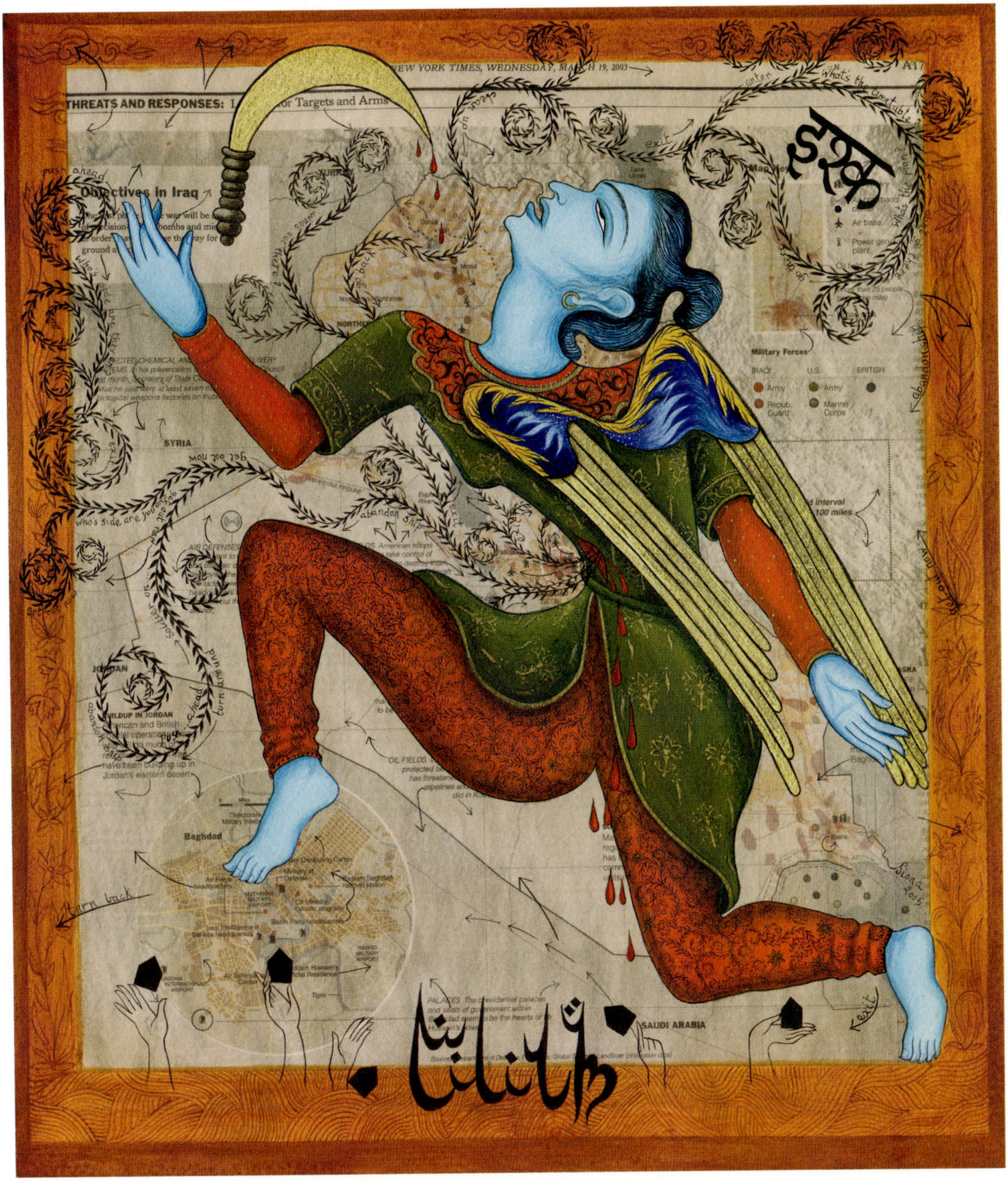

Fig. 4. Finding Home (*Fereshteh*) #79: Lilith (Ishq), 2006

This particular Lilith asks the question of what we are and whether we are worthy of divine love or even of whether we have a real desire for human love by being placed, splayed as she is in mid-flight, across a tawny—sand-colored—backdrop on which a map of the Middle East is drawn. Not merely any map, but a military map with strategic commandments and plans and objectives—specifically regarding Iraq. We can readily enough discern the contemporary context in which Siona has placed her avenging-salvational angel—her re-visioned Lilith. The second intrusion into Iraq, this one begat by lies to the American people from its highest leaders in a profound perversion of the American dream; the distortion of a republic into an imperialist nightmare.

There is another interesting visual component to this work. The splayed form that this particular Lilith takes may also be readily recognized as that of a broken cross—what in English was once called a gammadion (a Greek term) but which since 1871 has been known as a swastika. That word is pure Sanskrit: the prefix *sva* (*su*) means 'good', *asti* means 'to be' and the suffix *ka* is an intensifier. So the word means 'extreme well-being'. The symbol may be traced back, in the India of its origin as a specifically good-luck ornament, to at least 2500 BCE. It remains widely used in some Indian religions, such as Hinduism, Buddhism, and Jainism, mainly as a tantric symbol that evokes 'shakti'—auspiciousness. The notorious appropriation and transformation of the swastika by the Nazis—the rise of whom wreaked such worldwide havoc, to which the United States was both a dominant part of the solution and an insufficient place of refuge for would-be immigrants among the millions of Jews upon whom the Nazis exercised a particular destructive animus—adds another layer of interest to this particular Lilith.

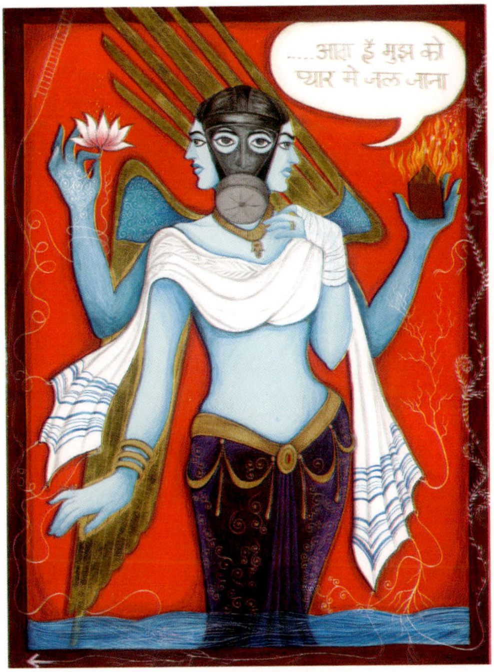

Fig. 5. Finding Home (*Fereshteh*) #105: Lilith, 2009

One can see further layers, both stylistic and conceptual, in two Liliths—#102 and #105 (Fig. 5)—that offer particularly overt reference to Lichtensteinian pop art and/or to Bollywood. The second of these has Lilith wearing an Israeli gas mask—for protection against Nuclear, Biological and Chemical dangers. She holds a burning house in one hand, while she contemplates a beautiful lotus flower in the other. The strings of her tallit extend and build ladders and form hooks to snare fish in the waters below. One string is tied around her little finger as a reminder. She recites a line from a Bollywood movie song '*Aata hai mujko pyar me jal jana*' (I know how to burn when in love), while she

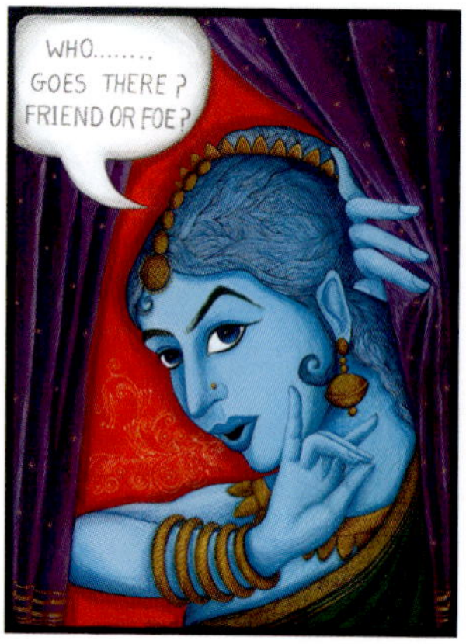

Fig 6. Finding Home (*Fereshteh*) #102: Lilith, 2009

nurses a bandaged hand. Will her wings promise to protect like steel swords? Will the strings extend themselves and build a web of protection?

Her sibling, #102, is inspired both by Lichtenstein's pop art and more specifically by the Amar Chitra Katha comic books of Siona's childhood (Figs 6 and 6a). Lilith looks seductively out of her window and asks 'Who goes there? Friend or Foe?' As the artist notes, 'In times like these, it is both ironic and necessary. Is it indeed a friend or it is a foe who comes by her window?'[11] She collaborated with a wood craftsman, Shifaz Usman, to produce the exquisite frame—inspired by the Moghul-era *jali* or netted window designs from palaces in India, Iran, and Pakistan (and in turn found distinctively on the upper reaches of the 1796 Sha'ar HaRahamim Synagogue in Mumbai).[12]

Siona's Liliths offer a concise articulation of how her diverse *Fereshteh*s and her conceptual approach to them are very often rooted in particular aspects of the Jewish tradition, interwoven with elements from other traditions. But the Jewish tradition itself cannot fail to offer questions to the careful student. As with so many faiths and cultures, Judaism's literature has traditionally been shaped by men, which means that the playing field of gender is an uneven one, although not always

[11] She comments this way in her website description of the piece.

[12] See Foreword, p. 12 and Chapter One, p. 75.

unsympathetic. Lilith's punishments are simultaneously approved and internally recognized as cruel.

Siona's paintings encompass an array of issues. Many of her *Fereshteh* figures have wings—but not all, which proves that wings do not an angel make. They all have blue flesh. On the one hand one recognizes this readily enough as a transformative allusion to Krishna[13] as he is often depicted in the Hindu tradition: the eighth avatar of the God Vishnu, in human form, who becomes a playful cowherd and the lover of Radha, the beautiful *gopi* (female cowherd). In fact, if for Vaishnavite Hindus, Krishna is merely an avatar of Vishnu, for Krishnaite Hindus—at least by the medieval period and the advent of the bhakti tradition—all gods, from Vishnu to Shiva to Brahma to Devi, are manifestations of the single, supreme godhead, Krishna.[14] But Vaishnavite and Krishnaite devotees neither disacknowledge the legitimacy of each others' spiritual emphases nor (for the most part) make war with each other—or with other Hindu groups—based on religion.

---

[13] The word 'krishna', in Sanskrit, literally means 'dark' or 'black' or 'dark blue'. Krishna is depicted early on as dark or black but eventually blue prevails as the pigment of choice in Hindu-tradition miniature paintings. The Bhakti tradition refers to his pigment as 'tinged with the hue of the blue clouds'.

[14] We may understand this paradox along two paths. One is to recognize it as a more complicated version of the belief within the Christian tradition according to which the One God is understood to be Triune—both divided and yet not divisable into Father, Son and Holy Spirit components. The other is to recognize the following parallel paradox: Hindu literature, (as noted earlier, in the introduction), is divided into *shruti* (literally: 'heard', essentially meaning divinely inspired) and *smrti* (literally: 'remembered', essentially meaning not divinely inspired) works. The *Baghavad Gita* (the words mean 'Divine Song') is a small piece of a larger whole. That whole is the epic poem the *Mahabharata*—a *smrti* work—but the *Gita*, which records at length the words of a god, Krishna, is *shruti*, even though it is embedded in a *smrti* work.

So, on the one hand, Krishna is invoked, with all the implications of that invocation, by the use of blue skin for Siona's *Fereshteh* as well as for figures in other works: they become associated with *bhakti* (love and devotion) and with broad-mindedness with respect to religious perspectives and the embrace of paradox. But on the other hand, the figures that the artist offers are typically female, so she has carried the idea of spiritual embrace to that of gender-diversity embrace. Her figures thus become embodiments of what in Hinduism is referred to as '*ardhanareshwara*'—a being half-woman and half-man. Ultimately, she has undercut, through the association of a skin color traditionally reserved most often for a male godhead, the implications of legitimizing male hegemony through associating God with maleness—whether that association is visual or verbal.

Her application of a skin color most popularly and familiarly[15] associated with a male figure to a series of females at the very least pushes the viewer who recognizes this aspect of the coloristic allusion to stop and rethink whatever (s)he thought (s)he knew about these images. But there is more. Siona has also synthesized the Hindu idea of *ardhanareshwara* to the Jewish kabbalistic idea of the *Shekhinah*: the female aspect of the genderless God that resides in all of us—both men and women—when we are 'gender-balanced' in our thoughts, words and actions. Moreover, '[v]ery often I look down at my skin and it has turned blue. It tends to do that when I face certain situations of people stereotyping and categorizing other people who are unlike themselves.'[16] So each of these figures is also

[15] The color is also associated with some female figures, notably Kali, but the image of Krishna is by far the most popular and familiar.

[16] From remarks made by the artist in conjunction with a 2007 exhibition of her work—'Blue Like Me: Paintings by Siona Benjamin'—at the Brooklyn Museum of Art.

a kind of self-portrait, and the entire series translates the personal to the universal with regard to two further interwoven issues.

The one is specific to race—skin color as a marker not only of 'Otherness', but to the observation she has made that, even within the context of feminist solidarity, it is not always so solid. Not only do 'even well-intentioned Western feminists often direct a Eurocentric gaze at sexual practices and politics elsewhere in the world', but more broadly, 'I have noticed and experienced myself that (regarding) non-western women… very often assumptions are made before we can open our mouths: "Do you speak English?", "Are you educated?", "Do you have our level of sophistication?", "Were you timid, oppressed, uneducated before you came to live in the west?"'[17]

So even within the feminist world, race can offer an unwitting definitional box for those whose perspective is insufficiently—not genuinely—global. The second issue, informed by the first, is that it actually isn't about race—or about gender or ethnicity or religion or nationality—but about all of these and whatever other ways in which we pre-judge others as other, as them, as different and, implicitly (or explicitly) less than we are.

Siona's figures are often both very specific—both because she labels many of them, thus identifying them as particular biblical or midrashic characters, and, to repeat, because they are all 'self-portraits'—and at the same time, universal. If on the one hand, 'in my case, if "them" did not turn out to be more like "us" then (my) skin turns blue, standing out as "the other", but also as a realization that "the other blue skin" can in turn

[17] These last two pairs of quotes come from the artist's remarks before a Morris Museum (New Jersey) audience on 21 May 2007.

be celebrated and accepted as normal in its difference'[18]—on the other hand, this is not about her, it is about all of us. And one of the things that we humans all share in common is our love of telling stories. Myth is universal, only its particular details differentiate one tradition from another. Siona's figures are bearers of myth, of story—they entertain as they educate, they wrap the past and its lessons around the future and its hopes. We also share the same sky across the entire planet, and yet another intention in her lavish use of blue for her figures and their contexts is to suggest the sky as a unifying element in the larger world that is mirrored in the microcosmic world of her paintings.[19]

There are diverse bridges that Siona uses to carry the personal to the universal, in the specific subjects and the particular symbols that are part of her ever-expanding vocabulary. The blue skin of her figures reflects other parts of the Indian miniature tradition and not only the portrayal of Krishna. She is also inspired by the larger Indic tradition and in particular its goddesses (like the ambiguous Kali). And if, as she says 'the blue skin has become a symbol for me of being *a Jewish woman of color*'[20] (italics added), which therefore identifies three specific aspects of her as a multiple subset of humanity; then the fact that her figures are nearly all women drawn from the Jewish tradition underscores those other two aspects (religion and gender) of her bridging personal to universal, together with the third (race).

---

[18] Brooklyn Museum of Art comments. Ibid.

[19] She has also commented on the blue as a reference to the unifying ocean that rings the planet—and for Jews, the unifying element of blue within the traditional *tallit* (prayer shawl—that then finds its way into the Israeli flag.

[20] Brooklyn Museum of Art comments. Ibid

The figurative aspect of her work is also wedded to an emphasis on background color and geometric, vegetal and floral patterns that are part of Muslim art—and in her most intimate art historical experience, in particular Persian Muslim art. Her lavish use of gold leaf to create spaceless space backgrounds for some of her works resonates from the world of Byzantine icons and medieval Christian paintings—as well as from the illuminated manuscript traditions within the Christian and Jewish European worlds. She is as conscious of and inspired by the bold Bollywood posters that plaster the city walls in the country in which she grew up—and the Amar Chitra Katha comic books familiar to her from her Bombay years—as she is of the poster-sized comic book moments re-visioned on that branch from the tree of Pop Art associated with Roy Lichtenstein, in the country that she now calls home.

The matter of 'Finding Home' is not only a matter of moving from one physical place to another. It is about—to come full circle to Siona's transnationality—being comfortable with being part of varied cultures and traditions and drawing from them to create one's art not only as a stunning aesthetic exercise, but as a teaching instrument to the next generation and the next—in a world the diverse parts of which are increasingly proximate through technologies like the internet. It is about being (in the artist's words) 'a transcultural artist… able to change his/her colors according to the environment'.[21] It is about being comfortable in one's own skin—a psychological metaphor which Siona has literalized visually.

Consider one of Benjamin's powerful and visually disturbing representations of 'Miriam': a small—10 x 7"—2006 gouache and gold leaf work on wood panel; #73 from the *Finding Home* (*Fereshteh*) series

[21] Ibid.

(Fig. 7). Miriam was the sister of Moses, the leader of joyful dances after the miraculous passage by the Israelites through the Sea of Reeds, and the finder of water in the wilderness. She was, moreover, the one by whose merit, according to a well-known midrash, God enabled a well of water to accompany the Israelites through the wilderness.[22]

But Miriam has been virtually passed over (pun intended) in the traditional narrative of the Passover Seder. That omission began to change two decades ago with the advent of the 'Miriam's Cup', a goblet that honors her, and that, filled with water, offers a female symbol of salvation to counterbalance the Elijah goblet filled with wine. Siona depicts Miriam with blue skin, like Krishna, and wearing a sari. She reclines in a goblet, connected intravenously to both water and blood as life sources, and surrounded by a grisaille mushroom cloud of faces, human and animal, beautiful and hideous. One might ask: Are these the faces of the people of Israel, present and future? Closer inspection suggests the faces of destroyers—the Egyptians—swallowed by the sea, turned gray and rising as a distant, threatening mushroom cloud. Are not all humans, though, Israelites, Egyptians and others, potentially creative and destructive, beautiful and ugly? Set in a field marked by dark-blue shadows (five of them, like the number of books in the Torah), the goblet is surrounded and framed by vegetal and floral imagery—including lotus blossoms, that close at night and re-open in the morning, thus symbolizing the ongoing cycle of life-death-rebirth, endemic to Indian culture and art. Vines that can overwhelm and even strangle but that, with their blossoms, are the imagery of fertility and life.

[22] See, e.g., Numbers Rabbah 1:2.

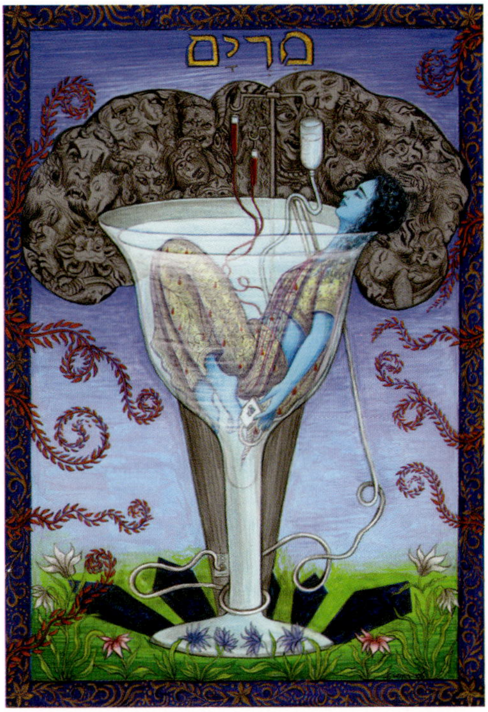

Fig. 7. Finding Home (*Fereshteh*) #73: Miriam, 2006

Like Lilith, Miriam is a character to whom Siona is drawn as an artist; she has portrayed her several times within her *Finding Home* (*Fereshteh*) subseries. The artist who wandered for many years before recognizing that her home is where she chooses to make it, could hardly not be drawn to a leader of the Israelites who wandered for 40 years in the wilderness, seeking home—seeking the Promised Land that they understood to be the land from which their ancestors had migrated to Egypt, so many generations earlier, but would not be theirs until they grew into it and made it their home again.

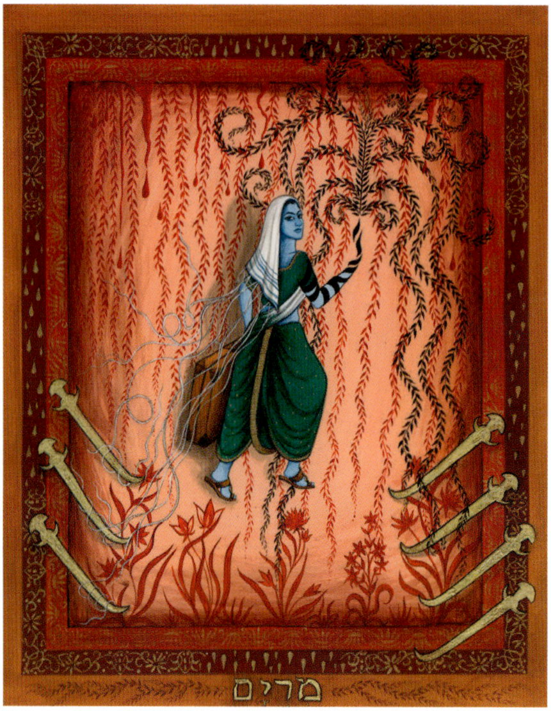

Fig. 8. Finding Home (*Fereshteh*) #77: Miriam, 2006

In Finding Home #77 (*Fereshteh*),'Miriam', (also 2006), the heroine carries a suitcase—the sort of suitcase that anyone might recognize as belonging to a ship-borne immigrant of a century ago, (or an immigrant arriving into JFK airport today, so that the story being told is as contemporary as it is ancient), with all of his/her old-world belongings and memories packed tightly, almost desperately, into it. Moreover, Miriam—who, as usual, may also be seen as a self-portrait, wears the green (and within the Bene Israel community, therefore wedding) sari of Siona's great-grandmother. The arm and hand wrapped with the leather

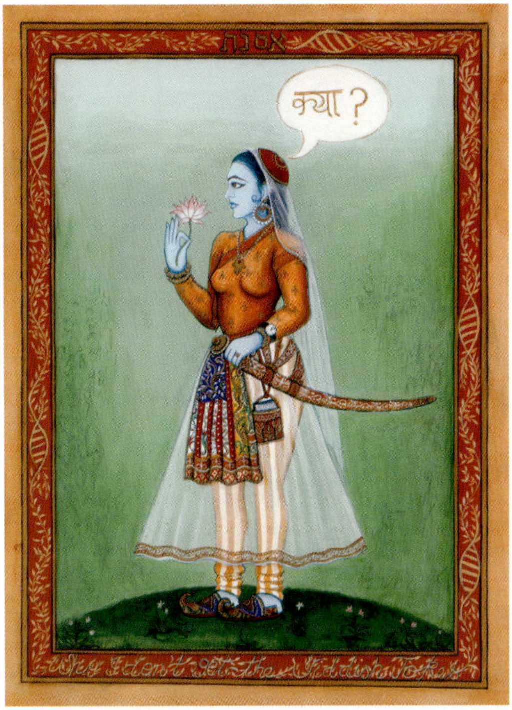

Fig. 9. Finding Home (*Fereshteh*) #62: Asnat, 2004

straps and box of the T'fillin—worn traditionally by Jewish males during daily morning prayers—terminates with the beginning of the endless vines of the Tree of Life (Fig. 8).

Other works from this same period in the artist's crowded oeuvre reflect on other women whose biblical stories in their profound ambiguity have necessitated intense rabbinic discussion. 'Asnat'—*Finding Home* #62 (*Fereshteh*)—depicts the Egyptian wife of Joseph, who bears him two sons, Ephraim and Manasseh (Gen 41:50-2)—and whom one midrash discusses as the daughter of Potiphar (whose wife had tried to seduce Joseph, which got him thrown into prison, which led to his meeting the cupbearer of Pharaoh, which led to his interpreting Pharaoh's dreams, which led to his Prime Ministership, which led the Israelites to Egypt, which led to…) (Fig. 9).[23] She is depicted by Siona in profile in the style of a Moghul imperial portrait[24] in a 2004 gouache and gold leaf on paper.[25] This 'foreigner' in Joseph's branch of the Israelite tree is identified by her name in Hebrew on the upper part of the painted 'frame'. But subtly interwoven with the decorative motifs along the lower part of that frame is the phrase 'Why I don't Get the Yiddish Jokes'—jokes in that Ashkenazi language—language that is as obscure to Siona's growing up as the *Devanagari* writing on the image is to Ashkenazi Jews. That writing is used to spell out the Hindi word for 'what?' in a comic-book-like bubble that begins to bring the world of Pop Art into that of the Moghuls.[26]

The other woman, besides Miriam, in the life of the adult Moses, is also portrayed by Siona. A small 2005 gouache and gold leaf on paper work depicts *Finding Home* #76: 'Tzipporah'—another 'foreigner', like Asnat. Both, according to the biblical texts, were daughters of priests, in fact—Asnat an Egyptian and Tzipporah a Midianite. Moses encountered Tzipporah while in exile from Egypt in the aftermath of his killing an

---

[23] There are, not surprisingly, other midrashic stories about Asnat—such as that she was the offspring of Dinah (Jacob's sole daughter and therefore Joseph's sister) and the son of the Pharaoh.

[24] She combines the general image of the princess with aspects of the emperor (e.g., the large sword) with a skullcap head-covering that derives from the Jewish (male) tradition.

[25] The rabbinic discussion is found in *Pirkei de Rabbi Eliezer* 37.

[26] '*Devanagari*' means 'city of the gods' and is so-called due to the implication that such a writing system was contrived by gods. It was used in antiquity to write Vedic and Classical Sanskrit, continued in use in the medieval and into the modern period, where it is still used to write Hindi and other related post-Sanskrit languages.

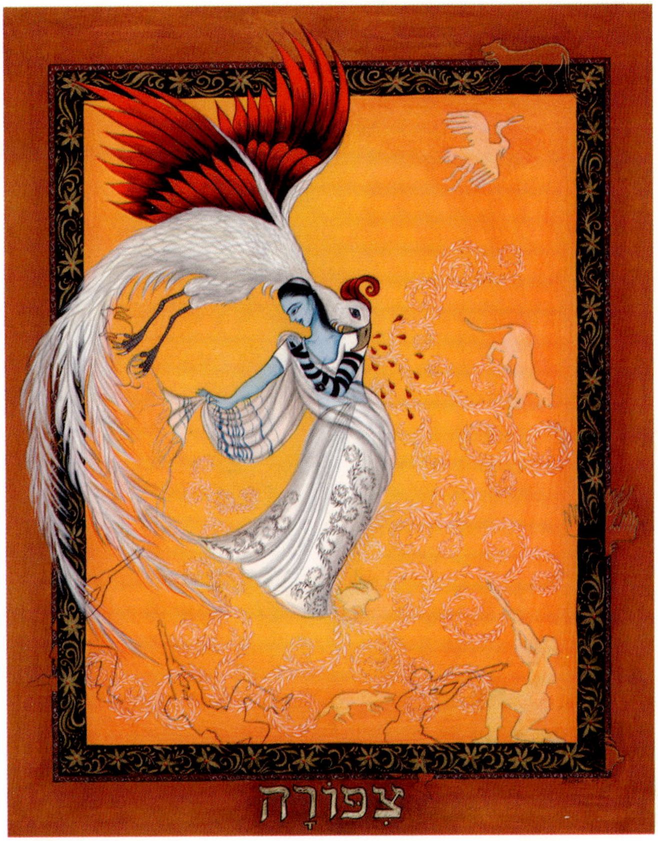

Fig. 10. Finding Home (*Fereshteh*) #76: Tzipporah, 2005

Egyptian task-master who had been beating an Israelite slave. Later, on the way back into Egypt so that Moses might obey God's commandment to him delivered at the Burning Bush, Tzipporah circumcises their son, Gershom, perhaps thereby saving Moses' life from an angry God's wrath, in an obscure biblical passage (Ex 4:24-6) that has provoked a good deal of rabbinic discussion (Fig. 10).

Siona has wafted her Tzipporah into the middle of the image; her left arm, wrapped in phylactery[27] thongs is pierced at the shoulder by a phantasmagorical bird—is it a Persian tawus (a peacock-like bird) or a hoopoe, who leads the flock of birds that make an arduous journey, from which 30 ultimately arrive to meet their Maker, the Simurg, at the end of Attar's *Conference of the Birds*; or is it the brilliantly-colored, benevolent Simurg itself, of which there is only one, like the Egyptian and Greek Phoenix, like the Russian Golden Cockerel, like the Slavic Firebird (for every tradition has its own of some sort)? Does the bird inflict the wound? Or is it gently and protectively removing her from the battlefield below? For one may discern there the shadowy figure of a contemporary-era soldier, his rifle raised to his shoulder, aimed at hers. If she is lifted above the bloodshed as she bleeds, she lifts herself up, for her name, Tzipporah, means 'bird'(*tzippor*) in Hebrew.

Ambiguities and an endless series of grey shades between absolute black and white drive the imagistic and symbolic language of Siona Benjamin's work, reflecting not only the diverse range of her personal experience in the world but also her sense of the world at large as fraught with ambiguity and with endless shades of grey. Nowhere is this clearer than in her 2006 image, *Finding Home #82* (*Fereshteh*), 'Joseph', which focuses on a male who is singled out in the text of the Torah for his physical beauty—it is that physical beauty that catches the eye of Potiphar's wife (Gen 39:6-7 ff) and leads to the narrative that will include Asnat.

And Joseph offers stereotypical male and female character traits. He begins as a spoiled, narcissistic child whose dreams are about his

[27] These are the T'fillin noted in Fig 7: small black leather boxes containing parchment inscribed with Torah verses and strapped on the upper arm (and forehead) of adult Jewish males during morning prayers.

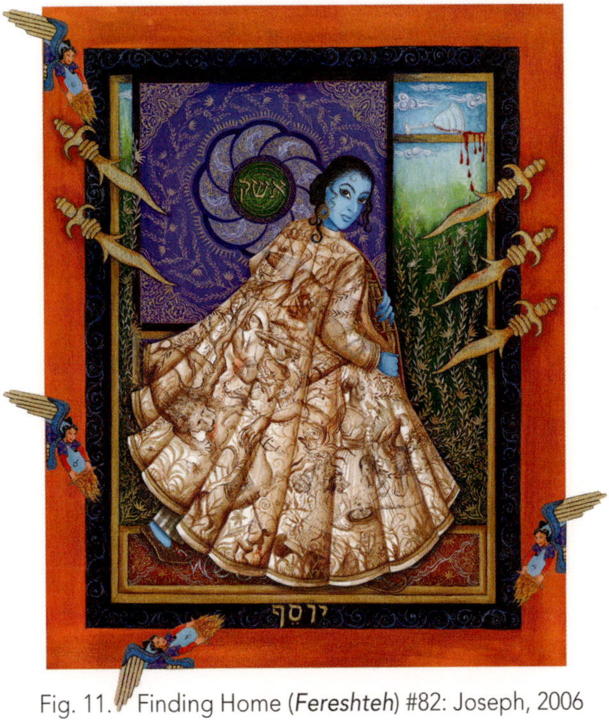

Fig. 11. Finding Home (*Fereshteh*) #82: Joseph, 2006

own glory, at the cost of his parents and siblings—and he plays with the fears of those siblings, years later, when he has them in his power, before revealing himself to them—all qualities that one might stereotype as male. But by the end of his story, after the death of his father, Jacob-Israel, he has recognized not only that God has been behind his enormous success, but more importantly, that the entire story had not been about him, but divinely guided 'to bring it about that many people should be kept alive' (Gen 50:20)—which conveying of credit elsewhere might be called stereotypically female. So one might say that Joseph eventually found his feminine side (Fig. 11).

Siona's Joseph is indeed, quite beautiful in an almost girlish way, with long, lush, dark hair, thick with curls, some of which spill out of his coif and down his blue-skin cheeks as she looks back over her shoulder winsomely, hurrying away from us. Joseph wears a rich coat-like garment—not one of many colors, in fact, but one where the viewer can almost feel the heavy silkiness, overrun in a grisaille-like manner with images of faces and figures: a kind of cross between a hunting carpet pattern out of Persia or India and the large cloud array that arises behind the goblet of Miriam (in *Fereshteh* #73, see Fig. 7). The coat is spread out like—well, like a dress whose feminine wearer has just turned suddenly, with a flourish.

Within the 22 x 17" painting, in the center of a floral motif at the center of a carpet-like image hovering in the air as if hanging on an invisible wall are the Hebrew letters aleph, shin, kuf. The letters spell out the Urdu word, 'Ishq', meaning 'divine love' or 'God-driven love' as noted above—the sort that Joseph came to understand had enveloped him even when his brothers hated him or Potiphar's wife sought to destroy him. Five elaborate golden monochrome knives with long blades 'decorate'—they might be said to overrun—the frame, their points directed in toward the figure. Their number alludes to the number of books in the Torah (the text in which Joseph's story is told and that connects Israel to the God who, Joseph observed at the time of his father's death, had guided his life and the lives of those around him, turning negative into positive, as just noted).

This is also the number of wounds in Christ's body (blood drips from a horizontal beam across the upper right of the painting) and also of the pillars of Islam. Indeed, the blood also suggests wine, dripping from the fallen goblet on that beam—consistent with the Sufi equation between human and divine love as intoxicants. Such imagery is embedded in the extended allegorical poem, Yusuf (Joseph) and Zulaikha, by the Perso-Afghan Sufi, Jami. In other words, the number five itself is a bridge, a connector among the three Abrahamic traditions for all of whom Joseph is, one way or another, an important ancestral figure.

The most obvious other figure in the Hebrew Bible noted for her beauty is Esther. It shouldn't surprise us to find her as a subject in Siona's work. After all, that savior of her people has an entire book devoted to and named for her—although, in strong contrast to the Joseph story, the text never mentions God in the course of its narrative. The book of Esther, in fact, was the last to be accepted into the biblical canon, largely for that reason. On the other hand, it was a necessary addition: the only tale placed entirely in the diaspora, it speaks of how courage and adherence to one's principles can lead to triumph over enemies bound on one's destruction. It is also unique in the biblical context in offering a female as its primary heroic figure.

More unusual than the expected Esther—but not for Siona's art—is her *Finding Home* (*Fereshteh*) #89, also from 2006, and also made of gouache and gold leaf (but on wood), and of very small dimensions (10 x 7"); 'Vashti'—the other female in the story, who, as queen of Persia, having refused to entertain her drunken husband's drunken friends, was removed from the throne (Fig. 12). That decision, by way of the beauty contest subsequently held in order to find a new queen, led to Esther's accession to the position of uncertain power through which she would end up able to save her people from their would-be destroyer, Haman, (the king's vizier)—albeit at great risk to herself.

Siona's Vashti is hugely, surrealistically proportioned—and blue-skinned, of course—with gold and blue *fereshtini* wings, as she peers through an opening in a stage-set-like structure; we can see one eye of

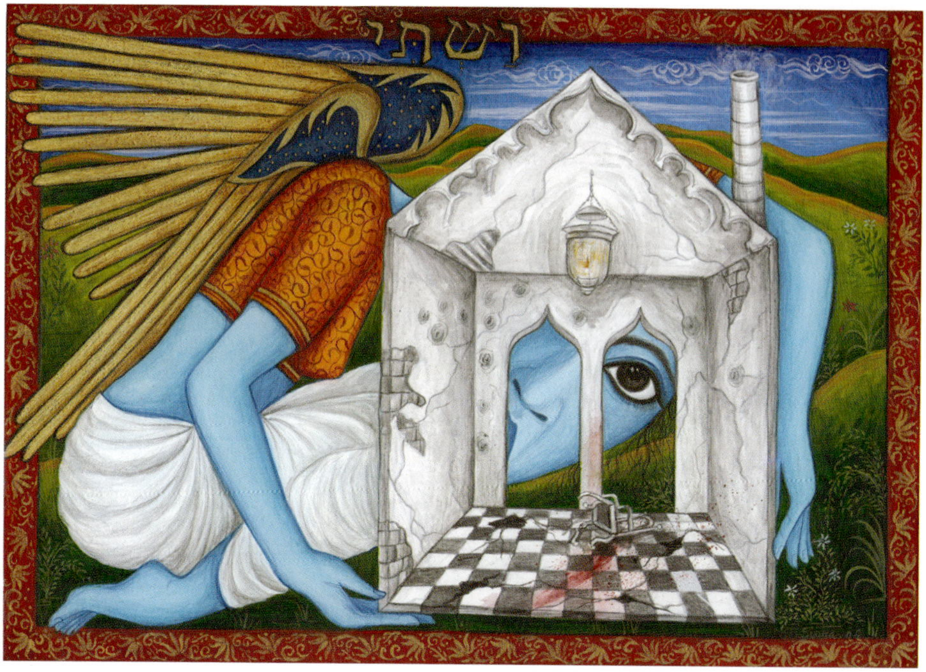

Fig. 12. Finding Home (*Fereshteh*) #89: Vashti, 2006

her enormous face, staring steadily and perhaps inquisitively out at us. The crumbling house, its wall on the viewer's side removed so that the dollhouse interior is open to our view, offers a chessboard-patterned floor—we are reminded that the game of chess originated in Persia and that the very word, 'chess' is a derivative of the Persian word for king, '*Shakh*'. A Louis XV-style chair has been knocked over, red pigment, suggesting blood (but its color also suggests wine) is slathered across the floor and Moorish-style arches elaborate the roofline as well as defining the openings through one of which Vashti looks simultaneously in (to the room) and out (at us).

Jewish tradition views Haman, the villain of this narrative, as the descendant of the Amalekites, the would-be destroyers of the Israelites in the wilderness beyond Egypt and, more recently, in more modern midrash, as the spiritual ancestor of Hitler. Is the chimney on this house-that-is-no-home, whose sole color, inside or out, is that of blood, derived from the iconography of Auschwitz? And is Vashti the indirect angel of salvation, without whose brave act of defiance the stage (this stage-set palace, its knocked-over throne empty of its queen) would not have been set for Esther and Mordecai to save the Judaeans—her outsized eye staring all the way through to twentieth-century destruction and redemption?

III. *Megillat Esther*

The entire story was taken up by Siona in a magnificent illuminated scroll presenting the Book of Esther—a *Megillat Esther* (Scroll of Esther) commissioned by a private dealer in 2007. Around, over, and above its extensive Hebrew text the visual elements flow with distinctly Indian and Persian illumination elements that resonate from Siona's multi-cultural and inter-religious background. That most prominent of flowers in the Indian tradition, the lotus—a symbol of the cycle of birth-death-rebirth because it closes up its petals at night and reopens them in the morning—decorates the opening edge as well as the lower edge of the first frame of the story (reading from right to left). Just above that edge, and below the opening lines of the text, are the words, 'Story of Esther' ('Esther che Katha')—written in the *Devanagari* writing system that conveys the Marathi language dominant in Mumbai (among other Indic languages, past and present).

The opening scene offers the king in a distinctive Mughal style: we see him ensconced on his throne from the waist up; a court dancer, swirls before him, her limbs splayed out in a kind of broken cross—recalling one of Siona's Liliths. By contrast, below, Vashti reclines in her boudoir, virtually unclothed and admiring herself in a hand-held mirror (Fig. 13). As the scroll unfolds (or, rather, unrolls), its components—aside from the beautifully calligraphed text—includes three primary elements. One is the cornucopia of diverse flora and fauna derived from the Indian landscape as well as Middle Eastern landscapes—from elephants and high-shouldered Indian bulls to lions and an array of camels. The second is the ongoing series of illustrations in gold-leaf frames running along beneath the text (one horizontally configured rectangle per register of narrative), in which some moments from the story are represented—beginning with the king's decision to elevate Haman to vizier status and continuing with Mordecai sitting mournfully, cross-legged, before the palace gates and on to the image of Haman and his advisers choosing a date upon which to purge the kingdom of the Judaeans—to the destruction of Haman toward the end of the narrative.

Most elaborate is the series of full illustrations between every pair of text columns. The first of these depicts the beauty contest, and the king using his scepter to indicate a very blue-skinned Esther as his bride of choice. The next offers a regal, blue-skinned—very Krishna-like—Esther serving the king and his leering vizier with tea (Fig. 14). Nearby, as Haman plots, sniffing the rose of his expected success, his large, curved knife spilling out of the picture 'frame', Esther dances her desperation; around her swirl white grisaille horsemen, brandishing spears.

By the next register, however, things are starting to go badly for Haman, who is shown, head bowed, garbage being poured on him by his unwitting wife from the balcony of their house, leading the white horse—a messianic, salvational allusion in the purity of its equine color—upon which a crowned, *tallit*-wearing Mordecai sits. Haman is forced to announce to all of the inhabitants of the city of Shushan that 'this is the man whom the king delights to honor!' The next series of texts is uniquely threefold rather than being a double register of texts; in each of the two spaces between them a sharp knife, dripping blood, is depicted, at different levels. Should it surprise us that, in the next interstitial illustration, all of Haman's sons are shown hanging, as in the story? But their heads are covered with sacks, as if the event is taking place in contemporary Iran—and the scaffolding is surmounted with sharp stakes upon which each of their heads is impaled, further shaping the image as a visual reflection of medieval and contemporary Middle Eastern executionary events.

The last interstitial illustration offers the Judaeans rejoicing over their victory over Haman; the central figure, in fact, carries on his head a large tray heaped high with *hamantaschen*—literally, (in Yiddish!), 'Haman pockets'—that are the primary treat distributed neighbor to neighbor in much of the Jewish diaspora during the brief festival of Purim, when the entire narrative of the scroll is read out in the synagogues of Mumbai, as in synagogues across the world. A blue-skinned Esther peers into the festive, music-making scene from the upper right. Her last appearance in Siona's scroll is in the final, lotus-decorated, gold-leaf framed lozenge below the last register of text. We see her from the waist up, dancing—not this time, however, in desperation, but in Thanksgiving and benediction. Her arms have multiplied like those of Shiva Nataraj

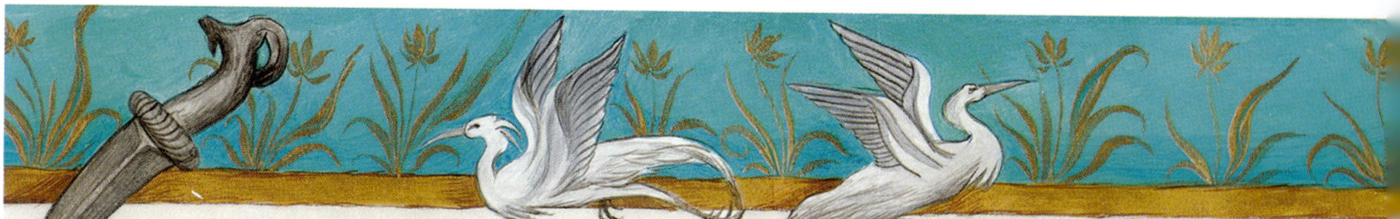

חשורוש הוא אחשורוש המלך
כוש שבע ועשרים ומאה מדינה
כשבת המלך אחשורוש על כסא
יר בשושן הבירה בשנת שלוש
ה משתה לכל שריו ועבדיו חיל
הפרתמים ושרי המדינות לפניו
ת עשר כבוד מלכותו ואת יקר
לתו ימים רבים שמונים ומאת יום
מים האלה עשה המלך לכל העם
שושן הבירה למגדול ועד קטן
עת ימים בחצר גנת ביתן המלך
ותכלת אחוז בחבלי בוץ וארגמן
סף ועמודי שש מטות זהב וכסף
בהט ושש ודר וסחרת והשקות
לים מכלים שונים ויין מלכות רב
והשתיה כדת אין אנס כי כן יסד
כל רב ביתו לעשות כרצון איש
גם ושתי
שתה משתה נשים בית המלכות
אחשורוש ביום השביעי כטוב
ביין אמר למהומן בזתא חרבונא

בגתא ואבגתא זתר וכרכס שבעת הסריסים
המשרתים את פני המלך אחשורוש להביא
את ושתי המלכה לפני המלך בכתר מלכות
להראות העמים והשרים את יפיה כי טובת
מראה היא ותמאן המלכה ושתי לבוא בדבר
המלך אשר ביד הסריסים ויקצף המלך מאד
וחמתו בערה בו ויאמר
המלך לחכמים ידעי העתים כי כן דבר
המלך לפני כל ידעי דת ודין והקרב
אליו כרשנא שתר אדמתא תרשיש מרס
מרסנא ממוכן שבעת שרי פרס ומדי ראי
פני המלך הישבים ראשנה במלכות כדת
מה לעשות במלכה ושתי על אשר לא
עשתה את מאמר המלך אחשורוש ביד
הסריסים ויאמר מומכן לפני
המלך והשרים לא על המלך לבדו עותה
ושתי המלכה כי על כל השרים ועל כל
העמים אשר בכל מדינות המלך אחשורוש
כי יצא דבר המלכה על כל הנשים להבזות
בעליהן בעיניהן באמרם המלך אחשורוש
אמר להביא את ושתי המלכה לפניו ולא באה

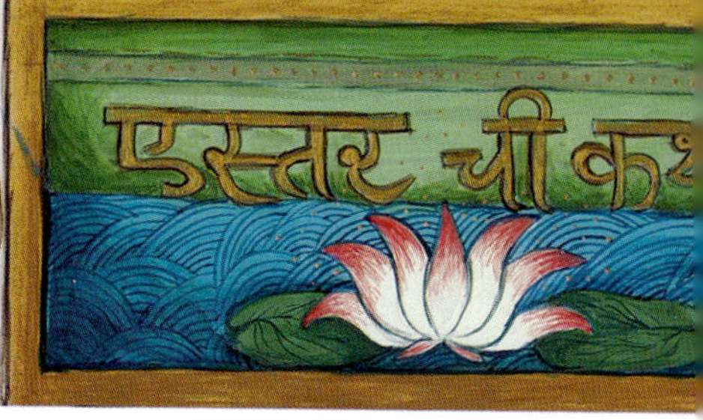

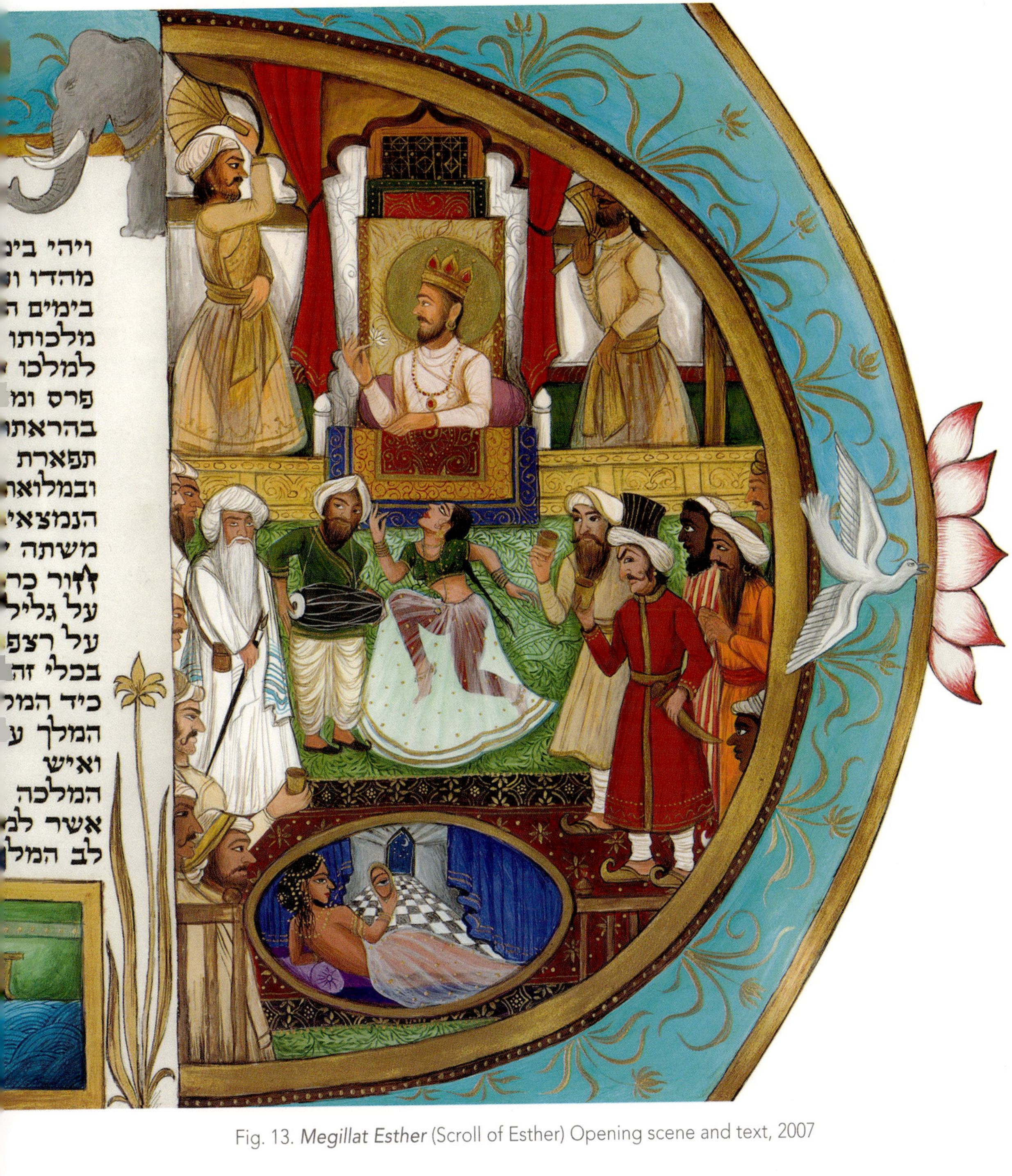

Fig. 13. *Megillat Esther* (Scroll of Esther) Opening scene and text, 2007

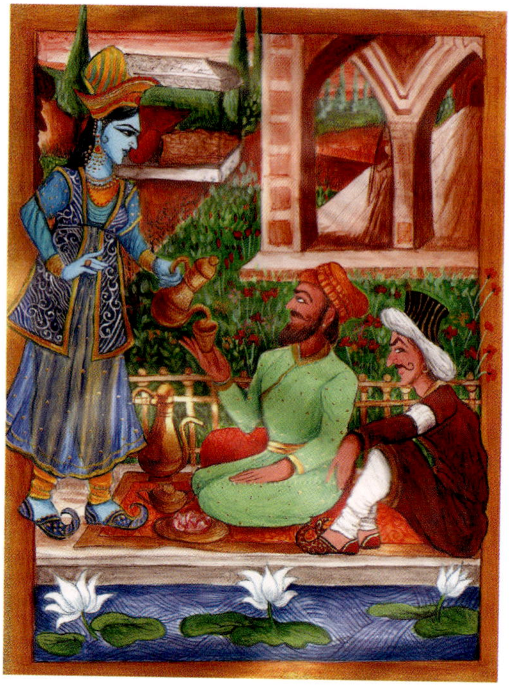

Fig. 14. *Megillat Esther* (Scroll of Esther) Esther entertains Ahasuerus and Haman, 2007

or Kali—there are five arms, like the number of books in the Torah (Fig. 15). Each terminates with a hand the fingers of which are configured—like those of the High Priest in the Temple, according to tradition, as he blesses the community—to form the Hebrew letter 'shin'. This letter stands for the word, Shaddai, which is used to refer to God in Its power-protective, warrior aspect. For Esther has triumphed, by way of her faith in her own capabilities and in the God never mentioned explicitly in the text, over a very dangerous enemy, on behalf of herself and her people.

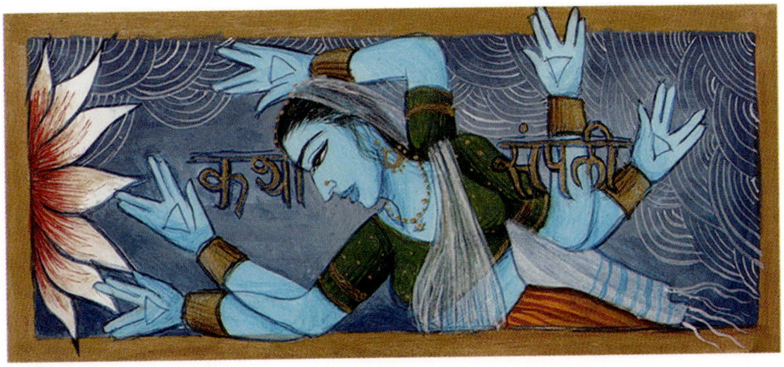

Fig. 15. Detail from *Megillat* Esther (Scroll of Esther) Esther's Triumph, 2007

One steps away from the details in this work with a strong feel for elements that are at once Hindu, Muslim, Jewish—even, by way of the gold-leaf elements, Byzantine Christian—Middle Eastern and Indian, medieval and modern, synthesized both comfortably and lyrically.

IV. From *Improvisations* to *Faces* to the *Exodus and Liberty* Series

In 2011, Siona began work on a new series called, as an entirety, *Improvisations*. Very different from the *Fereshteh* series and other earlier work, her palette was deliberately lighter and more monochromatic than previously—gray and tan, light green and deep light blue, sometimes inundated with a delicate web of floral and vegetal motifs, and sometimes with abstract yet organic patterns of gray, white, and gold leaf. Diverse figures—ghostly white cranes and oxen and more solidly depicted horses and dragons with human heads, and a dancing girl whose skirt is the sea itself—share the intricate space.

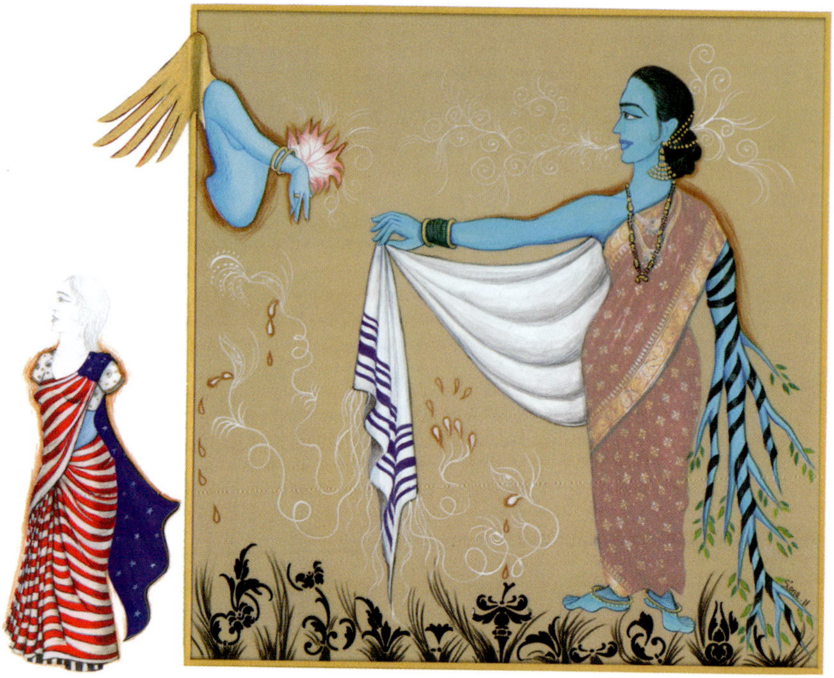

Fig. 16. *Improvisations* #14, 2011

'Improvisations #14' presents a blue-skinned Indian woman wearing a sari, her left arm evolving into a flowering tree branch, her right hand unfurling a *tallit* (Fig. 16). It extends toward a disembodied blue-skinned torso and arm with a bursting lotus blossom at its wrist, and a gold-leaf wing—suggesting that this is a kind of *fereshteh*—that spills outside the 'frame'. Fully outside that 'frame' the main figure is echoed by an armless figure: the pale white marble 'Venus de Milo', that icon of Western art; she is also wrapped in a sari that recalls the American flag. The work, like the artist who made it, offers multiple simultaneous identities.

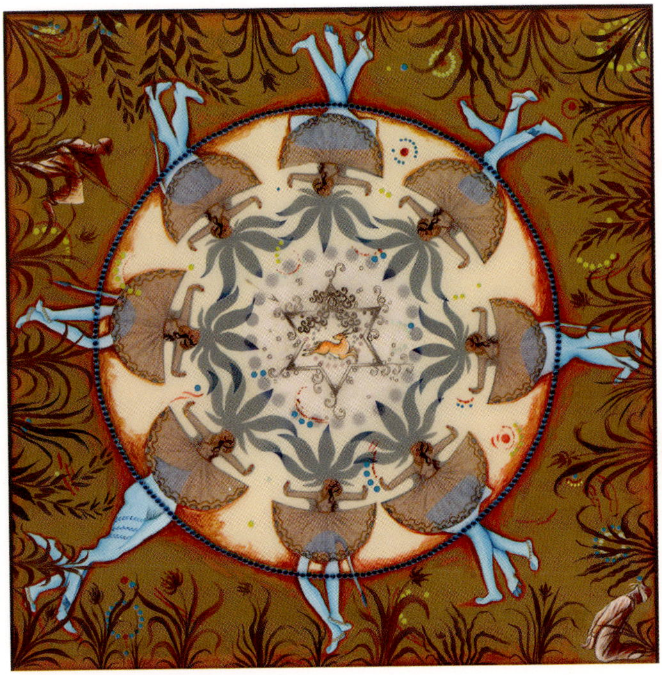

Fig. 17. *Improvisations* #18, 2011

Several among the *Improvisations* series—numbers 15, 17, 18, and 19—morph in part or in toto into kaleidoscope-like multiplications of their primary images. One of these is particularly mandala-like (#18): a circle the deep blue and reddish outer edge of which bifurcates eight dancing female figures facing in toward the center, a swirling seven-part effusion flowing out, it almost seems, from each of their heads and in turn, further in, a series of abstract vegetal elements and finally a six-pointed star with a small hind in full stride as the central element (Fig. 17). The bifurcating edge of the circle offers the outflowing skirts and outstretched arms of the dancers, suggesting a whirling movement—and outside the circle the blue-skinned naked lower parts. No two of these female figures are identical; four of them have two legs each and the other four have three; one, larger than the others, is visible all the way up, past her pubic area, to her waist. Outside the circle, a profusion of diverse flowers and plants populates a rich gold-leaf field, with two small figures barely discernible among the plants and flowers.

The November 2008, terrorist attack in Mumbai on the Chabad-run Nariman House—a Jewish outreach center established by an Orthodox Jewish group with roots in a mystical movement founded in mid-eighteenth-century Eastern Europe—and on the Taj Mahal hotel and six other locations, in which the young Chabad rabbi and his wife were among the six people who died, helped eventually to inspire Siona to create a further series, called *Faces: Weaving Indian Jewish Narratives*. She has observed that the news reports of the terrorist attack caused many Americans (at least those she encountered), to wonder about a community that they did not realize had existed. She repeatedly encountered the question: 'Did Jews first inhabit India with the establishment of Chabad House? If not, then what did the local Jewish population look and sound like?'

This led her to seek (and receive) a Fulbright fellowship through which she came back to Mumbai to create a new body of work, in 2012–13, that combined photograph-collages from among scores that she took as she interviewed 65 members of the Jewish community in Mumbai. She then embellished these images with gouache and 22-karat gold leaf to paint her subjects' stories—once again emulating the painting styles of Indian and Persian miniatures on the one hand and Bollywood posters and American Pop art on the other.

> Visualizing the Bene Israel Jewish faces and the painted ornamentation around them, they could be the ghost images from my past, my childhood in Jewish India, weaving new and old stories. Are these faces from dreams and memories or are they just other faces on passports or immigration cards or perhaps from my family's photo albums? It is with these faces and their stories that the rest of the world, I hope, will come to know the Bene Israel Jews in a very transnational India.[28]

These faces are wonderfully varied. Maayan Abraham (Sharpurkar) stares straight out at the viewer, her young, gentle, infinitely sweet face filling the space surrounded by a thick, mottled gold-leaf 'frame' across parts of which a wine-red pattern weaves itself (Fig. 18). To the lower left and right of the central image, the pattern takes the form of a pair of flowers, some of the blossoms of which suggest the form of hands assuming the positions—*mudras*—of Indian dance, but may also be recognized as repetitions of the hands of Leonardo da Vinci's renowned Mona Lisa, with whom Maayan also shares an enigmatic smile.

Very differently conceived is the portrait face of Daniel Elijah Benjamin (Gadkar)—who died shortly after he was interviewed (Fig. 19). His profile floats, skullcap (*kippah*) on his head, in a circle of gold leaf, like a Byzantine halo, that in turn floats within the Succath Shelomo Synagogue interior, just above the pulpit (*tevah/bimah*). Beyond it, in the background, the Holy Ark (*heikhal/aron*) draws one's eye, with its wine red-with-gold curtain (*parokhet*) sporting a six-pointed star and, hanging before it, the Eternal Lamp (*Ner Tamid*).

[28] I am quoting from Siona's Fulbright grant proposal.

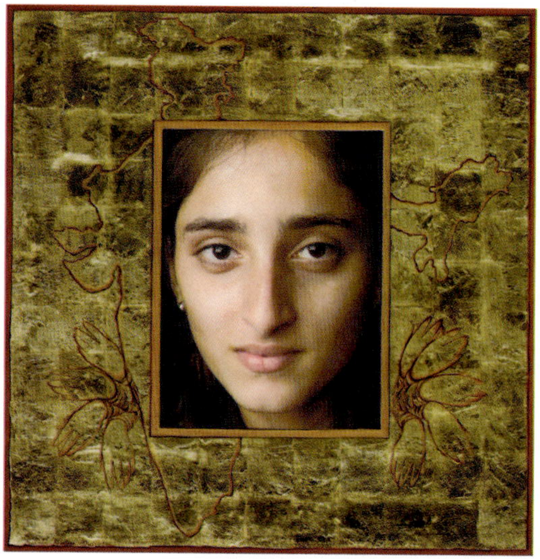

Fig. 18. Maayan Abraham (Sharpurkar), 2012–13

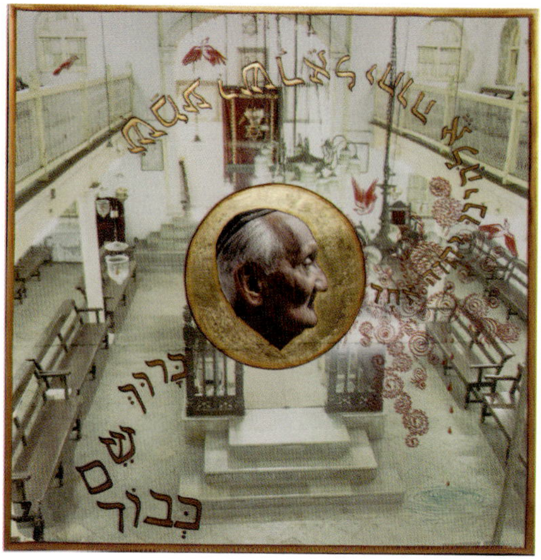

Fig. 19. Daniel Elijah Benjamin (Gadkar), 2012–13

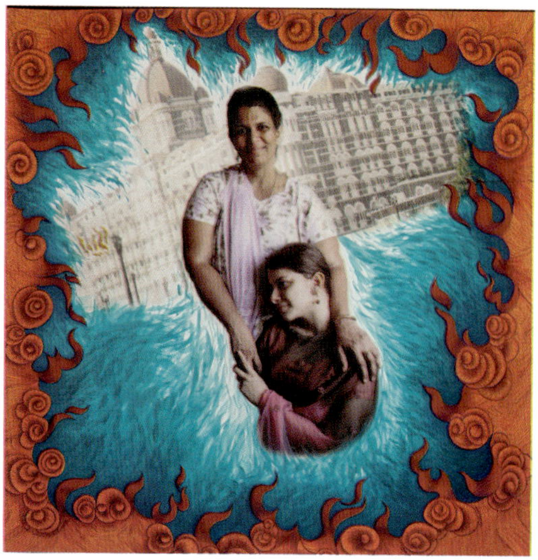

Fig. 20. Monica and Mozel Moses (Pugaonkar), 2012–13

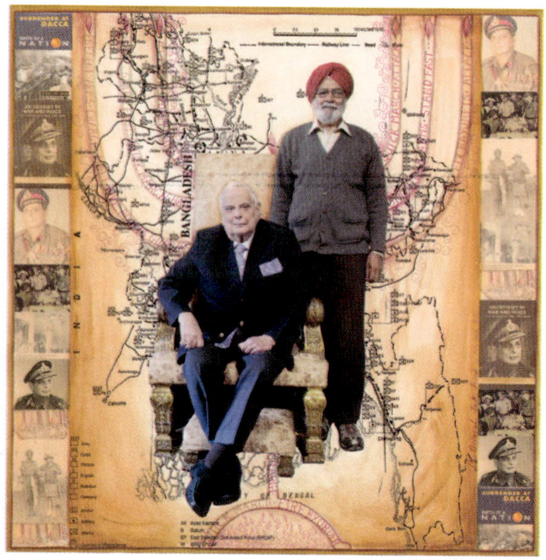

Fig. 21. Lt General Jack Jacob and Pal Singh Gill, 2012–13

Siona has inscribed the Hebrew words in gold—swirling upside down and right side up across the space, toward and from the central halo-medallion—of Judaism's central credo: 'Hear O Israel: the Lord is our God; the Lord is One. Blessed be the Holy Name...' Delicate vegetal circles in wine-red, their style a familiar part of her repertoire of abstract embellishments, dance to the right of the portrait with four dove-like birds—peace symbols, their number the number of letters in God's ineffable Hebrew name, (YHVH), but also universal symbols of the soul (for whom, according to the artist's grandmother, we must leave breadcrumbs on our windowsills)—while her brush enlivens one corner of the white-washed floor; the impeccable interior comes alive with a watery surface.

Some images are double portraits—like that of Mozel and Monica Moses (Pugaonkar)—mother and daughter (Fig. 20). Their husband/father was the only Jewish member of the Fire Brigade to be engaged in quenching the 2008 post-bombing fire at the Taj hotel—and so Siona has surrounded them and the majestic edifice with water and fire as their framing symbols.

Very different in sensibility is the double portrait of Lt General Jack Jacob (and Pal Singh Gill, his lifelong assistant) (Fig. 21). The Jewish Lt General—reminding us how frequently Jews served, particularly in the British army in India—and his turbanned Sikh assistant are situated against a backdrop that superimposes a seven-branched menorah inscribed along its stem and branches with British military sayings (for example, 'Stand fast!', 'Fire by order!') against a map of northeastern India, where Jacob served with distinction. Like a Byzantine icon, the main image is flanked up and down its two sides by smaller images of Lt General Jacob in uniform in earlier times of his life.

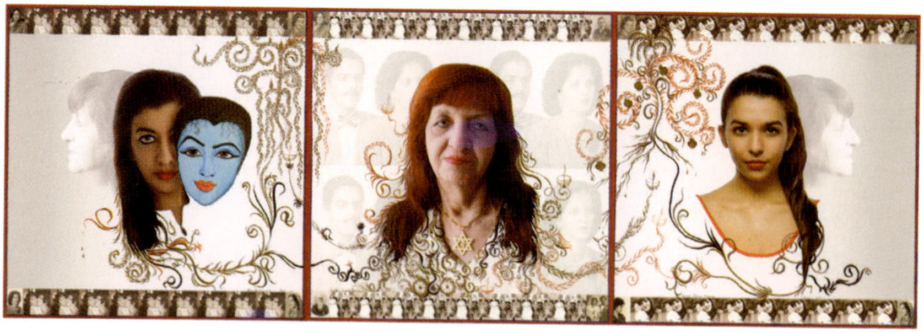

Fig. 22. Three Generation Triptych: Siona Benjamin, Sophie Judah Benjamin (Kasookar), Rachel Kruge, 2012–13

One of the more effecting images that present multiple figures is a triptych: a 'Three Generation Triptych: Siona Benjamin, Sophie Judah Benjamin (Kasookar), Rachel Kruge.' It is a portrait of Siona, her mother and her daughter, against the backdrop of ghostly images: her mother, profiled left and right behind the faces of Siona, Rachel, and a double portrait of the young Sophie and her husband (Siona's father and Rachel's grandfather), multiplied behind the face of Sophie (Fig. 22). The entire image is in the process of being overrun by delicate vines, their tendrils emerging from Sophie's image to encompass the other two (these are the conceptual echo of these faces that are part of a vine-rich tree of life)—and here, too, tiny repeating family photographs define the upper and lower frames of the triptych.

There are, in fact, any number of images with more than one face. Esther Sukkur (Belkar), Sukkur Enock and Queenie Sukkur are collaged in opposing profiles and one—Queenie—faces out to the viewer (Fig. 23). They are all encompassed in an arched 'window' form, over which the words 'Elijah the Prophet' are written in Hebrew. That opening is placed against a pale image of a dynamic Elijah whipping up

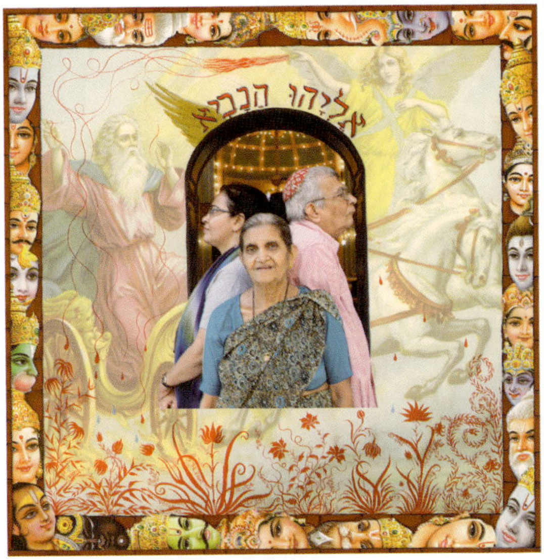

Fig. 23. Esther Sukkur (Belkar), Sukkur Enock and Queenie Sukkur, 2012–13

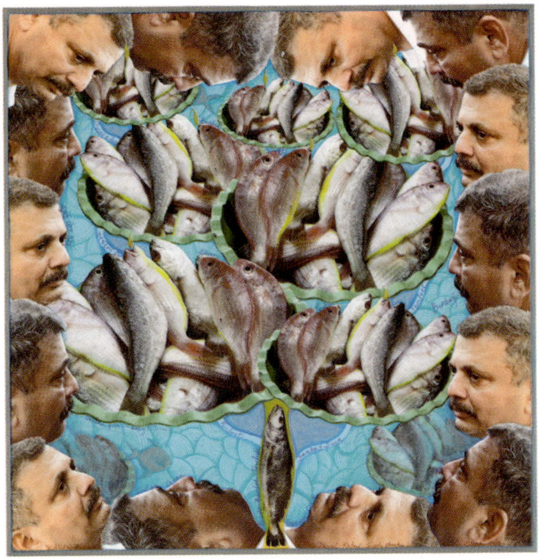

Fig. 24. Daniel Rafael Joseph (Bhonkar), 2012–13

the horses of his fiery chariot, an angel in attendance—but actively in attendance, for Siona has added, in bold, deep red, a blast of energy from its hand to the prophet's upraised hand, where the red becomes a kind of horse's reins. The red continues as abstract floral and geometric forms in the lower part of the image.

The Elijah image, harbinger of the messiah, seen in many Indian Jewish homes, is in turn 'framed' by a tumbling progression of gods, goddesses and gurus—including Krishna, Shiva and the elephant-headed god of good fortune, Ganesh. Indeed, as noted variously in Siona's memoir and in the discussion of the Bene Israel, a unique feature of the Bene Israel community in India is its Eliyahu HaNavi (Elijah the Prophet) traditions—that connect a particular place to a particular food and to particular occasions (see Chapter One, pp. 69–70 and Chapter Four, pp. 216–219). The Hindu gods are outside Esther's garden wall, for she respects and honors all religions but those that worship images must remain outside her home and garden.

On the other hand, the 'frame' of the image of Daniel Rafael Joseph (Bhonkar) is comprised of 14 repetitions—twice seven, that universal symbolic number, with its very particular reference to one of the more important origin stories of the Bene Israel (see Chapter One, p. 53)—of his own face (Fig. 24). The interior of the image presents a repeating collage of the photographic image of fish—grouped in seven 'platterfuls', with one fish vertically disposed as if standing on its tail, and therefore offering a kind of seven-branched candelabrum (each platter a branch, the single fish the stem) against a lush blue background. Thus the image of plenty (for which fish in general, in their ubiquity in the sea, are also a specifically Jewish symbol)[29] interweave the universal history of seven as a symbol with the idea of the menorah as the most frequent symbol in Jewish art across the millennia. And of course the fish all have scales, in accordance with the laws of *kashrut*: there is a Bene Israel tradition that when, centuries ago, David Rahabi brought a basket of all kinds of fish—as a kind of test—the women cooked only those with scales, throwing out the shell fish, validating their Jewish identity gastronomically.

One might say that each of the many images that use an infinitizing pattern in defining their frames—or that multiply some aspect of the main image into numerically significant or infinitizing patterns—offers a kind of statement of how culturally and spiritually rich the community

[29] Fish, particularly piles of fish, are also a symbol of plenty, among other places, in the Christian tradition—referencing the specific miracles effected by Jesus in the Gospel stories of the Draught of Fishes and of the Loaves and Fishes.

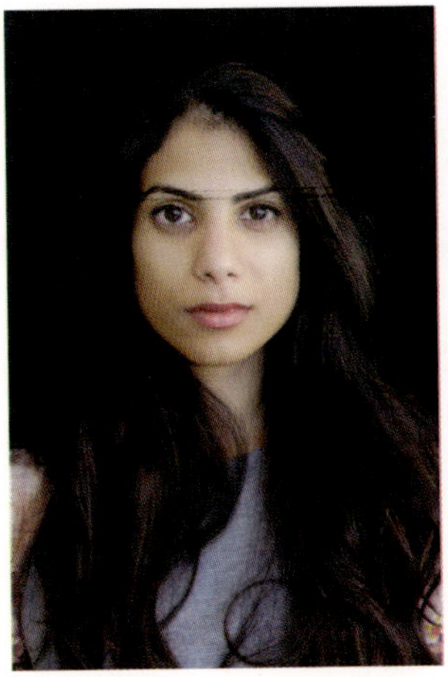

Fig. 25. Nogat Simon, 2017

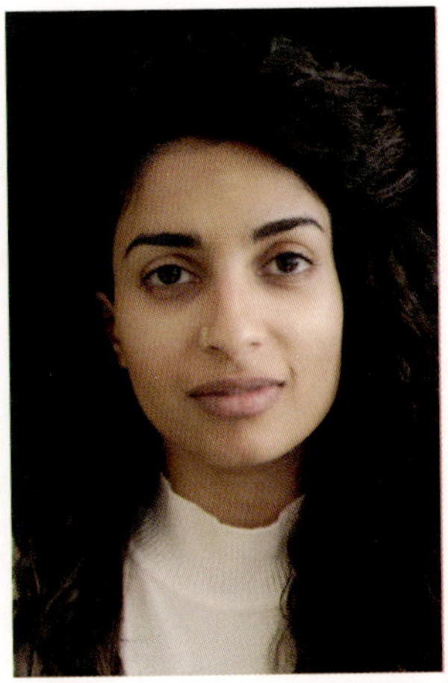

Fig. 25a. Livnat Simon, 2017

that Siona has re-encountered in the Mumbai of her past remains, even in its significantly diminished present numbers.

Consistent with the pattern of Jews, Indian Jews, and the Bene Israel, with which the narrative of this volume began—migration and diaspora, from the Middle East to the Far East, to India, within India, and out of India—Siona subsequently turned her vision to her community once more to follow it back to its geographic point of origin. A second Fulbright series, in 2016–17, engaged the Bene Israel community removed, since 1948, to Israel. Her images connected family members—twin sisters here, father and son there; grandfather and grandson here, nephew and aunt there, by means of 3-D printed Lenticular portraits. She has documented the faces and stories that tie them to each other and that tie her to the transcultural world that lives inside her memory and that has evolved and also re-located—finding home in diverse locales—and which is constantly being explored and re-shaped and expanded in her art (Figs 25 and 25a).

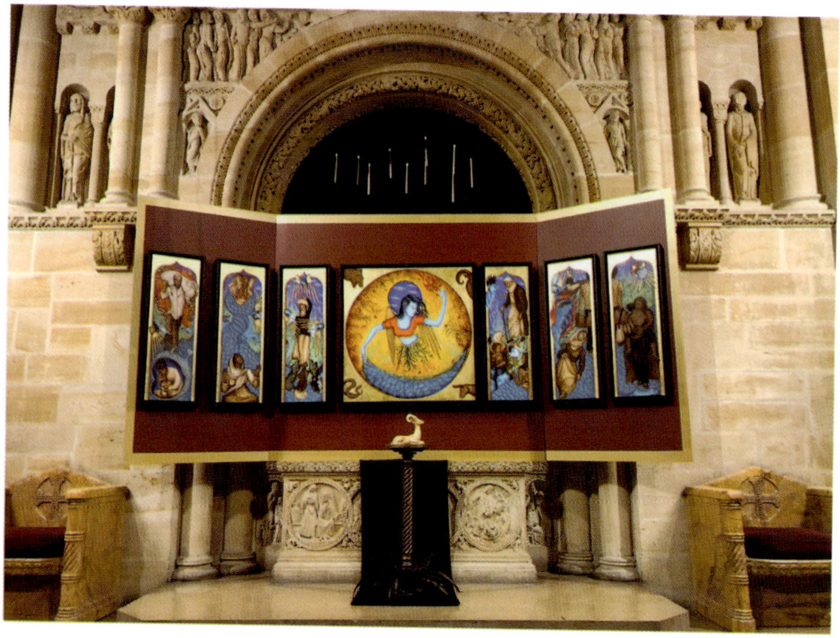

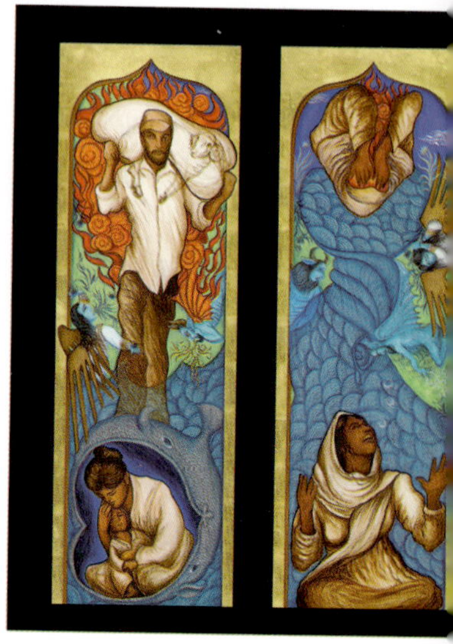

Fig 26. 'Exodus: I See Myself in You' in a church setting, 2016

She has, in fact, continued to be very visually active with regard to socio-political topics that extend beyond her own community. Her two most recent series—*Exodus* and *Liberty*—both offer a strong focus on the issue of immigration and of refugees of diverse ethnic, national, and religious backgrounds. The 2016 series, *Exodus*, is a complex compendium of images. 'Exodus: I See Myself in You', is both a part of the whole series and its own free-standing work: it consists of a polyptych—seven panels 3.5 feet tall and the totality 10 feet wide—with a small golden sculpture resting before the panels on a pedestal (Figs 26 and 26a). Male and female figures in light brown shades that suggest the contours of old sepia photographs are placed against and within

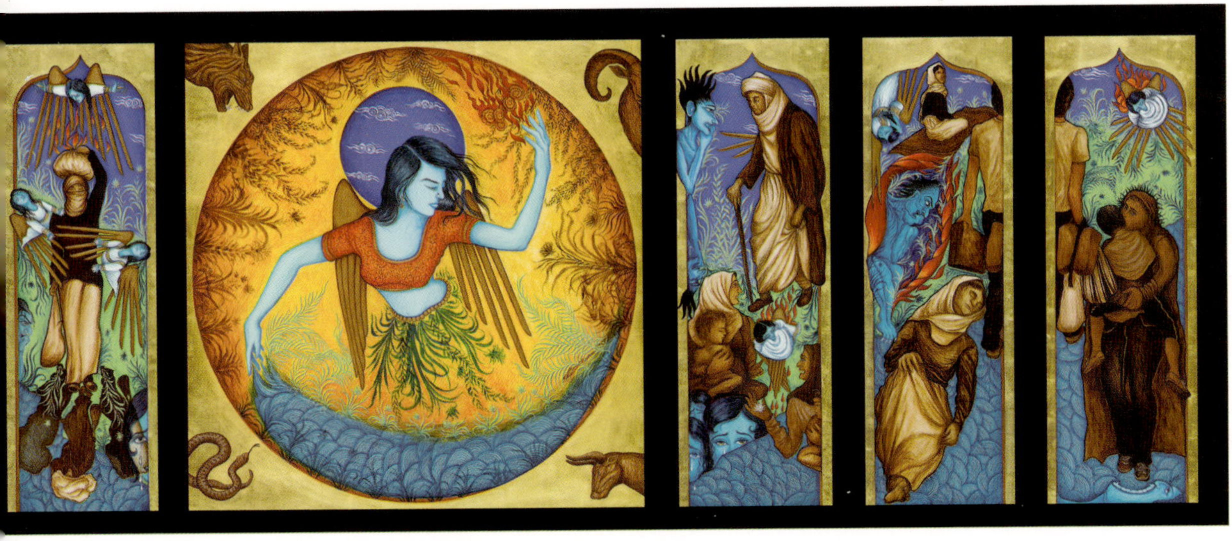

Fig. 26a. 'Exodus: I See Myself in You', 2016

sky-blue and greyer blue—the latter as if it is the scaled surface of a serpent—and pointed arched frames of gold-leaf. The central panel, dominated by a light blue-skinned *fereshteh*, is twice the size of the other six, connoting the sabbath-as-moment-of-paradise seventh: that is, to say, paradise in time, rather than in space. Before these panels, a gilded ram, at rest—the pedestal-supported sculpture—presides: this is the ram that was offered by Abraham in lieu of his son, to God. A sacrifice, he reclines in a dish colored red—as if, that is, kneeling/reclining in its own sacrificial blood.

The large series of works of which this heptaptych is part is, overall, inspired by the terms for Paradise in Hebrew and Urdu: *Pardes* and

Jannat.[30] Siona's intention is to raise questions regarding Paradise: what does it mean to us and why do we pursue it? Moreover, how much are we willing to give up in order to gain it—in a contemporary context in which thousands upon thousands of people have lost their homes and wander, seeking new homes and re-constructing their old homes in their minds as a remembered Paradise.

There are two other elements within the overall series. First, a series of drawings of diverse faces—portraits of everyday people, floating within the space of the image as within the world—presents her personages. Then there are other paintings, aside from the polyptych—it is both part of and independent of these paintings: single images and, in one case, a triptych, a male, 'Tupac', bare-chested, with a crucifix hanging against his chest from around his neck, within a ground of bright green; in the side panels a pair of *fereshteh*s dance within a ground of blue. Each of the three panels is framed by the swirled marbling associated with the Ottoman Turkish ebru-on-paper patterns.

Among the individuated images is one dominated by a soaring bird with a multi-colored tail that resonates from a range of traditions: the Hoopoe in Faridud-Din 'Attar's 1177 Persian-language epic Sufi poem, *The Conference of the Birds*, as well as the ancient Greek story of the Phoenix and the Slavic tradition of the Firebird (Fig. 27). The yearning for Paradise, like the yearning for home, is universal: the language of that yearning offers an infinity of particularized dialects derived from the specifics of ethnicity, religion, race, nationality, and culture. The stories we tell that distinguish us are the stories that also unite us.

---

[30] As Siona is aware, the Urdu term is borrowed from Arabic, and the Hebrew term is actually derived from Persian—*Para Desu*—which makes the linguistic substratum for these words even more complex. *Pardes* is rendered in Biblical Greek as *Paradeisos* and in turn, St Jerome creates *Paradisus* in his Latin Vulgate translation—which thereafter yields a range of variant forms in diverse European languages, including 'Paradise' in English.

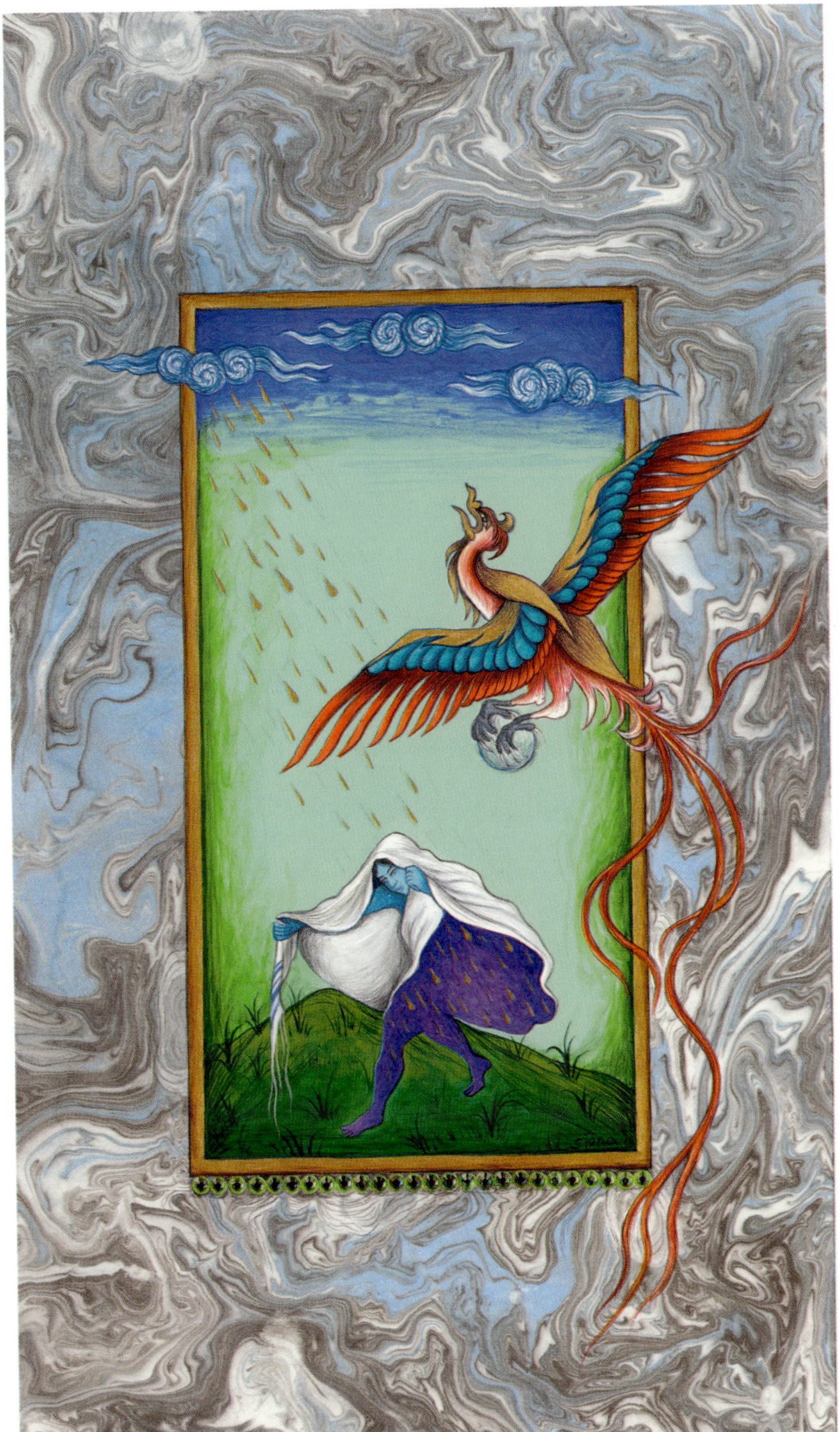

Fig. 27. 'Exodus #5', 2016

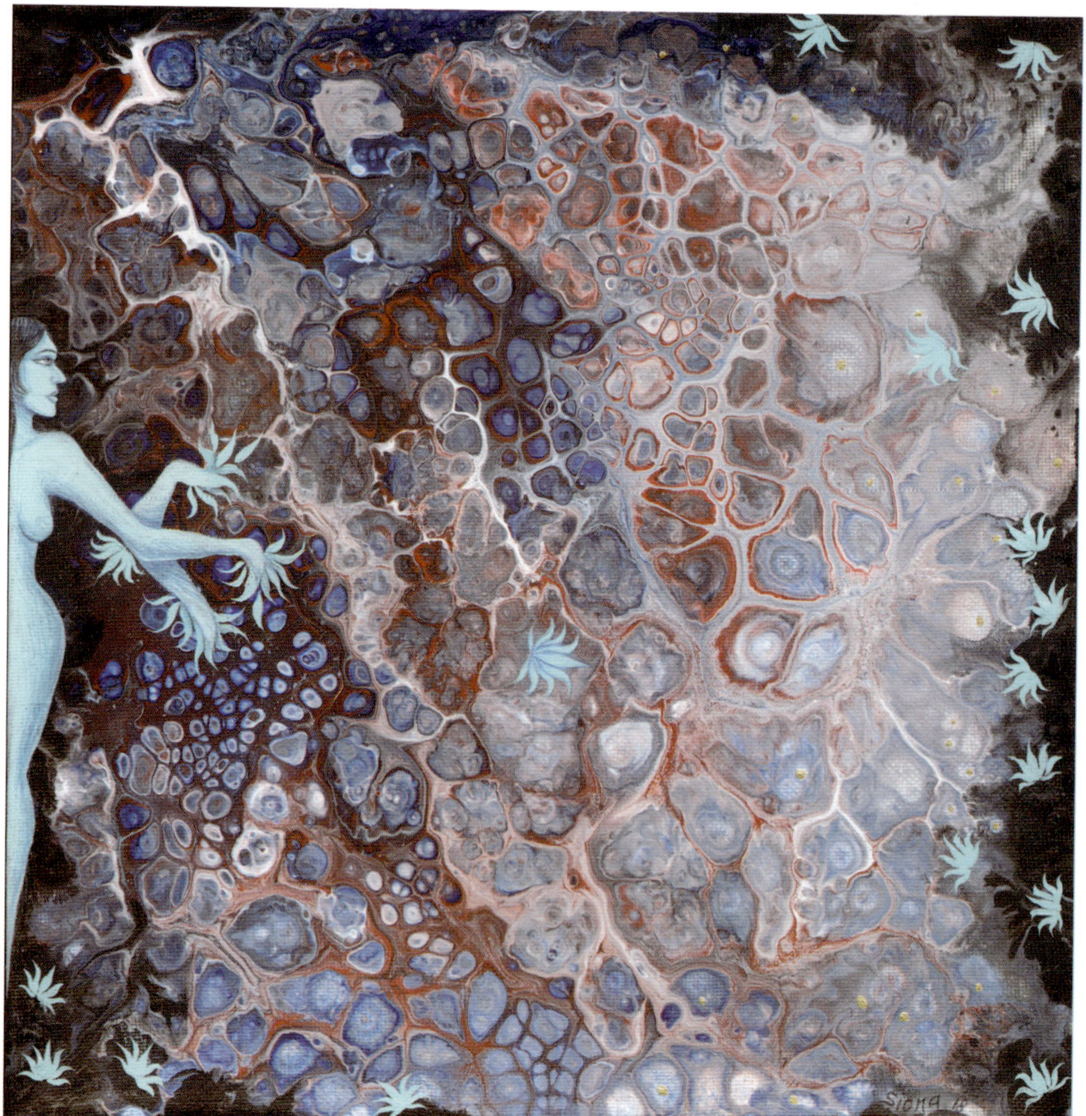

Fig. 28. *Liberty* Series #1: Give Me, 2018

The 2018 *Liberty* series offers 14 images—twice seven—to narrate a particular tale within the universal human story. In it, Siona has taken the renowned 1883 poem, 'The New Colossus', by the Sephardic immigrant, Emma Lazarus, which has been affixed to the base of the Statue of Liberty in New York harbor since 1903, which begins with the words 'Give me your tired, your poor, your huddled masses, yearning to breathe free…' and concludes with the words 'I lift my lamp bedside the golden door'. Each of Siona's images focusses on a different key word or phrase, in sequence, from the poem, (eg, Give me/your tired/ your poor…) providing a background of lush textured color against which a foreground figure falls or crouches or flies—energized or tired, sleeping or tempest-tossed, homeless and vulnerable: yearning to breathe free (Fig. 28).

Each figure possesses a blue-skinned pigment, connecting them all both to the artist in a personal way and to her earlier, landmark *Finding Home* (*Fereshteh*) series (see earlier in this chapter, pp. 251–278), and each offers attributes familiar from Siona's other bodies of work—multiple arms here, gold-leaf wings there, a fiery halo here, an unfurling lotus blossom there—but all float in a newly conceived environment of spectacular torrents of abstract viscous color that suggest both the cosmic explosion of the universe in creation and the embryonic waters of the womb (Fig. 29).

From one end of Siona's work-cycle to the other, she interweaves microcosmic with macrocosmic imagery and ideas with narratives that draw their details from the particularities of a range of traditions and that offer those details as threads in a vibrantly diverse tapestry. Her concerns combine eye-pleasing aesthetics with an ever-present interest in the socio-political, and not only cultural contours of humanity and

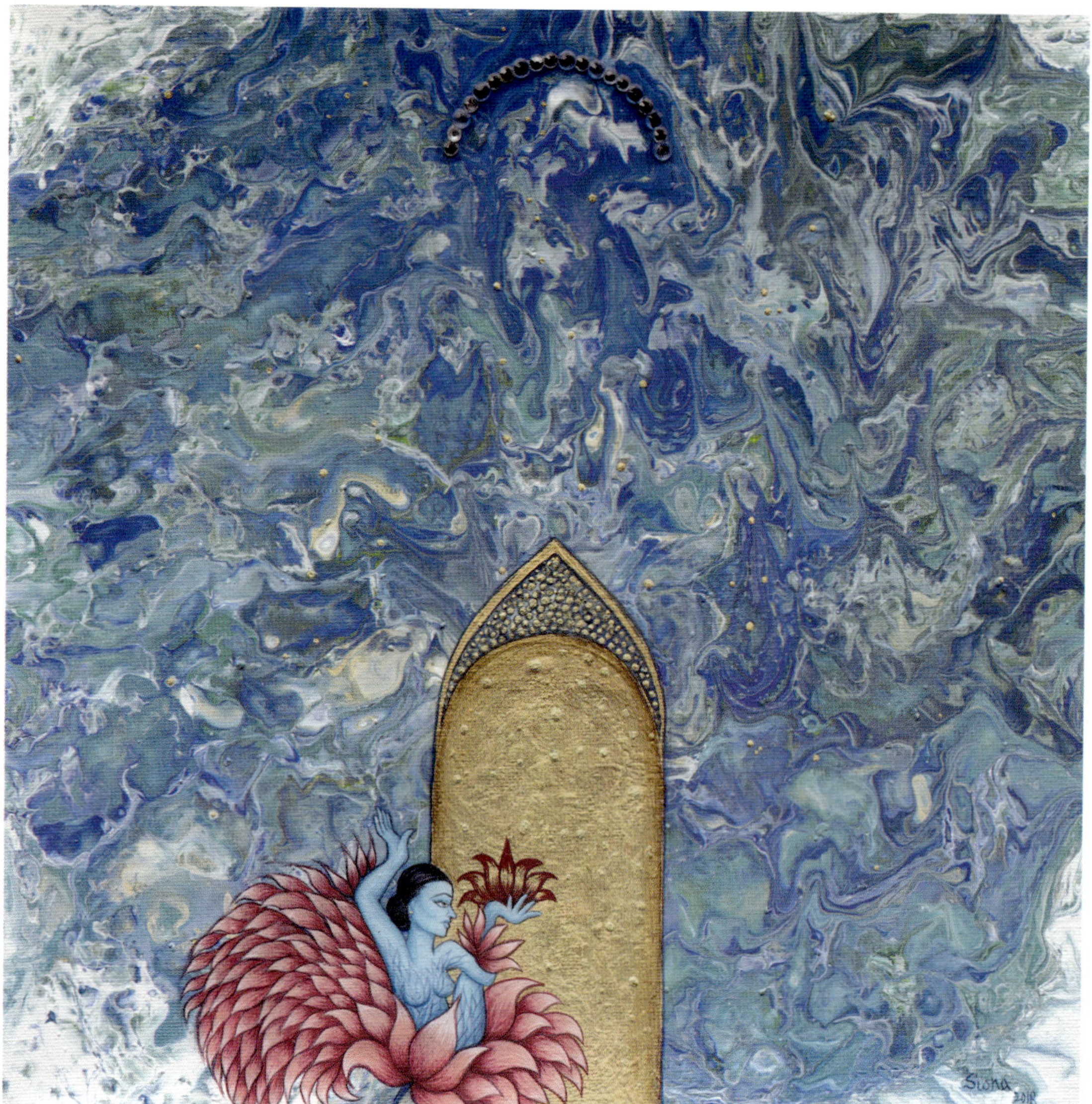

Fig. 29. *Liberty* Series #14: The Golden Door, 2018

a never-waning hope for the improvement of the human condition, within which process of improvement her art is intended and designed to play a serious role.

Siona's work is drawn from the well of her experience of growing up Jewish in Mumbai, India, and her similar and dissimilar experiences in the three decades since she left one home to seek others in the United States—coming to understand that 'home is wherever I pitch my tent, once I have made it home'. She expresses a diversely articulated hope that we humans can ultimately arrive at an understanding of the important ways in which our universal commonalities can be harmoniously interwoven into a lush fabric—of which we are all part, as we extend and intertwine the threads of our boundless forms of individualized uniqueness toward and with each other.

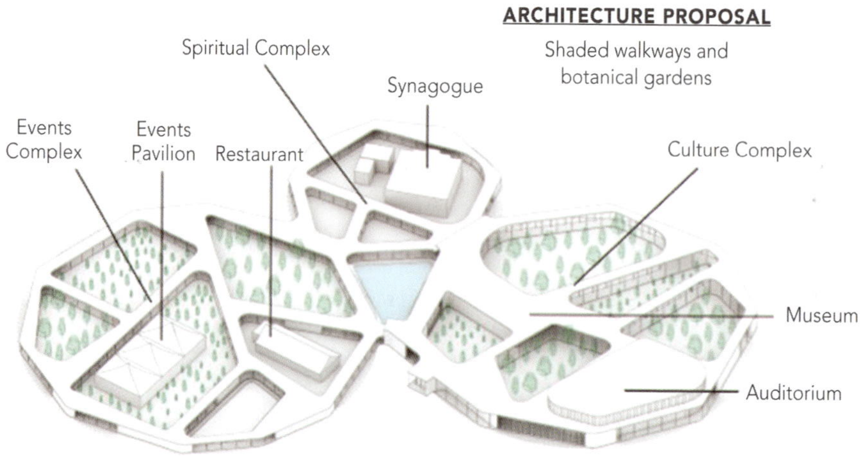

Fig. 1. Indian Cultural Center, architectural plan

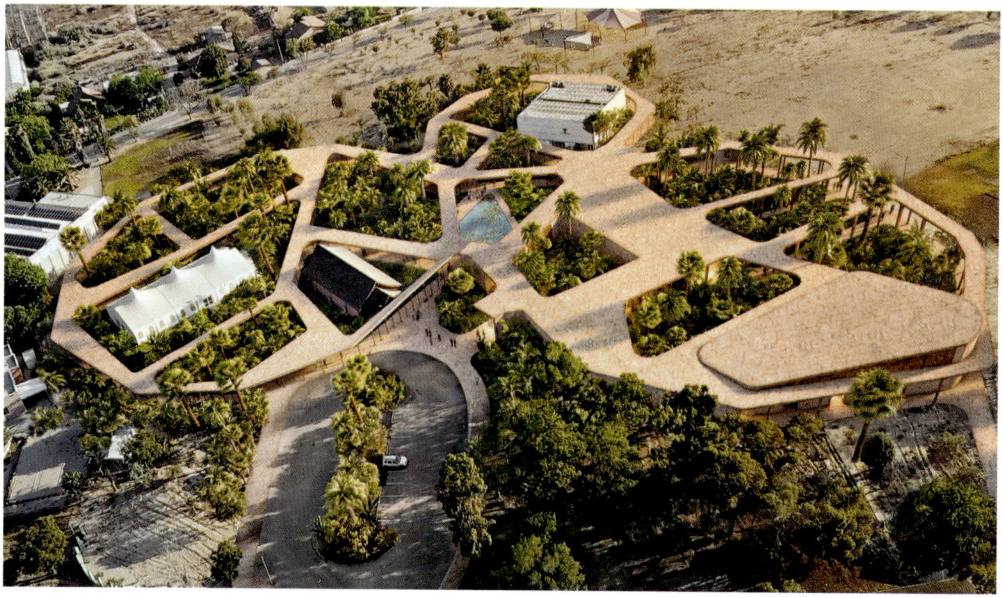

Fig. 2. Indian Cultural Center, aerial view, artist's conception

CHAPTER SIX

Epilogue

INDIAN JEWISH COMMUNITIES BETWEEN PAST AND FUTURE

Ori Z. Soltes

This volume has followed a very distinct, if slightly unusual, trajectory. We have begun with a wide-angled focus on the arrival of Jews into the southern and eastern parts of Asia overall, as a context in which to embed a general reflection on the arrival of Jews into parts of what is now India, at different times, from different places, as different kinds of Jewish groups. One of the consistent emphases in introducing the subject of Jewish arrival and settling in India has been the tendency of the Hindu-majority (and Muslim-minority) populations to be welcoming of other religious and ethnic groups, such as members of various Christian denominations as well as of the Jews.

It was against this broad statement that, in three individual chapters, we have explored the three primary Jewish communities in India—the Bene Israel, Cochini, and Baghdadi Jews—and placed a certain amount of emphasis, in both the narratives and their accompanying illustrations, on the development of the architecture and décor of their wide array of synagogues. We have considered how, when, and where these structures have emerged over the centuries, and in many cases, their repurposing, abandonment, or destruction, with the emigration of so much of the Jewish population of India in the wake of the shaping of the State of Israel.

Indeed, there are two distinct directions, during the last 70 years or so, for the Indian Jewish communities, that are suggested by the introduction and first three chapters of this volume. The first and most obvious, perhaps, is the significant just-noted emigration with the vast majority of the communities reconstituting themselves in Israel. That reconstitution is spread throughout much of the country, so that the story of the synagogues, too, is a story that continues in multiple directions. To offer one example as symptomatic of the flourishing of these communities in Israel alone (because there is also a critical mass of Indian Jews within the United States): there are Bene Israel synagogues in two dozen locales throughout the country.[1]

The shaping of the state of Israel, however, has also been accompanied by the reshaping of the communities of Indian Jews who have arrived there and thrived there in the last few generations. Nothing is more significant and symptomatic of this reality than the current project of creating a substantial Indian Jewish Cultural and

[1] Thus, there are synagogues of various sizes and configurations in Arad, Ashdod (where there are four of them), Beer Yaakov, Beersheva (where there are three of them), Dimona (where there are two), Eilat, Haifa (where there are two), Hedera, Karmiel, Kiryat Ala, Kiryat Bialek, Kiryat Gat, Kiryat Shemonah, Kiryat Sprinzak, Kiryat Yam, Lod, Or Akiva, Or Yehudah, Petah Tikvah, Ramle, Rishon leTzion, Rosh ha-ʿAyin, Yavneh, and Yerukham—at the very least.

Heritage Center. Sponsored mainly by the Bene Israel community, it will use as its starting point an already existing heritage center for the Cochini Jews, but will encompass all of the communities of Indian Jews, particularly since all of them are currently found in Israel. The vast complex will be located in Nevatim, not far from Beer Sheva, the capital of the northern Negev.[2]

The structure being planned will take the form of a large stylized lotus blossom. The elements within each of two large and one small 'blossoms' include a centrally-located synagogue within the smaller 'blossom' as the centerpiece of the spiritual complex; a cultural complex in one of the two larger 'blossoms' that includes a museum (in which, among other things, models of synagogues from all over India will be exhibited), and an auditorium for performances and lectures; and in the second large 'blossom' that will be an events complex, there will be an events pavilion, a modern convention center, a place for yoga and for meditation, a business center, and a restaurant. Shaded walkways and botanical gardens—into which plants and flowers specific to India have been introduced as a prominent feature—will contour the many outside spaces that are interspersed among the buildings (Figs 1, 2, and 3).

On the other hand—and perhaps a more unusual epilogue to this discussion—is the shaping of at least two new Jewish communities in India, as noted in the introduction to this volume. Thus, (to repeat), there is a group of approximately 9,000 individuals who refer to themselves as the Bene Menashe. Comprised of formerly animist Mizo and Kuki headhunting tribesmen in Manipur and Mizoram who converted to

[2] For more information on this extraordinary project, please contact Avner Isaac at avnerisaac@gmail.com.

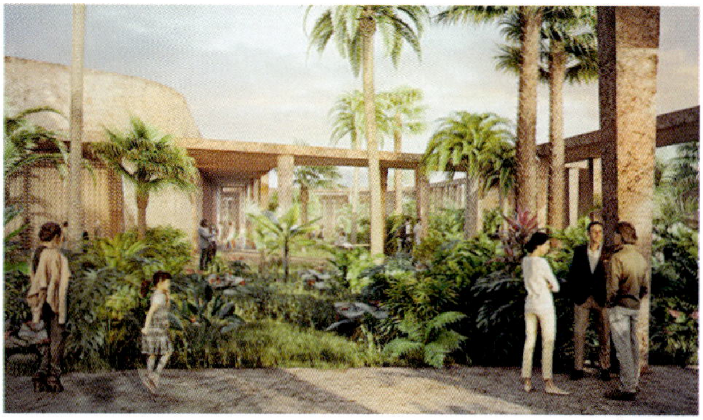

Fig. 3. Indian Cultural Center, artist's conception—detail

Christianity at the beginning of the 20th century, they began to convert to Judaism in the 1970s—asserting that they are returning to their original faith, having descended from one of the lost Ten tribes (that of Menashe, one of the two sons of the patriarch, Joseph) who disappeared from history after the Assyrian conquest of northern Israel in 722–721 BCE—which would make their ancestors Israelites. In fact, the form of Judaism that they follow is more akin to biblical 'Israelitism' than to mainstream Judaism. They follow the Bible without filtering its texts through the rabbinic tradition that has evolved for most Jews during the past two millennia.

The second such recent addition to the overall Indian Jewish community (repeating, too, what was noted in this text's introduction), is the smaller group in Andhra Pradesh on the southeast coast, referred to as the 'Telugu Jews'; they speak Telugu and embraced Judaism in 1991. The 'Telugu Jews'—some of them came to follow an ultra-Orthodox lifestyle—refer to themselves as Bene Ephraim, tracing their ancestry in a manner analogous to the identity-sensibility of the Mizo and Kuki Bene Menashe, to the other son of the Israelite patriarch Joseph—Ephraim—and to the lost Israelite tribe that is traditionally understood to have descended from him. These two groups are also now represented among the Indian Jewish communities residing in Israel—and will be part of the story told in the new Indian Jewish Cultural and Heritage Center.

This narrative with its primary emphases, nonetheless, on the Bene Israel, Cochini, and Baghdadi Jews, has, in turn, led to a memoir by the artist, Siona Benjamin—a member of the Bene Israel—which was, in a distinct sense, the inspiration for the overall volume: hers is a particular and particularly arresting story of growing up Jewish in India. Her memoir explores her experience in evolving as a child and as an adult in Mumbai (Bombay)—through the relations between her family and their friends, neighbors, and associates; and through the schools that she attended and the diverse friends that she made in those schools. Her personal account reflects a life that offers a rich interweave of distinctly Jewish features, distinctly Indian Jewish features, distinctly Bene Israel Indian Jewish features, and the intertwining of all of these elements with the Muslim, Christian, Zoroastrian (Parsi), and above all, Hindu worlds of which she and her family were also part—and a further refraction through the layered lenses of living for several decades in the Midwestern and Northeastern United States. As much as Benjamin's essay is a personal one, it resonates with aspects of the larger Indian Jewish experience through its lenses in an array of interesting ways.

Most obviously, those lenses and their refractions are visible—literally—in the evolving body of Siona's art work, which is discussed in the final essay in this collection. The thrust of that essay is first and foremost to articulate how three particular truths reverberate throughout her art and its myriad details: Hindu India's historical hospitality to non-Hindu groups, and in particular to the Jews; the complexity of the Jewish identity, in general and with regard to producing visual art; and how the wrestling with these two issues has continued to evolve in Siona's art from one body of work to the next. On the one hand, her art undergoes dramatic visual changes as one follows it through the past 30 years or so, but on the other hand one feels throughout those transformations a continuum of both conceptual and visual aspects. As discussed in that essay, one may discern elements that connect to illuminated manuscripts from the Hindu, Persian, and Moghul traditions; allusions to Bollywood posters and American Pop Art; references to Christian icons; and the engagement of the ongoing question of what exactly 'Jewish' art might be—this last by way, in part, of a constant dancing with the Jewish textual interpretive traditions known as Talmud and midrash, and Siona's own additions to that pattern of thinking.

Her art has taken her from her own eventual home in the United States back to her former community in India to study what remains of it, in the places where she grew up—thus exploring it both as an insider and as an outsider—and out to the eventual venue into which much of that community has emigrated: Israel—and back and forth among these three locales. Thus her exploration of the Bene Israel in diverse contemporary contexts reflects the ways in which the community has interwoven its own diasporic patterns within the diasporic patterns that are part of the overall Jewish experience. Her art in a very distinct manner brings the entire narrative within this volume back full circle to its beginnings with its exploration of the arrival of Jews into southern and eastern Asia and into India itself. So, too, it offers a distinct visual summary of India and its diverse religious, cultural and ethnic communities, Jewish and otherwise—as it articulates her intention as an artist: to use her work as an instrument that promotes *tikkun olam* ('repairing the world') by weaving its myriad human elements into a new tapestry of colors and shapes, images and words, concepts and qualities.

One of the unfortunate ironies for this story is that, in the present political dispensation in India, where Hindu nationalists are in power, India has, for the moment at least, ceased to be the country the long history of which shapes the context of this narrative and its magnificent tapestry of interwoven cultural, religious, and ethnic threads. And in the case of Siona Benjamin's art, there is much to contradict this new development, given the intention of her art as a reflection of her own international and multi-cultural identity, and her desire to use her art as a palliative: to repair the world of its painful fractiousness and to bring its diverse human components together.

Perhaps even this turn is appropriate in a particular way to the larger story of India, which is an intense and not only endlessly varied country—and therefore both reflects and reminds us about humanity in all its rawness and (to use a favorite turn of phrase from Siona) 'without being discreet. It's open and in your face, it's difficult and it's amazing at the same time': full of colors, sounds, smells, tastes, and touches that assault all of the senses. India never hides; it is even shamefully blatant and revealing and unabashedly addresses our flawed, imperfect human existence. This is not for everyone—but richly rewarding and endlessly fascinating for those who embrace it—who embrace humanity—with all of our flaws and imperfections.

As one juxtaposes the art of Siona Benjamin and all that it represents in terms of the history of India and her coming of age as a Jew in a Hindu and Muslim nation, one might also keep in mind the degree to which her adopted country, the United States of America, particularly at this moment in history, has also strayed so very far from the principles articulated by the Founding Fathers, as well as from its long history as a nation of immigrants who are both welcomed and end up contributing to the vibrancy of the nation, and one where being a member of a minority cannot prevent one from rising—even rising to prominence—in the world. In the case of both of these countries—and arguably the third, Israel, to which this story is ultimately connected—if the present fails to live up to the ideals articulated and lived in the past, there is always hope, embodied in the narratives contained within this volume, and in the art still being produced at a feverish pace by Siona Benjamin, for the future and a reclaiming of those ideals.

Ultimately this volume addresses both the complex diversity of the Jewish communities of India, against the backdrop of India's own complex diversity as a nation and as a culture; and how one artist in particular filters that doubly diverse complexity into her art, yielding an outcome that is both visually lush and conceptually compelling. The shaping of her art resonates from the process of growing up Jewish in India, with all of its wondrous qualities and questions. As the narratives that have unfolded in these pages—from that in the preface to that which explores the most recent of Siona's work—offer a connection between the Jewish and various non-Jewish communities of India, they also suggest positive liaisons between the richness of history and the potential vibrancy of the future.

Contributors' Biographies

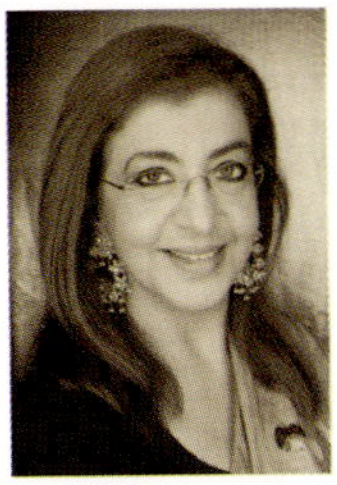

Siona Benjamin is a painter originally from Bombay, now living in the USA. Her work reflects her background of being brought up Jewish in a predominantly Hindu and Muslim India. She received her first MFA in painting from Southern Illinois University-Carbondale, Il., and a second MFA in Theater set design from the University of Illinois-Urbana/Champaign. She has exhibited her work in the US, Europe, and Asia. She was awarded a Fulbright Fellowship in 2010–11 for the art project titled: *Faces: Weaving Indian Jewish Narratives*. The first exhibit for the India Fulbright was in 2013 at the Prince of Wales Museum in Mumbai and several others followed. Siona received a second Fulbright fellowship in 2016–17 to Israel and her project is titled *From Motherland to Fatherland: Transcultural Indian Jews in Israel*. A documentary on her work was made by filmmaker Hal Rifken in 2015, entitled *Blue Like Me: The Art of Siona Benjamin*. Her website is: www.artsiona.com.

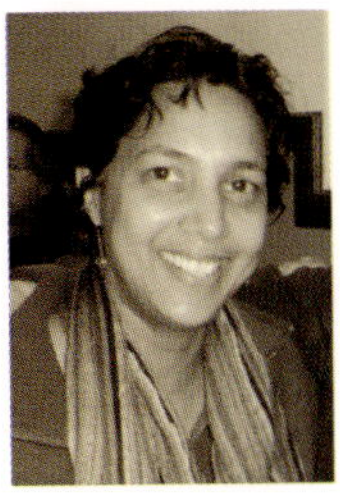

Orna Eliyahu-Oron, M.A., is an art historian and ceramic artist based in Seattle, USA. Born and raised in Israel to parents who immigrated there from Ernakulam, Kerala, in the 1950s, Orna earned a B.A. in archaeology and art history, and an M.A. in Jewish art history, both from the Hebrew University. In 1996–2002 Orna served as the curator of the Cochin Jewish Heritage Center in Nevatim, Israel. Her Master's Thesis, '*Heichalot* (Torah Arks) from the Synagogues of Cochin Jews in India' won the 2004 Ben Zvi Institute Prize for research of Jewish communities in the East.

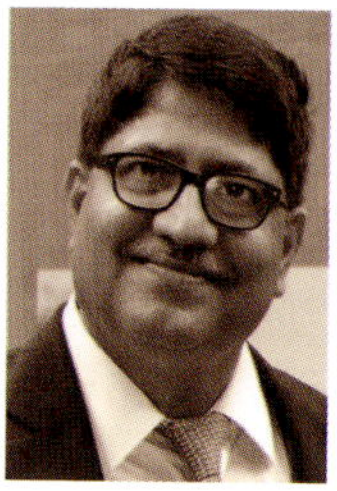

Ralphy Jhirad is the Founder and Managing Trustee of the Bene Israel Heritage Museum and Genealogical Research Centre. He is the faculty for the Jewish Heritage of India for the Guides Training Course of the Government of India. Ralphy has developed diverse itineraries for *Tours of Jewish Heritage in India*, and has published several books on India's Jewish Heritage and Culture, including *Bombay: Exploring the Urban Jewish Heritage* by Prof. (Dr) Shaul Sapir; *The Jews of Pakistan* by Yoel Reuben; and *Bene Israel of India – Heritage and Culture (An Encyclopedia)* by Nissim Moses. He is the recipient of the Herzl Award from the World Zionist Organization and the Man of the Year Award from The American ORT Federation, among others.

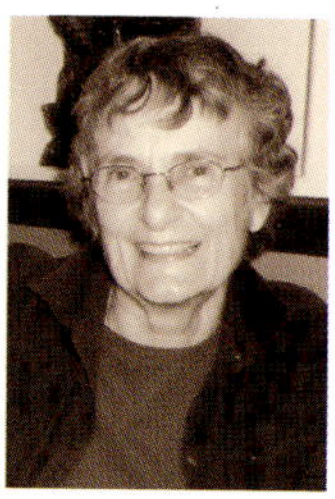

Barbara C. Johnson is Professor Emerita from Ithaca College, where she was founder and Coordinator of the Jewish Studies Program. She lived for four years in South India during the 1960s, after graduating from Oberlin College, and then began her long-term research on the Jews of Kerala, completing her PhD in anthropology at the University of Massachusetts. In addition to many published articles on the Kerala Jewish communities of India and Israel, she co-authored, with Ruby Daniel, the memoir *Ruby of Cochin: An Indian Jewish Woman Remembers* (Jewish Publication Society, 1995). Johnson's book on the Malayalam-language songs preserved and performed by Kerala Jewish women, with translations, transcriptions, and commentary on 79 of these songs, is forthcoming from the Jewish Music Research Centre, Hebrew University, Jerusalem. She edited the 2004 CD and booklet *Oh, Lovely Parrot!: Jewish Women's Songs from Kerala*, also published by the Jewish Music Research Center.

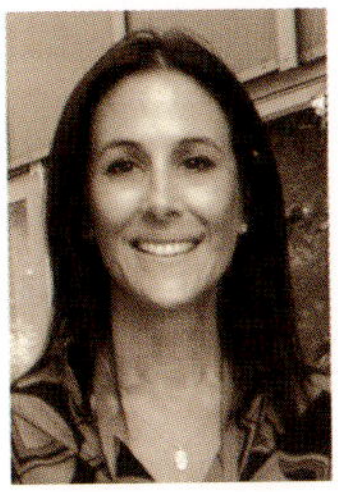

Erica Lyons is the founder/editor-in-chief of *Asian Jewish Life – a journal of spirit, society, and culture* that celebrates the diversity of the Jewish experience in Asia. She is the chair of the Hong Kong Jewish Historical Society and is the Hong Kong Delegate to the World Jewish Congress. Her work appears in a wide variety of books and media publications. She is an active member of Hong Kong's Society of Children's Book Writers and Illustrators and has recently begun work on a series of Jewish historical fiction books. She has also served as regional consultant for the American Jewish Joint Distribution Committee and spoken at a number of international conferences about the history of Jewish Asia as well as contemporary Jewish communities. She participated in the Schusterman Foundation's ROI Summit for Young Jewish Innovators, the Tikvah Fund's Advanced Institute for Jewish Studies, and was a fellow with the Anti-Defamation League's Glass Institute.

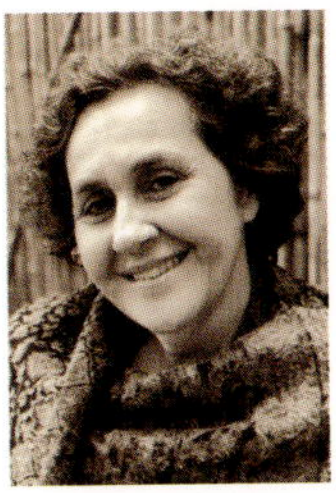

Jael Silliman is an independent scholar, consultant and writer. She is a former tenured Associate Professor of Women's Studies at the University of Iowa and a Program Officer at the Ford Foundation, New York. She is the author of several books, scholarly papers and popular articles on gender, development, race, social justice and women's rights issues. She contributes to scholarly journals and books on the subject of her community, the Baghdadi Jewish community, and is the author of *Jewish Portraits, Indian Frames: Women's Narratives from a Diaspora of Hope* and two novels—*The Man with Many Hats* and *The Teak Almirah*. Her co-authored book *Where Gods Reside: Sacred Places of Kolkata* was published in 2018. She is the curator of www.jewishcalcutta.in and spends much of her time in Kolkata.

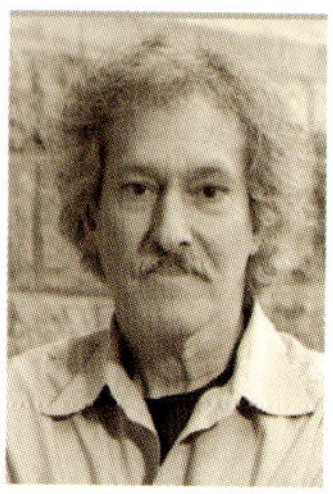

Ori Z. Soltes teaches art history, theology, philosophy and political history at Georgetown University. He is former Director of the B'nai B'rith Klutznick National Jewish Museum, and has curated more than 85 exhibitions on history, ethnography and modern and contemporary art there and at other venues across the country and overseas. He is the author of nearly 300 books, articles, exhibition catalogues, and essays on a variety of topics. Recent books include *Our Sacred Signs: How Jewish, Christian and Muslim Art Draw from the Same Source; Searching for Oneness: Mysticism in Judaism, Christianity and Islam; Untangling the Web of the Middle East; Magic and Religion in the Greco-Roman World: The Beginnings of Judaism and Christianity,* and most recently, *God and the Goalposts: A Brief History of Sports, Religion, Politics, War and Art.* Professor Soltes leads study tours to different parts of the world, including many parts of Europe, Asia, and Africa.

Index

Note: Page numbers marked in italics denote images.